ARKANSAS

MISSOURI

Memphis

TENNESSEE

KENTUCKY

TRACE

14
13

12

11

10
9
8
7
6
5
4
3
2
1

ALABAMA

Tennessee River

Cumberland River

Nashville

CHEROKEE NATION

A WAY THROUGH
THE WILDERNESS

Also by William C. Davis

A WAY THROUGH THE WILDERNESS

The Natchez Trace and the Civilization of the Southern Frontier

WILLIAM C. DAVIS

HarperCollins*Publishers*

FIRST EDITION

Designed by Alma Hochhauser Orenstein

Library of Congress Cataloging-in-Publication Data

Davis, William C., 1946–
    A way through the wilderness : the Natchez Trace and the civilization of the southern frontier / William C. Davis. — 1st ed.
        p.   cm.
    Includes bibliographical references and index.
    ISBN 0-06-016921-4
    1. Natchez Trace—History.   2. Southwest, Old—Civilization.   I. Title.
F217.N37D38   1995
976.2'04—dc20   94-42289

95 96 97 98 99 ❖/RRD 10 9 8 7 6 5 4 3 2 1

CONTENTS

Illustrations follow page 144.

PREFACE

This book began its life as a biography of David Crockett, but then it was learned that one or two other lives of that quintessential frontier character were in the offing, and prudence suggested a change of tack. It proved to be a fortuitous shift, for while the Wag of the Canebrakes is a wonderfully colorful character who still boasts, jests, and blunders through the pages that follow, he now walks in company with a number of equally intriguing people who might otherwise never have stepped into the story. Old Anthony Hutchins, the perpetual revolutionary. Lorenzo Dow, the apparition in a preacher's garb. Martha Martin with her bad-luck leg and incredible spirit. Mushulatubbee, Pushmataha, the Colberts and LeFlores, and a host of Choctaw and Chickasaw. The absolutely incredible Sir William Dunbar, scientist, philanthropist, friend of Jefferson and defender of slavery. Merchants, bankers, planters, soldiers, the larger-than-life "Kaintucks," and the low-life gamblers and whores. Best of all, perhaps, the man who virtually defines the Old Southwest from 1790 to the 1830s—the farmer-cum-teacher-cum-physician-cum-lumberman-cum-soldier-cum-public servant—that perpetual seeker of opportunity Gideon Lincecum.

Moreover, they all get to live their lives on one of the most exciting stages in American history and are all tied in one way or another to that enchanting, storied, and oft-mysterious highway of the American frontier, the Natchez Trace. So much fable and fiction has grown up around the shadowy Indian path and the road that followed that the even more interesting and often exciting facts of its career have been almost lost in the popular mind. By this trail virtually everything came originally to the Old Southwest. Settlers moved by it through the forest fastnesses of the native inhabitants. Education, religion, and the spread

ix

of enlightenment radiated first from its dark lanes. Community and the growth of white civilization planted themselves at its termini, poised to spread into the interior of the new territory. Crime and punishment both plied its reaches, and all these things and more, originally perched precariously on this edge of the wilderness, eventually rolled through the woodlands and across the prairies to cement the white man's grasp on this rich new land. In the process, elements of the frontier character emerged and took shape—not a few of them attributes that defined Americans of all regions in their juggernaut roll across the continent. And here, too, as sadly as anywhere, comes the tragic story of the men who lived there before the whites came, made the more poignant because, far from being "hostiles," as they were often called, they mostly just wanted to be friends.

As usual in preparing a book, many thanks are due, perhaps first of all to M. S. "Buz" Wyeth of HarperCollins, who suggested not scrapping the Crockett idea, but rather reshaping and directing it to offer a portrait of his era and people. Thanks again for a lovely job to Susan H. Llewellyn, whose marginal comments make the drudgery of going over a copyedited manuscript *almost* pleasurable. In a special category must stand Assistant Chief Ray Claycomb and the staff of the Natchez Trace Parkway. They administer arguably the most varied and beautiful national park in the whole system, and beyond cavil the most stunning stretch of highway in America. Their park is nearly 450 miles long and only a few hundred yards wide, but so wonderfully designed that a day or two spent driving its length at a sane fifty miles per hour, unvexed by billboards and eighteen wheelers, is time spent in another century. Writing this book would have been a delightful experience if for no other reason than the excuse it offered to drive the full length of the parkway half a dozen times. And in the parkway headquarters at Tupelo, Missis-sippi, in their wonderful library that contains a storehouse of material available nowhere else, Ray Claycomb stretched the definition of hospitality.

Certainly vying for equal importance in the research is the magnificent Natchez Trace Collection, now housed at the Center for American History of the Eugene C. Barker Texas History Center of the University of Texas at Austin. Comprising more than one hundred subcollections, this massive accumulation of material is still being cataloged, with many of its treasures remaining untapped. Sincere thanks are due to Katherine Adams, Ralph Elder, and Sarah Clark for opening this chest of riches to me.

While a host of other archives made their materials available, special note must be made of the continuing friendship and aid offered by the wonderful staffs at the Alabama Department of Archives and History in Montgomery, especially Norwood Kerr and Rickie Brunner, and Ann Lipscomb of the Mississippi Department of Archives and History in Jackson. Wilbur Menery of the Special Collections branch of the Howard-Tilton Memorial Library at Tulane University in New Orleans answered every plea. Then there are the friends and fellow historians whose aid cannot go unnoticed. T. Michael Parrish of Austin went out of his way to make me aware of sources, as well as to make some of those sources aware of this project. John Saleeby of Natchez opened the door to an understanding of that fascinating river community, so like and yet so unlike the Southwest whose capital it was. Charles and Alice Shewmake of Montgomery, Alabama, deserve a special medal for putting up itinerant historians at their lovely home, all the more for providing such delightful evening companionship in contrast to long days spent researching amid dusty manuscripts. Sylvia Frank, who should be spending her youth doing other things, gave far too many hours turning her perceptive editorial eye to the excesses, omissions, and sometime mysteries of a messy first draft.

One of the delights of working with the materials left behind in the sometimes awkward, occasionally illegible, but always interesting hand of these frontierspeople has been their spelling. No Webster for them. In their way of creating things for themselves, they carved their own variety of the language, including spellings that often amuse and frequently amaze. It would be possible to follow every one of these idiosyncrasies with the scholar's "[sic]" as a way of assuring the reader that the word is indeed misspelled in the original, and to show off that I the historian know that it is misspelled. However, in deference to the ingenuity of the authors I have left their words exactly as they wrote them, uncluttered by pedantic and anachronistic insertions except where actual understanding might be obscured. Call a rose what you will, it still smells lovely, and whether Crockett "took hold" of Old Betsey or "took a'holt" of it, the meaning of his grip was just as clear to the man or beast in his sights, and so should it be to us.

They have all been so nice, both the living and the dead. Too bad that Sylvia and Charlie and Alice and Mike and Ray and all the rest cannot sit down with Gideon and Lorenzo and Martha and Mushulatubbee and more. Over a cool glass in a saloon in what little remains of Natchez Under-the-Hill, or perhaps picnicking on the bluff or spending a warm fall afternoon under the cottonwood shade along the Trace, they would have a lot to share and enjoy. For my part I would just inhale the fragrance of the wilderness, wrap myself around one of George Vennigerholtz's notorious mint juleps, and listen to the sounds of the Trace and its people, past and present. They have all been so companionable.

A WAY THROUGH
THE WILDERNESS

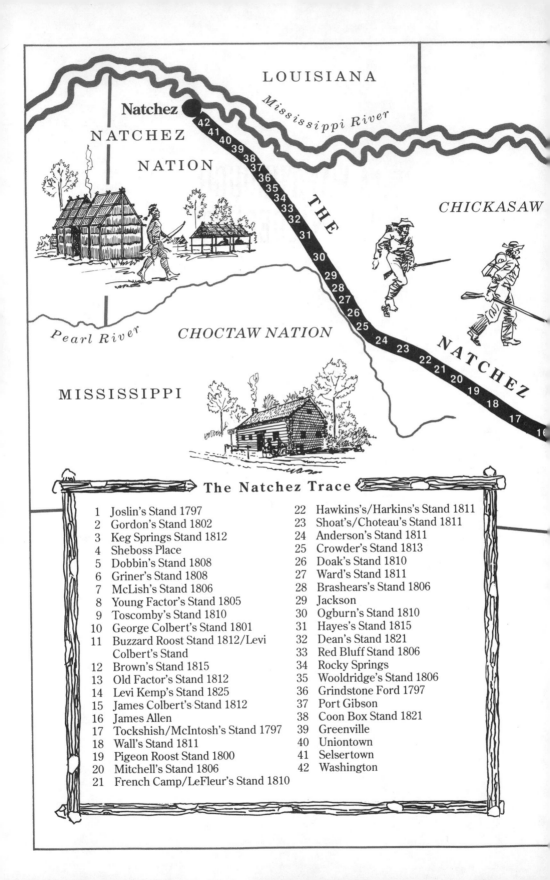

LOUISIANA

Mississippi River

Natchez

NATCHEZ

NATION

42
41
40
39
38
37
36
35
34
33
32
31
30
29
28
27
26
25
24
23
22
21
20
19
18
17
16

THE

CHICKASAW

Pearl River

CHOCTAW NATION

NATCHEZ

MISSISSIPPI

The Natchez Trace

1 Joslin's Stand 1797
2 Gordon's Stand 1802
3 Keg Springs Stand 1812
4 Sheboss Place
5 Dobbin's Stand 1808
6 Griner's Stand 1808
7 McLish's Stand 1806
8 Young Factor's Stand 1805
9 Toscomby's Stand 1810
10 George Colbert's Stand 1801
11 Buzzard Roost Stand 1812/Levi
    Colbert's Stand
12 Brown's Stand 1815
13 Old Factor's Stand 1812
14 Levi Kemp's Stand 1825
15 James Colbert's Stand 1812
16 James Allen
17 Tockshish/McIntosh's Stand 1797
18 Wall's Stand 1811
19 Pigeon Roost Stand 1800
20 Mitchell's Stand 1806
21 French Camp/LeFleur's Stand 1810

22 Hawkins's/Harkins's Stand 1811
23 Shoat's/Choteau's Stand 1811
24 Anderson's Stand 1811
25 Crowder's Stand 1813
26 Doak's Stand 1810
27 Ward's Stand 1811
28 Brashears's Stand 1806
29 Jackson
30 Ogburn's Stand 1810
31 Hayes's Stand 1815
32 Dean's Stand 1821
33 Red Bluff Stand 1806
34 Rocky Springs
35 Wooldridge's Stand 1806
36 Grindstone Ford 1797
37 Port Gibson
38 Coon Box Stand 1821
39 Greenville
40 Uniontown
41 Selsertown
42 Washington

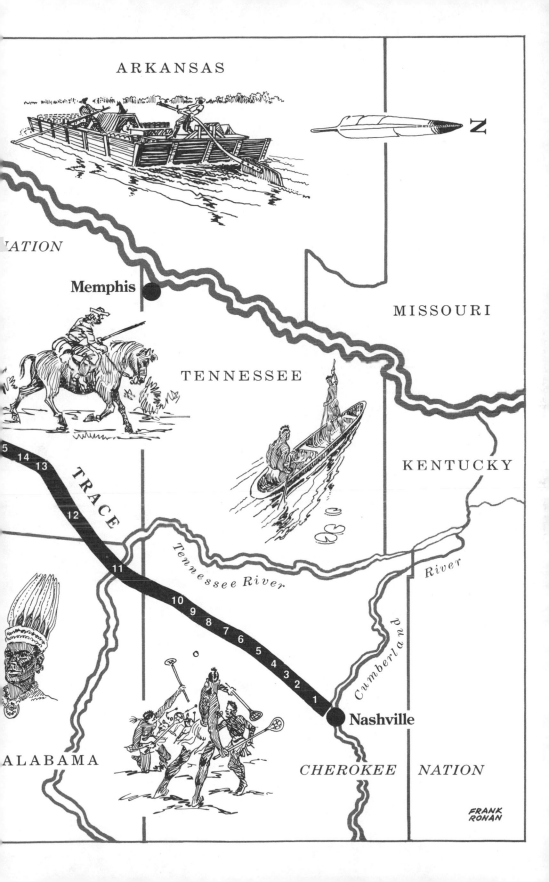

1

The Road to Empire

First came the earth. Ages before there were names or men to assign them, ages even before the idea of time gave some order to the passing eons, a mighty river flowed—a river beyond the imagination. Between the two great northern oceans rested a vast continent. A huge gulf sat beneath it, and next to that a sea to be called in a later time the Caribbean, and into it flowed the great river. More than a hundred miles wide at its mouth, it stretched northward many times that and more, extending in its tributaries into the peaks of the great mountains far to the north and west, and almost as far into the older, lower ranges hundreds of miles to the northeast. From either bank along its lower course to the sea, the river simply stretched to the horizon and disappeared.

Yet gradually over the millennia the horizons grew closer, until land appeared. In the way of rivers, this greatest of them all wandered back and forth from east to west. In time—which still had no meaning—it slowly ate its way through the soil and the bedrock. Moreover, its waters brought uncountable billions of tons of earth south from its tributaries, and with each shift of its course it deposited more and more of these effluvia along its banks. Slowly, ironically, the great river choked itself even as it built the banks and bluffs that gradually contained it. By the beginning of historical times its once immeasurable expanse had dwindled to little more than a mile's width in most places—still mighty proportions by any measure, yet a fraction of what once it had been.

In its place, across tens of thousands of square miles where once

1

the river flowed, there now sat new land, new parts of the continent. Soil from places that would later be known as Pennsylvania, Ohio, Kentucky, Illinois, and Indiana now sat on banks and grassy savannas in what men would one day call West Tennessee. Pieces of mountains from faraway Montana and Wyoming wedded with earth from the prairies of Nebraska and Kansas when the river placed them in the Delta and gentle rolling hills of Mississippi and northern Alabama. Even as the river kept at its work of bringing more land south, great winds from the west blew across vast central prairies, lifted dust from the ground, and carried it east to deposit it in great bluffs along the river's eastern bank. Yet no sooner—in geological time—did the soil settle than the river picked it up again and carried it south once more, this time to make the marshy bayous and prairies of Louisiana.

All the while, with the land itself in constant motion, the great builder kept bringing more from the north until, by what men chose to name the 1700s, its finest creation met European eyes. In time—a notion by then firmly fixed on this most unfixed of firmaments—those men called the region the Old Southwest. The name meant nothing, of course. Other men had come centuries earlier, giving place-names that would dominate the geography. Yet those names, too, stood of little consequence beside the achievement of the great river: It made a land where none had been, by bringing it from east, north, and west. The earth itself was the first immigrant.

Long before the first men came to start naming the new land, the region began to assume its distinctive character. Flora came on the winds, in the beaks of the birds, and out of the droppings of the migrating herds of bison from the western plains. Deer spread south from the north and east, the hulking alligators shifted west along the new coastline from future Florida. The white heron and the pelican shadowed the skies above the southern bayous. Hardwood forests and great spreads of pine covered much of Mississippi and Alabama, separated in places by sandy prairies or swampy bogs where only the cypress could flourish, and with it reptiles great and small. Breezes carried the spores of clinging mosses that spread through the forests, cloaking the trees in funereal vestments. Poison ivy crept along the dank forest floor, coiling so densely about the timber as to seem a part of the trees themselves. Everywhere lay green lushness, teeming life, and lurking death—a picture of creation itself, a window on Eden.

Against the background of those ageless eons of growth in the region, its habitation by man seems little more than a heartbeat. While the first Asian migrants crossed the ice bridge between Siberia and

Alaska perhaps fifteen thousand years ago, not long after the final retreat of the glaciers from the last Ice Age, their descendants took another three or four millennia to spread down to the southern banks of the still-great river that some of them would call Mississippi.[1] A few came directly along the river, from its confluence with the Ohio River, where the great mound-building Adena and Hopewell peoples once flourished.[2] Many more came from the west, crossed the Mississippi, and began the settlement of future Mississippi, Alabama, Louisiana, and Tennessee. They came as Muskogee but in time split into smaller families, the two greatest being the Chicacha and the Chacta—later anglicized into Chickasaw and Choctaw. The former settled in much of what became northern Mississippi and Alabama and western Tennessee. The latter in time populated much of the region south of the Chickasaw lands. When they came they already knew the rudiments of planting and supplemented their corn, beans, squash, and melons with chickens, which they domesticated, and bison from the herds that still migrated across the landscape, mostly north to south, seeking water and salt at the riverbanks.[3]

Smaller families splintered away from the larger tribes, even while others migrated from some of the more easterly aboriginal settlements. The Alabama, the Mobilien, the Colapissa, the Tonica, the Houma, and others chiefly inhabited the eastern bank of the Mississippi and the shores of the Gulf of Mexico. Among those small families of natives clinging to the dust-built bluffs overlooking the great river were the Natchez. They were neither the first nor the last in population, wealth, or civilization. They simply chose a good place to live, high above the river's occasional floods. Neighboring tribes knew them as fierce and well organized, at one time the rulers of a loose confederation of several lesser groups. Still, only about twelve hundred of them inhabited their half dozen villages on the bluffs. Indeed, none of the Muskogee peoples' cultures were overpopulous. The Choctaw made up no more than twenty thousand people scattered among their seventy or so villages, while the Chickasaw counted barely five thousand in their five major villages. Both cultures actively kept their populations up by absorbing other smaller groups into their "nations"; thus—thanks to the merging of so many other bloodlines—the true Chickasaw had disappeared long before the coming of the white man. Their penchant for such incorporation led early whites to call them simply "Breeds."[4]

Thanks in part to their small numbers, and even more to their ancestral descent from the woodland dwellers of the North, they kept to the forests for the wood to build their houses and fuel their fires, and to defend themselves against surprise in their occasional wars. They came to know the woodlands intimately and traveled them extensively. But the Choctaw and Chickasaw and the rest were not road builders. Like the migrating wildlife from which they learned so much, they followed the lines of least resistance. Rather than labor to carve great highways through the primeval forest, they used narrow tracks and moved in single file. They trod where the bison and deer had walked for centuries in their migrations, and like the animals they preferred the high ground, along the ridgelines and divides, to avoid the bogs and swamps and lands flooded in spring and summer. Not even the Indians themselves could number all the paths, especially since their "roads," like the great river that built this land, tended to meander and shift from time to time in response to mud, collapsing riverbanks, and ravages of weather that could send a hurricane to level a forest. Their more important trails led from one village to the next, past the burial and ceremonial mounds that the Chickasaw built, to shallow crossings on the streams and rivers, and to places where they found the best hunting or the richest yield of fish and shellfish. The Indians knew these roads intimately and kept them marked by blazed trees and painted sticks. Still, to the newcomer, these heathen highways could be almost imperceptible.[5]

The first white men to meet these natives, walk their trails, and covet their land were the French. The bold explorers Marquette and Joliet came down the Mississippi from Canada in the summer of 1673 and got as far as the Chickasaw country before turning back, only three hundred miles short of the river's mouth. Nine years later René-Robert Cavelier, Sieur de La Salle, retraced their voyage and pressed on all the way to the gulf. Along the way he saw Indian mounds on the banks to his left. He passed the home of the Natchez on the high bluffs formed by the west winds so long ago, and he envisioned a chain of forts running the entire length of the mighty river, built on such eminences, to guarantee the French hold on the New World.[6] When he returned two years later with an expedition from France to start his enterprise, his paranoia and autocratic behavior so alienated his men that two of them assassinated him before he could locate the mouth of the great river. The rest of his men succumbed either to disease or to Indians, with only two or three finally surviving and being absorbed into the native community.

Undeterred, the French came back, seeking to take and hold the new land before their rivals the Spanish. Pierre Le Moyne, Sieur d'Iberville, came in the spring of 1699 and rowed up the river almost to the Natchez villages. Assisted by his brother, Jean-Baptiste Le Moyne, Sieur de Bienville, Iberville firmly planted a French presence on the Lower Mississippi. Soon after the turn of the century, King Louis XIV had outposts on Mobile Bay and near Biloxi, and his Jesuit missionaries and traders were traveling up the river to the Natchez in search of wealth and souls. Iberville wanted to build a fort on their high bluff, but—significantly—settlers and commerce won the first footholds. As early as 1705 a white family moved to the vicinity, despite the prevailing notion that the Natchez, far from being friendly, were vicious barbarians.[7] Later, in 1714, the brothers Ursins built a trading post on the low riverside bottom directly beneath the bluff. It took two more years, and the first of several small skirmishes with the Natchez, before the French finally built their tiny Fort Rosalie des Natchez. At once the French began cultivating tobacco, indigo, rice, and cotton, while also experimenting with silkworms as well as a far more lucrative trade for Indian furs and pelts. Within seven years this outpost at the edge of the known New World grew to 303 inhabitants, more than a third of them slaves used to work the fields.[8] Small as the colony was, the colonists regarded it as considerably more important than the equally infant settlement downriver at New Orleans. By 1719 they were already calling the place "Nathez" after the Indian population of the same name. When new men like Joseph M. Pellerin reached New Orleans and heard of the number of people who went upriver to establish themselves on the bluff, he felt secure in taking his wife and himself there to join them. It was not an easy trip, for if they waited until August the river current could be too strong to paddle against.[9]

For the next half century the French held almost undisputed white hegemony over the Lower Mississippi. Spain scarcely contested the region. The Natchez, however, proved less passive. Inflamed by French outrages against their women, demands for more land, and the virtual exaction of tribute in the form of supplies, the Indians grew increasingly troublesome to the settlers. In 1729, when a blustering commandant at Fort Rosalie haughtily announced his intention to relocate the tribe, they struck without warning. On November 28 they entered the fort by a ruse and launched a devastating attack, slaying nearly one-third of the inhabitants of the settlement and taking another 450 or more prisoner. A month later the Natchez's neighbors the Yazoo launched another attack fifty miles upstream at Fort Saint Peter, with similar results. Yet what seemed a devastating blow to the Europeans proved in the end the undoing of the Natchez themselves. A month later the French, aided by Choctaw allies, struck back and then relentlessly pressed the Natchez into the interior. For two years the pursuit continued, capturing and killing hundreds. Slowly, on the run and in hiding, the Natchez lost their identity. Many of the survivors settled with the Chickasaw and became "Breeds" themselves. Others finished their lives as slaves. In 1743 Bienville boasted that the once-proud Natchez had been "totally destroyed." Not one of them ever again gazed across the Mississippi from their ancestral perch on the bluff. Only their name remained.

Indeed, the name of the Natchez was about all that outlasted the 1729–30 uprising, for the French themselves, despite Bienville's urgings, would not return in numbers. A small outpost remained and sporadically worked at rebuilding Fort Rosalie, but a visitor in 1751 found the site practically uninhabited. France had other things on its national mind. The whole Louisiana colony went through administrative turmoil, and then France and England went to war for seven years, with results that virtually forced the French out of the lower half of the continent. In 1762, in the face of the inevitable, France turned over its domain west of the Mississippi to Spain, and the next year ceded the remainder east of the river to England.[10]

The British quickly dubbed their new territory West Florida but did little to rebuild the Natchez settlement. After three years a small garrison occupied the renamed Fort Panmure on the bluff, then left it two years later; and a scare caused in 1770 by drunken Choctaw led to the near-abandonment of the area by its remaining settlers. When Captain Philip Pittman visited in 1769, he found the road from the landing up the bluff in a miserable state, unfit for carriages, though he added that once on the bluff "the trouble of going up is recompensed by the sight of a most delightful country of great extent." Another visitor, in February 1771, suggested that "an asthmatick man" could never make the climb; however, he agreed with Pittman that once atop the bluff "you have as noble and extensive a Prospect as can gratify the eye."[11] Some of the old French garden plots and fences still remained, and their fruit trees yet blossomed. The fort was in disrepair but usable, the mixture of moss and mud called *barbe Espagnole*—literally "Spanish beard"—still in place behind the walls of its buildings to provide insulation and prevent draft.[12] Slowly newcomers replaced those who had left, and Edward Mease in 1771 found several settlers' houses, their inhabitants striking him as "very industrious and healthy." As Britain and its North American colonies approached war in 1775, the population spread along the Mississippi from just above New Orleans to old Fort Saint Peter increased to nearly five thousand.[13] The next February, while Continental armies and Redcoats sparred in earnest, Governor Peter Chester implemented an order to lay out a town on the landing below the bluff. By the end of the year perhaps two hundred white settlers inhabited the spot. More important to its future, and that of the region, four trading houses operated at the river landing, one of them run by James Willing of Philadelphia. Louis Le Fleur operated a fairly regular boat service to and from Pensacola, Florida, that both brought outside supplies to Natchez and conveyed the produce of the area to English colonial markets. At last, and tenuously, Natchez linked itself and the potential riches of the Upper Mississippi and the wilderness interior to the world outside.[14]

But with outside commerce came outside attention, and inevitably the warring colonists turned their gaze to Natchez and the Southwest as a region of potential embarrassment to their British foes as well as commercial advantage to themselves. Both purposes would be served if Natchez could be wrested from its small and somnolent masters. In the summer of 1776 a Yankee captain, on his way to New Orleans, actually managed to raise the American colors briefly at Fort Panmure, only to see them come down again just as quickly. Perhaps the ease with which he did it, however, put an idea in the head of merchant Willing. His business failed the next year, and he went home to Philadelphia mired in debt yet mindful of the potential riches of Natchez. Through family influence he obtained authorization to lead a small expedition to secure from the Spanish in New Orleans several boatloads of supplies for the Continental Army. In the process, if he could, he was to seize British property. In the back of his mind lurked the possibility of taking West Florida itself.

Willing and twenty-seven others left from Pittsburgh in January 1778 aboard the small gunboat *Rattletrap* and made their way down the Ohio to the Mississippi, attracting more recruits along the way until the party numbered one hundred or more. On February 19, having already seized Loyalist property on the way, they reached Natchez and arrested Anthony Hutchins, one of the most prominent and successful landowners in the area, a man against whom Willing harbored a grudge quite possibly related to the failure of his store at the landing. Two days later Willing exacted a pledge from the citizens neither to fight the United States nor to aid its enemies, and then set out southward, pillaging and burning, until he reached the safe environs of Spanish New Orleans. Willing's personal motivation for taking booty revealed itself when he also seized property from British subjects living on the Spanish side of the river and, under Spain's protection, causing a minor diplomatic incident and some embarrassment for all parties involved. As a result the Spanish refused for some time to let Willing get away for the trip back up the Mississippi.

Finally they allowed him to leave on a sloop out of New Orleans, and none seemed too dismayed when the British captured him soon thereafter. His expedition failed in most of its official objects and disgraced Willing and his cause thanks to his party's quick descent from the lofty perch of patriotism to the scramble for plunder and slaves. Moreover, instead of taking West Florida for the United States, Willing only demonstrated to the neighboring Spaniards just how easily it could be done.[15] It did not take them long to act. Already relations between Spain and England teetered on the brink of war. When it actually came in 1779, one of the first acts of the authorities in New Orleans was a sweep up the Mississippi. Almost without resistance the British commander on the river, Lieutenant Colonel Alexander Dickson, surrendered his post at Baton Rouge, sixty miles upriver from New Orleans. On October 4 Captain Anthony Forster, commanding the post at Fort Panmure, received an order from Dickson to yield his garrison, and the following day he did so. It was a sad day for the British subjects in Natchez, "His Majesty's dutiful & loyal Subjects" as they styled themselves. While complimenting Dickson on his less-than-heroic defense, they did not waste a moment in commending themselves to their new Spanish rulers by flattering Governor Bernardo de Galvez as "a brave and generous Conqueror." First and last the people of Natchez felt their greatest loyalty to themselves. They were planters and traders at the edge of a wilderness, yet also on the verge of potentially the richest trading highway of the continent—the great river. Rigid loyalty could prove costly in days like these for men with eyes cast to the future. Almost all of these leading planters like Anthony Hutchins, John Blommart, Alexander McIntosh, and more, owed their original land grants to England.[16] For the first but hardly the last, time, Natchez's citizens leaned with the prevailing political breezes.[17]

As they would do often, they read those winds perfectly. It helped that the people of Natchez were by this time already a polyglot. Besides the British grant holders, a fair number of Americans from the Atlantic Seaboard colonies came during the 1770s, some due to British encouragement before the outbreak of the Revolution and others once the fighting began. Now under Spanish dominion, the settlement's actual Spanish inhabitants were and would always be among its smallest minorities. Indeed, the permanent influence of Spain's years of rule would prove elusive. Few place names remember them. Few settlers came, and fewer still stayed. Only some soldiers, appointed officials, and a handful of merchants actually settled in the province for a time. Their longest-lasting stamp on the infant community proved to be the utter confusion of the Spanish land-grant system, one that would take future rulers years to settle, rarely to the satisfaction of all.[18]

Captain Juan De la Villebeuvre took possession of Fort Panmure on October 5, 1779, and immediately required an oath of allegiance from the landholders in Natchez. Those declining to sign had to leave. But soon thereafter more American settlers arrived from the East, happy to swear loyalty since their colonies were now allied with Spain against Britain. De la Villebeuvre ruled his domain with a gentle hand, but he saw all too well how thin was the support for his king. "I know of no one faithful in all this district," he lamented to his superiors late in 1779.[19]

It did not help that Fort Panmure was crumbling, and authorities in New Orleans showed little inclination to help. Worse, the British in nearby East Florida kept a watchful eye on affairs along the Mississippi and proved only too happy to take advantage when possible. Repeatedly British commanders urged citizens, white and Indian, to rise against De la Villebeuvre, but only a portion felt receptive. As Anthony Hutchins, perhaps the most prominent of the colony's leading men, noted a few years later, a majority of the Natcheans, after some unease under Spanish rule, very quickly adapted to it, especially when Galvez offered them "the prospect of future indulgences, accompanied with many natural advantages that presaged a plentiful living & the accumulation of wealth."[20]

But winds shifted, and when Britain sent unsolicited commissions to men like John Blommart, with encouragement to rebel, a loose coalition of about two hundred Loyalists, American colonists, and thoroughly confused Choctaw rose under his command. They attacked Fort Panmure on April 22, 1781, but someone had warned De la Villebeuvre in advance, and he was ready. The siege lasted for nearly two weeks. Finally, on May 4, after being fooled into thinking that the upstarts had undermined his fort with explosives, the Spaniard capitulated. Almost at once the rebels fell out among themselves. Some wanted to execute their captives, despite the fact that most of them—like their attackers—had eighteen months before been signers of a testimonial to their benevolent rulers. With allegiances shifting almost daily, Hutchins, long a vocal supporter of the Spaniards, now came to the side of the rebels as their success seemed assured. He and Blommart managed to spare the lives of the garrison and then also defeated a faction within their following who wanted to declare for the United States. They had little time to gloat, however, for the Spaniards soon took Pensacola from the British and were on their way back toward Natchez. Many of the rebels left the region, some to take cover in the interior with the Indians, while others, including Hutchins, made the dangerous overland trek to refuge with the British. In June 1781 Spaniards approached Fort Panmure once more, and Blommart yielded without resistance, finding himself sent in irons to New Orleans, together with many of the other leaders of the rebellion.[21]

Predictably the surrendered rebels quickly renewed their oaths of allegiance to Spain, and in time even Blommart and the other leaders obtained release and Hutchins returned to his home. Thereafter the Natchez settlers remained docile until European powers decided their immediate fate. In 1782 the initial treaty between the United States and Britain ceded the territory to the Americans, despite Spanish occupancy. The next year the Treaty of Paris did much the same, also guaranteeing to American traders the right of free passage down the Mississippi, even though doing so meant crossing Spanish territory—a confusing diplomatic tangle and one that Spain determined to ignore, since Britain was giving things it did not have to give to the Americans. Natchez would remain part of the far-flung Spanish dominions, and that was that.

As peace came to the continent once more, Natchez itself lay in danger of being forgotten. Though happy to have it, the Spaniards paid scant attention to their West Florida possession. By 1783 its population, always variable, now counted no more than five hundred. True, there were the large landowners like Hutchins, but the community itself seemed dormant. Worst of all, it lay so far out on the edge of white civilization that communications could be a nightmare. Its only potential markets were New Orleans, and from there Europe, or the spreading American settlements five hundred miles northeast along the upper reaches of the Tennessee and Cumberland Rivers, in what is now Tennessee. The New Orleans route lay open only at Spanish whim, while the other offered seemingly unsurmountable obstacles. Commerce coming to Natchez virtually had to float down the upper tributaries into the Mississippi, and then down its wide expanse for hundreds of miles through sometimes hostile territory controlled by Indians, Spaniards, and scattered banditti. Once in Natchez or even New Orleans, no vessels could run back upstream against the current. It was a one-way trip, and voyagers' only alternatives for returning were either to book ocean passage out of New Orleans or to attempt to find a way through the wilderness along the myriad confusing Indian and animal paths. Neither option offered much encouragement. Yet at both ends of that wilderness, in Natchez and among the British inhabitants, and in the faraway United States, a growing interest fueled hopes of somehow bridging the gap. Over such a bridge could pass trade, always the first interest of these pragmatic settlers by the bluffs. For the infant republic to the north and east, such a link also offered the promise of access to vast new territory, a pathway to empire. Even as the Spaniards doggedly ignored the treaties and continued their indolent rule of the district, men of vision and ambition turned their thoughts to a potential future for an American Natchez, and to a way to join it to the new nation.

In the ensuing decade more and more Americans acted on that vision by making the long journey down the rivers to Natchez, and even on to New Orleans, content—for the time—to dwell as Spanish citizens, or at least on the sufferance of indulgent Spanish authorities. Once more Natchez's people were asked to swear allegiance to Spain— and did so, of course. In 1787 Spain elevated the status of the colony by sending a genuine governor to rule from Natchez. Manuel Gayoso de Lemos proved to be the best single decision the Spaniards ever made regarding their possession, for the young, efficient, and personable governor secured the amity and regard of almost all in his small realm. He married a local woman, entertained lavishly, and wore a gloved hand in his dealings with the potentially troublesome colonists. Though he was hardly responsible for edicts from Madrid, locals also saw him as the embodiment of a gradual liberalization of government policy. In 1784 Spain closed the Lower Mississippi to American traffic bent on reaching New Orleans. But there was rising pressure far upriver in the settlements along the Cumberland and Tennessee. Before long almost fifty thousand pioneers flocked out of Virginia and the other Eastern Seaboard states to populate the new land. This increase required an immediate safety valve, both to vent the flow of population and to give it an outlet for trade.

These westerners looked only to the rivers that served the Mississippi, and to the great river itself, as an avenue for their goods to reach markets. The eastern overland route through the Appalachians simply was not practical. Within only a few years, denied access to New Orleans and its port, these new entrepreneurs spoke increasingly and openly of acting on their own, without the sanction of government, to spread south and seize what Spain denied them. Sensitive to this danger, in 1788 Spain—through Gayoso—changed its policy. Already hundreds of illegal immigrants had come down the river from Kentucky, many of them attracting notice for lawlessness and thievery once they arrived, and found themselves unable to trade. Now the king in Madrid decided actively to encourage such immigration. Many of these frontiersmen felt alienated from their eastern American brethren, who seemed indifferent to their interests. It was thought that allowing them to move south would discourage incipient invasion conspiracies and at the same time weaken a potential national foe looking covetously at the Louisiana Territory, including Natchez. Besides, with these new men under his eye, Gayoso could better prevent them conspiring than if they were hundreds of miles upriver. Spain even offered land grants to those who swore fealty, and opened the Mississippi once more, though charging a hefty duty on exports.

The scheme worked well for a time. That same year Natchez got nearly one hundred new settlers, more than half of them from Kentucky alone, and by 1790 they arrived at the rate of forty-three a month, almost half of them slaves to work the new land grants. For the first time the lower landing at Natchez—soon to be called "Under-the-Hill"—almost teemed with craft, chiefly flatboats, two-thirds of them from Kentucky. By 1792 the population of the district swelled from 500 to 4,346, with more than 1,000 of them settling in the growing community on the bluff itself.[22] Almost all came by river, for no practical overland route afforded access from the Cumberland settlements.

Yet the Spaniards ultimately failed. Rather than siphoning significant population from upriver, their immigration policy only temporarily eased pressure rather than released it. Kentucky became a state in 1792, Tennessee four years later, and each experienced an attendant surge in settlement, which only renewed the pressure downstream. Spain's open navigation edict, combined with this enhanced population perched on the Upper Mississippi, resulted in a rapid increase in traffic on the river, and most of those moving south, whether for settlement or temporary trade, brought with them ideas not entirely consonant with Spain's notions for the district. Conflict was almost inevitable.

On October 16, 1795, chiefly in response to international affairs not directly related to the Mississippi Valley, the Spaniards concluded the Treaty of San Lorenzo, by which they ceded to the United States all the territory it claimed east of the Mississippi above the thirty-first parallel, or roughly from a point about forty miles downriver from Natchez. Madrid saw this as a stopgap measure, chiefly to prevent the Americans getting too friendly with its rivals the British in East Florida. Indeed, given the opportunity, Spain would have repudiated the treaty, and when President George Washington's appointed commissioner, Andrew Ellicott, arrived in Natchez the next year to commence surveying the new boundary, he encountered little cooperation from Gayoso. Though polite with each other, they squabbled over matters great and small, and Gayoso presented one pretext after another to postpone commencing the work of the survey for more than two years.[23] In the end Gayoso did not finally order the evacuation of Natchez by Spanish troops until 1798. Then at last, on March 30, Ellicott arose at four o'clock in the morning and walked to Fort Panmure to find the last of the Spanish guard just in the act of leaving. He walked through the gate they had left open and climbed to the parapet. There, in a gray predawn glimmer, he could see all of the great river beneath him. Directly below, on the flatland "under the hill" that stretched perhaps an eighth of a mile from the bottom of the bluff to the water's edge, he saw Gayoso's men boarding their boats. Silently he watched "the pleasing prospect of the galleys getting under way." Before full daylight they passed downstream out of sight. Natchez, at last, was American.[24]

The departure of the Spanish hardly put an end to its difficulties, however. Ellicott finally started his survey, but political factions that had arisen during the past several years renewed their agitation, threatening the district with anarchy. Congress began the work of organization on April 7 when it created the Mississippi Territory, but that was only a start. "This is a Hot Country & peopled in a very chequered manner," complained Captain Isaac Guion, commanding the small American garrison at Natchez. It seemed full of desperate characters, many of whom he believed had fled authorities upriver in Kentucky. They seemed at the same time to clamor for government and yet to fear it, and the firm hand of a resident governor was needed to get the district and the new territory on track. Four months later, on August 6, 1798, that new governor, Winthrop Sargent, recently governor of the Northwest Territory, arrived in Natchez, now designated the territorial capital, and almost at once the factions began to settle and the population to quiet with the prospect of final stability.[25]

In the past four decades Natchez had been French, then British, then Spanish, and now at last American. No wonder Natcheans felt confused and paid allegiance chiefly to themselves and their own individual interests. Only with the coming of sustained communication and trade with their new American compatriots would they finally, in time, feel a single loyalty, and with the organization of the territory and the further opening of opportunity there for new settlers and entre-preneurs from the United States, that increased level of contact would come. It would come on flatboats and rafts and keelboats and more, but that would not be enough. For the region to thrive, and for white civilization to spread and flourish in this new southwestern bit of America, there had to be another artery of commerce and transportation, one not subject to the whims of the great Mississippi. Only when they found or carved an overland link with the rest of the nation would they be truly bound together on the road to empire.

2

The Road to Natchez

On the Fourth of July, 1797, Francis Baily arose from his bed at the Job Routh house, just a few hundred yards outside the village of Natchez.[1] He had arrived on the river four days earlier, concluding part of a major tour through the wilder parts of America, and now rested on this edge of civilization before the journey to the East. It was a significant day, of course, and the American element in Natchez celebrated in what style it could afford, in part just to aggravate the Spaniards in Fort Panmure, who still delayed acting on the provisions of the Treaty of San Lorenzo. Andrew Ellicott hosted a party—an indoor affair, since Ellicott rarely ventured outside during the summer for fear of poison ivy—to which he invited Baily, but the Englishman, anxious to be on his way, declined. Besides, he had other matters to settle. His horses were rested from their recent exertion, but he had to lay in a store of supplies to last him for some weeks on what he expected would be a tedious journey. He paid Routh to kill an ox and dry the meat to preserve it. Bread, of course, was out of the question; hard biscuit was a traveler's staple. Unfortunately the only man in Natchez who could make it was a Spaniard in the fort, and though he agreed—for a price—to provide the article, he had to make it secretly, baking some twenty-five pounds for Baily and his companions. While seeing their horses freshly shod, they bought the rest of the necessary staples, every man providing himself with six pounds of flour, twelve pounds of bacon, three pounds of rice, and some coffee and sugar as well as the dried beef and biscuit. The coffee and sugar might have seemed frivolous to some, but, expecting to be in the wilderness for three weeks at least, Baily and his friends needed the small cheer these modest comforts afforded. And in anticipation of hazards along the way, they put in their bags something at the far end of the scale of luxuries. Each man secured a pint of roasted corn, ground to a fine powder. From the Choctaw these whites had learned that when all other food was gone—lost, stolen, destroyed—a man could survive by taking a spoonful of corn every morning to stave off hunger. Baily regarded it as a "preventative against want," little imagining that he would need it before journey's end.[2]

That afternoon, while the Americans in Natchez drank their toasts and glowered at the Spaniards in their lonely fort, Baily rode a dozen miles out of town on the road leading northeast, on what locals called the "Path to the Choctaw Nation." It was the same route that some of the refugees from the abortive 1781 revolt used to escape to American settlements far to the north.[3] While hardly a road, the trail nevertheless stretched some sixty miles or more until it reached a stream called Bayou Pierre, and Baily and his companions made a leisurely trip of it, taking three days to reach Grindstone Ford on the bayou. They moved slowly through the piney woods to allow others of their party to catch up, sleeping outdoors at night for want of taverns or other accommodation and occasionally finding meals at plantation homes they passed.

Grindstone Ford was the last limit of civilization, the outer edge of the Natchez district settlements. Once they crossed the bayou and struck out into Choctaw and then Chickasaw country, they would be in the wilderness. Baily keenly observed the land and its people as he rode, those first three days, and concluded with a charity rare among Englishmen of his time that because of the youth and rawness of the territory "we ought rather to anticipate what it will be than to dwell upon what it actually is." Once under the gentle governance of the United States, and with all its potential for commerce and cultivation, he expected the region to blossom with "the arts of civilised life" and become first among the American peoples for "commerce and the diffusion of general knowledge in the western territory of America."[4] That was a lot to foretell as he stood there, looking across Bayou Pierre into the edge of the wilderness.

That last night at Grindstone Ford could hardly have encouraged Baily. He shared the house with his companions, his host, all their baggage, a supply of the owner's lumber, and the few articles of furniture belonging to any frontier habitation. There in that single room they cooked their simple dinner of mush and milk, and there they all bedded down for the night. Baily tried to write in his journal, but the sounds and smells of a dozen men drove him outdoors, where he walked along the stream for a time, then laid his blanket in the owner's garden and slept there. Even for that, the keeper of the house charged him twenty-five cents for lodging.

The next morning Baily's party, thirteen strong, crossed the bayou on a rude ferry and set out into the virtual unknown, armed only with what information they had been able to obtain back in Natchez as to paths and hazards. Almost immediately they encountered the first of a host of difficulties facing any traveler in this wilderness. They came to a small creek that proved too deep to ford. Fortunately a fallen tree bridged its steep banks, and the men unloaded their animals and precariously carried all their baggage across. The horses had to swim, then be reloaded. But for the serendipitous accident of the presence of that tree, they would have had to risk their belongings to the swimming horses or else find a suitably located tree to fell themselves.

The morning after that they met their first Choctaw, a war party of forty, brandishing scalps just taken on a raid against a neighboring tribe. The Indians posed no outward threat to the travelers, energetically shaking their hands and offering a pipe to smoke as a sign of friendship. They spoke no English, and the whites had no Indian interpreter with them, so all communication lay in grins, laughs, nods, and crude signs that laboriously but eventually conveyed a message. Most important of all to these men, the natives managed to confirm that they were on the right trail. With a score of dim paths and trackways evident as the routes of animals and men, finding the right one was as much a matter of chance as intent, and the reassurance from these Choctaw considerably cheered Baily and his companions.[5]

Already they saw along the path evidence of eerie times ages earlier, part of the mystery of the territory. Between Natchez and Bayou Pierre they passed at least two sets of ancient Indian mounds, and once across Grindstone Ford they immediately encountered more as they peered through the forest. The Indian paths they covered, in fact, seemed to lead from one set of mounds to another, hinting that these strange places perhaps held some ceremonial significance to the Choctaw. Unable to converse with the natives, Baily and his friends could only guess as to the meaning of the mounds.

Soon they rode along ridgelines and above bluffs and then out onto the sandy prairies along the Pearl River, until they came to a place called "Forks of the Path." Here one trail pointed eastward to the Choctaw villages, while the other led northeast toward the Chickasaw. Baily wanted the latter, but since the trail east looked more traveled, he almost took it until a passing Indian managed to set him right. Using his hand to his head as a sign, he told the whites that it would take them "five *sleeps*"—five days—to reach the Chickasaw nation. That done, the Choctaw used a stick to sketch on the ground the principal trails that lay ahead of them, indicating by pointing and grunts just which they should take at each fork.

The ground turned increasingly sandy and gravelly and then almost abruptly became rough and broken, more so as they progressed. The path almost disappeared in the dense underbrush, and Baily noted that the trail generally led over the worst possible ground as it clung to the ridgelines to avoid swamps and low places. Though the thirteen men and their thirty or more horses walked single file, they still sometimes lost the path. Then the saddle girth on one animal loosened and its pack slipped, sending the horse off in a panic, and several others with it. They lost all of that day and most of the next trying to recover the horses as well as the baggage that spilled out along the way as the frightened animals bolted through the woods and brush. In the end, however, all they lost was a tin cup, thanks largely to the wonderful ability of another Indian whose path crossed theirs to track the passage of the animals through woods and grass. But then, that second night, having unknowingly been followed by a party of other Indians, they found two of their horses stolen when they awoke in the morning, and an attempt to track them proved fruitless. All they could do to console themselves was spend that night resting men and animals beside a cool, clear stream and parcel out a bit of their precious coffee and sugar.[6]

They arose refreshed just before dawn the next morning and went through what had by now become a daily procedure. First they removed the hobbles that kept their animals from wandering in the night, packed them, and then traveled for several hours until near midday, when they stopped wherever they found water. There they unpacked the horses, ate a meal, and rested for two or three hours during the hottest part of the afternoon. Then they packed once again and moved on until dark.[7] The ground they traveled over this gravelly prairie afforded scant pasture and little more water, forcing them now to move on after dark some nights before they found a spring or stream. Sometimes they passed by water unseen as it lay covered by heavy brush, and on a few occasions Baily confessed shouting for joy at the discovery of "*a nasty dirty puddle.*"

Drinking water like that hardly encouraged good health, and the day after the loss of the two horses, three of their party fell ill, unable to continue. The next day Baily and the rest went ahead, promising to send back the first Indians they encountered with some of the herbal remedies for illness that the natives often carried. It was all they could do for men no longer able to ride or walk. Hardly had the travelers resumed their journey than they nearly lost their way in an impenetrable thicket of brambles and downed trees left by a recent hurricane, almost completely obscuring a path none too clear at the best of times. Two "sleeps" later they finally saw signs of Indian habitation, first a cornfield and then a small village. It proved a triple blessing. They filled themselves with fresh roasted corn now that their supplies had already dwindled. They sent a Chickasaw back to aid their ailing companions. And finding the village confirmed that despite all the possible wrong turns along the way, they still rode the right path.

The Indians showed great curiosity about the travelers, and even more for their horses and baggage. Only constant vigilance prevented pilfering from their packs, for to the Chickasaw and other tribes in the region petty theft was a game, a source of some pride and jest when successful and little or no shame when caught. Baily marveled at the life of these people. Whole families slept in the same bed. They sat on tree stumps for chairs and drank from hollowed gourds. When not hunting, the men spent the entire day lying about "in a state of constant indolence" in the sun, while the women tended the fields of corn and tobacco. With them Baily also found a white man, "one of those of whom there are a great number, who, from habit and disposition, prefer the Indian mode of life." The man interpreted for the travelers their wants, and it was he who arranged for a native physician to make the trek back to the ill travelers. He also told them where the path ahead of them lay and offered to accompany them on their way.[8]

It is well that Baily had knowledgeable company, for now the trail became even more intricate and confused with side lanes and overgrowth. Fortunately they went only nine miles before coming to a place probably already known as "Tockshish" or "Estokish." Supposedly it derived from a Chickasaw or Choctaw word, but just as likely the spot took its name from the "plantation" of John McIntosh, the first white habitation travelers encountered since leaving Grindstone Ford. McIntosh's father had moved to the region as a British agent to the Chickasaw before 1770 and simply remained, insulated by distance from all the political upheavals of the ensuing quarter century. Like him, his son was literate, educated, influential with the Chickasaw, and undoubtedly reclusive. Yet, as frontier custom required, he welcomed at his home the few white travelers who passed his way. He planted corn and tobacco on his farm, with the assistance of a few black slaves and apparently with the goodwill of his Indian neighbors. Nevertheless

McIntosh knew how quickly amity could turn to enmity in the wilderness. The Chickasaw had just commenced war with their Creek neighbors some distance to the east, and only recently a party of Creek got close enough to the Chickasaw village a few miles north of McIntosh's to kill some of their foes. Prudently, the Englishman was in the act of surrounding his house with a high plank palisade when Baily arrived.[9]

The house itself Baily found to be a sorry place, little better than some of the Indian huts he had seen, but he could not fault McIntosh's hospitality. With their supplies dwindling, the travelers purchased for two dollars some dried beef and venison and a quantity of Indian bread but declined the offer of a homemade cheese that proved so dreadful they could not eat it. Their host also warned them that the road ahead would become even more difficult until they reached the big Chickasaw village, and recommended a white guide who for six dollars would lead them on the right trail.[10]

Early on July 19 Baily and the rest bade farewell to McIntosh, went once more through the monotonous routine of packing their animals, and set off behind their new guide. Along the way they accepted the hospitality of some Chickasaw under a half-breed leader, entered their hut, and shared a meal of bread and venison. Each of the men pulled a spoon from his pack and joined their hosts in sipping milk from an iron kettle. "Picture to yourself a dirty hole of a place," Baily wrote that night, "without any other light but what came in at the door, plastered up on each side with mud, with a rough-hewn stool, formed with a tomahawk out of the trunk of a tree, an iron kettle which had served for all the purposes of life, together with all our spoons dipping into it alternately." Presumably Baily did not mean that the offensive kettle served "sanitary" as well as culinary purposes.[11]

Refreshed, the white men continued their journey until they came within about five miles of the great Chickasaw town. Fearing the "pilfering disposition" of the Indians, and realizing that amid such a large number of them there would be no way to guard the animals against every hand, they decided to camp quietly—and they hoped secretly—outside the village. Besides, there they could dine on peaches and apples still growing wild in abandoned Indian fields and now turning ripe. The next morning they went on and crested a small rise to see the "town" spread before them. Like most Indian communities, it was no town at all but rather a number of clusters of four or five huts, each separated from the others by fields of corn, small vegetable gardens, and fruit orchards. This was what the Chickasaw called "Bigtown," though other, smaller villages lay scattered in the vicinity.[12] Indeed, Baily and the others had already encountered signs that the Chickasaw had long inhabited this area, for they passed several sets of ancient mounds during the day.

The next morning Baily and his friends approached the village, first observing the Chickasaw men amusing themselves at sport. Beyond them they came to the main part of the town and stopped to try to buy a few souvenirs to take north. Unfortunately they tarried too long, and before long half the village surrounded them, paying especially curious attention to their horses and packs. Some looked longingly at their firearms while others shook saddlebags loaded with silver dollars and smiled knowingly. Knowing objection to be futile and possibly dangerous, Baily could do nothing but acquiesce. But he did refuse to trade them his hat, despite the Chickasaw repeatedly shouting a word they had recently learned from Kentucky travelers, "Swop!" Sensing that prudence suggested a speedy departure, the whites gathered their arms from the hands of the admiring natives, secured their packs, and mounted to leave, Baily himself at the end of the line.

At the edge of the village two Indians met them, shaking each traveler by the hand as he passed. Baily's companions did not look back to see that two natives detained him when his turn came. One started very carefully examining his packs, grabbed his pistols from their holsters on his horse's neck, and then demanded his hat. Baily handed it over, declined to "swop," and was about to recover it when the other Chickasaw grabbed it and ran off. In a rage, Baily dismounted and chased him, threatening to throw his own tomahawk if the man did not return his hat. Baily finally recovered his headgear, but when he turned to retrace his steps, he found that both his horses had bolted on their own and disappeared. Almost miraculously, the remaining Chickasaw returned his pistols, and Baily, feeling very much alone and without a guess as to which direction his animals had taken, set off in hopes of finding his companions, now well out of sight. In an hour or so he caught up to them, glad to find that his horses had naturally followed their companions. Although it was a narrow escape, leaving Baily nothing the poorer except for a fright, like so many of their adventures, it owed entirely to the disinclination of the Indians to take advantage of them.[13]

They moved into hilly country then, frequently encountering the innumerable tributaries of the Tombigbee River. Some of these creeks proved too deep to ford, and once again they relied on trees obviously felled on purpose to bridge the banks. With the Chickasaw—whom they still feared—safely behind, they encountered a new danger, poison ivy, which they heard called "*poison vine.*" Every time they walked their horses on the narrow trails, they exposed their legs to the offending leaves. Baily's legs swelled ominously. He could not wear his boots or shoes and then had to slit his trouser legs to get them over his swollen feet. He cut the leather uppers from his boots and fashioned moccasins to wear, but then as they passed into hilly country covered with small sharp stones, every time he dismounted to rest his horse he found the jagged gravel piercing his makeshift shoes and even the soles of his feet.

In this condition, and with only an Indian herbal poultice to relieve his discomfort, Baily felt no small elation when he crossed Bear Creek and after a few more miles beheld from a steep rise the wide, majestic Tennessee River before him. It meant that the trip was three-fourths completed. Having planned for three weeks on the journey, they had already been eighteen days on the road, their supplies dwindling rapidly and their stamina with them. The Chickasaw villages had been the last opportunity to purchase any food until they came within a few miles of Nashville on the Cumberland.[14] But any excitement cooled rapidly when they realized that now they would have to cut timbers and build rafts to get themselves across nearly a mile of water to the opposite bank. Worse, the river ran with a swift current that season, and if it carried a raft or a swimmer downstream from the sandbars on either side at the crossing, the banks below rose perpendicular, with no foothold for escaping the river.

The first raft crossed successfully, as did the second, but Baily and his companions on theirs were so exhausted by their labor in building and then trying to pull the raft across by swimming and towing, not to mention the swelling in their legs from poison ivy, that they made no headway and the stream carried them below the sandbar. "Imagine us, I say," he would write, "our heads just above water, our hands clinging to the raft and supporting our weary bodies, our provisions before our eyes, but ourselves unable to touch them, as the least disturbance given to our raft would instantly overwhelm it." "What was to be done?" he thought in retrospect, and his answer was simply "Nothing." As the current swept them out of sight of the rest of their party, they saw downstream other men in a boat. At first they feared it might be an Indian war party, but they proved to be friendly Cherokee rather some distance from their usual homelands. Soon the natives loaded Baily's men and their baggage into their canoe and paddled them back upstream to the rest of their anxious companions and a happy reunion.

They celebrated with a meal and then commenced the laborious process of carrying their baggage piece by piece up the steep, slippery, twenty-foot banks, a task so exhausting that it took them half the day even with the assistance of the Cherokee. That called for another meal, and then the Indians managed to convey by signs that Nashville lay only another three sleeps distant. In fact, it was about fifty miles and would take them another week, a journey not commenced auspiciously by having to spend that night in a mosquito-infested lowland. The next morning they felt some relief at climbing back out of the bottom and onto the ridgeline of what locals called the "high lands." From here onward they traveled on elevated crests and plateaus, still densely wooded but dry. But that day their renewed spirits received a shattering blow when they encountered a white man on the trail who told them—quite in error—that they had another two hundred miles to go to reach Nashville. He may have been playing a cruel joke or just unable to gauge at all accurately the distance he had himself traveled. In either case Baily and friends recoiled in shock. Their provisions were all but depleted, since they had counted on encountering some of Nashville's outlying settlements on the morrow. Worse, he also told them that the Creek were on the warpath and could be expected to be watching the trail ahead.[15]

They rode on until eleven that night, then halted, in some disarray from fear and hunger. All that remained to them was their ground corn, and at least they found that it did seem to swell in the stomach and assuage their pangs for a time. They tried hunting, but their pistols proved too inaccurate for them to take any game, and they had earlier accidentally ruined the stock of their only rifle. Besides, with the Creek about, the noise of firearms could summon swift and brutal death. "In this predicament," said Baily, "we hurried on as fast as we could." One of them rode constantly a quarter mile ahead of the others as a scout. At night they tried to conceal their whereabouts by each walking singly a mile or more to a preagreed location, where they slept without a fire, speaking only in whispers even during the dark hours. Their sole cheer was a spoonful of their ground corn mixed with a little water, and that had to last them all the next day.

Despite their precautions the whites could not evade the careful eyes of two Chickasaw who had been traveling the same path a day ahead of them. Doubling back, the Indians came up to Baily's camp one night and, seeing that the sleeping men were whites rather than Creek, actually walked unannounced into their midst and were only discovered when one of the travelers saw a face in the darkness that he did not recognize. It put a terrible fright into Baily at first, but soon they were talking with the Chickasaw about the dangers on the road and exchanging stories of paths and trails. Nevertheless, from then on the party moved with depressed spirits in tempo with the hunger in their bellies, made the worse by the constant sight of deer and turkeys that they could not approach close enough to shoot with their pistols, even if they dared chance the noise.

The second day after leaving the Tennessee, they stumbled into a party of Cherokee sitting at a cook fire, and after mutual assurances of friendliness, the Indians shared their freshly roasted venison, which they all dipped into honey spread in a deerskin. "No meal was ever so grateful as this," Baily wrote later, and even the watching Cherokee seemed to take pleasure in their guests' gluttony. When Baily asked the distance to Nashville, they told him it would be another three sleeps, and gave the party enough venison to get there, for which the whites exchanged salt, gunpowder, and some silver in small denominations.

Their spirits revived by the meal and the prospect of avoiding starvation, and with Nashville seemingly within reach at last, they set out again July 27 and soon came to the bluff overlooking the Duck River. Only a few hundred feet wide and not too deep to ford, it presented no obstacle at all compared to the Tennessee, but on the other side they encountered some difficulty in finding the right path once more. In times past, this side of the river between the Duck and Lick Creek, some distance away, was heavily traveled by bison herds moving to the latter for its salt licks. They created the main trail now used by men, but they also stamped out a host of lesser ones, and in the end Baily had to guess which to take, and guessed right.[16]

At least from here on they left their fear of the Creek behind them, for they believed that that tribe rarely if ever operated north of the Duck. As the ground became even more broken and hilly, they sometimes had to dismount to clamber up steep slopes and then almost slide down the other side, trusting their horses to follow on their own. By Saturday, July 29, with only that day's provisions left from their supply of venison, they redoubled their efforts to move quickly in hopes of reaching a settlement before nightfall. By now some of their animals were suffering so badly from the exertions of the long trip that they slowed the party, while Baily and others still walked only with difficulty, thanks to the poison ivy. The solution seemed to be for each to go at his best pace. Three men with heartier constitutions and less fagged horses struck out ahead, Baily and another came behind at a slower pace, and the worst-off two brought up the rear. They agreed that as soon as the first reached civilization, he would send back help for the rest.

Even traveling after dark, Baily still could not see a sign of human habitation, and when they lay down that night they really collapsed, unable to walk farther or even to try to build a fire. In the morning, a little refreshed, they boiled some coffee then set out, expecting every time they topped a ridge or came out into a clearing to see a white settlement ahead. Noon came and went without a sign of civilization, and as they made a fire and ate the very last of their paltry provisions, their spirits once more took a downturn. Too exhausted and depressed to continue, they slept under the shade of some trees for three hours while their equally depleted horses grazed. Then they moved on slowly until past sunset, when they came to the Harpeth River. In fact, had they but known, they only missed the home of Hugh Leeper, who settled on what—with typical frontier nonchalance about spelling—would become Leiper's Creek in 1788, barely a mile from the path they followed that day.[17]

What they did discover, however, were two Indians on the trail ahead after they crossed the Harpeth. Coming up, Baily found that they were the same two who had surprised their camp a few nights before. Now they agreed to travel together, but it was too late to continue, so they all bedded down without anything to eat, taking cold cheer from each other's company. The next morning, July 31, their twenty-seventh day on the trail, the Indians went their own way and Baily left early. At about 9 A.M. he noticed that for the first time the path ahead of him seemed to widen from the narrow single track it had been for hundreds of miles. Then he saw the prints of cattle and other domestic animals, and two hours later he beheld a farmhouse. "Nothing could exceed our joy," he wrote in his diary. He and his companion jumped up and down and shouted their relief, only to find themselves turned away by the lady of the house when they came to the door. She could offer neither provisions nor shelter but said that the more established plantation of a Captain Joslin lay less than half an hour ahead. Baily hurried on and soon saw the horses of his three friends who had ridden ahead grazing in a pasture. Moments later the parties happily reunited, and Joslin himself warmly welcomed them into his strong log house. Already steaming in the fireplace, boiled bacon and heaping bowls of beans awaited them, as well as bread made of Indian cornmeal. "As it was *quantity*, not *quality*, which we stood most in need of," Baily gratefully recalled, "we made a very hearty meal, and devoured with great avidity." Then, just as they finished their meal, they heard the shouts of the last two of their party, now seeing for themselves their first signs of white civilization since leaving Natchez.

They spent the afternoon in welcome conversation, comparing their several adventures while separated. Most chose to remain a few days sampling Joslin's hospitality and recovering their stamina, but

Baily and his companion of the recent days felt an undeniable desire to push on to Nashville at once despite their fatigue. They set out that evening, now able to admire the countryside thanks to the disappearance of their anxiety. They saw a lovely, rich country, dotted with seemingly prosperous plantations that increased in frequency as they moved forward. A couple of coaches even passed them on the road, which had now become a fair highway, and private carriages rumbled by them in the twilight. Finally, about 7 P.M., they saw in the distance Nashville itself. "The sight of it gave us great pleasure," Baily wrote, and to them the homely buildings of the rude frontier community took on a beauty as if they had been the stateliest mansions of the East. In quick time they found which of the community's taverns offered the best accommodations and, wasting no time, went there, turned their horses over to the stabler, and "entered the house and sat us down, completely happy in having performed this laborious and troublesome journey."[18]

Their road had been many roads, and with many names, where it had a name at all. This last part from northern Mississippi to Nashville men called the Chickasaw Trace. Below that it was the Choctaw-Chickasaw Trail, and from there to Natchez simply the Path to the Choctaw Nation. But other names were even now coming to mind. Baily and his band were hardly the first to make the trip. As early as 1742 a Frenchman had made the journey, remarking chiefly on the miserable condition of the paths. A few other whites certainly undertook the trek before him, and several afterward, in increasing numbers, until the time Baily set out. At least seven different paths comprised the lower portion of the trail, and only as Mississippi became at last an American territory did men begin to think seriously of making something of this overland route linking the Cumberland settlements with Natchez. Reflecting the objects of those who undertook its passage, within four years of Baily's trip men at the northern terminus started referring to all of the trails collectively as the Natchez Road. At the other end of the line, northbound travelers spoke of the Nashville Road. It would be almost three decades later before it took on a single name—north and south, and in the frontier mind and legend—as the Natchez Trace.[19]

Empire, even at the turn of the eighteenth–nineteenth centuries, turned on communications and trade, for both prosperity and defense. With Spain and Britain still uneasy neighbors on the southwestern frontier, the fledgling government of the United States could ill afford to be isolated from its most distant lands. The rivers were fine for drifting commerce on the way to Natchez, but it was a slow trip, and from the edge of secure American borders in Kentucky they led voyagers along two sides of a triangle. Very soon after admitting Mississippi to territorial status, authorities saw the need for a direct land route, the hypotenuse of the triangle. They needed it for the movement of military forces to guard their frontier, for commodities too precious to trust to the uncertainties of river travel, for the return of soldiers and boatmen alike who could not practically come back by any other route.

And first and most immediately, they needed it for communications. Immediately upon the establishment of the Mississippi Territory, Governor Sargent implored Secretary of State Timothy Pickering to look into establishing a line of blockhouses along the Indian trails as way stations for the passage of mail and travelers. Pickering hardly needed convincing. "At present," the secretary lamented, "a letter is as long in travelling between Philadelphia and the Natchez, as between Philadelphia and Europe."[20] Sargent thought it could be done for $1,300 a year, but he underestimated the challenge. Pickering, complaining that a letter from Natchez could take three months to reach him, better appreciated the dilemma. He proposed establishing a number of inns at intervals along the trail, where riders could rest, eat, and find fresh mounts waiting.[21] Even while Sargent investigated the best locations, the postmaster general awarded Abijah Hunt a contract to carry mail between Nashville and Natchez, commencing on the second Monday in January 1800. For the rather princely consideration of $2,400 a year, he would make one round trip a month, which seemed quite ambitious considering that it had taken Baily and his party almost a month to travel it one way. But Postmaster General Joseph Habersham also looked ahead even as he gave Hunt his commission, expressing the hope that Congress would soon designate the overland route between Nashville and Natchez as a post road.[22]

Congress did just that on April 28, 1800, but initially it acted in name only. Meanwhile the first riders made the journey. John L. Swaney found his mail sacks filled with newspapers, some government dispatches to Sargent, and a scattering of personal letters, all packed into a deerskin pouch well treated with oil to prevent water from ruining its contents. Besides his mail he carried half a bushel of corn for his horse, to supplement pasture along the way, provisions for himself, and a tin trumpet, presumably to announce his arrival.[23] Shortly thereafter Habersham established a schedule calling for a post rider to leave Nashville every other Sunday at 9 A.M., arriving at John McIntosh's by 8 P.M. the following Friday, a distance of 230 miles in six days. He would meet the rider coming up from Natchez about six miles from McIntosh's, at Hoolky Creek, where they would exchange mail and rest a little less than a day before each retraced his steps. The bag from

Nashville was to leave McIntosh's Sunday at 5 A.M., and after a 270-mile ride reach Natchez at 2 P.M. on the subsequent Saturday. Thus, if all went well and the riders did not lose the road, a letter from Nashville could be in Natchez within two weeks. More important, in spite of the impossibility of upriver traffic for return mail, a letter from Natchez going north could reach Nashville in the same time.[24]

It all depended on the "road." Only days after establishing his schedule, Habersham complained to the army that the "badness of the road" made it not only difficult but expensive to run his riders, calling the trail nothing more than an "Indian foot path," as indeed it was. He suggested that troops stationed in the western reaches of Tennessee would be well used if put to work cutting a wagon road out of the wilderness, bridging creeks, and clearing obstructions. Happily General James Wilkinson, commanding the United States Army, agreed.[25]

Before a single tree could be felled, Wilkinson had to secure permission by treaty with the Chickasaw and Choctaw, through whose lands his road and mail riders would pass. The Indians rarely if ever interfered with solitary groups or travelers like Baily, but armed soldiers coming into their lands posed another matter. Secretary of War Henry Dearborn appointed commissioners to meet with the tribal leaders, and then proposed a route for the road, and that white families be allowed to settle at intervals to operate the inns needed by riders and wayfarers. In two treaties formalized October 24 and 27, 1801, first the Chickasaw and then the Choctaw agreed in part. They granted the right-of-way for the road but declined to allow the white settlers to establish inns. Meanwhile they also reserved to themselves the exclusive right to operate ferries on the Tennessee and other unfordable streams. Wilkinson at once ordered eight companies of the Second United States Infantry to journey to the Tennessee River crossing and from there, under the guidance of an Indian appointed to mark the route, commence the work.

The next spring the soldiers started cutting, first opening the section between the Tennessee and the Duck. Then they extended it north to Nashville, but after that it progressed slowly, enough so that Dearborn complained of it to Wilkinson. Only in the spring of 1803 did the work continue, as Wilkinson transferred his soldiers to the southern end of the line and started working north from Natchez. Each month he sent a party of thirty men out to work, relieving them with a new gang at the end of thirty days. Dearborn instructed them to clear close to the ground all trees and stumps to a width of up to eight feet and then in some degree grade or smooth the surface, meanwhile clearing brush and other growth to an additional distance of up to four feet on either side to prevent overhangs and brambles from injuring riders. No one envisioned this road for vehicular traffic as yet, only riders and people on foot. A better road could come someday in the future if needed. The soldiers also had to bridge all but the wider rivers and creeks, and erect causeways over the swamps where they could not go around them. For a new nation with little money, it represented an ambitious public project at the edge of its own frontier.[26]

Not surprisingly the work took longer than expected. By 1805 the soldiers had completed the road only from Natchez to Grindstone Ford. For 40 miles beyond that they had cleared much of the right of way—at too great a width, in fact—but had yet to remove much of the underbrush to ground level. Thereafter for the next 186 miles they had not cut a single tree, and for the balance of the road, another 154 miles to Nashville, undergrowth reclaimed the original cut, which in any event was not as wide as required. And all along the way streams remained for the most part unbridged. The next year, largely in response to the quickening political pulse in the Mississippi Valley, Congress took a more serious attitude toward the road.[27]

To finish the job quickly the new postmaster general, Gideon Granger, divided the road into three sections and put out the work of finishing each to civilian bid. In the process he revised the requirements. The road must be twelve feet wide and cleared of all logs, trees, and brush. No stumps were to stand more than sixteen inches above the ground, so as not to hinder the passage of wagons. Every stream less than forty feet wide must be bridged, using logs or trees where possible. Wider rivers should have their banks planed or sloped so that wagons could safely reach the waterside. Swamps and bogs must have causeways composed of submerged logs topped with earth. Most important of all, the job must be finished by October 1, 1807. Predictably it remained in part unfinished when the deadline came, but by 1809 a final inspection ordered by Washington revealed that the wagon road was substantially complete at last.[28] For years thereafter, especially in Tennessee, locals referred to the new route as "the Road Opened Up by the Federal Troops."[29]

This still left unsettled the issue of accommodations for the post riders and other travelers along the 450-mile length of the new "road." At first reluctant to allow whites to operate such inns, the Indians relented to the extent that they consented to a few, and in 1805 the government advertised—at first unsuccessfully—for potential lessees. By now some places in addition to McIntosh's offered a traveler rest and recuperation, but not many. South of Nashville the road passed by the new community of Franklin on the Harpeth, where scattered settlements afforded some hospitality. Then, farther south, at the Duck crossing, John Gordon of Nashville and his wife, Dolly, with their five sons, built a house near the work buildings of the military road builders. In 1802, as that section of road opened, he concluded an agreement with Chickasaw chief George Colbert's half-breed son William. Under the stipulations of their treaties with the United States, only Indians could operate ferries and inns along the road, but there was nothing to prevent them from going into business privately with white partners. Consequently, when Wilkinson's soldiers moved on, leaving their buildings behind, young Colbert and Gordon appropriated their flatboats for a ferry operation and turned the houses into a "stand," as the frontiersmen called wilderness inns. Colbert supplied a slave to help work the place, and Gordon provided a cook and other hired hands as well as the hardware and equipment needed. They agreed to share all profits equally between the partners, a spirit of equity probably made possible only by the fact that for the moment the Chickasaw still held the upper hand in the region. Despite good intentions there were few profits to share, however, for Gordon's operation lost money almost from the first, as did a general trading store that he opened in hopes of outfitting travelers on the southbound road.[30]

In 1805, the year that the Chickasaw eased somewhat their restrictions on white operators, David Dobbins established a stand on Swan Creek some ten miles south of Gordon's Ferry, and a few miles farther on William McLish built a house on the north side of Buffalo River, the jumping-off place for the Chickasaw country. From there it was another ten miles south to a stand located on the banks of Factor's Creek, a name itself probably taken from the presence of the stand known as "Young Factor's." In a usage later lost to history, a factor operated a trading store. Ten or fifteen more miles led to a stand run by an Indian named Toscomby, a dirty cabin with few amenities other than corn for horses and warm Indian bread for journeyers.[31]

One of the seemingly innumerable Colbert brothers—George, William, Levi, James, and Joseph—secured the crossing of the Tennessee sixteen miles below Toscomby's. The fact that George Colbert's mother was a Chickasaw was enough to win the half-Indian, half-Scot permission to move from the main Indian town farther south in 1801. On the lower side of the Tennessee he established a stand on high ground a few hundred yards back from the river, and he also appropriated abandoned army flatboats to operate a ferry over the stream. Colbert proved to be a sufficiently crafty businessman to persuade General Wilkinson to erect new buildings for him, including a kitchen, storehouse, and stables, at no cost, and to build him a new ferryboat as well. Moreover, once in operation he charged exorbitant rates by frontier standards, including six cents for a single dried fish and a dollar for a quart of whiskey, when it customarily sold for a quarter at most. No wonder one visitor characterized Colbert as a "very shrewd, talented man and withal very wicked," while another, admitting his intelligence, thought him an "artful designing man." R. J. Meigs, who visited him in 1806 and dealt with him extensively before that, concluded that Colbert was "extremely mercenary, miscalculates his importance, & when not awed by the presence of the officers of the Government takes upon himself airs." Perhaps so, but in the years ahead he proved to be one of the most important men in the region, to Chickasaw and whites alike.[32]

Once across the Tennessee and out of Colbert's greedy clutches, the traveler moving south went past a modest stand at Buzzard Roost after seven miles, passed a small Chickasaw village a few miles farther on, and then launched himself into the wilderness for thirty miles before he came to James Allen's modest stand near the Tombigbee. Married to a daughter of William Colbert, Allen merely allowed occasional travelers to stay at his home. So did his wife's uncle, James Colbert, who also grudgingly accepted an overnight guest now and then a mile north of Allen's. Not as hospitable—or avaricious—a man as his brother George, James Colbert offered scanty fare and sometimes granted hospitality only after every other door in the vicinity refused to open to the traveler.[33]

On leaving Colbert's, the last stand before the traveler departed Chickasaw territory was McIntosh's. In 1805 more than twenty miles then awaited before the first stand in Choctaw country, the half-breed David Fulsom's modest place near Pigeon Roost Creek. Visitors remembered little other than the voracious gnats and mosquitoes, and the terrible water Fulsom had to offer. Yet to travelers moving north it was still welcome, and for those going south in 1805 it represented a last chance, for Fulsom's was the only stand in Choctaw country. The southbound mail rider had fifty miles ahead of him after that. Finally he came to Turner Brashears's stand. This Marylander came with a sense of entrepreneurship. He established his home there sometime in the late 1790s and was ready for the growth of traffic as the roadwork commenced. A considerable land-and slave owner, he was the first of the stand operators actually to advertise his establishment. In 1806 he ran a line in the *Mississippi Herald and Natchez City Gazette* announcing his "House of Entertainment on the road leading from Natchez to Nashville, about 40 miles from William Smiths at the Indian line." Early visitors paid testament to his "fine public house" and to his gentlemanly manners but added that he "knew how to make a high bill."[34]

And as his advertisement suggested, in those early years Brashears's lay forty miles north of the next stand. William Smith's newly opened inn perched directly on the boundary between Choctaw country and newly formed Claiborne County, part of the old Natchez district. Accommodations were sparse, but there was at least the promise of better, for from here on the road improved and white settlements were increasingly frequent. Grindstone Ford lay only eighteen miles beyond, and a few miles past it the outlying settlements and towns began to appear, with Natchez itself only twenty miles distant.[35]

Over the ensuing decade, the gaps between the stands filled rapidly as increased travel on the Natchez-Nashville road afforded more opportunity for profit and more demand for accommodations for men and animals. By 1816 three new stands opened between Smith's and Brashears's. William Dean, Phillip Hayes, and Noble Osburn each put up inns about five miles apart. North of Brashears's, in the great empty expanse of the Choctaw lands, as many as nine crude establishments vied for passing business. John Norton charged sixty-two and one-half cents for a night's lodging at his stand, where travelers shared the house with him and his Choctaw wife and were often forced to make do with a dinner of water and cold hominy gone sour. Several miles from Norton's, William Doak began operation in 1810, soon making his stand one of the better known on the road, especially after it became a terminus for a stagecoach service several years later.

"Very dirty and disagreeable" accommodations met visitors at Crowder's stand five miles beyond Doak's, not the worst of them being the host's constant profanity and the necessity of sleeping in a room filled with Choctaw. Rooming was no better at Anderson's a few miles farther north, but at Choteau's—often called Shoat's or Chote's—the price of a night indoors at least came down to a mere quarter. And it certainly beat what waited ten miles on, for a man named Hawkins or Harkins opened a stand where he only grudgingly sold travelers venison and grain for their animals, and then gave them sleeping places even poorer than the usual low standard on the road.[36]

Choteau's presence attested to a remaining memory of the one-time French presence in the region; even more did French Camp, only a mile or two beyond Hawkins's paltry place. Louis Le Fleur came from France some years earlier to trade with the Choctaw, and simply remained, marrying into the tribe. Around 1810 he opened his stand, variously known as Leffloe's, La floure's, and Lafleur's, but soon commonly called French Camp. He prospered sufficiently to allow him in ensuing years to open other stands in the Choctaw lands, becoming one of the dominant men in the region.

Samuel Mitchell was one of the few who originally applied for the lease of a stand back in 1806, and opened his inn some ten or more miles north of French Camp. North of Fulsom's, Noah Wall, brother-in-law to both Fulsom and Mitchell, opened his stand on Line Creek, the natural boundary between the Choctaw and Chickasaw territory, and he, like so many others, seems to have cared little for the comfort of his guests, one complaining that he could get nothing to eat but some cold cornbread. Once back in the Chickasaw lands, the stands became more spread out even with the addition of Perry's, north of Wall's. After McIntosh's and the less-than-hospitable Allen's and James Colbert's, the weary road wore on across the Pontotoc Ridge and the black prairies into the Tombigbee hills, before coming to one of the more ironically named establishments. Despite the existence of Young Factor's many miles to the north for some time, when this new stand opened in the lower Chickasaw lands, people soon came to call it Old Factor's. The name of its proprietor is lost to history, but he was apparently appreciated for his good coffee and venison, and his reasonable rates of fifty cents for lodging.

Between Old Factor's and Colbert's Ferry on the Tennessee, two more stands opened by 1815, that of James Brown—a Chickasaw despite his Anglo name—and that of yet another Colbert, Levi, at Buzzard Roost. Brown could offer no indoor accommodation, but at least he provided good cornbread and fodder, while his sometime partner Levi Colbert, was far more ambitious, operating a grist mill and a plantation with a number of slaves, in addition to his stand on Buzzard Roost Creek only a few miles below brother James's ferry. Unlike his brother, Levi Colbert impressed visitors as an intelligent and able host who fed his guests well and treated them openly, many travelers remarking on his hospitality—and his prosperity.

Having crossed the Tennessee, the wayfarer in 1815 found no new stands since the decade before until he came to John McLish's on the Buffalo Ridge, run by yet another half-breed. It hardly compared with another inn barely a mile distant, opened in 1807 or 1808, and at first generally known as Indian Line stand. Robert Griner and his wife, Priscilla, built a substantial house, in fact two log cabins several feet apart connected by a roof over a central breezeway—a "dogtrot," the frontiersmen called it. Sticks and dirt made its chimney, clapboarding its roof, and yellow poplar logs the structure itself. Mud chinking sealed the gaps in the logs but could be knocked out in the summer for ventilation. Some distance behind the house Griner built a kitchen, and a stable not far away. Located as it was on the outer edge of land open to white settlement in 1808, Griner's—people soon mistakenly called it

Grinder's, the name that would stick—became a prominent, and one day an infamous, stop on the Natchez road.[37]

Beyond Griner's, two routes to the Duck were in use by 1815, one leading to Gordon's, where the proprietor even then planned his new brick home, eighteen by thirty feet, with four rooms in two stories, on the rise some distance back from the ferry landing.[38] Not far from him, on the south side of the Duck, an obscure stand called the Sheboss Place went into operation briefly, supposedly taking its name from the exclamation of a Chickasaw married to the proprietor, who always referred questions to his wife by saying "she boss." On the other route, a few miles to the east, travelers stopped at Keg Springs stand, run by a widow named Cranfield, the sight of whom relieved travelers going north that the Indian country was safely past and they could be "thankful to be with white people again."[39]

With the passage of another decade, stands came and went, hostage to the vagaries of white-Indian politics and the ebb and flow of the river-borne economy that influenced travel down the Mississippi and, thereby, foot and horse traffic back up the road to Nashville. By 1825 most of the stands between Gordon's and Colbert's Ferry were gone. In the Chickasaw country Brown's closed, but Levi Kemp opened a stop near Allen's and James Colbert's. Farther south Perry's and Wall's had closed, and in the Choctaw country Anderson's and Crowder's were no more. Doak's now lay within the limits of newly formed Yazoo County, and below it only Ward's and Brashears's remained as white settlement spread steadily northeast along the old Path to the Choctaw Nation. Grindstone Ford had disappeared as the town of Port Gibson grew just to the west. With the coming of civilization and real inns, better roads, increased demand for better services, and at last a way to go upstream against the currents of the mighty rivers, the need for the old Natchez-Nashville road dwindled, and with it the need for the old stands. Only in the Indian interior did they continue to operate after 1830, and even then their operators saw traffic curtailed substantially as the military and civilian authorities cut new roads that followed easier ground parallel and to the east.

By 1825 the post road had shifted to the new routes, further lessening use of the old trail. In the short span of three decades, traffic on the route grew from a trickle to the hum of a major artery of communication, then receded once more to barely more than a dribble. Ironically, only long after its use began to recede from 1820 onward did people start to call the old route by the romantic name that stayed with it for the rest of time.[40] Indeed, in frontier usage a "trace" was little more than an obscure woodland path, not even sufficiently used or marked to merit designation as a trail. In 1801 in Tennessee a court docket actually referred to the series of Indian and animal paths leading south as the Natchez Trace, the first recorded usage of the term, but farther south in Mississippi it never came into use until after 1830 and the road's official abandonment.[41]

At the very commencement of the construction of the thoroughfare, Wilkinson indulged in the prediction that "this road being completed I shall consider our Southern extremity assured, the Indians in that quarter at our feet & the adjacent Province laid open to us." A decade later, when Congress appropriated money to repair the road, the politicians agreed with the general, thinking it unnecessary even to state the obvious advantage of such a connection with the Lower Mississippi. Yet if they thought that the road would also become the backbone of frontier community, they erred. For all the travel along the Trace, very few people actually settled beside it other than the Indians and half-breeds who derived their modest income from its travelers. Because the old original trails avoided lowlands, they also tended to skirt most sources of water other than the rivers and creeks they crossed. Settlers needed the springs and creeks that the Trace shunned. Moreover, the ridgelines that the road followed held shallow soil, unsuitable for the plow. Farmers wanted bottomlands. "There is not a spot over which the road passes which would make an eligible farm," wrote an 1801 wayfarer between the Duck and the Tennessee. Instead, farmers and their future communities tended to locate some miles from the Trace, and in a few years, as they became centers of population, the postal route naturally diverted to serve them, and the post roads and military roads being cut moved in the same way.[42]

Thus, gradually, piece by piece, the Trace saw itself shunted aside. Instinct and logic of both animals and men had located it where it best served the interest of travel in the rough wilderness. The spread of settlement made possible in part by that travel and communication, however, listened to other imperatives, the demands of those who came to stay and live rather than those merely passing through. The result was an aberration in American civilization's spread south and west. While everywhere else community and commerce sprang up all along most avenues of movement through the wilderness, not a single lasting community of substance arose along the Trace during its heyday. Instead it gradually saw itself abandoned, turned back to the Indians and the animals and the occasional country wayfarer, a victim of its own success.

3

The Road to Travel

In the spring of 1785 the Spanish soldiers in Fort Panmure, as well as the few inhabitants of Natchez itself, saw the harbinger of the future for themselves and the Southwest. Slowly floating down the Mississippi there came a scow, or flatboat, that soon made for the landing under the hill. On its deck were stacked hogsheads of flour and probably of bacon, maybe even whiskey. The boatmen, eyed suspiciously by the soldiers, said they came from Fort Pitt in the western reaches of the new state of Pennsylvania. They had floated down the Ohio, run its falls on the northern border of what would become Kentucky, then swept down the broad Mississippi. They came to sell their goods in Natchez, or New Orleans if possible.

They also presented a problem for the Spanish authorities. Territorial law forbade such trade. The Lower Mississippi was closed to the Americans. But the Spaniards, and even more the Americans, Indians, and Frenchmen in the Louisiana colony, wanted those goods from upriver. Recognizing a pressure it could not resist, Spain made the best of it by opening the river to trade two years later and slapping a hefty duty on all goods so imported. That same year Wilkinson himself, a congenital adventurer, floated a boatload of Kentucky goods to New Orleans, and within three years the landing at Natchez hosted at least sixty-four flatboats laden with goods from all along the Upper Ohio. Bacon, flour, tobacco, iron, salt, and more found their way up the steep incline to the bluff and the people of Natchez.

Though international relations remained icy, when Spain ceded Louisiana back to France, and then President Thomas Jefferson purchased the whole territory in 1803, the rapid increase in the flow of goods and men was assured. In less than twenty years the trickle started by that lone scow from the future Pittsburgh became a flood.[1] In the first six months of 1801 the total number of vessels of all kinds, chiefly flatboats, bringing cargoes to Natchez and New Orleans, came to 486, every one laden with the trade goods of Kentucky, Pennsylvania, Tennessee, Ohio, and even faraway Virginia. They brought more than 93,000 barrels of flour; 882 hogsheads of tobacco; bacon, pork, beef, and apples; and at least 500 barrels of whiskey and more of brandy and cider. Furs and animal skins from the North and West rode side by side with tons of pig iron, flat lengths of "strap" iron for wagon wheel rims, and nails. Household goods like soap, lard, and butter made the same journey as window glass for the increasingly refined homes on the bluff. And more than four thousand bales of cotton came down, the first produce of the staple that would support much of the South for the next two generations.[2]

"No form of water craft so whimsical, no shape so outlandish, can well be imagined, but what, on descending from Pittsburgh to New Orleans, it may some where be seen lying to the shore, or floating on the river." Timothy Flint spent ten years along the Mississippi, and knew what he was saying when he recalled in 1828 the incredible variety of boats on the river carrying people and goods on the long float south. While a few sailboats managed to make the trip, the overwhelming majority of the cargoes came on barges or flatboats, the two often confused as one. Barges could be the size of an oceangoing schooner, with sails and masts and a low covered deck over their hundred-ton cargoes, all managed by a crew of thirty or less. Despite their size they could go upriver, but only by the laborious process of a small sailboat running ahead a hundred yards or so trailing a hawser that it secured to some tree on the bank. The men on the barge then pulled themselves upstream by main strength alone until they reached the tree, when the whole process was repeated. In this cumbersome fashion they could make six or seven miles a day and take more than two months to haul themselves up the Mississippi to the mouth of the Ohio, hardly a practical means of return. The barges often had names, like the *Nancy* that ran between New Orleans and Natchez in 1808 carrying liquor by the barrel, as well as cigars. Some took their name from their owners, as with "Mrs. Morrison's Barge," which conveyed slaves as far north as the Walnut Hills at $15.00 each, promising delivery "death or desertion excepted." The bargemen measured their freight for its cubic area, then converted that to "barrels" as a unit of conveyance, generally at $1.25 to $1.50 per each five cubic feet or barrel.[3]

More prevalent were the scows, sometimes called "sleds" or "skiffs." Single families going south to the Mississippi Territory most often built them of a few dozen logs tied together, with a rude shed on the "deck" for shelter and to keep their provisions and household goods dry. Others sometimes emigrated from the north aboard canoes or even *pirogues* made of hollowed tree trunks. More unusual still were the "wheel" boats, generally two flatboats or keelboats side by side, with a paddle wheel between them driven by a cow or a horse walking the interior of the wheel. Flint even saw one craft driven by a man who sat turning a crank that propelled a paddle.[4]

Most prevalent were the flatboats, sometimes called "Kentucky flats" or "broadhorns." They were nothing more than oblong boxes up to fifteen feet wide and fifty to one hundred feet long, built on a bottom of huge sturdy beams to hold tons of cargo while withstanding the rigors of the river journey. Some could take several hundred barrels of goods, while others carrying whole families floated lazily along while the occupants used them as virtual houses, with bedrooms, kitchens, and stoves. "We see in them ladies, servants, cattle, horses, sheep, dogs and poultry, all floating on the same bottom," wrote Flint, "and on the roof the looms, ploughs, spinning wheels and domestic implements of the family."[5] They were propelled by wide oars called "sweeps," which also gave them the name *broadhorns* and afforded them stability and some momentum beyond that of the current. Generally only three or four stout hands were needed to man the side sweeps and the stern oar. In time, regardless of where they came from, the downriver people assumed all flatboats and their crewmen to be from Kentucky, and called their occupants, in the vernacular of the day, "Kaintucks."[6]

Less ungainly and more manageable, even able to move slowly upriver by clinging to the shallows where the current ran less swift, keelboats came into increasing use thanks to their large cargo capacity and their relative comfort for the crew. The average vessel measured forty to eighty feet in length, and a mere seven to ten at the beam, with a pointed prow at each end. So shallow was its draft that, fully loaded with tons of cargo, it might still rest easy in only two or three feet of water, with clearance for the keel that gave it its name to provide stability in its course. A cabin some six feet high or less generally stood in the center of the deck, providing shelter for passengers and protection for perishable cargo. A runway extended along either side of the cabin at the gunwales, and on this a dozen or more men with long poles walked in easy time, from fore to aft, leaning against their poles planted on the bottom, and thus propelling the boat along, while a steersman managed the rudder. Oars at bow and stern allowed for rowing as well, and most could even unfurl a sail, though they were little used. Unlike the flatboats they moved far less at the whim of the current and steered themselves around sandbars and floating obstacles like trees or the submerged trunks called "sawyers," which could wreak disaster on a flatboat.[7]

Whether conveying cargo or passengers, the captains of the broadhorns and keelboats and barges almost always issued a receipt or bill of lading stipulating delivery of people and possessions "in good order and condition, the danger of the river only excepted."[8] It was an important proviso. Friends who had already made the trip offered lots of advice to those about to embark on the Ohio for the run down, and from 1801 onward Zadoc Cramer published his guidebook *The Navigator* for those planning on making the journey. His opening advice that they should first "procure a boat" may have seemed a bit self-evident, but he took the matter of selection very seriously. Too many people came to grief or ruin because they bought a vessel constructed of faulty planking or otherwise not well made. "It behooves every purchaser of a Kentucky boat," he said, "to get it narrowly examined before the embarkation."

Travelers should time their trip for the spring and fall, he advised, leaving either in February right after the winter ice broke up, or else in October after autumn rains raised the level of the rivers from the summer drought. Running the river after a "fresh," or sudden rise due to rainfall, was best done by getting into the middle of the stream and then instead of rowing or trying to steer, simply permitting "your boat to have pretty much her own way." The immigrant boatman should tie up to a tree on the bank—"choking a stump," they would come to call it—no more than necessary, for it lost time better spent on the passage. He ought also to take a canoe with him for emergencies and for speedier and more maneuverable travel up side creeks for hunting or visiting the shore from an island. If at all possible, said Cramer, they should travel all night, posting a good lookout at the bow, and especially when the moon rode high and full.[9]

Matters of crew and provisions rightfully commanded careful attention from the prudent. A flatboat could get by nicely with a crew of three to five, and men bound for Mississippi often banded together with others both to save the expense of hiring a crew and also for company on the journey. For the four- to six-week trip from Kentucky to Natchez, a single crewman expected about $40.00 in wages, while a captain or *patron* commanded an extra $10.00. On top of that expense, the owner of the broadhorn paid up to $110.00 to have the boat itself built, and perhaps another $45.00 for provisions for the voyage. That made a total cost of $365.00 for the trip. Such a boat might carry 250 barrels of goods on the way, which, at $1.25 each for transport, would yield $312.50, plus another $5.00 or more for the boat itself, which would be broken up and sold for lumber in Natchez or New Orleans. Thus a man might get himself and his family and household goods to the new territory for a net cost of $50.00 or less.[10]

What to take on the voyage depended largely on what was available, but in the main immigrants packed their flats with hard biscuit, bacon, flour, dried beef and pork, perhaps a few chickens, certainly a quantity of whiskey or brandy, and some trade goods or a small amount of cash to buy necessaries from the Indians along the way. Also before going, every man, crew or working passenger, received an assignment from the *patron*. "There is no distinction of persons," Baily discovered on his voyage in 1797. "Every one must put his labouring hand to the oar, and keep his appointed watch if they float by night." Often the last man to sign on found himself deputed cook, a position of little esteem, given the anything but extravagant nature of their provisions.[11]

The trip down the river was one that none ever forgot, regardless of whether they came as tradesmen, settlers, or just crewmen who would make the trip, walk back home, and then make it again, sometimes twice in a year. The Mississippi awed its witnesses. "She appears with a superior Kind of Dignity," wrote a voyager in the late fall of 1803, immediately after the Louisiana Territory became American. "We see her Tremendous Work at Every Moment She Seems to make and Unmake Islands in mere Sport—and at her pleasure, Snatches off or Adds large Territory to the Main Land—the Ohio indeed is but a Child compaired with her—I have little doubt but the Islands in this River if sold by the United States would pay the money which we are to Pay for Louisiana. . . . Even her waters declare the Superior Richness of her Islands."[12]

By day, in good weather, the Kaintucks had little to do but keep a good lookout as the flat floated with the current at five or six miles an hour. "The boat takes care of itself," said Flint. "Meantime one of the hands scrapes a violin, and the others dance. Greetings, or rude defiances, or trials of wit, or proffers of love to the girls on the shore, or saucy messages, are scattered between them and the spectators along the banks."[13] If the boat started to drift too close to either shore, a few pulls at the long sweeps gently shoved her back toward the main stream again.

Inevitably, despite the fact that all floated in the same current, some boats overtook others or else pulled in to shore to allow others to come up. "It is always most pleasant in going down the Mississippi," wrote Baily, "to have as many boats as you can in company." They needed the companionship of the other boatmen floating with them, as well as their help in emergencies. Sometimes they even lashed several boats together and let them float as one while the crews "enjoyed the advantages of an extended society." When four or more made a convoy downstream, they agreed to put in together at night at the signal of a gun from the lead flat. The best place to spend the night was around a tight bend, where the water ran a little slower, and preferably under a willow-covered bank, where the trees provided shade and some protection from the winds and rain. Once the boars were tied together, the crew and passengers brought out their jugs of whiskey and kindled a fire; the lowly cook did what few miracles he could with stale biscuit, salt pork, and river water; and they passed the night in camaraderie that Baily, at least, found helped make "amends for the loss of friends and distant situation."[14] In a bend below New Madrid, Flint encountered nearly one hundred boats landed in a single day. "The boisterous gaiety of the hands, the congratulations to acquaintances, who have met here from immense distances, the moving picture of life on board the boats, in the numerous animals, large and small, which they carry," deeply impressed him, "and, more than all, the immense distances, which they have already traversed, afford a copious fund of meditation."

The boats from Kentucky, loaded with their whiskey and hemp and tobacco, moored together in one spot, while the Ohio boats with their New England trade goods quartered in another. Tennessee flats carried cotton, while the broadhorns from the prairie territories north of the Ohio and west of the Mississippi brought cattle and horses, along with lead and valuable pelts for the fur trade. Their crude wooden surfaces covered literally acres, making wooden islands that the chickens and geese cackled over in dissonant tune to the lowing of the cattle, the snorting of the horses, and the grunts of the swine. "In travelling over the roofs of the floating town, you have a considerable walk," said Flint. They bartered, bought and sold, quarreled, parted, and made up again. One broadhorn of enormous proportions actually called itself a "town," boasting a tavern, retail shops, and the sheds of a number of inhabitants. In 1822 a large flat went down the river as a floating furniture store, pulling in to the banks at every settlement, displaying cabinetry in the "warehouse" located on deck, and selling tables, dressers, chairs, and more.[15] "They have come from regions, thousands of miles apart," Flint marveled. "They have floated to a common point of union."[16]

Dr. John Bedford left Nashville on the Cumberland, sailed down it to the Ohio, and thence into the Mississippi for the voyage to Natchez. Some days he made thirty miles, he thought, but others the head winds, the height of the river, or occasional heavy rain, slowed his progress to a crawl. He watched for the snags and sawyers on the Mississippi that the French first named the "Devil's Race Ground" as the current tore through them, and took advantage of any opportunity when the barge tied up at the shore at night to go to a white habitation for some food to replace the "rough fare" that the crewmen on the boat served. When it rained, voyagers—usually without shelter of any kind on the barge—simply got wet or at best pulled planks over themselves to fend off the worst of the downpour. One flatboat occasionally meeting another, two vessels traveled together until the current's whims separated one from the other. A not uncommon sight on the banks or against the islands was another flatboat wrecked, run aground, or stuck on the snags, often with its cargo still intact and awaiting the first scavenger.

For Bedford and others making these trips in the early days of the Mississippi's commerce, the sounds and sights filled them with wonder. Strange birds flew overhead. The croaking of frogs announced the coming of spring. The lazy lap of the water against their boats lulled them into a somnolent reverie that seemed somehow to be the very song of the stately river. From their positions in the middle of the stream, they saw Indian villages on the banks as they passed south, and occasionally they encountered French hunters in canoes and more and more Americans wandering the wilderness in search of game, riches, or simply isolation.

Only fools became unwatchful, however. A fog could hit the river at night that made it impossible to land or even to see beyond the bow of the boat, and one night Bedford's barge had no choice but simply to float along with no idea of its direction or of what might lie just a few feet ahead. In months like March the weather could turn from sultry to freezing overnight, the travelers awakening in the morning to find their barge surrounded by half an inch of ice along the shore. At least the Indians posed no threat and seemed generally indifferent, if not friendly, to the passing boats.

It came as a relief to the early travelers when they saw their first signs of substantial civilization. Walnut Hills, a small community about one hundred miles above Natchez, was "the most beautiful place on the Mississippi," thought Bedford. The bluffs and hills rose two hundred feet or more above the river and presented a delightful aspect after many days of floating through the wilderness. Several hours downstream lay Palmyra, a community on the east bank, settled in

1801 by New Englanders who now produced cotton that could make a single planter more than one thousand dollars a year from a sixteen-acre plantation.[17]

Just the next year Henry Ker passed exactly the same scenes on his way down the Mississippi, and he, like others, thought the great river seemed almost to look on the lesser Ohio with disdain. He might have added that the river's current regarded his little flatboat rather disdainfully as well, for when his companions tried to reach shore to get out of the swift water, it carried them several miles beyond their anticipated landing point before they could tie up safely. Then they found that, having stopped on the outside of a large bend, they and their boat were directly in the path of driftwood including large trees careering downstream. Faced with being battered to pieces along the bank, they stayed up all night using their poles to try to fend off the larger flotsam as it approached. As if that were not enough, the next morning a terrible storm arose that Ker believed to be a hurricane. He had pulled his boat out of the main channel into a small bayou, but the force of the storm broke the hawser securing the vessel to a tree, and then from time to time he heard the crash of other trees being blown into the water. If one of them came down across the mouth of the bayou, he and his boat would be trapped. As it was, he waited out the storm and the next morning still had to cut a path through the fallen timber for his boat to reach the river again.[18]

Commenting with no attempt at wit, Ker later concluded that "the navigation of the Mississippi is rendered somewhat difficult, and often dangerous." There were the sawyers, trees literally standing upside down, their tops stuck in the mud, while their trunks and roots stuck anywhere from one to twenty feet out of the water. The current kept them bobbing up and down and sometimes moved them, but a stubborn sawyer could be a landmark for twenty years and was enough to scuttle a boat of fifty tons or better. Then he saw "planters," trees that the current had jammed into the mud with their jagged tops facing upstream, and usually just beneath the surface. The boatman who did not see the telltale disturbance they made in the surface of the water could find himself scuttled in an instant. Driftwood catching on planters sometimes formed small islands, and the unwary steersman who did not keep clear of one could find the current driving him into it, forcing his bow down under the accumulation and sinking him. Whirlpools, "boils," and "sucks" only added to the river's hazards, and worse than that its changing course and the tendency of sawyers and planters to move, along with the growth and retreat of sandbars from time to time, meant that no boatman or Kaintuck could count on the river being exactly the same on any two trips. He must learn it and relearn it again and again.[19]

Little more than two days after escaping his "hurricane," Ker saw the sun disappear behind "an awfully formed cloud," and, taking its meaning, hurried to tie up at the bank. Within minutes a tornado swept past, uprooting most of the trees and brush in a path a quarter mile wide on the opposite bank. In twenty minutes it was gone, followed by a beautiful sky of remarkable serenity contrasted with the devastating act of nature just past.

The farther down the river Ker went, the more its wonders and dangers impressed him. Sometimes he hit giant eddies in the stream that set his boat spinning around and around, out of control, for some time until he regained his course. Still, when not fearing for his life, he admired the beauty of the scenes before him, concluding that "it only wanted time to make this a country of wealth and happiness." Imagining himself in discourse with the wilderness, he mused that "your hills and vallies, believe me, will one day be the resort of men of genius and enterprise, who will add to your future glory."[20]

At night, when the flatboats often lashed themselves together for safety, their crewmen socialized or, more often, drank, since most cargoes carried at least a few barrels of Pennsylvania or Kentucky whiskey. Choctaw along the east bank sometimes came down to the water to sell turkeys, venison, or pumpkins that the boatmen eagerly devoured in preference to their monotonous diet of salted and dried beef and pork. Despite the outward friendliness of the natives, the Kaintucks and their passengers needed to have a care for their actions. In 1811 men on a flat loaded with lead bartered for turkeys with some Choctaw, only to hear a shot fired by someone out on a boat. Immediately the Indians flew into a rage, accused the boatmen of shooting their dog, grabbed their own weapons, and began a heated debate over whether to take the whites prisoners or just kill them on the spot. Only the providential barking of the dog once more, demonstrating that it was alive and well, calmed the warriors, who immediately went back to their trading. John Bradbury, nervously conducting the negotiations for the boatmen, rather hastily concluded his dealings despite the feeling that he was giving them too much money and gunpowder in trade. "I was not very exact in measuring," he confessed, "being rather anxious to get away."[21]

And then there were the earthquakes. In the first years of the 1800s the Mississippi Valley suffered unusual seismic activity, and inevitably it hit the boatmen with bewildering speed and shock. No sooner did

Bradbury and his colleagues approach the Devil's Race Ground, or the "Devil's Channel" as others called it, than they moored, exhausted, to rest for the night of December 15–16, 1811. About 2 A.M. "I was awakened by a most tremendous noise," he wrote, "accompanied by an agitation of the boat so violent, that it appeared in danger of upsetting." His French crewmen erupted in panic. *"O mon Dieu! Monsieur Bradbury, qu'est-ce qu'il y a?"* they shouted. He had no idea of what was happening, of course, but when he rushed out of the boat cabin he saw the whole surface of the river in agitation. "The noise was inconceivably loud and terrific," he said, but above it he still heard the sound of hundreds of trees crashing on the banks and into the stream. Above it all the wild fowl screeched in panic. He told his men to rest easy. *"C'est un tremblement de terre."* That was obvious, and it hardly quieted them.

In a few moments the shocks ceased, but then the effects manifested themselves. Whole chunks of the banks, shaken loose, tumbled into the stream, bringing trees with them. Their splashing created such swells that Bradbury feared they might swamp his boat. He asked the French captain what they should do to save themselves, but even the *patron* fell into a panic, just yelling *"Mon Dieu!"* over and over. When one of the crew went ashore on the island to which they sat moored, he discovered that a chunk of it eighty feet long now lay separated from it by a four-foot chasm, and in danger of floating away or sinking into the river and dragging them down. Only the shallowness of the stream at that point saved them. Worse, half an hour later came an aftershock, less severe than the first, but still strong. Then came two more in rapid succession, and throughout the balance of the night, as they huddled around a deck fire unable to sleep, more tremors hit every six to ten minutes. Twenty-seven of them came and went before dawn, and then they saw the whole river seemingly blanketed in foam and drifting timber, and several feet higher than the day before. Two canoes came drifting past, filled with provisions but no occupants, testimony to the destruction of three Kentucky broadhorns they had passed the day before.

It should have been an omen to them that their own danger was not past. Just as Bradbury and crew began loosening their lines, another major shock hit, as great as the first. Some of his crew ran up the bank in panic, only to have a tree fall almost atop them. Worse, Bradbury saw the bank itself start slipping down into the river. He yelled for his men to get back aboard and they cast off before their piece of the island disappeared. But now the Devil's Race Ground lay before them, choked with trees and driftwood lodged hard against the underwater planters. The French *patron* and his crew were too frightened to think or act, and Bradbury simply ordered them to find another piece of bank on a more secure island. There they would wait for everyone and everything—including the earth—to calm.

While the men prepared breakfast, Bradbury walked along the island to look downstream and survey their chances of a passage. Another shock almost threw them to the ground, then two more followed as they ate and reboarded their boat. One man stood on the bank as the last tremor hit and found himself almost sucked into the river as the sand beneath his feet gave way. Still they embarked safely and surprisingly got through the rapids without mishap. The relief was so great that the French boatmen dropped their oars, crossed themselves, and gave a shout of joy.

The next great shock hit at 11 A.M. "All nature was in a state of dissolution," Bradbury noted wonderingly. The wild geese screeched overhead as the earth shook, the banks on both sides caved in, trees fell by the hundreds, and those still standing waved like grass in the quake. The oarsmen panicked once more and begged to go ashore, but Bradbury reasoned that they were probably safer in midstream. The Frenchmen refused to listen, but in fact after gaining what appeared to be a firm bit of bank, they rested untroubled by quakes for the rest of the day, though deeply disturbed by the evidences of tragedy upriver as canoes and bits of boats floated past. The next morning the shocks began again, however, and continued sporadically through the day. Bradbury put in to the bank in the afternoon, when he saw a log cabin with about twenty very distressed people milling about. They had come for shelter and to pray together, and while some studied a Bible open on a table, one of their number presumed to explain the earthquakes by stating that the planet had just passed through one of two tails of a comet seen in the sky some months before and now bounced back and forth as it tried to pass through the other. If the Earth successfully cleared the second tail, all would be well. If not, the planet was doomed. "Finding him confident in his hypothesis, and myself unable to refute it," Bradbury wrote later, "I did not dispute the point."[22]

In fact, despite the imaginative explanation of Bradbury's acquaintance, they had all just experienced the great New Madrid Earthquake—not a single quake but an innumerable series of shocks commencing December 16, 1811, and continuing for two months with considerable activity. Later tremors occurred into the following November, and a few shocks were felt as late as December 12, 1813, almost two years to the day from the first.[23] It took its name from the small Missouri town where the quakes centered, and which they almost destroyed. Lakes emptied into the Mississippi; new lakes formed in minutes as riverside land sank. Islands disappeared, and the river changed its course dramatically in places. For a time, as the shaking sent huge waves surging northward, the Mississippi actually appeared to be running backward. None who experienced it ever forgot. Bradbury and his companions were among the fortunate voyagers south who survived. No one could calculate how many perished when caught on the river during the quakes, especially the first great shock of December 16, though in March 1812 the number of vessels and crews unaccounted for approached sixty.[24]

The flatboats and their cargoes of goods and immigrants generally waited until the rivers were at their highest, from late October until early June. The low water of summer made the trip the more hazardous thanks to the sawyers and planters, as well as innumerable sandbars.[25] Between November 24, 1810, and January 24, 1811, for instance, 197 flatboats and four keelboats passed Louisville alone, by the falls of the Ohio. The cargoes they carried told not only of the trade done at Natchez and New Orleans but also of the needs of the immigrants going down with the boats. More than fourteen thousand turkeys and chickens went south in that period. Horses to draw plows, slaves to till fields, pine planking to build houses and stables, bagging for cotton, shoes, boots, furniture, crockery—all the staples of settlers going to stay made the long float downstream to the Southwest Territory.[26]

All who took the trip on the rivers, whatever their reason—trade, settlement, or merely to turn around and go back north on the Nashville road—met the same scene when they reached the bluffs crested by Natchez. "The sight of this landscape interrupted the monotony of the noble Mississippi," said an 1817 arrival, who found the town "pretty and as regular as the uneven terrain permits."[27] As many as 150 or more broadhorns and keelboats could be tied at the wharf under the hill, all of them teeming with crewmen just arriving, preparing to depart, or else sleeping off the effects of a good night at the taverns.[28]

"Immediately after landing [we] throwed off our very dirty clothes, that had not been in contact with water since Nashville," Bedford wrote in his diary on March 5, 1807, "except when we were wet with rain or by an accidental tumble in the river." Boatmen and passengers alike dressed in their best, even when, as Bedford confessed, their best often still "barely then reach[ed] common decency." That done, they "tripped up into the town" along the steep slope leading down the bluff.[29] The boatmen, of course, were anxious to be paid. A keelboat captain might be due one hundred dollars a month for his time, and a crewman half that. A barge *patron* commanded twenty-five dollars a month, and a crewman twenty or less, and as soon as they got it, there were ways and places to spend.[30]

Food and lodging presented the first demands, though in earliest times Natchez actually acquired a reputation for opening the doors of its homes to travelers without charge. By 1820, however, as the influx of boatmen and settlers made possible by Mississippi's organization first as a territory, and then as a state in 1818, grew to major proportions, such hospitality rapidly disappeared until only the more wealthy or socially prominent found free lodging, and usually with others of their own class. To replace that earliest rude frontier courtesy, several of those who had granted it started inns and taverns instead. In 1803 John Walton opened his tavern, an "elegant stand at Natchez landing," with buildings both atop the bluff and under the hill, and soon took in $107 a month or more from nightly lodgers.[31] Thomas Winn opened Travellers Hall in 1808, and at Christmastime that same year the Franklin Hotel opened its doors. The amenities were in keeping with the time, though as traffic to Natchez progressed, so did the services the town could offer. Eventually even fresh ice was available almost year round.[32] When it came to feeding the visitor, Natchez beef tended to disappoint, as did its pork and fowl. But the Mississippi catfish, and those from the creeks and rivers feeding it, provided legendary fare, some of the fish running to the incredible size of two hundred pounds, though the larger they were, the less tasty they became.[33] The Natchez fish market early acquired a considerable reputation, boasting also fresh catches from the gulf brought up river from New Orleans.

Once the would-be settler reached Natchez, of course, his travel was nearly done. He had but to sell his flatboat for lumber, load his worldly possessions aboard his animals, and set out through the wilderness to find his newly purchased property, much of it turned over by the U.S. government as bounty lands for veterans of the two wars with Great Britain. If his land lay to the west across the river, he paid a ferryman a quarter for himself and each other person, a dollar for each horse and rider, fifty cents a head for cattle, and half that for sheep and hogs.[34]

For the man bent on moving on or returning whence he came to make another voyage down, however, no ferry to the north presented itself. Only the Nashville road beckoned, that and a walk or horseback ride of five hundred miles or more. Innumerable boatmen, as well as traders and simple upriver farmers who used the fallow season to float their goods to market, all gathered in Natchez as the jumping-off place. They banded in groups of fifteen or twenty or more, determined to travel together for mutual company and protection.[35] For some of them who intended to go all the way to the Ohio River, the whole journey ahead could be sixty-five days or more, which required laying in a good store of supplies. A group of sixteen, for instance, would spend $227.50 for their supplies and an additional $6.00 for tobacco. Making the long trek to the Ohio, they would thus spend a bit more than twenty-one cents per man per day for their food and drink, not counting their overnight expenses at stands along the way.[36]

There were seldom enough horses for all in a party to ride, so those with animals rode ahead while those behind walked. In time the riders dismounted, tied the horses to a tree by the road, and walked on. When the first walkers caught up to the horses, they mounted the by-now-rested animals and rode on, up to and past the men now walking, repeating the process. With them as they walked or rode, the boatmen carried tents and provisions and other baggage, and when they could afford it they trailed an extra horse or two to handle it all. They preferred small Indian or Spanish ponies called "Opelousas"—hardy, resilient, and able to subsist on grass and even tree bark.[37]

The boatmen presented quite a picture on the old Trace. "They appeared to be a very good sort of men," noted Baily, "though not the most refined of those I have seen."[38] "These men were as dirty as Hottentots," a witness recorded in May 1810; "their dress, a shirt and trousers of canvass, black, greasy, and sometimes in tatters; the skin burnt wherever exposed to the sun; each with a budget, wrapt up in an old blanket; their beards, eighteen days old, added to the singularity of their appearance, which was altogether savage." Falling in with them for a time, one Alexander Wilson noted how they coped with obstacles. When they came to a stream, they walked up and down the bank looking for a tree that might have fallen across it. Failing that, they put their goods on their heads and waded across, sometimes repeating this ten or more times a day.[39] They were tall men, lean and sinewy, who stepped with the broad pace of the western man accustomed to walking long distances, and to adopting an air of supreme confidence while doing it. In the warm months, even along the Trace, they could well be walking with their shirts off, their bodies bronzed like an Indian's. They ate plainly, walked as long as there was daylight, and spent their evenings enjoying whatever blandishments a stand might offer, or else in the open in their tents, passing the dark hours with the ever present whiskey, fiddle, and boasting and tall tales.[40]

By 1815 there may have been as many as three thousand or

more men working the Mississippi as barge and keelboatmen. Some achieved considerable notoriety, especially Mike Wolf, James Girty, Bill Sedley, and most of all Mike Fink, who typically preferred to spell his name *Miche Phinck*. This prototypical frontier character was only in his late twenties when he started keelboating, but his wit quickly became legend, and his own imagination and penchant for boast added a host of mythical stories to his genuine exploits that soon entered western lore. Tall, robust, quick to laugh or fight, he boasted that "I can out-run, out-hop, out-jump, throw down, drag out and lick any man in the country. . . . I'm a Salt-River roarer; I love the wimming an' I'm chock full of fight." He drank whiskey literally by the gallon, and even though frontier spirits were generally weaker than the kind that Southerners distilled generations later, still his consumption became a matter of comment, especially since he evidenced immunity to its effects. He could also be brutal, threatening any man who failed to laugh at his jokes and reputedly nearly setting fire to a lady friend because she winked at a man on another boat.[41]

Boast and brag were a part of the rude frontier ethic, and Fink excelled at it, especially when it came to his marksmanship. He thought nothing of risking his woman's life by shooting tin cups from her head for the amusement of fellow drinkers. His practical jokes were even more outlandish, usually ending in some profit to himself, and in Louisville, Kentucky, when about to be arraigned in court for one of his innumerable transgressions, he supposedly put his keelboat on an oxcart and "poled" his way up the town streets to the courthouse. In 1823, having left the now-crowded river to go west as a trapper, Fink inadvertently killed an associate when shooting a cup from his head, and a friend of the dead man's ended the river legend's own life in retaliation.[42]

The boatmen entertained themselves and those bold enough to travel with them on the Trace, though not a few who encountered them felt a bit of relief when they had passed. Wilson encountered by his own estimate some forty to sixty every day on the road, more than five hundred during his journey on the Natchez-Nashville road. Some travelers found it a bit difficult to understand these companions on the road, for the boatmen developed a peculiar slang and a species of colorful metaphor that sometimes baffled. Still, their humor helped on the long trip up the trace. As the new stands and inns began more and more to break up the longer parts of the journey, the boatmen and others moving north also found accommodations marginally more inviting than did the first travelers. Washington, the new capital of the Mississippi Territory, sprang up about seven miles from Natchez, and there

Abram Defrance opened a tavern "at the sign of the Compass." Another five miles or so farther on George Seltzer commenced an inn at "Selsettown," worth visiting if for no other reason than the inventive spelling on his sign outside, announcing INTERTAINMENT FOR MAN AND BASTE.[43] All along the way the men on foot and horseback encountered signs announcing the accommodations within, whether a black horse or a compass or a rudely painted name like TRAVELLERS REPOSE.[44]

On the road they often as not took their water from puddles filled with mosquitoes and gnats when no stream was nearby.[45] If they ran low on food, they purchased hominy or rough Indian bread called "kuntee" or "coon te," made from a brierroot. They could also buy provisions from the better stocked travelers they met who passed on their way south. Despite the fact that the predominance of the civilian traffic on the road was northbound, there were always others moving the opposite direction. Missionaries came this way to preach to the Chickasaw and Choctaw. Others, like Alexander Wilson, passed south from Nashville to study the wildlife. Government surveyors came to lay out lands open to settlement, while Indian traders and other men from Washington followed the path to negotiate land cessions from the natives.

Those making the trip south followed a somewhat different imperative than the immigrants and traders on the flats and keelboats. Friends advised people leaving Nashville to come in September, when the worst of the summer heat was past and the streams would be low and fordable. People leaving Nashville also banded together—one traveler called them "caravans"—in small groups for the trek. A man on his own generally inquired at the several public houses in town looking for others intending to make the trip.[46] The knowledgeable recommended horseback as the best way by far, though after the road clearing lay chiefly completed, at least a few came by carriage all the way, their only serious obstacle being the Tennessee crossing. In 1817 William Willis went from Nashville to Port Gibson in a carriage in thirteen days without difficulty, thinking it "a record."[47] But a carriage or "chaise" moved slower than a horse, meaning that some nights the journeyer would not be able to reach a stand and have to sleep in the open. One man in 1811 made the Nashville-to-Natchez trip in twenty days in a carriage, and estimated that he could have shaved five days or more from the time if he had been on a horse.

Whether north- or southbound, the travelers appreciated their tents once they passed into the Indian country, for the stands there teemed with insects and vermin. Indeed, people who made the trip in the summer months warned of insects of all varieties everywhere, especially the yellowjackets, and then there was the poison ivy to contend with. At least the southbound traveler did not want for white companions. "The road is full of travellers and company is easily had," Francis Martin told a friend in March 1811. In fact, however, he advised that one should not fear to make the trip alone, for the Indians, if difficult at times, never acted hostile. The only time they really posed a threat to a white was when he accidentally encountered a bunch of them who were intoxicated. Still it was best to travel with others, for "it would be a gloomy journey without company."[48]

Accommodations and prices varied on the upper end of the road as much as on the lower. Coming out of Nashville a man could pay twenty-five cents for a meal at a tavern and three dollars for a week's board and lodging. In Franklin, Tennessee, south of Nashville, a drink of whiskey cost him twelve cents, and a day's room and board seventy-five. More thirsty patrons paid a dollar for a gallon of whiskey, twenty-five cents for a quart, and thirty-seven cents for a quart of brandy. Outfitting themselves for the trip south, they handed over a dollar for four pounds of coffee, and another dollar for eight pounds of sugar.[49] Not a few people finished the trip complaining of "the exhorbitant charges of this plentiful country, which in reality is as scarce & extravagant as our own."[50]

With every succeeding year and the occasional improvements to the road, travel over the trace became more tolerable. Some thought its northern reaches "a much more pleasant trip than the other part of the road" by 1817, and Tennessee helped to enhance the convenience of passage through its borders by erecting mileposts along the way showing distances from courthouses or principal towns. When no tree stood near at hand, the state put in place posts with signboards shaped like "index hands" to point the directions at crossroads.[51] As the hundreds became thousands by the 1810s and 1820s, and with the widening of the Trace by the military and the passage of wagon traffic, the way gradually smoothed, easing passage. Moreover, with ensuing years, rains falling on the cleared road tended to wash away some of the soil, and that and the traffic itself gradually wore down the surface so that by the 1820s the trace "sank" in places. Where once it ran across the surface of the forest floor, now it nestled between banks that rose two, three, even four feet or more on either side. The overhanging trees perched atop these banks only added to the sense of passing through a verdant tunnel of wilderness. "These are covered with a prodigious growth of cane and high woods," wrote Wilson in 1810, "which, together, shut out the whole light of day for miles."[52] And yet the road changed course from time to time, especially where subject to large amounts of standing rainwater. When the surface turned to a muddy loblolly, travelers just moved around it for a few hundred yards, establishing a new path, and then another when that, too, turned into a morass.

Surprisingly enough, one of the most common dangers to the travelers in either direction came not from Indians or bandits or even the weather, but from the spookiness of their animals. Hardly one of the people who trekked the Trace and wrote of it afterward failed to mention at least one incident in which a horse or mule took fright and ran away. Baily, of course, lost a whole day because of a slipped saddle girth. William Richardson, traveling south from Nashville in 1815, barely got on his way before a companion's horse became frightened at some unseen peril and bolted, strewing its load of corn and fodder all along the way.[53] Yet few if any suffered more from such a mischance than twenty-two-year-old Martha Martin. In 1814 she, her husband, and their infant daughter, Jane, left Natchez in a buggy. They got only about twenty miles beyond Washington, however, when they crossed Bear Creek, and somehow in the crossing the animal pulling the carriage took fright and bolted up the bank and off onto the prairie. "I thought my only hope of saving myself & child would be to jump out," Martha recalled afterward. She stood and leaped out of the racing buggy, throwing her daughter aside into some soft grass as she did so. The driver (not Martha's husband) stayed with the careering vehicle and suffered an arm and several ribs broken. Jane providentially emerged entirely uninjured, but her mother landed on her left ankle and shattered it so severely that splinters of bone pierced her flesh and stuck out of her gaiters. After a servant carried her to a nearby plantation, Martha waited for two doctors, who examined the shattered limb and told her that it must be amputated or else she would perish.

Her husband at first refused, but after she turned deathly ill in the night he relented. At dawn they were ready. "My heart seemed it would burst," Martha remembered. "I felt like soul & body were about to separate." She grasped her little daughter in what she feared was a final embrace, then told her husband a last wish that Jane be raised by her mother. After that the doctors worked quickly. They carried her out onto the gallery of the house, laid her on a table, and began cutting at once. There was no sedative or anesthesia of any kind, and Martha could only say afterward: "My suffering was only known to God & myself." She spent twelve days recuperating at the plantation and another six with nearby friends before her own doctor came to take her back to Natchez. In a nightmarish déjà vu, the horse pulling the doctor's buggy spooked when some Choctaw seated at the roadside arose to wave as they passed. The animal began kicking the front of the carriage with its back legs until Martha feared it would break through and injure her. Entirely forgetting her own recent injury, Martha jumped out of the carriage on instinct and came down on the end of her amputated limb, driving the remaining bone clear through the still-healing stump. "Blood flowed from the wound," she said, "like pouring water from a pitcher." Only her doctor being near at hand saved her life, and even then she spent two weeks in bed before the physician determined that he would not have to amputate even more of the leg. After another month of recuperation, she set out with her husband on the Trace once more and this time reached Nashville, though not before she made a show of independence by throwing her crutches in a creek and refusing ever to use them again. For the rest of her ninety-four years she hopped on her right foot instead, living testimony to the spirit and resilience of a frontier woman, and of the unexpected dangers that lay on the road.[54]

With more and more men and women traveling in the Southwest, more and more roads came into use for them, gradually extending and connecting communications between the still scattered settlements. Like the Trace itself, most of them started as dimly outlined Indian and animal trails. In 1806 the federal government negotiated with the Creek and other Indians the right to run the so-called Federal Road through Georgia, and across the southeastern part of the Mississippi Territory to Mobile, then on to New Orleans. In 1807 a spur extended to Natchez itself, connecting with the post road and marked by a triple blaze or mark on trees on either side, giving rise to its nickname, the Three Chopped Way.[55] Soon it saw almost as much traffic as the Trace, as first men and horses and, later, wagons used it to penetrate the wilderness to the new lands of the Southwest. It even saw a novel new kind of vehicle, a barrel or hogshead with a single axle run through its ends so that wheels could be attached for drawing with an animal.[56] The Federal Road, too, became a post road, and a military highway in time of war, and over it surged a flow of population to the eastern half of the Mississippi Territory that was to become the State of Alabama in 1819.[57] Along it, as along the Trace, stands and later villages appeared to serve the travelers, and accommodations were equally as spartan. At Lewis's tavern near Fort Bainbridge a single towel served all twelve guests.[58] By 1830 more than sixty taverns operated along the main frontier roads through Alabama, some of them former stands on the part of the Trace that passed through the northwest corner of the state, like Levi Colbert's Buzzard Roost Tavern.[59]

In that same northwest corner of Alabama, George Strother Gaines carried out the instructions from Washington to survey a wagon road connecting Colbert's Ferry on the Tennessee with the Tombigbee River. The Spanish in West Florida were interfering with American goods coming to their port at Mobile, and this Tennessee-Tombigbee connection would allow a route for goods to come into Alabama via Tennessee and northern Mississippi instead. Meanwhile another route, known as the Gaines Trace, was surveyed by Edmund Gaines in 1807–8 as a way for immigrants to settle northern Alabama.[60]

The coming of war with Britain in 1812 vastly increased American concern for travel and communications in its Southwest, and after the successful conclusion of the conflict General Andrew Jackson drew a lesson from his experiences. He led a small army to New Orleans to defend the city in 1814, drawing on Kentuckians, Tennesseans, and Mississippians in particular. Although the Natchez-Nashville road had been vital in moving men, it was still slow and indirect. As soon as the war concluded he recommended that a new road, a military route, be constructed connecting Nashville directly with New Orleans. It would save untold miles of road travel and move over better ground for men and animals. In 1816 Congress approved Jackson's recommendation, appropriated ten thousand dollars for the task, and work started almost immediately. Once the surveyors finished, construction began in May 1817 and finished almost three years to the day later. It passed through 483 miles of wilderness, spanned more than thirty-five streams and rivers with bridges, laid down a full 4 miles of causeway over swamps, and cut 208 miles from the previous distance via Natchez. It kept three hundred workers busy almost continually, and if Jackson exaggerated when he announced its completion by saying that "this will become the most important road in America," still it represented a wonderful feat.[61] Moreover, it opened yet another section of the Southwest to immigration and settlement, and the spread of frontier communications.

One year later another new road connected with the old Trace between Doak's and Brashears's stands. No sooner did Washington commence mail carriage over the Trace than a problem arose. Because of its location on the ridgelines where soil discouraged settlement, the road saw no towns spring up along its path between the Harpeth and the Mississippi settlements above Natchez and Washington. Settlers preferred to locate generally east of the Trace, on better ground. With each new community, pressure grew to relocate the post road so that the riders actually passed through places where people could send and receive mail. Jackson and Columbus, Mississippi; Florence, Alabama; and Franklin and Columbia, Tennessee, all pressed their demands for service. Their taverns offered better lodgings and amenities, and the roads connecting them, being more traveled, became in time better built and maintained.

But their communications remained terrible. To get from Columbus, Mississippi, to Jackson on the Pearl River, a distance of 140 miles overland, the traveler had to go up the Tombigbee to Cotton Gin Port, take the Gaines Trace to Pontotoc near the Tennessee, and then down the Trace, a total trek of 260 miles. This and similar inconveniences finally prompted Congress to authorize a new road from near Brashears's to Columbus on the Tombigbee. It took more than five years to complete and took its name from its surveyor, Raymond Robinson. Even when done it failed to satisfy entirely, and for years Congress and locals continued to toy with the best ways of having it suit its purpose and pay its way, even making it a toll road for a time. Stands sprang up almost instantly, nevertheless, some of them run by operators like Fulsom from the Trace or relatives of Doak and Le Fleur. Though it too would fall into disuse after a time, it supplanted much of the older Trace in northern Mississippi in the later 1820s and contributed one more connection in the frontier network of roads that made settlement and exploitation of the wilderness possible.[62]

Even with the once-great impenetrable landscape gradually quartered into smaller and smaller pieces by the spread of a rude frontier road network, communications remained limited to the current of the rivers flowing south and the speed and endurance of a man or horse going north. But then came something that, if it did not exactly make the roads obsolete, produced a revolution in the way men and information moved and spread through the Southwest: steam. While Robert Fulton and others had experimented with steam-powered vessels for some years in the East, they had always had their eyes on the route from Pittsburgh down the Ohio to the Mississippi and New Orleans as an ultimate goal. Finally, in 1811 Nicholas Roosevelt used plans by Fulton to build at Pittsburgh a vessel that he named, significantly, the *New Orleans*. Twenty feet in the beam and 148 feet long, she struck one viewer as almost the size of a frigate and wasted little time before setting off down the Ohio on her historic voyage.[63]

She encountered more than anyone could have imagined and certainly produced reactions along the way that few if any ever forgot. Her steam whistle terrified Louisville, but then she amazed the city even more by demonstrating that she could do what no other vessel could under its own power: She went upstream against the current. That done, the *New Orleans* went on down the Ohio, terrifying white men and Indians along the way, and then steamed into the middle of the New Madrid earthquakes. Almost lost in the completely disorienting stream as it teemed with trees, driftwood, and bits of dismantled islands, the pilot simply kept the ship where he felt the current to be the strongest.[64] His relief at last to round a slight bend and see Natchez ahead on the bluff in January 1812 almost turned to terror when the ship lost power just before landing and started to drift downstream out of control. But the engineer got steam up once more, the paddle wheel began to turn, and she astonished the hundreds of apprehensive spectators on the bluff when she breasted the current and steamed safely up under the hill. Natchez made Roosevelt the lion of the moment, and the captain of the ship celebrated by marrying Mrs. Roosevelt's maid.[65]

"You will have many visitors now that you would have never seen had not the power of steam been invented, or found out." William Kenner proved to be a prophet in his prediction to Stephen Minor a few days after the *New Orleans* completed its voyage to its namesake city. At once Roosevelt began demonstrating just what his vessel could do, selling rides downstream and back a few miles for three dollars apiece. "He has been astonishing and amusing the multitude here," said Kenner, "and has exceeded the most sanguine expectations." The vessel could take ten to twenty passengers on the upstream trip to Natchez and thirty or more coming down, and Roosevelt set rates at thirty dollars for the one-way passage. Before her first voyage back upstream, Kenner quipped that "the boat will sail, no, that won't do, will *fumigate* for Natchez," loaded with oysters and "other odd notions." With his freight rates fixed, Roosevelt projected realizing sixteen hundred dollars from the four-day downriver trip, and half that for the return, which, though slow, still overcame the current and made three to four miles per hour headway.[66]

Roosevelt never intended that the *New Orleans* should attempt the trip all the way back up the Mississippi. She was merely a prototype, destined to spend the rest of her brief career plying between New Orleans and Natchez. In 1814 she struck a snag and sank, and the next steamboat, the *Vesuvius*, also never went farther upriver than Natchez, and also suffered the ignominy of being stuck literally for months on a sandbar while trying to return to Louisville.[67] But then Daniel French of Pittsburgh built and steamed his *Enterprise* south. She spent March and April 1815 on the New Orleans–Natchez run but in May attempted and succeeded in going back up the rivers to Louisville, inaugurating at last the possibility of round-trip steam travel.[68]

"There is no portion of the globe," wrote Timothy Flint in 1828, just thirteen years later, "where the invention of steam boats ought to be so highly appreciated, as in the valley of the Mississippi. That invention ought to be estimated the most memorable era of the West."[69] The people of the Southwest did not wait for Flint to conclude for themselves just how important the new mode of travel could be. They embraced it as the inebriate clutches his bottle. Where it took a keelboat a backbreaking three months to pole itself upriver to Pittsburgh, and boatmen a full month to walk up the Trace to Louisville, a steamboat could now make the trip in three weeks, with every year seeing more time shaved off the record as engines and designs improved. By 1820 some did it in fifteen days, and in 1830 they had cropped that down to ten. The end of 1817 saw at least nine boats plying the Lower Mississippi, making occasional trips to the falls of the Ohio at Louisville, and in the dozen years that followed that number increased severalfold, with twenty-six steamers working just the rivers of Alabama by 1830. Five years later the tally of steamboats that had churned the waters of all the western rivers together came to more than seven hundred.[70]

It was a remarkable mode of travel. By 1829 the boats offered passenger saloons running their whole upper deck, with a ladies' cabin and a gentlemen's bar and smoking room, a dining room on some vessels, and all of them carpeted, the woodwork of fine hardwoods and the glass stained or etched. Staterooms ran along the sides of the public rooms, containing all the amenities of a fine eastern hotel, while outside ran promenade decks for enjoying the scenery and evening breezes. Some vessels held a hundred or more in their cabins and that many more paying lesser fares to sleep on the lower decks. As builders experimented with designs and gained increasing experience, their vessels became more and more sleek, stately, and comfortable. Meanwhile, belowdecks and on the bow, hundreds—in time thousands—of bales of cotton lay stacked for transport to New Orleans.

"A stranger to this mode of travel would find it difficult to describe his impressions upon descending the Mississippi for the first time in one of these steam boats," declared Flint. "He contemplates the prodigious construction, with its double tiers of cabins, and its separate establishment for the ladies, and its commodious arrangements for the deck passengers and the servants. . . . You read," he went on. "You converse, or walk or sleep, as you choose." Little or no formality characterized people on the boats. They watched the verdant scenery glide by, looked at the birds overhead, listened to the hypnotic splash of the paddles in the water and the low chugging of the engines. "The trees, the green islands, the houses on the shore, every thing has an appearance, as by enchantment, of moving past you," said Flint. Often that scenery was nothing but a pathless wilderness. "A contrast is thus strongly forced upon the mind, of the highest improvement and the latest pre-eminent invention of art with the most lonely aspect of a grand but desolate nature."[71]

Not every passenger waxed so eloquent, of course. On the Alabama River and its tributaries, the vessels were far more spartan and utilitarian in the early days of steam—smaller and with far fewer amenities.[72] Even on the Mississippi not every boat was a floating palace. In 1829 Joseph Cowell took the *Helen McGregor* south to New Orleans, boarding at Louisville. He found her overloaded with too many passengers and too much cargo, more than a hundred people jammed together in the open to sleep on planks and with only a canvas awning for protection. Passengers' chickens cackled in rude coops, while scores of cabbages hung from the overhead and slowly rotted. Immigrants spoke a babble of Irish and German, intermingled with the yelling of the children and the barking of dogs. "All moral and social restraint was placed in the shade," complained Cowell. "*There Jack was as good as his master*—and never was Republicanism more practically republicanized than it was during the twelve days of confinement I passed on board this high-pressure prison."

The *Helen McGregor* offered no staterooms, no saloon or social hall, not even a washroom. Those concerned with cleanliness stood on the "guard," a fender or platform only about two feet wide on the side of the vessel. A chunk of yellow soap sat on a stool chained beside two tubs of water, and there bathers took their chances between the danger of leering passengers on one side and falling into the river on the other. The interior sleeping compartment contained a mere thirty-two berths in a room that also served as the main cabin, so even when a man could lie down, he had to attempt to sleep with the noise of drinking, gambling, laughter, and conversation—not to mention snoring—right in his ear. Food at least was plentiful, if inelegantly served. A table was cleared at mealtime in the cabin, and the cooks brought out venison, ducks, geese, turkeys, and a variety of overcooked vegetables, and the passengers simply lined up and started past.[73]

For most of those riding the steamboats, concern about finery and accommodations was no more uppermost in their minds than it had been for their predecessors who made the trip on the broadhorns and keelboats, or those fewer souls who made the trek on the Trace. The steamboat was just one more way of reaching their new opportunity in the Southwest. More than one passenger, looking at the mass of expectant settlers, surrounded by children, a few belongings, and a coop of chickens, commented on the tide of emigration: "The steam navigation, & the trade for the raw materials for manufacturing, ensure the migrating woodsman a supply of cash & the boundless & fertile soil around him & the domestic labour of his family, secure to him a full supply of all which the rude habits of his life give him a desire for."[74]

Indeed, steam so revolutionized the use of the river for transportation and the expansion of the trade and civilization of the Southwest that Mississippians, especially the people of thriving Natchez, came to resent their dependence on boats operated by New Orleans or Louisville owners. Two or three boats a day stopped under the hill to disgorge passengers and take on freight, but their rates soon left growers and travelers alike disgruntled. In 1819 planters paid $1.50 to ship a bale of cotton to New Orleans. Shipment of a cask of wine up the river to Natchez cost $1.00, and fifty cents for a bag of coffee. A quarter of a cask of other spirits could cost $1.75, and boxes, hampers, and other casks cost thirty cents per cubic foot. One recipient paid $2.25 for transport of a barrel of sugar, a box of soap, and two small packages aboard the *Alabama*, while even cigars cost fifty cents a bundle to ship, and a demijohn bottle of perfume a dollar.[75] Passenger rates could be just as capricious. Passage to Natchez from Louisville cost $25.00 in 1822, $6.25 for a child, and $9.33 for a servant. On another vessel four years later one slave cost as much to board as two white children, while adults cost four times the rate for a child.[76]

Even before the *Enterprise* inaugurated successful upriver transport, the tradesmen and planters of Natchez realized that their future and that of their region lay inextricably joined with this new phenomenon. In 1815 they organized the Natchez Steam Boat Company and commenced selling stock.[77] Shares went at $100.00 each, $10.00 on subscribing, $15.00 within sixty days, and the balance as demanded by the directors.[78] The work of raising capital went slowly, and by 1818 the company had sold only 682 of the anticipated 1,000 shares needed to raise $100,000.00 to build or buy one or more vessels for Natchez.[79] Meanwhile, elsewhere on the river planters had the same idea. Protesting "the extravagant price of freight on board of Steam Boats," twenty-five planters downstream of Natchez around Baton Rouge also created a subscription to raise $25,000.00 to buy or build their own vessel.[80]

Nothing came of most such private endeavors, and the flow of people and goods into and out of the territory remained largely in the hands of companies at either end of the mighty rivers. It had to wait for the dawn of yet another revolution in transportation before the people of the Southwest began truly to rule some of their own commerce. The steamboats, for all their wonder, were dangerous. The *Helen McGregor* exploded on her next voyage after Cowell disembarked. The *Boonslick* suffered a steam boiler explosion while carrying a lot of female passengers on the Lower Mississippi. Moreover, captains could not resist the temptation to urge more steam on their engines in order to push a record or race a neighboring boat. Shipping clerks in Natchez often made note of the record arrivals of the vessels passing through, then afterward set down their subsequent mishaps from burst boilers or sawyers and planters unseen until too late.[81] But by 1830 another wonder, one that could move more swiftly, was beginning to make its way into the Southwest. Better yet, this one could go where the rivers did not, and it proved far less prone to accident.[82] The steam locomotive and the railroad began first in the East, and gradually swept westward and into the South. Eventually it would do to the steamboat what that vessel did to the Natchez Trace, making it obsolete. For now it remained just a dimly seen and imagined possibility. But it would come.[83]

Ironically, by 1830, just as the name "Natchez Trace" was actually starting to take hold on the ancient route to Nashville, the road itself lay in the twilight of its life, retired by the coming of steam. Besides absorbing a great deal of the immigrant traffic moving south, the vessels virtually swallowed the upriver flow of returning flatboatmen and keelboaters and then later all but put the Kaintucks out of business. Much of the mail service to the river cities shifted from the overland traces to the rivers as well. Speed, reliability, and cost all worked in favor of the newest mode of transportation and against the oldest. It was a part of the inevitable march of progress that came hand in hand with the tide of settlement.

Samuel Clark lived on the shore of the Red River, one of the Mississippi's lower tributaries, and like everyone else liked to watch the graceful smoke-belching steamers ply up and down past his plantation. On one he actually saw a friend who wanted to tell him something, but the boat could not stop, so the friend scribbled a hasty note, tied it to a billet of firewood, and threw it ashore. As he retrieved the note Clark pondered the way the Southwest had burgeoned. New faces jammed the roads everywhere, he noted almost sadly. Whatever the route they took, over the Trace, along the Federal Road, down the rivers, their tide did not ebb. Already they spilled across the Mississippi toward lands farther west.[84]

4

The Road to the Fields

On a winter day in the early decades of the nineteenth century, one southern observer on the Mississippi swore that he saw a continuous line of immigrants more than a thousand strong.[1] Even allowing for the now maturing propensity of southwestern settlers to exaggerate in their stories, still the tale is not improbable. Millions of acres of public land beckoned as the country finally opened itself to American settlement following the Revolution. As early as 1796 word spread to the East of what one land agent called "surveys of a most excellent quality" lying vacant, almost begging for occupancy.[2] In a few short years the increasingly colorful stories of abundant land available almost for the asking proved a powerful lure. "There are I believe no lands in the U. S. that repay so well the toil of the husbandman," Francis Martin wrote in 1811 after traveling the full length of the Trace to New Orleans. "The best place to settle is in this territory." Governor Sargent boasted that he realized a $270 yield from the labor of each of his field hands, and Martin reported seeing cotton plantations that were "very superb indeed."[3]

The land *was* rich. "Happy Valley," settlers called the land along the Tennessee in upper Alabama, while men working the bottomlands along the Alabama thought of themselves as tilling Arcadia itself.[4] In 1806 a single planter with twenty-eight slaves on his fields anticipated that he would earn between ten and twelve thousand dollars, not counting some produce from sugarcane that he put to plantation uses.

Yet at first the soil did not come easily under the planter's plow. As late as 1801, when Congress was just starting to think about widening the wilderness path into a frontier road into the Southwest, actual ownership of the land remained in doubt. The Chickasaw and the Choctaw, of course, felt secure in their ancestral title to their lands in central and northern Mississippi, as the Creek did their lands in later Alabama, and the Cherokee theirs north of the Tennessee. For the rest, the federal government claimed ownership under the cession from Spain, and then after 1803 from that portion of the Louisiana Purchase that constituted the territory south of Natchez. The legislature of Georgia also claimed some of the ground on the basis of an early vague definition of its western boundary, and a later legislative action that simply tried to push its limits all the way to the Mississippi, to territory it had not settled or even explored, and which it could not occupy or defend. Even in 1801 the state and the national government still debated the matter, which impeded the opening of offices to begin surveying and selling the vacant lands.[5] Moreover, private South Carolina, Virginia, and Georgia companies held title to millions of acres under largely fraudulent speculations enacted and endorsed by their legislatures. In 1789 Virginia's Yazoo Company laid claim to virtually all of the upper half of Mississippi north of the Pearl River, while the South Carolina Yazoo Company maintained proprietorship of the territory south of the Pearl to Natchez. Six years later the Virginia and South Carolina companies were out of the picture, but the Georgia Company now held "title" to all of Mississippi and most of central Alabama between the Walnut Hills and the thirty-fourth parallel, while the Georgia Mississippi Company claimed almost all of the ground south to the line of Spanish West Florida, some distance below Natchez. Other combinations also laid claim to the northernmost reaches of Mississippi and Alabama.[6]

It was a mess, tainted by sloppiness, avarice, and more than a little corruption, and in the end resulted in bankruptcies. "A many-headed dog of Hell," one congressman termed the whole sordid affair, and ultimately, in 1818, the government itself wound up making marginal restitution to the investors in what had been the largest land speculation the continent would ever see.[7]

Meanwhile other obstacles to retard the flow of settlers presented themselves. The San Lorenzo Treaty in 1795 ceded much of future Mississippi to the United States, and its territorial organization by Congress three years later seemingly set the stage for the influx of settlers. But when Governor Sargent arrived he found the non-Indian portions of the territory already checkered with a host of different, and often conflicting, existing land grants and occupants from the British and Spanish years, not to mention the Georgia claims.

In one of his first acts Sargent decided that he should honor the Spanish grants, chiefly centered around Natchez and south of the Choctaw lands. That, and the confusion over existing titles, actually decided some early immigrants to give up and return to their homes or else move on to available lands in the territory still held by the British and the Spaniards.[8] The British grants from 1763 to 1779 were somewhat haphazard, often unsettled, and just as often used for speculation by absentee owners who never actually improved the land to validate their claims. Even a few old French grants added spice to the bubbling legal stew. When Spain took over some order ensued. First, land went only to those who actually lived on and improved their plots, and then all such claims had to be registered to differentiate legal owners from the often itinerant squatters who planted themselves on vacant land until or unless driven off. Then when Spain left the territory, in a last defiant act it granted a host of new titles and backdated them prior to the San Lorenzo Treaty to provide an air of legitimacy.

Thus, when Sargent took over in 1798, a mess met him. He told the squatters not to worry. They could stay put for the time being. But in deciding to honor the old Spanish grants, he alienated a large faction of new immigrants who had hoped to seize some of the best property around Natchez and elsewhere from the Spanish grantees. Worse, he soon appeared to be far too close to many of those beneficiaries personally, and a clamor went up for his replacement. Newly installed President Thomas Jefferson sent William C. C. Claiborne in his place in 1801. Claiborne enjoyed a bit more success than Sargent, but still the situation remained muddy until March 3, 1803, when Congress stepped in and passed legislation formally recognizing all British and Spanish grants dating prior to San Lorenzo and on which the grantees were actually settled and cultivating. It further gave grants of up to 640 acres to settlers without Spanish grants who could establish that they had been planting their acreage at the time of the Spanish evacuation in 1797. Beyond this it also allowed first purchase options to those squatting on tracts at the time Congress passed the act. Rarely then or later did Congress move in such a thorough manner to settle equitably such a muddy dispute.[9]

But it did not satisfy all. The act failed to establish policy for new settlers, and that especially worried those scattered inhabitants of the future Alabama, where proximity to sometimes hostile Creek made them feel their own insignificant numbers most painfully. Still, on the whole the act put the Southwest on the road to future settlement, and toward that end it also established at last two land offices in the territory to commence the orderly sale of public lands to the tide of immigrants now expected to flow into the region.

Edward Turner assumed the post of land commissioner in the eastern half of the territory, making his headquarters at Washington, the territorial capital. At first he found houses so scarce that he feared he could rent nothing, and would have to build his own office. He found something, however, and in January 1804, while complaining that "office rent is very high in this Territory," he moved into a drafty wooden shack and began setting up his office, starting literally from nothing. He first sent out orders for the making and binding of the necessary deed and survey books, which took four months to reach him from Philadelphia and cost $273.5625 when finally they arrived.[10] While he waited he tried to scavenge two large blank books from a court clerk's office. Then he had to persuade the holders of the Spanish grants to come forth and present them in order that their titles might be converted under the new congressional act. Despite being warned that their claims might be invalidated if they failed to do so, some feared to step forward. "The claimants are very backward in filing their claims," Turner complained. Some held back out of fear of the trouble and modest expense, and in time became surly enough that the land agent feared they might "abandon the government." Then there was the problem of dealing with their actual grant papers, written in Spanish. He wanted a Spanish clerk, suggesting to his superiors that "such an one may be had from N. Orleans, by offering extraordinary wages," and fearing that none could be found in the territory. Finally Turner located two men in Natchez who could read and translate the documents into English, but they refused to come the seven miles to Washington to earn only twenty cents for each one hundred words translated.[11] And all of Turner's work was further complicated by the fact that it took twenty-five days for a letter from one Washington to reach him in another.

Still, Turner got his work done with relative dispatch, certainly faster than his counterpart working in the Alabama lands to the east. That did not stop the grumbling, of course, especially among those now required to pay for squatted new land. No matter how Congress established terms and credit for the payment, the settlers complained, leading Congress to conclude only half in jest that the immigrant would not be satisfied even with absolutely free land. Petitioners flooded Congress with appeals for exceptions, which harassed politicians all too often managed to grant. In the end, once the registration of all the preexisting grants and the settlement of most of the disputes lay complete, Secretary of the Treasury Albert Gallatin forcefully urged Jefferson to start selling the unclaimed lands at once before Congress just gave it all away. In January 1809 the first land office opened in Washington, with two others soon to follow.[12]

Of course, many settlers did not wait but simply squatted, generally on the Indian side of the public lands, trusting to the peacefulness of the Choctaw and Chickasaw not to force them out, and to governmental inefficiency not to notice their presence. In 1809 federal authorities removed seventeen hundred of them from Chickasaw and Creek lands by force. With the announcement of the formal sale of remaining lands, even more prospective settlers appeared. Typically they either purchased their parcels in advance through agents or else journeyed to the territory and "shopped" themselves. In 1816 Richard Breckenridge left his home in Tennessee and rode south into the territory soon to become the state of Alabama. All along his path he looked at the land with the eye of a settler and exploiter. When he crossed a substantial creek, he saw in it not a pretty stream but a potential site for a mill. He looked carefully at the land to see if the topsoil was too thin for cultivation or sources of water too distant for livestock. In the forests he saw not firewood or simply timber to be cleared but selected hardwoods with market values. Two weeks into his journey he wrote in his diary: "I have seen no place since I started that I would like to live in."[13] Finally, ten days later, he found the place he sought, good land not far from a small river, with creeks and springs abounding. "There is as handsome a situation for a town as ever I saw," he proclaimed. He commenced work at once on a sixteen-by-twenty-foot log cabin. A few years later the town of Tuscaloosa would grow up there and briefly become Alabama's capital.[14]

At first the settlers paid $2.00 an acre—those who paid at all, that is—and in time the price came down to $1.25. They paid it for land that was excellent for several miles back from the rivers and major creeks, and especially in the central portion of the territory, where a rich belt of black loam passed from east to west. They paid it for higher ground that was less friendly to the plow but offered excellent stands of hardwood timber for exploitation. Some regions actually looked as if they held potential for viticulture, while the prairies, though often strewn with gravel, still held enough grass to support grazing livestock. Holly, wild peach trees, the stately magnolia, red oak, walnut, cherry, elm, mulberry, ash, and more abounded in the forests. Below Natchez huge canebrakes covered miles of open lands. Moreover, the land benefited from a climate very friendly to a long growing season, if uncomfortable to man and beast. "Temperate" was a mild term to apply to it. The temperature could and often did rise above one hundred degrees, with a killing humidity thrown in that made early-afternoon work almost impossible for field hands but could add inches of growth to corn in a single day. Not a dozen days in the winter provided sufficient cold to warrant a heavy coat.[15]

While some visitors complained of the quality of the beef that planters raised on their new farms, the cattle themselves seemed to thrive. In fact, cattle first came to the territory with the French, and by the time of the British occupation the raising of livestock meant a good deal more to inhabitants than did planting. Then came the Spaniards, who took advantage of the natural savannas and grasslands for grazing, and soon the Lower Mississippi region teemed with small herds. When the Americans came to take over, they found animals of good size and fair quality, with many planters keeping herds of two hundred or more. Sheep, too, flourished, producing excellent mutton but rather coarse wool. And livestock of all descriptions exhibited considerably less domestication than elsewhere in the country, thanks to being allowed to run free from restraint and to the rich growth of the grasslands, which required little contact with herders for feeding and care. As for swine, Ellicott thought them in no way inferior to those found anywhere else in America.[16]

By 1805, as the old Spanish grants were being registered by Turner, the five counties then comprising the organized parts of the Mississippi Territory numbered more than thirty-five thousand cattle.[17] Indeed, while planters still struggled to find a profitable cash crop, beef loomed with surprising potential for sale to the New Orleans and West Indies markets. Prices varied wildly, but in the main in the early 1800s a cattleman could get from $6.40 up to $13.00 a head, with fat steers bringing up to $25.00. Dressed as beef they commanded prices around six cents a pound by 1800. Certainly a good steer was more than valuable enough for the owner to spend money on advertising in the press for its return when one strayed.[18]

People in the East not familiar with the southwestern planter would come quickly to assume that his definition of his home as a "plantation" meant that planting was all he did. In fact, some of the great planters of the Natchez area, like Anthony Hutchins, owned herds exceeding fifteen hundred, and their slaves devoted perhaps as much as a quarter of their time to tending these and other livestock. The story was much the same with swine, which were so ubiquitous and so essential to the frontier community—and to the nation—that one wag of the time suggested that America ought really to be called the "Republic of Porkdom." Bacon and pork were such staples of the frontier diet that they frequently appeared three meals a day. For every two cows or steers in a planter's fields, he usually had three pigs. Moreover, a good sow produced more than twenty offspring a year that were simplicity itself to raise. They could almost fend for themselves in the wilderness, rooting and grubbing for much of their provender and fattening quickly until ready for slaughter or market.[19]

Poultry, of course, added some variety to the plantation sights and sounds, and to the meal table, but the immigrant to the Southwest hardly looked to the lowly chicken and goose for a market profit. His horse was another thing, however. Horse-trading came instantly into demand in early Natchez. The Spaniards brought fine animals with them when they came, and inevitably left many behind. Wild ponies from the other side of the Mississippi were brought across and broken to saddle and plow or sold in New Orleans at fifty dollars and more a head. The planters soon learned that they could be difficult, uncomfortable to ride, and easily spooked to throw a rider or set a carriage off careering wildly, as Martha Martin discovered to her dismay. Better animals came down the river on the flats and over the Trace, and with them the planters began to refine the bloodline of their stock and, like Americans everywhere on the frontier, rapidly turned their best horses from pleasure and work to sport.[20]

The settlers in early Natchez, and then along the lower Trace as settlement spread, enjoyed a brisk livestock market in the town on the bluff and some considerable trade with downriver New Orleans. Moreover, from the animals slaughtered for local consumption their owners derived hides and tallow, leading to a small leather industry. So ubiquitous was livestock of all descriptions in the territory that as early as the Spanish days, colonial government imposed regulations on grazing and fencing to keep the animals from wandering loose in large herds. Law required owners to register brands to be used on their animals, and those planters who found stray animals with their own herds had to advertise every six months the description and brands of the creatures in order that their rightful owners might reclaim them. The regulation of stray beasts, in fact, assumed considerable importance, showing just how many there were in the territory, and their value. Visitors and men passing through could not, under penalty of law, take up a stray, and the owner of any wandering animal that damaged a planter's fences in entering his property must pay restitution.[21]

Making a living from his land was the concern of the small farmer; making a profit occupied the energies of the larger planter. In 1822 Andrew Marschalk lamented that "with more than $10,000 of real property in my possession, I am in danger of prison for $100."[22] Others found themselves in similar positions in the early days as they tried to find a cash crop. Virtually everyone raised some corn—perhaps six or seven acres for a small family, the same acreage per field hand on the larger plantations. The grain fed the hogs and perhaps the poultry, as well as providing meal for pones and Indian bread. But no one looked to it for cash or wealth. Wheat, rye, barley, oats, and most other grains also appeared in their fields for domestic use.

They tried tobacco first, and by the time of the Revolution planters were already exporting it to Spain. It was difficult to cultivate and exhausted the soil, but in a good season a single acre yielded almost a ton of the leaf. Planters harvested the leaves and hung them in sheds to dry before packing them in hogsheads carrying from six hundred to eight hundred pounds. Spanish merchants paid an inflated price of one hundred dollars a hundredweight—subsidized in part by the Spanish government—which meant a yield of two hundred dollars per acre. For the planter working several hundred acres, the rewards could be substantial, and for a time it appeared that the Southwest had found its staple crop. By 1792 the annual production just in the Natchez district came to half a million pounds. The profits led to a natural desire to put more land under cultivation, which in turn increased the demand for more slaves to work the fields. But then the Spanish authorities abandoned their price support and started buying better—and cheaper— tobacco from Kentucky instead, and almost overnight the commercial tobacco business in the Southwest dwindled.[23]

The result at first was almost devastating. The planters had gone into debt to acquire more land and slaves to work their crops, and when the market died, they almost went with it. Until the authorities stepped in and imposed an eight-year grace period, many farmers faced the probability of losing their property to creditors. Even then, since all they had to sell was their tobacco, the planters approached ruin trying to get out from under their load of debt. By 1800, as a result, the Natchez area ceased to be an important producer.

The earlier settlers had tried planting indigo, a weed from which blue dyes could be extracted, and now they returned to it for a time as a possible salvation from the tobacco collapse. It was easy to cultivate, though immature plants needed careful attention. After that stage, however, they grew well with little or no care. Workers cut the plant just prior to its going to seed, tied it in bundles, and piled it into large steeping vats filled with water. Once the indigo had soaked for some time, the planter drained the liquid into another vat, where he churned the broth and then left it to sit in the sun. Fermentation soon set in, and the actual dye itself settled to the bottom of the vat, from which, after the rest of the liquid was drained off, workers shoveled the sludge into canvas-lined draining boxes. They later dried it in molds, cut it into cubes, and shipped it to market.

The darkest hue of blue became the most prized, while a lighter shade called "floton" emerged in great quantities but brought a lesser price. The problem with indigo, however, was the odious nature of its processing. Men found the stench of the rotting plants unbearable, and disposing of them presented a pollution problem. Draining the water into local streams killed the fish, and made humans who drank it seriously ill. Throughout its life, from cultivation to processing, the plant also attracted millions of flies, and in the end its attraction proved its undoing as an insect arrived that delighted in dining on its leaves and buds and sapping the precious juice from the plant. The vermin devastated the crops and almost entirely put an end to its commercial cultivation. Where the dried cakes of indigo sold for $1.50 to $2.00 a pound prior to the insects' arrival, afterward the quality of the crops dwindled and the resulting dye brought only $1.00.[24]

Necessity forced on them by the decline of tobacco and indigo led more by chance than design to cotton. The French planted it in a small way in the earliest days of settlement, and throughout the 1700s the planters and farmers grew small quantities of it for their own use in making homespun garments. Unfortunately the fiber that emerged from the cotton boll when ready for harvest contained myriad small seeds that had to be separated by hand. One slave could generally seed only about a pound or two of cotton per day.[25] Still by 1760 a few Louisianians began commercial cultivation of the crop, encouraging authorities to import some of the crude roller gins that could laboriously separate lint from seed, but only at a rate of about seventy pounds per day. The process thus remained so time consuming that there was no way for the crop to assume major commercial possibilities. By 1795 the Mississippi farmers grew cotton and roller-ginned it, but it held little promise for them.[26]

Then came a set of plans based on the new gin designed by Eli Whitney in the East, and reportedly very effective. Daniel Clarke of Wilkinson County looked at the drawings brought through by a visitor who had seen and sketched Whitney's machinery, and at once put John Barclay, a local mechanic, to work building one on his own plantation. "Barclay will soon have his gin sufficiently forward to essay how it will work," Clarke wrote to Anthony Hutchins in August 1795. "I have done a great deal to bring this brat into the world, and if it succeeds shall put in a claim for my share of the honor."[27] Local planters frequently visited Clarke's plantation to observe the progress of the construction, and not a few stood in attendance when he first set the completed machine in operation. The result startled planters. It worked easily and cheaply and could process their long-staple (long-fibered) black-seed cotton at five hundred pounds a day. Overnight the new gin made cotton a profitable potential crop for commercial cultivation. In 1796 Natchez mechanic David Greenleaf began commercial manufacture of the new gins and himself operated the first public gin at Selsertown, a village that had grown up around one of the old Trace stands outside Natchez.[28] Not long after the turn of the century further improvements and modifications, including the harnessing of horse- and waterpower, revolutionized production.[29] Soon almost every planter had his own gin on the plantation, and if he did not he could take his crop to a commercial gin that charged him about 10 percent of his cotton as a fee for processing.[30] In an era when hard currency was scarce, the gin operators gave the planter a receipt for the poundage of the cotton processed, and growers soon found that they could use their receipts virtually as paper money, acceptable by any and all.

"We continue to cultivate cotton with very great success," Sir William Dunbar wrote from Natchez in 1799. "It is by far the most profitable crop we have ever undertaken in this country."[31] He predicted a long and brilliant future for the staple. By 1800, with the industry just getting into sway, cotton brought from twenty-two to twenty-three dollars per hundredweight at Natchez, and about three dollars more in New Orleans.[32] The planters packed it in large bags for transport, but it was cumbersome and occupied a great deal of space on the flats and barges. Fortunately Dunbar, one of the region's most inventive characters, conceived the idea of a press that could compact up to four hundred pounds or more into a cubical bale that made it easier to transport and required fewer vessels to get a crop to market. His screw press cost him a thousand dollars to build in Philadelphia but proved so effective that it soon became as ubiquitous almost as the gin itself. Many a planter paid more than fifty dollars for a set of "screws" to operate his own press, and bought rough gunny bagging at twenty-seven cents a yard for wrapping the pressed bales.[33] Ironically, Dunbar thought more about the oil that could be extracted from the cottonseed itself and hoped thereby to recoup his investment, but decades would pass before its uses for fertilizer and animal feed supplements became known. Until then the cottonseed simply went up in flames or else was dumped in refuse piles and allowed to rot, "considered of no use whatever, and really a nuisance."[34]

Soon the repercussions of the sudden profitability of cotton spread throughout the settled parts of the territory. Men made profits importing the bagging and hemp ropes from upriver to sell to the planters. Others opened warehouses in Natchez and New Orleans for storage of the finished bales until ready for shipment abroad, charging twenty-five cents per bale per month. The steamers charged twenty-five cents per hundred square feet of cotton for transport, and the manufacture or sale of cotton gins themselves spread clear up into the southern parts of Tennessee along the Trace. The price of the cotton itself fluctuated, but went down considerably from that early twenty-three dollars per hundredweight as supply increased dramatically. By the late 1820s a good bale brought forty-two dollars in New Orleans, and the introduction of steam power to ginning by 1830 only increased output and profits.[35]

But the sudden explosion of the new cash crop did not come without hardship. Mississippi Territory planters grew only the Georgia long-staple black-seed variety, because it worked so well and was all they needed. In 1811, however, a variety of rot appeared in the fields that in two short years was ruining half of some planters' crops. "The rot has been so destructive in Wilkinson," one resident of Natchez wrote of a neighboring county in 1818, "that half crops will not be made, notwithstanding the fine season we have had for picking."[36] Shortly planters introduced a new variety of cotton, shorter-stapled and coarser in texture but impervious to the rot, which then disappeared. Then in 1806 a Natchez man named Walter Burling went to Mexico on a business trip, and while there looked at a Mexican variety that appeared to have both the resilience to rot and the softer, longer staple that Mississippi planters most needed. He asked permission to import the seed into the Southwest, but Spanish authorities refused. To a seemingly unrelated request, however, they offered no objection. They told him he could buy and ship all the Mexican dolls he wanted, apparently unbothered by—or unaware of—the fact that their dolls were stuffed with that same cottonseed. Burling bought as many as he could and took them back to Natchez, where he introduced the variety to a hungry soil in which it throve.[37] If the story has perhaps the ring of myth about it, still the fact remained that this seed became the basis for all of the subsequent developments and hybrids that made the planters' fields look like a new-fallen snow. In fact, producers of the seed itself came in time to reap rewards almost as great as those who harvested the lint.[38]

The spread of cotton through the territory that became Mississippi was dramatic. By the time the Mexican seed came into use, cotton had already become the dominant crop in all of the settled areas in the southern third of the country occupied by whites. The balance, of course, still belonged to the Choctaw and Chickasaw, and even they cultivated a little of the staple, but only for their own use. In the land to the east that would become Alabama, the story was largely the same, and after 1832, when the Indians were finally forced from their lands and the entire region was opened to white settlement, cotton instantly moved in with the planters. By 1834 Mississippi itself would be the leading U.S. producer.[39] With further developments in methods and seed varieties, cotton growers could get 2,000 pounds and more of unseeded cotton from a single acre, or about 800 pounds a year for each field hand needed to tend and harvest. That translated to two bales per year per man, which in flush times brought one hundred dollars per bale. A planter working one of the average 640-acre grants might theoretically expect to send almost 250,000 pounds of cleaned and seeded fiber to the press, yielding him more than sixty thousand dollars for his crop.[40] In 1801 alone, with most of the refinements yet in the future, cotton brought seven hundred thousand dollars of income to its planters in just the region around Natchez. That meant an annual income averaging more than seven hundred dollars for each of the 9,000 citizens of the area, a phenomenal sum by frontier standards, and higher even than most areas in the affluent Northeast.[41] And at the same time that cotton virtually swept over these southern fields, sugarcane began to be planted in some of the southernmost reaches of the territory, and even more in Louisiana. In the summer of 1800 a planter put in an experimental crop just north of the Louisiana line, and enjoyed sufficient results that he and others determined to capitalize on the crop where the soil seemed suitable.[42] Within two decades planters were shipping bundles of harvested cane by the hundreds aboard the steamboats bound for market.[43]

Out of this seeming miracle crop grew a whole new class in the Southwest, men whose rise to affluence, power, and station came not from birth or bloodline but solely from their almost overnight wealth. Half a century would see Natchez itself inhabited by more millionaires than any other city in the nation, all of them made either by cotton or by trading with those who planted it. With their wealth came a yearning for a social station based on something other than money, a way of standing equal to the aristocrats of Virginia and South Carolina, and by 1830 they had evolved an aristocracy of sorts. It derived chiefly from money, of course, but those who could point to grandfathers who had settled there in the 1700s laid claim to status thanks to tenure in the territory rather than ancestral distinction. More and more they intermarried on the basis of these new social distinctions instead of the ways their parents and grandparents had wedded. As a result, out of a virtually classless society in the 1780s, the Old Southwest, and especially the burgeoning territory at the end of the Natchez Trace, grew into a class-ridden culture in the span of two or three generations. Men whose grandfathers might have floated down the Mississippi in a broadhorn, or braved the loneliness of a horseback trip down the Trace together, now stood on either side of an invisible line that one might actively seek to prevent the other from crossing. When young John A. Quitman sought to marry the niece of Edward Turner, who had himself acquired considerable property and wealth, he managed to secure her family's permission but had to sign a prenuptial contract stipulating that any property coming to her from her family should only go to her own heirs and assigns and not to his. Only Quitman's own rise to wealth and position some years later finally made him almost the equal of his wife's family.[44]

One other, even more important factor helped to reinforce the growth of class feeling and distinction. The wealth coming from the great crop was wholly dependent upon a large supply of cheap labor. Planting, tending, and especially harvesting cotton required extensive work by many hands, not to mention all the other tasks necessary to running one of the larger plantations. In the early days, with the white working population small, and so many of them intent on building holdings of their own, hired labor was in short supply and, in any case, too costly. Slavery, however, offered the perfect solution. The first African slaves entered the territory with the Spanish explorers and then settled with the French, who followed. In 1723, 111 slaves, a third of the whole population, lived near the site of future Natchez. Their number doubled in the next four years, but they came and went with their largely military masters, few actually staying permanently. More arrived with the influx of Americans, commencing in the 1770s; and then in 1793 as the plantations began to show real promise, the Spaniards lifted all duty from slaves and encouraged their import.

From then on the slave population burgeoned. Between 1784 and 1792 it rose from 498 to 1,893. The year after the lifting of the duty that number rose to 2,100, and it never stopped climbing. By the turn of the century the population of black slaves approached half of the entire non-Indian population of the territory, and thereafter maintained that same proportion almost unchanged.[45]

"We require more slaves," William Dunbar wrote in 1799 as cotton planting spread across the territory. "Negroes and particularly tradesmen are in demand here. Ordinary men are worth $500 cash, women $400 and upwards," he continued the next year. "There is no country where they are better treated. They are supplied with winter and summer clothing of good materials, heavy blankets, and hats and shoes." Planters fed them plenty of pork and beef and allowed the blacks to raise livestock of their own, "and every thrifty slave has his pig pen and poultry house." Bread, milk, and vegetables were theirs in abundant supply, and most planters allotted each slave family a piece of ground for growing its own produce, and sometimes even the use of a team for plowing.

Moreover, in 1800 Dunbar and others practiced a bonus system whereby they rewarded slaves with an incentive for any day in which they picked more than the usual seventy-five or eighty pounds a day. Masters did not work them after dark and provided cabins for their families and fuel for their fires. Indeed, typical of most slaveholding aristocrats throughout the South, Dunbar saw in slavery only a benevolent institution, as well as one necessary for preserving the social order. Whites must have absolute mastery over blacks. "If this principle be not admitted," he warned, "the alternatives are, insurrection, with all its horrors, or emancipation with all its evils. . . . Slavery can only be defended perhaps on the principle of expediency," he confessed, "yet where it exists, and where they so largely outnumber the whites, you must concede almost absolute power to the master."[46]

Prices reflected the increasing value of and demand for able field hands. In 1781 a man might bring $330 to $350 and a woman about $280. Children commanded prices around $100. A decade later blacks could cost $450 each, but by the time Dunbar was writing, some especially strong or otherwise desirable field hands could fetch prices of $1,450 or more, with the average price topping $700. Even the price of females rose to more than $400 as some planters began to discover that they could equal males at picking cotton.[47] Through the early decades of the 1800s, despite financial recessions and occasional falls in the price of cotton, the slave population increased steadily on the plantations.

The Natchez slave market, along with another across the Mississippi from New Orleans, became the most active in the whole South in the days immediately after the end of the second war with Britain. Dealers sold slaves at the landing fresh from the boats, in the market and auction houses in the city on the bluff, and out on the plantations themselves. In 1817 alone some fourteen broadhorns pulled in under the hill, loaded with blacks. Buyers went to established dealers or to traveling salesmen for their purchases, but most of the business was done at a place called "Forks of the Path" just on the outskirts of Natchez. One of its proprietors, Isaac Franklin, who had been credited with importing two-thirds of the slaves brought into the Southwest, made himself a personal fortune exceeding $2 million.[48] He employed an agent in faraway Alexandria, Virginia, who bought blacks there and shipped them to Natchez for sale.[49] Others sent agents to Virginia as well, and considering the prices in excess of $1,000 that were quite common by the 1820s, the profits available in this ebony trade were indeed substantial.

Samuel Coborn went to Virginia on a buying trip in 1828 and spent $520 for a male of twenty-two, $526 for an eighteen-year-old, and prices ranging from $330 to $385 for four others of lesser potential, aged fifteen to twenty-five. Boys and girls aged fourteen to sixteen cost him from $250 to $330, and even though all these people would surely bring twice their price on the Natchez market, still Coborn complained that they cost him too much. "I am afraid negroes are not to be bought in this part of Va.," he lamented.[50] Because of the expense of transporting the blacks by sea, and the fact that few vessels were fitted out for such human cargo, most of the slaves either came south by the rivers or else walked in "coffles," or gangs, the fifteen hundred miles from Washington to Natchez via Nashville and the Trace. Traveling with them on the seven- to eight-week journey on foot, their white dealers came well provisioned and heavily armed for fear of an uprising, but nothing of the sort is known to have happened. It helped that the Chickasaw and Choctaw, who generally did not approve of slavery, still did not want runaway blacks in their territory. As the owners and their stock of blacks crossed the Tennessee and entered the Chickasaw territory, those slaves contemplating escape—if they could read—saw disheartening signs advising travelers to "Take Notice" that the Indians would arrest and return any blacks who tried to run away.[51]

During just a portion of the year 1833, sales by itinerant slave traders in Natchez alone came to nearly a quarter million dollars, and that did not include men like Franklin or the other resident merchants or the markets growing up by then in other communities in Alabama and Mississippi.[52] Such an influx inevitably had a profound impact on the growing white community and the planter class itself. Indeed, without the slaves, the distinctions of class so dear to socially ambitious planters would have been much less clearly defined, for in the early 1800s slave ownership came to be one of the marks of aristocracy in the new states. It denoted not only wealth but the most visible sort of evidence of superiority and mastery, giving to the planter class the air of people born to command. Though they would have been loath to confess it, the whites' burgeoning society needed slavery almost as much as did their economy.

The existence of a growing black minority—that would become a majority—within southwestern society carried with it an inherent fear of slave revolt. Almost from the time that they began importing blacks, then, the planters commenced enacting increasingly rigid legal controls on the slave trade, and on black behavior, all designed to preserve white security. Ironically, in 1798 when Congress organized the Mississippi Territory, it left in place earlier legislation that tacitly prohibited slavery. No one seemed to notice this, and certainly the owners of the few thousand slaves then in the territory did not call attention to the anomaly. Four years later, when they organized their territorial government in 1802, they specifically omitted all mention of the prohibition in their constitution, and that settled the matter. Once Mississippi itself became a state, its first constitution addressed itself to trying slaves for breaches of statute law and commenced the legal attempt to intimidate would-be rebellious blacks. Yet government approached the slave with two hands, one holding the rod, and the other offering comfort. The slave must have an impartial trial by jury when indicted. Moreover, masters could be made to meet certain minimum standards of conduct with their chattels, must "treat them with humanity," clothe and feed and house them properly, and "abstain from all injuries to them extending to life and limb." A master could whip an unruly slave, but he risked facing the law himself if he mutilated or killed his "property." Those who failed to behave humanely with their chattels could see the authorities forcibly take them away to resell to more law-abiding whites.[53]

This high-sounding blanket of law protecting the slave's basic right to life covered a host of lesser enactments to follow that not only severely restricted his ability to enjoy that life but also provided sometimes brutal punishments as a means of control. Almost inevitably the punishment came in "stripes"—strokes of the lash across the back. While laws fixed the maximum number, anything up to that lay at the discretion of the justice of the peace. Moreover, those stripes were to be "well laid on." Ten lashes comprised the general minimum, for minor infractions like merely walking onto a plantation without prior leave from the owner, the fear in this case being of outside slaves agitating a planter's blacks and perhaps inciting them to misbehavior or even revolt. At the other end of the scale, officials doled out a brutal thirty-nine-lash maximum for the worst offenses, including theft and, oddly enough, "buying and selling without a written permission from his master."

Law forbade the slave to leave his plantation without the master's permission, sometimes in writing. Nor could he have a weapon of any kind. Especially after 1830 was he enjoined against meeting in groups of other slaves in numbers greater than five, and in Alabama in 1832 state law prohibited formal education of all blacks, slave or free. Knowledge, they feared, tended to make the slave less content with his lot. Moreover, it could give him the tools of communication to spread his discontent, while school itself constituted a place of assembly where blacks could meet in greater numbers than five.[54] The larger the slave population became, the more the whites came to fear a mass uprising.

These laws also forbade the slave from attending church except those services that many planters provided on their own property. For that matter, a master might take it on himself to offer the rudiments of reading and writing to his slaves, so long as he did so on the plantation, and many owners did. Statute prohibited the slave from owning any livestock or doing any cultivation on his own, though of course most owners allowed exactly the opposite to happen. Still, since a slave was property, anything belonging to him, including the chickens he raised, could be taken from him at any time and considered the master's property. The whites showed their continuing fear of slave violence by their specific prohibition against dogs, however. If a master caught his chattel with a horse or a chicken, he simply punished the offense by taking the animal from him. However, if a slave were caught with a dog, he could suffer up to twenty lashes. A horse posed little threat to a master, of course, but a dog could be trained to attack. Meanwhile, if the master meted out excessively cruel punishment to his chattels, he could be fined up to five hundred dollars, and many owners did find themselves taken to court for mistreatment of their slaves, though few ever paid the maximum penalty.

Whites certainly recognized that a slave had a right to defend himself when unlawfully attacked, even by a white, yet in the end it was often up to the unfortunate slave to prove himself the victim rather than aggressor. Lifting his hand, or even uttering offensive language to a white, could set the lash to whistling through the air for the first of thirty-nine times. In cases where the slave clearly—or white judges so decided—attacked a white, his life could be forfeit. If he did so with intent to kill, he would be hanged. In a mitigating circumstance, he could suffer up to one hundred lashes—each day for three days in a row, a fate perhaps worse than hanging, and one that would see many strong men dead before it came to an end. Law required an impartial jury trial, of course, with counsel provided for the slave, but the jurors were all free whites and generally from the master's own class. Juries might spare a slave his stripes but order that he be branded, and most crimes not punishable by hanging involved "burning in the hand" along with a number of lashes. Manslaughter, rape, arson, and assault and battery could all bring such a sentence, as also could any attempt to incite or conspire toward rebellion.

White juries occasionally summoned slaves to give testimony but declined to give them the same oath taken by whites, promising to tell the truth with the help of the Almighty. Instead, after enjoining the slave to be truthful, the judge offered a stern warning against perjury and stated that the punishment could be terrible. In fact, law in Mississippi provided for thirty-nine lashes, plus standing at a pillory for an hour with one ear nailed to the post, after which it would be severed and the same thing repeated to the other ear. While the punishment may never in fact have been inflicted—or only so rarely as to escape record—it offered a powerful inducement to veracity.[55]

"In some respects slaves may be regarded as chattels," a state justice ruled in 1821, "but in others they are regarded as men." The jurists of the Southwest chose to view them as men when it came to the punishment of whites for murdering slaves. "The law views them as capable of committing crimes. This can only be upon the principle that they are men and rational beings," he continued. "Has the slave no rights because he is deprived of freedom? He is still a human being and possesses all those rights of which he is not deprived by the positive provisions of the law. . . . Because slaves can be bought and sold it does not follow that they can be deprived of life," he concluded. "It gives the master no right to take the life of the slave." To kill a slave was murder, he concluded, and he sentenced the white man guilty of the crime to be hanged.[56]

In practice, and despite the harsh laws on the statute books, the treatment of slaves by most masters was humane and, at times, familial. On the one hand, it was only good sense and sound business practice. A slave was an investment, like a horse or a cow. Well treated, fed, and housed, he could give many years of good service and return the cost of his purchase and upkeep many times over. Senseless abuse or overly harsh punishment only risked physical impairment, detracting from the black's productivity, and encouraged a sullenness that could fester into rebellion. Masters who abused their slaves often found themselves ostracized from the rest of the slaveholding society and looked upon as brutes or men of bad breeding. On the other hand, most of the second and third generation planters grew up playing with the children of their fathers' slaves. They knew them first as friends and playmates, and even after they reached an age when such informal and intimate association had to stop, they continued to look on their bondsmen with a parental—if condescending—affection and even trust. After all, the slave was like a child in their view, unable to take care of himself and needing the firm but gentle hand of the master as the child did that of the parent. Thus, willful mistreatment of their slaves came no more naturally to most planters than did brutish behavior with their own children. By and large, white children and plantation slaves found themselves the recipients of considerably indulgent attentions from their parents and masters—until, that is, the masters felt threatened.

When slaves fell ill, the master's wife treated them or else called for a doctor to come. A call and a prescription for a sick black could cost the owner $4.00 to $5.00 plus the expense of the medicine itself, whether $1.00 for castor oil or $1.50 for some indeterminate pills of dubious efficacy.[57] Owners hired ministers to come preach to their slaves and perform marriages and baptisms, and the more enlightened paid for teachers as well, sometimes in spite of law. Some masters allowed their people surprising freedom to move about, and sent them into towns like Natchez without escort for errands. James Buell saw many a slave walk into his Natchez store carrying a list of merchandise sent by a planter, and sometimes appended to the list would be an instruction to "please to let gimbo have 3 bits in your store." As he might with his own child, this planter was giving his slave a little treat for running the errand.[58]

Not surprisingly, even amid the affluence that cotton and slavery brought to the territory, there were those who found it uncomfortable to dwell in the midst of bondage. The Reverend William Winans settled in Wilkinson County, just below Natchez, in 1815, and at his marriage came into possession of several slaves through his wife. While he preached, she ran their farm and bondsmen, but he never managed to ease his conscience. Slavery, he thought, was a practice "so bad that an argument in favor of it would only be an aggravation of crime." Indeed, by 1820 he averred that he would be willing to spill his own blood to prevent enslavement of the Negro and went farther to advocate—in the abstract—the emancipation of those already enslaved. However, he feared that emancipation "would *ruin* them absolutely" and perhaps even endanger the nation, for he shared the common belief that they could not take care of themselves and would naturally become a public burden, if not a menace.

"May a Christian hold them?" he asked. His neat rationalization was "Why not?" They had lost their freedom before the Christian bought them, so it was not he who deprived them of their liberty. Moreover, by owning them, the Christian saved them from the proprietorship of the ungodly. "The Christian does real service to those Negros whom he purchases from unbelieving masters." But in a better world, he believed that slavery would not exist at all. "It is a curse upon our, otherwise, happiest country in the world," Winans lamented, and he saw that curse as one inflicted equally upon the white as well as the black. Given the fact of slavery, he felt a moral obligation to protect the slave both from unscrupulous whites as well as from himself. "I could not, in good conscience sell them, unless my conviction was that I could place them in as favorable situation as they are with me," he told his brother, "and, I have already told you, I cannot give them free-dom."[59]

Some years later Winans would help organize the Mississippi Colonization Society, dedicated to the goals of the American Colonization Society: encouraging voluntary manumission of slaves and then transporting them back to Africa to the new colony of Liberia. It was a way out of the dilemma. Slavery could be eradicated, and with it the potential problem of the free Negro in southern society. In fact, manumission in the Southwest dated back at least to the 1790s, and perhaps earlier. A twenty-one-year-old man named Caesar was given his freedom on November 16, 1795, in Natchez in what would become Adams County. The next year immigrant Isaac Smith freed six of his slaves and announced his intention to manumit the remainder. Such wholesale freeing of numbers of slaves became not uncommon. Margarita Bently freed five of her New Orleans slaves in 1797. Daniel Clark—not the gin builder—and his wife, Jane, freed one man in 1799, four females in 1800, and another in the following year. Charles Bird freed three in 1803, George Fitzgerald a mother and her four children the next year, and in 1815 William Barland manumitted thirteen. A significant number of the whites giving freedom to their slaves were women, and the rolls also included some of the territory's social nabobs, including the heirs of Anthony Hutchins.

Significantly, some of the masters were also allowing their slaves to purchase their own freedom. A slave woman named Milly paid Charles Bird a thousand dollars for freedom for herself and her two children. In 1804 Robert Moore freed his woman Esther "for her exemplary services," and a consideration of one hundred dollars. Slaves named Monday and Phillis paid their owner, Susanna Scott, two hundred dollars for the manumission of their daughter Clarinda. Since Mississippi law sought to inhibit manumission with extensive paperwork and delay, some owners handled it in out-of-state courts as far away as Cincinnati, whose proceedings in such cases were still legal throughout the South. Members of the Mississippi Colonization Society stood up for their ideals by manumitting their own slaves as well as by letting them buy themselves. Men purchased their own freedom first, then saved until they could buy their wives and children. Obviously, despite the legislation designed to prevent slaves from having their own crops or marketing their own produce, enough masters encouraged such activity that their chattels could save the money for freedom. The courts were even willing to right old wrongs. Somehow Caesar, the black manumitted back in 1795, was taken into slavery once more despite his protests, and seventeen years later won his freedom again when yet another owner checked the court records of his original manumission. Perhaps most unusual of all, on February 22, 1828—a date already symbolic of freedom in America—Thomas Foster freed a sixty-six-year-old man known as Prince who had been on his plantation for forty years. It came as the result of a request from President John Quincy Adams himself, when it was discovered that Prince was actually Prince Abd al-Rahman of the Fouta Djallon region in Africa (in present-day Guinea), captured in battle and enslaved in 1788.[60]

Emancipation, while never widespread, represented for many like Winans a compromise between conscience and social practicality, and by 1830 was on the increase as the Mississippi Colonization Society's efforts bore fruit. A few years later William Foster freed twenty-one of his slaves and put them on a ship for Liberia. But other pressures worked against freedom. In 1822 the Mississippi legislature required that benefactors secure legislative permission before manumitting any further slaves, out of alarm at the small but growing population of free blacks in the Southwest. The rising fear of slave revolt following Nat Turner's electrifying slave rebellion in Virginia in 1831 also inhibited emancipation, as well as encouraging renewed repression of slave freedoms. And the outcry of the growing abolitionist sentiment from press and pulpit in the North turned many in the Southwest against the whole idea in reaction to the attacks upon them from outsiders. Not to mention, of course, the continuing demands of the expanding cotton economy. It had taken the region years to find its ideal cash crop and the best means to exploit it, and having done that, planters were hardly about to see the only economical means of capitalizing on that crop slip through their fingers by loosening their own grip on their "property." Cotton literally made the fabric of life in the Southwest possible, and slavery was and would continue to be the loom upon which these Southerners wove their fortunes.

5

The Road Home

While the planters had most of the slaves and almost all of the wealth, they were never more than a minority within the white community of the Old Southwest. Overwhelmingly the majority were the simple families of immigrants, squatters and legal landowners, who came to eke out a new life on the cheap land. They came, said some, like a flock of birds, alighting on a fresh field to pick it clean, and then taking flight once more in search of another. Birds are, after all, opportunists, and so were the men and women who came along the Trace and down the rivers. They had no initial notions of making states or extending a nation. They came to build lives for themselves and to capitalize on the opportunity to do so on an unpopulated frontier where birth and family name—as yet—did not stand in their way. They came, as had the very first white immigrants to Virginia in 1607, simply looking for something better and expecting to find it.

They showed that spirit of opportunism by the way they followed the behavior of the birds. They refused to stay put. Time after time the families who first arrived went through the same process. They built a rude cabin, burned off the canebrakes and cut timber to clear fields for planting, sowed their crops, and then settled for a season or two, digging a well, penning their cows and pigs, planting a subsistence garden, and waiting for the harvest. Yet after "one or two crops," as one settler put it, they got the itch for better land, a larger parcel, something closer to the river or nearer a settlement. William Ramsey came to the territory in 1808 and subsequently moved, with his family, eight times in the following twelve years. Always he sought someplace less exposed to Indians or the elements, or a patch with earth a little blacker than what he had. "I think father made a mistake in moving so often," his son said later, but in so doing Ramsey sat in the mainstream of the immigrants building lives and a civilization at the end of the Trace.[1]

Gideon Lincecum was another who watched his father go through the "one or two crops" process over and over again. "He, being naturally of a restless disposition," said the son, "was very willing." "Three years of successful farming had tired him out." His father sold his very profitable cotton farm in Georgia and, typically, disposed of everything that would not fit in a wagon with his mother of eighty-eight, his four children, and four slave children. With just a chest and four beds for furniture, they moved west only a few miles before Lincecum stopped and rented a farm for the season. But the itch for new land near the Trace in Tennessee never left him. "So he fixed up again," after only one crop, said Gideon, and moved on. But along the way he saw a farm he liked in western South Carolina and decided to rent it. The next year he bought a new piece of land back in Georgia. "We were soon on the road again," lamented the son, and that season they got in and harvested a good cotton crop that earned the family a few hundred dollars.

"He again became restless," however, and packed the family for the third attempt to get to Tennessee. Unfortunately, the elder Lincecum, in addition to wanderlust, suffered from a more than occasional inclination to disappear for two or three days with drinking companions, and on the return from one of these forays along the way he announced that Tennessee was off again, and he had bought another piece of ground in South Carolina. They had a peach orchard and abundant fields of corn. "It was an easy place to make a living, and my father seemed to be quieting down to a settled state of mind." Almost plaintively the younger Lincecum recalled how happy he and the rest of the family would have been to remain there. But then an uncle passed through on his way east, filled with tales of the land to the west in Tennessee, and the elder Lincecum had to go once more. Indeed, the word "again" is ubiquitous in Gideon's recollections, as are a certain fatalism and not a little wit. "The next time we stopped it was at a place a mile from where we lived the previous year."[2]

The next year they moved again to a double cabin on a small farm, and somewhere along the way the son seems to have inherited the father's wandering instinct. He left home for a time, took a wife, then came back to sell out with his father and move once more, still trying to reach Tennessee. They got as far as the border between

Georgia and the Creek nation in the Alabama territory before father Lincecum got "a little 'tight'" in company with another fellow, and in the process bought his farm from him. "Being satisfied that my father would not remain more than a year, I concluded to stop also and do what I had never done in my life; idle away the time until he got tired of his bargain and made ready to move again." The son read the father well. After a few months the elder Lincecum chafed at seeing people starting to settle farther west than he. "My father loved a border life," said the son, and once more he sold out and set off to find a new edge of civilization.

This time they actually got somewhere, covering several hundred miles to a small village of log cabins that was to become Tuscaloosa, Alabama. Gideon built a small clapboard house in the village, and his father went a few miles beyond to a cabin in the woods. A month later he told his son that he had found land seventy-five miles to the west on the Tombigbee and, better yet, that there was no road to get there. "It was the wildest, least trodden and tomahawk marked country he had ever explored," said the old man. That would deter settlers from passing him by. The son, like the father, now expected to pull up stakes and relocate every few hours, and he happily agreed to go along. "We were in a perfect ecstasy over the prospect of a wagon journey through a roadless wilderness," said Lincecum, and on November 1, 1818, they set out. The family by now had been in more or less constant westward motion since the turn of the century.[3]

Twelve days of hacking their way through the wilderness brought them to the Tombigbee, near where Columbus, Mississippi, would later appear. Gideon pitched his camp on its banks but his father, true to form, had to move on another four hundred yards in order to be that much farther from the civilization he left behind. "You have found the right place for us to stop at," Gideon's young—and tired—wife told him. They started making a home. In a single day Gideon cut the logs to build a modest cabin. In another he split the clapboards for its roof, and in one more had it assembled with the aid of his brothers. On the fourth day he split trunks lengthwise into puncheons, setting the rounded side down into the dirt inside the cabin, and the flat surfaces turned up to form a floor. Another day saw a log chimney and fireplace built, then lined with mud to prevent their burning, and that same evening the small family moved into their new home. Having no bed of their own, they slept on the wooden floor. With the gathering cold of late fall, they set a large fire in the chimney, crackling with pitch-loaded pine knots. "The light was as bright as day," remembered Gideon, "making the whole house which was lined with newly split board fairly glitter." His wife looked lovingly about her at the new walls of their home as she lay down for the night. "This is fine," she said.[4]

Gideon Lincecum would move again, and again, and while he and his family may have appeared to overdo their wanderlust in roamings through the Old Southwest, they were not at all out of the ordinary. "I have no elbow-room," one Mississippian complained in 1832 as settlement of the Old Southwest neared completion. "I cannot move without seeing the nose of my neighbor sticking out between the trees."[5] Too many men saw those noses in the woods. Following the end of the War of 1812, the eastern lands of the territory experienced a surge in settlement as the Creek were displaced from much of their land, and what some called "Alabama Feaver" ensued. They came by the old Federal Road, as did Lincecum and his family, or they swept down from Tennessee. Like the Lincecums, they were for the most part not simply squatters. They came with the intent to settle, and to pay for their new lands whenever territorial organization came into place and formal sales were held for the property. "They are quiet, peacable, *extremely industrious*," one government surveyor said of the Lincecums and their kind.[6]

That surveyor might have rethought his words had he encountered another of those coming into Alabama to seek land. In the fall of 1816 a Tennessean named David Crockett, a veteran of the recent war and a typical peripatetic frontiersman, crossed the Tennessee River and began exploring through northern Alabama until he reached the Black Warrior River, near where Lincecum later found the small log village that became Tuscaloosa.[7] He nearly died on that trip, thanks to a bout with malaria, and rumors of his death got back to his wife, and eventually to him when he recovered. "I know'd this was a whapper of a lie, as soon as I heard it," he quipped later in his very studied frontier vernacular. The trip to Alabama proving a bust, he went back to Tennessee, but soon found that "the place on which I lived was sickly, and I was determined to leave it." In January 1817 he leased his thirty-eight acres, and the next fall went some eighty miles west to former Chickasaw lands near Shoal Creek, north of the Tennessee River, and selected some 160 acres at the head of the creek.[8] "No order had been established there," he recalled, "but I thought I could get along without order as well as any body else.[9]

"We lived in the back-woods, and didn't profess to know much, and no doubt used many wrong words," Crockett recalled, but there he built a simple twenty-by-twenty-four-foot log home, and eventually erected and operated a gristmill for a time, and a distillery nearby. Both were wiped out by a fall flood of the creek that Crockett, writing some years later, referred to with typical wit by saying that when it destroyed his distillery the flood "just made a complete mash of me." His wife's solution to their ruin, more typical of frontier men than of their women, was to pay their bills as they could, pack their belongings, and "scuffle for more." "I therefore gave up all I had," said Crockett, "and took a bran-fire new start."[10]

"Bran-fire new starts" were what all of them sought, and Crockett, Lincecum, and Ramsey all followed the same pattern. These small farmers were the first to enter the wilderness, usually before they were supposed to. They cleared their few acres, planted them, raised their rude dogtrots, and commenced their lives. There was a remarkable sameness about the homes seen all across the southwestern frontier, the dogtrot being almost ubiquitous. The family often occupied one of the cabins, while lumber, grain, leather harness for the animals, and anything else that needed to be kept dry and out of reach of prying Indians filled the other. Sheds and lean-tos backed against the main cabin or stood on their own in a patternless scatter about the clearing, most for storing more grain, or providing some shelter for the more valuable animals. When there were neighbors near, the new settler held a house-raising party. All who could came to help in lifting the pre-cut logs into place, finishing the house in a day, and then celebrating with food and drink at the new tenant's expense, and leaving him obligated to help them when they built new homes. To make holes for windows, they used short logs set in waist high or else cut pieces out of the whole logs from the roofline down. Then, with no glass practical or affordable, they filled the openings with wooden shutters or animal skins. In an attempt to allow light into the cabin, some settlers scraped deerskins as thin as possible so that light could filter through, or else used greased paper that served the same purpose. They made a door in the same fashion and hung it on wooden hinges, then set about filling the gaps between the logs with mud chinking.

Next came the fireplace and chimney, made of "cats and clay," as they called it. They built a clay fireplace inside the log house, pounding it hard until tightly compact, and sometimes making it extend from one side of the cabin to the other, twelve feet or more. A chimney made of sticks rested on the sides of the fireplace, and on a lintel thrown across the top of the opening; then they covered it with a layer of mud several inches thick to prevent the chimney itself taking fire. A year or two after raising their first cabin, a family—if they decided to stay put—built a second a few feet away, and connected them by a roof to make their dogtrot. Then, with the luxury of double the space, they could spread out. If they decided not to fill the second cabin with lumber and supplies, they might use the first as a kitchen and dining room and the new addition for the rest of their living. Lofts above both, accessible only by ladders, contained sleeping and storage space.[11]

There was nothing lovely about these homes, and romance only came to them in recollection many years after the more fortunate occupants prospered enough to move to more conventional dwellings. "Our houses were very rude and rough, built and covered without nail or hammer," John Hutchins wrote of the first home his father, Anthony, built at the end of the Trace near Natchez in the 1770s. "Very few farm utensils were brought by the emigrants."[12] They could also be intolerably cold and drafty. Heat came solely from the fireplace, which burned constantly for both warmth and cooking. In the larger hearths farmers actually used a horse to drag a huge log into the house, then rolled it into the ashes. The fire commenced in the center of the log and might burn for days, the family gradually levering the ends of the log inward as the timber burned away. Unfortunately, in the way of fireplaces, most of the heat went up the chimney, taking with it much of the warmth from the house as well. The chinking between the logs dried and shrank, then fell away, exposing gaps that allowed the draft of the chimney to pull cold air from the outside inside. Some wags thought the warm air of the house actually attracted the exterior cold, and one veteran of many a frontier winter complained that the interior of his home had been nothing but all the winter weather come indoors. In the lower reaches of the territory the weather hardly required heat, of course, with even windows and doors left open year-round for ventilation against the heat and humidity. But snow could fall in northern parts of the Chickasaw country and in southern Tennessee, and cold blasts occasionally swept even to Natchez and beyond. When they came children discovered that the best place of all was right inside the fireplace, sitting in its corners or on the ends of the great log, smoky but warm.[13]

In most cabins at first the only floor was the earth itself, but in time most settlers built their own puncheon floors, and then covered them with animal skins as a protection against splinters. There were no closets and very few had wardrobes—or clothes to fill them. "Clothing and covering were scarce," said Hutchins, "and such as we had was of the coarsest and roughest kind made by our mothers and sisters from the spinning wheel and the loom."[14] Both vital tools sat in a corner of the cabin, and the few articles of clothing that the family had simply hung on wooden pegs driven between the logs, or else dangled from the horns of deer and bison and other game animals taken on the hunt. Indeed, except for what few treasures they kept in a dresser or cabinet brought as a lonely memento from some now-distant home in more settled parts of the country, everything they had hung from the walls, often side by side with their smoked joints and their drying onions and herbs.

A cupboard perhaps, some plain crockery or pewter plates and cups, drinking vessels sometimes make from hollowed animal horns, and perhaps just rude wooden platters for dining, filled out the family's living ware. Of course, every cabin had at least one rifle, and perhaps a pistol or two, virtually all of them, up to 1830, working on the old flintlock system. They put meat on the table, defended the home against intruders, and provided some entertainment for the men. They also constantly enhanced and reinforced the frontier ethic of independence and self-defense. A man was not a man without knowledge of firearms and some skill in their use. They personalized their muskets and Pennsylvania long rifles with little brass inlays in the shape of the religious and superstitious signs that otherwise influenced their lives, and many a woodsman gave his rifle a name as well. He taught his sons to use it from the age of ten or earlier or got them a small squirrel gun that shot small loads of scattershot. When a little older they went out with him to hunt the deer and bear that filled their dinner plates, and in the worst extremities, when the Indians came prowling or on the warpath, the boys became men all too soon in defending their lives and property. Marksmanship was essential, because lead could cost fifty cents for a small bar, including some buckshot, and most hunters tried to retrieve and recast their bullets after firing.[15] All those sets of antlers used as hangers inside these cabins were more than utilitarian relics of kills. A few stood as reminders of a coming of age, when the sons of the family became old enough and adept enough with the rifle to add to the family's welfare and support.

The flintlocks could be cantankerous, of course. When the hunter pulled his trigger, the hammer snapped forward, striking a piece of flint against a steel "frizzen" covering a small pan of powder on the outside of the breech of the gun barrel. As it drove forward, the hammer pushed the frizzen open while at the same time the flint struck sparks from the steel. The sparks ignited the powder in the pan, which in turn sent a fire into the main charge in the barrel. If all these things went well, the gun fired. Often it did not. Once, when aiming at a chicken not too far distant, a settler pulled his trigger but the rifle failed to go off. Instead, he said, "she sputtered, an' spootered, and sizzled till the chicken got tired waitin' an' went over in the field to hunt June bugs. I had both eyes shet, fur the sparks wuz jest a b'ilin' out'n the tech hole, an' I dasn't take 'er down from my shoulder, 'cause I knowed she'd go off *some* time that day." Finally the rifle stopped sputtering and the fire got to the powder charge behind the bullet. It went off just as an old sheep wandered in front of the gun "'n got the whole load right behin' the shoulder, an' keeled over deader'n a shad."[16]

For the family that prospered or chose to move from the isolation of the outlying farm into a village, or even a growing town like Natchez, a new house took on a much more civilized look—or should have. As early as 1781 a typical house for a village dweller on the bluff could be eighteen feet deep, and forty feet wide, the broad side galleried and facing the river to take advantage of cool westerly breezes. It might still be built on the old dogtrot pattern, with a wide center hall flanked by two large rooms, or else three or four rooms wide, each to be entered from a door off the gallery rather than by a hall. Other Natchez houses were even larger, twenty by forty feet, with floored galleries front and back, and containing a parlor, two bedrooms, two "cabinets" or storage rooms, and a kitchen, with real glass in the window sashes. Even a simple cabin would still have planked exterior walls instead of rude logs, and a real roof rather than split boards laid shed fashion.[17]

Building such a modest yet handsome town house could be very costly. Simple "cut" nails, so called because they were literally chopped out of sheets of iron, brought eighteen and three-quarter cents a pound in 1821.[18] Then there were the other expenses. Planking ran three cents a board foot. Shingles cost one-half cent each. Cypress planking for flooring ran three and one-half cents a foot. Walnut or cherry planking for finer interior woodwork could cost four cents a foot.[19]

Emery Wilson, one of Natchez's more successful house builders, calculated that the necessities for building a house thirty-six feet wide and eighteen feet deep came to:

756 feet of sills	22.68
2000 feet of joists	60.00
2000 feet of siding	60.00
2000 feet of flooring	60.00
17,000 shingles	85.00
700 feet of studding	21.00
700 feet of rafters	21.00
200 pounds of nails	20.00
1000 feet of sheating	15.00
1,500 feet of lumber for windows and doors	85.00

amounting in all to $449.68.[20] In 1835 he built a house in town for Robert Bradley that had weatherboarded sides, six glazed windows, two doors, cypress flooring, a front gallery, a post and rail fence with a gate around the yard, and a nearby milk house. The bill came to $433.93. Windows alone cost $4.00 apiece, and each door came to $5.00.[21]

Then came the interior and exterior appointments, which even on a modest town home could add up. Door locks cost fifty cents to install, on top of the cost of the hardware, and window hinges from the local blacksmith ran $1.75 a set.[22] Window glass went at six and one-fourth cents per "light" in 1817 when installed in new sash, and double that if fitted into old sash that required removal of broken glass. By 1835 the price for an eight-by-ten-inch light quadrupled. Wallpapering cost $1.00 per roll just to put up, and hanging a paper border cost another $2 per roll.[23]

Then came the painting. The most popular colors in the territory at the time were Spanish brown, chrome yellow, rose pink, verdigris green, Prussian blue, sienna, and combinations of them, along with London white, all lead-based paints. Painters mixed the pigments on the premises with linseed oil, and used lampblack to darken them. The oil to mix the paint cost $2.00 a gallon, and the pigments themselves from twelve and one-half cents a pound for white to $2.00 for verdigris. Paintbrushes could run up to seventy-five cents each, and resin, or copal, varnishes for woodwork ran $3 a bottle.[24] Then came the labor. Benjamin Fuller and Joseph Sylvester, house painters, charged $25.00 for the front of a house, $7.00 for the back, and another $25.00 to do two interior rooms. And for those who wanted more than bare wood floors, painters decorated oilcloth "carpets" by painting them at $1.25 a square yard.[25] For the man who wanted something more substantial looking, and requiring less maintenance, Wilson could also build houses of masonry, but bricks came high at $2.00 per thousand. A modest house could require thirty-eight thousand of them.[26] And so simple a thing as the ubiquitous craftsman's sandpaper could cost as much as a dollar per quire.[27]

Yet these were no mansions, and houses of similar size, certainly with less-refined appointments, hardly impressed many visitors. Louisa Bowie reached the southern frontier in 1821 after a five-week journey and almost turned away in disgust at the house awaiting her. "Found a very dirty house and yard," she moaned; "we have not yet got them clean. I don't think I ever saw a dirtier house, the walls were once white washed but they are more like a yellow wash." It was a simple four-room affair of good proportions except for a tiny breakfast room.

Galleries, or piazzas, extended the full width of front and back, with a pantry and dairy under the rear gallery. When not purchased outright, such places fetched a rent of fifty and even seventy dollars a month and were still in high demand.[28]

Of course, genuine mansions were emerging in the territory, almost all of them in and around Natchez. Indeed, as cotton prosperity brought wealth to more and more, some of the planters maintained two homes, one on the plantation, and the other in the town where they might see and be seen and flaunt their wealth before a larger audience. Indicative of the early "grand" houses was William Dunbar's Forest plantation outside Natchez. When he first arrived, in 1790, like many other planters he erected a simple but comfortable home then started to build his fortune with his wife Dinah, "make our little crops and dis- till brandy together." He built a typical raised colonial "cottage," with the living quarters elevated above ground level on piers, and a gallery extending across its front, much in the manner of the same houses being built on the plantations in Louisiana at the time. It was neither elaborate nor ornate but large and spacious, "neat and comfortable" one visitor called the place. Dunbar died in 1810, perhaps without knowing that his wife had great plans for their cottage.[29]

In 1816 Dinah Dunbar started construction of a new Forest, on a far more elaborate design. The list of materials indicated the scale of the project she envisioned, as well as the kind of wealth that some planters were enjoying only a few years after basing their economy on cotton. The frame alone involved 65,622 board feet of lumber costing $2,624.88, almost six times the cost of the modest town homes built by Wilson. The cypress flooring cost $655.00, and the roofing shingles cost almost exactly what Robert Bradley's Natchez town home cost him. At least thirty-two windows would make the interior a blaze of light, most of them triple-sash affairs stretching from floor almost to ceiling. The elaborate cornice moulding held medallions that them- selves cost $2.00 apiece, while the gallery that extended more than six hundred feet around the entire perimeter of the house cost nearly as much as a house. Large Doric columns stretched from the main gallery to the eaves, and two exterior staircases led to the upper gallery. The windows alone held 856 panes of glass, some of them col- ored with gold leaf. Ninety-one interior and exterior doors gave access to a score of rooms, while the interior staircase ran one hundred steps, up fifty-five feet in a graceful curve. That stair alone cost $1,500.00. There would be a library, a breakfast room, four main rooms on the ground floor with two smaller back ones, and an upper hall from which several more opened.

When she was done, Dinah Dunbar had spent $13,647.48 just on materials. The actual construction of the new Forest plantation house probably cost several thousand more, and a member of the family later recalled the total price, probably including furniture, as more than $30,000.00.[30] "The rooms are magnificently large and high," wrote a visitor, "higher by a foot than any parlor I've seen in Philadelphia." The descripton continued, "My own room is lighted by one magnificent window, regal in size, opening upon the gallery, and overlooking the wooded porch." Dunbar's son Archibald missed the smaller, earlier Forest house. "Shall I never see the old mansion again!" he lamented in 1817, after it had been demolished to make way for the new house. "I certainly have a great attachment to the house I was born in and the *back room* I have had so many frolics in. But as I suppose it is necessary for a new one to be built I shall not repine."[31]

The Forest was typical of the grand mansions that cotton began building in the early 1800s and decidedly untypical of the home of the average man at the end of the Trace. The middle ground were those Natchez town homes built by Wilson, or the smaller plantations like Mount Locust, which grew up around one of the early stands fifteen miles up the Trace from Natchez. It started as a one-room cabin in 1780 built by John Blommart and then passed to William Ferguson, who by 1800 was operating a stand and trying to make it the base of a new village to be called Union. It started as a simple sixteen-by-twenty-foot one-floor house, with galleries on three sides, one of them closed off to make small rooms. Gradually over the years additional rooms sprouted until by 1830 it was a seven-room plantation house, ample, comfortable, yet still modest. At the same time, its conversion from an inn to a cotton farming home around 1820 also reflected the decreasing trade from travelers on the Trace, as the steamboat gradually attracted more and more of the northbound traffic. Becoming planters was the only alternative open to the Ferguson family.[32]

Furnishing these homes reflected every bit as much variety as the homes themselves, from the rude stools and split-trunk benches in the log dogtrot to the imported mirrors and French draperies in the cotton lords' palaces. In John Blommart's Mount Locust home in 1781, his sum of furnishings included a cypress table; a corner cupboard, or "press," with the unusual feature of glass in its doors; a chest of drawers; two portraits; a writing box; two tea boxes; a flambeaux, or candle lamp; eight teaspoons and thirteen silver spoons; and a calico bedspread, damask robes, and a velvet coat, all of them in his favorite color, green.[33] By some standards, that was rather a lot. Forty years later in 1821 Louisa Bowie complained that "we cannot get any furniture here it is very scarce, what is, is very extravigant, chairs such as your yellow ones are 25$ a dozen." Often people like the Bowies took the loan of chairs from a neighbor, while another might make them a pine table.[34]

The tools and implements needed to keep a modest frontier house running were also simple, and yet precious and costly both to buy and repair. Mending a broken shovel could cost half a dollar. Putting a new hoop on a well bucket might run $1.50, while a new ax cost almost $4.00 and sharpening an old one brought the blacksmith fifty cents. A branding iron for livestock cost $2.00 to make, and something as simple as a clapper for a field bell could run four bits. A new handle on a coffee mill cost 37½ cents, and mending a candlestick was a quarter. Saul Ferguson paid a dollar for a garden hoe in 1821, John Hardin paid $1.50 for a chisel, and John Davis, having broken his weakest one, paid 37½ cents for a new chain link. A seven and one-half pound broadaxe cost $7.25 new.[35]

At the other end of the social scale, the planters in the houses like the Forest spent their money on much the same tools, but often had them made or repaired right on the plantation by skilled slave artisans whom the poorer settlers could hardly afford. Some plantations were almost completely self-contained communities, providing virtually every service and product needed to sustain themselves. As a result, instead of spending money to repair buckets and broken candlesticks, the wealthy men and women of the Southwest went instead to Natchez to paw over the contents imported from abroad by the latest ship. As early as the turn of the century importers brought in luxuries that the squatters out along the old Trace had never even heard of, much less coveted. Just the ship *Carlisle* out of Baltimore in a single voyage in 1801 brought to Natchez 770 casks of French claret, 15 "pipes" of brandy, and an incredible 2,400 bottles of Saint-Estèphe. There came as well cambrics and linens, white silk stockings and kid gloves for the men, almost ten thousand pieces of French soap, demijohns filled with soft-shelled almonds, reams of fine writing paper, wallpaper for houses like the Forest, and even eighteen gross of white playing cards for the planters' leisure.[36]

There was one realm in which the nabobs and the squatters alike shared a common need. They all ate, and though what they dined upon varied increasingly as the gap between them widened in the years approaching 1830, still the difference often lay more in preparation than ingredients. The early settler, regardless of social caste, consumed whatever came to hand. He depended at first upon wild game for his meat—deer, bear, bison. The last especially delighted the pioneer, though the shaggy beasts were a rare sight by the time the Mississippi Territory came to be settled. Men ate everything but the intestines, and then roasted the bones until they cracked in order to extract the marrow for soups. By the 1790s they were almost all gone east of the great river. Bear provided a rich fat used in place of shortening, and though it smoked and smelled terrible, the tallow would also smolder enough to keep a rude lamp flame alive and provide light. The settlers salted, smoked, and cured bear meat, preferring it as steaks, though some thought it "too strong and gamey for the average taste." Venison, of course, the settler ate in a variety of ways, many of them learned—like so much else—from the Choctaw and Chickasaw.

Wild turkeys so teemed in the forests and on the savannas that some Louisianians claimed they rode them down, roping them like cattle. So plentiful was the fowl that when a settler had no bread, he used a slice of white meat from a turkey instead to accompany other food and wipe the gravy from his plate. Turkey often joined venison in the ubiquitous stewpot, along with whatever vegetables lay at hand. They might also find themselves in company with squirrel, raccoon, even opossum, as well as rabbit, quail, and bobcat. In short, anything that moved—except for armadillos and poisonous reptiles—could be a meal. Of course, that also included anything that could swim, including the alligator.

While the newcomer gradually established his own livestock, to replace the bear and bison with pork and beef, he also exploited all of the native plants and vegetables available. In the spring he picked and boiled "poke weed" with fat meat. Wild fruit and berries went straight to his table, along with wild grapes for crude wines, and persimmons for pies and puddings. He picked nuts from a variety of trees and sometimes had to depend on them in lean times or through hard winters, when they could make soups, bread, oil, and seasonings the squatters called "Tom Fuller." But as soon as possible he replaced these serendipitous finds with domestic plantings of his own, most especially his corn. His wife parched it until hard, then ground it to a meal, mixed it with water to make a hoecake, literally named because it was baked before the fire on the blade of a hoe. She served it as mush. She soaked it in lye until it swelled several times its size to become hominy, and either cooked it like that or dried it once more, ground it, and made hominy grits.[37]

For many the lowly sweet potato was the king of vegetables and almost everywhere on their tables. A traveler through the interior in those days found that in some counties the sweet potato was the principal crop, chiefly because it grew in poor soil and asked for little or no cultivation. Yet an acre could produce several hundred bushels in a good year.[38] At some tables everything not meat derived from the tuber. William Claiborne's nephew John F. H. Claiborne, on a ride through the pine woods country of Mississippi, just finished a hair-raising race to get away from a wolf when he heard the reassuring sound of a farm bell and suddenly saw through the evening gloom the dim light of a settler's window. The woman of the house told him to "light"—dismount—and stay the night. He took his horse into the stable, where he found a trough filled with sweet potatoes and a rack of vines instead of hay, all of which the animal ate with gusto. Claiborne himself went into the house for dinner. "The repast was abundant, excellent and scrupulously neat—but almost every dish was composed of *potatoes* dressed in many various ways." He saw them baked and fried alongside bacon, boiled beside a joint of beef, mixed with wild turkey into a hash, stuffed into a roasted chicken, baked into biscuits, dried hard and ground to make coffee, and baked into a pie for dessert. To finish the dinner off, one of the daughters of the house set a brimming tumbler of potato beer in front of him, and while he drank the sparkling beverage, the girl suggested that if he were still hungry she could get him a couple of hot potatoes from the fire ashes. Her mother informed him that she also sometimes made whiskey, molasses, and even vinegar from the ubiquitous tuber.

When Claiborne went to his bed, overfull and perhaps rather overimaginative after his beer, he soon dozed, but only after discovering that the mattress in his bed was stuffed with potato vines. He slept badly. "The night-mare brooded over us," he remembered. "We dreamed that we had *turned into a big potato*, and that some one was *digging us up*." He awoke in a sweat and could not sleep for much of the rest of the night. His hostess found him with a sore throat and a mounting fever and treated him with a roast potato soaked in vinegar tied around his neck, as well as a tea brewed from potato leaves. Instead of resurrecting Claiborne's nightmares, the "simples" seemed to work, and he soon mounted and went on his way, sent off by the lady with some jerked venison in his saddlebag, and a handful of sweet potato chips.[39]

Turnips, squash, peas, pumpkins, beans, and more made up most of the rest of the vegetable diet in the southwestern larder, though most were simply used to add bulk and body to the meat, fat, and water in the boiling stewpot. And vegetables on any regular basis really did not figure largely in the thinking of those men, who like Lincecum's father, stood always on the farthest edge of the frontier. They rarely bothered to clear and plant a garden, since it was only one more thing to leave behind when they moved on to some new border.[40] But once they stopped to stay, the backyard vegetables began to sprout. "Mother cannot do without a garden," wrote one woman. "The day after we got here she had the yard clean'd out." Beans, peas, cucumbers, tomatoes, cabbages, and radishes went into her little clearing right away. "It is very small," said her daughter, "but it answer'd the purpose."[41]

The actual dining in the rude frontier cabins made no pretense at etiquette. People ate with their fingers or used rough spoons fashioned from hollowed gourds to dip the stew from their plates. Cutlery was a rarity among the poorest of the settlers, and a fork proudly given to a guest at table might have but a single tine. When crockery plates cost seventy-five cents a half dozen, and cups and saucers a dollar in the same quantity, settlers were not inclined to waste their precious money on such breakable goods.[42] "Nobody ever heard of dinners being served in courses," one plantation girl recalled. "The soups, meats, and vegetables were all served on the table at once." The day's three meals might well be as unvaried as salt pork and corn bread for breakfast, the same with some sour milk and sweet potatoes for lunch or "dinner," and the same again, cold, at supper. Every traveler from the East or abroad who passed through the Southwest left behind his or her horror story of the plain fare of the plain people, some maintaining that they saw no variety on their tables for up to six months.[43]

Perhaps the only real variety in their diet came in what they drank, and even there it was not much. They took water from the nearby spring or creek, of course, and few of the first settlers bothered digging wells. Cows gave them milk, and they drank it both sweet and sour, sometimes mixing a quantity of the two in order to make the sour milk last longer. Given the questionable quality and taste of the latter, it is no wonder that almost all of the Southwesterners—like people of the rest of the South—greatly preferred spirits instead. Almost everyone brewed or distilled something. Berries and grapes made wine. Sweet potatoes and persimmons produced a rough sort of beer. Apples yielded a good hard cider, and from peaches he could distill brandy.

But the most prevalent drink of all was whiskey, and they distilled it from corn, producing a distinctive liquor uniquely American. The planter or settler ground it to a coarse cracked texture, then put two bushels of it into a barrel with fifty gallons of water. A natural fermentation soon set in that could be hastened with yeast, and when the "mash" was ready, he boiled it in his still, the liquid and alcohol leaving the mash as steam, then condensing as whiskey in another container. He could get five gallons or more of "corn" from a single barrel of mash, and then tested its strength by dropping a bit of tallow in a glass of the liquid. If it sank too fast, the whisky needed another distilling. Too slow, and it would be too strong and he added water. Generally they preferred it strong, though, and double distilling or "rectifying" was commonplace.[44] Besides what it did for the maker, whiskey added to his meager store of hard cash and gave him something to trade at the village store. In 1800 retail whiskey brought 62½ cents a quart in Natchez, but two decades later, after the influx of settlers and a seeming explosion of home distillers, not to mention commercial competitors, the same article brought only 68¾ cents for a gallon in the Natchez trade.[45] Travelers on the Trace, of course, paid considerably more, because they were tired and thirsty, and had no choice.

There were staples of the diet that neither squatter nor planter lord provided for himself, though, and these he had to buy. White wheat flour simply was not made in the region. Merchants in Natchez imported it from the North on the river and charged $7.50 for a barrel, more than enough to ensure that white bread and cakes only appeared on the tables of the affluent, especially when a man might have to work a month just to buy fifty bushels of the infinitely cheaper corn.[46] Coffee ran from thirty-five to forty-five cents a pound, and a whole barrel of it cost $63.70 in 1819, making it largely the beverage of the wealthy. Sugar to sweeten it cost fourteen to fifteen cents a pound, and $34.80 for a full barrel, which meant that while the Dunbars and the Hutchins could have candies and spun sugar delicacies on their tables, the yeomanry settled for honey taken at some risk from a tree of bees.[47] Salt cost $7.50 a barrel in 1819 and a dollar less the following year, explaining why some of the most remote settlers chose to dig earth from the salt licks used by animals and add it to water to extract a brine.[48] For all the sweet potatoes growing in the territory, very few planted or had time to tend white potatoes, yet even at only $3.00 a barrel, they were still beyond the average settler.[49] And none but the wealthy paid the $1.00 per bushel for fine Egyptian oats, but then only the affluent rode the kind of thoroughbred horse that needed the grain.[50]

Not surprisingly the indifferent nutritional quality of the food they ate, and even more that it was cooked in ever-present pools of grease, made sickness more than a frequent companion of people on the southwestern frontier. If the food did not get them, their own doctors and remedies could. Professional medical training had scarcely any representatives in the region other than in New Orleans, Natchez, and Nashville at the other end of the Trace. Stomach ailments, complications from bad food, malaria along the lower river, and a host of other enemies lay in waiting for the new inhabitants. As if the loss of her foot had not been enough, Martha Martin barely recovered before facing a greater danger. "During that year there was much sickness throughout the Country call the Cold Plague," she recalled. "Very few ever recovered that were attacked with the terrible disease. Many families were all taken." It was "more fatal than Collery," she wrote, referring to cholera.[51] The true diagnosis of the "plague" is uncertain, but it perhaps does not matter, since the quality of the medicines available, and equally that of the doctors, afforded little hope of recovery.

Gideon Lincecum spent some of the months of 1810 and 1811, while his father was between moves, in studying medicine—this despite the fact that he was only sixteen years old and had only been able to read for less than two years, following a total of five months' schooling. Nevertheless he applied himself single-mindedly to whatever medical reading was available, and decided therefore that he was qualified to practice medicine. On this frontier, determination counted for as much as a diploma, though in Lincecum's case the adage "Physician heal thyself" proved almost to be his undoing. After the last move to the Alabama Territory, he took one of the fevers that sometimes raged through whole villages, and while his wife and others finally improved, he seemed to remain the same, hovering in a dangerous state. "All the doctors—they were my friends—came often to see me and to note the progress of the case," he lived to recall. "Their opinions and prescriptions were as varied as their faces." Some thought his problem an enlargement of the heart; others thought it an aneurysm, still others a swollen aorta; and one said his heart had simply gone soft. "So one and another of them, first and last, suggested treatment for all the heart complaints known to the faculty," he complained. "No two of them, when alone with me expressed the same opinion in reference to the nature of my complaint." One can only wonder at the extent and origin of their own medical education, which may have been no more extensive or systematic than Lincecum's random readings. The one thing they seemed to agree on was the treatment—bleeding.

Drawing blood with a lancet, generally a spring-loaded device that on being tripped thrust three or more razor-sharp blades through the flesh and into the wall of a major vein in the arm or leg, was presumed for centuries to aid in almost every illness by drawing out foul "humors" with the blood. After the loss of a pint or more, the subject could feel light-headed and relaxed, a symptomatic relief that doctors ascribed to healing, but which only meant, of course, that the patient's own ability to fight off disease had been diminished by the loss of blood. Bleeding was the hallmark of the blind leading the blind, but

Lincecum believed in it just as did his doctor friends, and so he applied the lancet—too much. He bled himself daily, drawing by his own account some twenty-two and a half pounds of blood in twenty days, perhaps a pint a day. Hoping to "salivate" himself, as he put it—to cause humors to be purged in excessive saliva—he also swallowed every day ten grains of calomel, a mercury chloride purgative that failed to work, though he never realized that he could hardly "salivate" when he was dehydrating his system radically from loss of blood. He also rubbed a pound and a half of "strong blue ointment" on his body daily in hopes that it would somehow aid in his recovery. In fact, of course, he was putting himself through a race to see which would kill him first, blood loss or mercury poisoning.

The doctors continued their visits, shook their heads, clucked knowingly, and continued to disagree, meanwhile flattering the waning Lincecum that his was an interesting case, "and they wanted to watch it through all its changes and variations." In the end they watched him for three years—presumably he did not continue the bleeding and the calomel all that time—yet "nothing they prescribed seemed to act on my side of the question." Finally his wife began to see through the quackery and ignorance of the would-be medicos. She told Gideon that these men were not only doing him no good, but they might be killing him. Moreover, with all their lengthy visits, they and their horses were eating his larder and their stable empty. She advised him to send them all packing, and when Gideon seemed unsure of how to do it, she prescribed that he "run away from them" and go to an acknowledged physician in Columbus, Mississippi. Lincecum did as she asked and visited the doctor, who asked him what all the others had diagnosed and prescribed, then wanted to know what Lincecum himself believed to be the source of his ailment. Hearing his patient's response, the doctor announced that he believed Lincecum knew more about his complaint than anyone else and could very well treat himself. "Here is the key of my shop, in which you will find a choice selection of fresh medicines," he said. "Go there and help yourself to such of them as you may think your case requires, and welcome."[52] Eventually Lincecum recovered, no doubt in part due to his own system's fighting back, as well as to escaping the clutches of a gaggle of quacks, and the fact that most of the medicines in the Columbus doctor's shop posed as little danger to his health as they did to his disease.

As John Claiborne noted, the simple people of the backwoods "could scarcely form a conception of a physician such as we see here, riding day and night, keeping half a dozen horses, following the pestilence to enrich science with its spoils, attending the poor from charity, accumulating fortunes from the infirmities of the human family, but not infrequently losing life in the effort."[53] Most settlers never saw a doctor at all, and those few who secured "professional" medical services got them from a few itinerant medicos or by walking into town themselves or sending a child or slave with a note describing symptoms. Most of the cases that came to physicians in the Southwest related to stomach ailments and indigestion, no doubt due to bad nutrition, rancid food, and perhaps too much poorly distilled whiskey. "Sally complains of them panes being wors than they was yesterday," came a typical note to a Natchez doctor, who either made a house call or simply sent a bottle of Epsom salts, a cathartic like cream of tartar, or a laxative of magnesia of elixir vitriol—a concentrated metal sulfate or even sulfuric acid![54] If the physician wanted to dazzle his patient with science, he could send a bottle of Bateman's Drops for thirty-seven and one-half cents, the presumably more powerful Lee's Antibibulous Pills for 62 ½ cents a bottle, or the even-more-impressive sounding "Stomach Elixir of Health" for $1.50 a bottle.[55]

For heart problems they sent digitalis by the vial, at sixty-two and a half cents, or Bateman's Drops. For snakebite they sent snakeroot or saltpeter, or Bateman's Drops. For a cold the physician might suggest a bag of asafetida, which cost $3.50 for a quarter pound, and a narcotic cough syrup chiefly composed of laudanum that, like so many other things, cost 62 ½ cents a vial.[56] "Plasters," poultices designed to raise a blister on the chest, also enjoyed considerable popularity as cures for colds and fevers, while oil of clove and cinnamon was used for sore throats. No one could yet diagnose high blood pressure, but when its symptoms appeared the doctor generally suggested cream of tartar and folio senna—dried leaves from a cassia shrub—and of course Bateman's Drops. Malaria constituted an annual danger. "I am very apprehensive that it will be sickly in Mississippi," a friend wrote to Dr. Abram Barnes in June 1825. "We have Information of the Yellow fever having commenced its ravages in New Orleans & fear for Mississippi." To deal with the malaria so common in the lower part of the territory, they gave sufferers quinine, along with "sudorific drops" to induce sweating and "febrifuge powder" to bring down fever.[57]

The best that could be said for most of the medication dosed into trusting patients is that it did not pose a danger to their health worse than the maladies it supposedly treated. But that does not apply to all of these cures. Doctors administered arsenic, at thirty-seven and a half cents a vial, to an alarming degree. Moreover, it appeared as an ingredient in a number of the more popular mixtures. Laudanum, too, commonly walked out of the doctor's shop and into the home. The druggist sold quantities of white lead. It may have been used in paint, but it just as easily found its way into home cures, as did mercury in a host of remedies and poultices and something simply called "Blue pills."

Patent medicines abounded, generally based on a foundation that involved far more alcohol, opium, and imagination than any genuine pharmacology. Besides Bateman's and "Dr. Lee's North London Bilious Pills," the doctors prescribed Anderson's Pills, Jessuit's Drops, Davis' Powder, Henry's Magnesia, Stoughton's Bitters, "Stomach Elixir of Health," Hoopes's Female Pills, and the inauspiciously named "Drastic Pills" and "Daffey's Elixir."[58] Even the physicians knew little of the ingredients and sold and prescribed them almost solely on the claims of the packagers. Most included heavy quantities of herbs and roots and provided about as much symptomatic relief as a good drink of whiskey.

More painful, and certainly more dangerous, were injections. Both male and female syringes allowed for treatment of urinary and other genital complaints, and the fact that some doctors purchased considerable numbers of them from their suppliers, while others did not, suggests disagreement over whether or not injections in those areas really worked. When the doctor himself administered a shot, he charged $1.00 regardless of the medication used. More disturbing is the number of syringes sold directly to planters and small farmers, indicating that they dosed themselves. Doctors and druggists also sold large numbers of the bleeding lancets to people over the counter, while the physicians themselves actually wore out the instruments at an alarming rate, though at $4.00 per bloodletting the profits were great when a lancet cost only $2.50. John Griffith of Natchez went through three of them in 1819 alone. With all this quackery in equipment and medicines so readily available, the people of the Old Southwest often as not simply diagnosed and treated themselves, since doctors were few and far away. The druggists sold "plantation medicine chests" filled with syringes, lancets, and a host of patent and other remedies, at prices ranging from $30.00 to $80.00. Some planters went through an amazing quantity of the contents, or allowed their overseers to do so. Benjamin Farrar bought one for $80.00 in March, and so much enjoyed dosing his slaves and family that he had to have it refilled just two months later.[59]

The doctor and his colleague the dentist thought nothing of advertising their services, and for most of them business was good enough that they bought their glass vials and corks for prescriptions several dozen at a time. Their fees were usually just the cost of the medicine, unless something more was required at the office visit or a plantation call was neccessary. A night visit and a prescription ran $10.00 by the 1830s. Dressing a fractured limb in the office cost $5.00 and double that at home. Setting a broken bone and then dressing it could run as high as $30.00, however.[60] The doctor also cleaned teeth and often pulled them if no dentist was at hand. He performed amputations as well as setting fingers and limbs, and treated white and black alike. Indeed, planters often showed more solicitude for their slaves than for themselves—one more way of protecting an investment.

Some cases were naturally beyond the frontier physician's skill, such as it was. Eye problems especially defeated curative efforts, and—with surgery on the internal organs nonexistent—most internal medicine was a mystery. When a man complained of a slight pain in his left eye in 1814, Doctor A. Barnes prescribed a cooling remedy that only made the eye hurt more. So Barnes bled him and administered a cathartic and applied a plaster to his neck—none of which in any way addressed the problem. The eye only got worse and swelled to a "considerable size." The doctor applied leeches and then more leeches around the eye, then another eye potion, none of it to any avail. He sent for another doctor, fearful that his patient might lose the eye, while the sufferer himself confessed he thought the eye would simply swell until it exploded. What happened to the poor man remains a mystery, but his sufferings are testimony to the medical ignorance of the time, compounded by quackery.[61] Arsenic, mercury, opium, leeches, and Bateman's Drops made for a sad prognosis for anyone suffering from just about anything.

The doctor, like his patients, came to the frontier for opportunity, and in the hazards of living, working, and eating he found plenty of fields of his own to cultivate. But he also faced risks, from infection by his patients to the irrational wrath of the bereaved who blamed him for the loss of a loved one, and the almost universal inability to be paid in a timely fashion. Settlers and planters alike showed a remarkable indifference to paying their accounts, often because of the shortage of hard cash. And when they did pay their doctors, they might do it only once every year, or else do it with hams and chickens instead of dollars and cents. Not a few paid in cotton, though at two cents a pound, a simple broken arm could cost a man half a ton or more. Yet it was worth it if he survived to use that arm again. The men and women who came to this frontier had to survive so much, from clearing their land and building their homes to the elements, reptiles, and wolves, even their own food and physicians. But when they had their rude homes and their plots of sweet potatoes or their mansions and their cotton fields, they needed only their health to look beyond their own hearths to their neighbors', and the foundations of society.

6

The Road to Community

Gideon Lincecum's father was by no means an exception in his aversion to the sound of his neighbor's ax. "In the United States a man builds a house in which to spend his old age, and he sells it before the roof is on," wrote a visitor in 1830. "He brings a field into tillage and leaves other men to gather the crops." Only death itself could stop him, and that "before he is weary of his bootless chase of that complete felicity which forever escapes him."[1] Yet such men soon became a minority, as others came along with different notions of settlement, men and women who wanted to bring with them a sense of society and culture from their old homes and transplant them to the new. Lincecum may have come to the Southwest to be alone. Most of the rest immigrated to find safety and contentment in numbers.

The Mississippi Territory was to be a new Canaan, the "Garden of America." "Abundance spreads the table of the poor man, and contentment smiles on every countenance," boasted a settler. Once he had his piece of ground, his cabin or house built, his livestock in their pens, and his cotton in the ground, the immigrant looked around him for something to add to that contentment—the company of friends and associates—people of like mind.[2] It was that human need for associations, along with the imperatives of travel, communications, and trade, that largely determined when and where communities arose.

Settlement began in the Natchez vicinity, of course, and by 1798 the district had a total of about 4,500 inhabitants. Divided into Adams and Pickering Counties the next year, its population grew by half. By 1811, with now five counties lying along the Mississippi, that population had soared to 31,306 and just kept growing. By contrast, the settlements along the Tombigbee grew at a slower pace, being much more removed from the Mississippi, harder to reach, and just as hard to supply. By 1810 they counted not quite 3,000 known inhabitants, and all told the population of what would later become the state of Mississippi stood at something over 34,000 whites, and another 16,000 or more slaves.[3]

Once the War of 1812 concluded, of course, the influx that came to be called the Great Migration accelerated. In 1816 one man along the Federal Road said he saw 4,000 immigrants on the road in the space of a few days. Men in the East actually feared that the "Alabama Feaver" might result in the depopulation of states like North Carolina and Virginia, and some wrote despondently of seeing abandoned farms and houses east of the Appalachians, left by their owners who went to the new territory in search of a future.[4] "When a man once gets to the limbs on the tree of fortune," one settler wrote to a friend, "'tis not hard for him to climb in this country,"[5]

By 1820, with both Mississippi and Alabama carved out of the territory as new states, the former counted 42,176 white and 33,272 black inhabitants, while the latter rose to 99,198 whites and 47,665 slaves. Many in the new Southwest and in the older East as well felt some concern not only for the size but also the quality of the population shift. Timothy Flint found the settler "generally an amiable and virtuous man," but others thought quite the opposite.[6] The Reverend Thomas Barnard felt an early suspicion of the kind of men who went to the new territory. In 1758 he remarked on their "Habits of Idleness and Intemperance," saying that the ability to prosper on cheap land "by the spontaneous Products of Nature with Little Labour," encouraged in such men "a solitary State and distant Neighborhood."[7] That matter of "Neighborhood" concerned many. Congress in 1784 looked to the new land to the west and debated how to provide "security against the increase of feeble, disorderly and dispersed settlements in those remote and extended territories," and "against the depravity of manners they have a tendency to produce."[8]

Congress need not have worried overmuch. If the Southwest showed any wildness, it was of the sort that largely came with the immigrants rather than springing spontaneously out of the new soil along the Mississippi and Tombigbee, and the same civilizing influences of society in the older states rather quickly exerted themselves when real frontier communities emerged. Alabama got started later than Mississippi and grew more slowly until after the War of 1812. Settlement in earnest began on the Tombigbee and Tensaw Rivers, and the nearby Alabama, in the last years of the 1700s. Saint Stephens grew up on the Tombigbee, where the Spanish had established a frontier fort and then abandoned it in 1799, some years after the San Lorenzo Treaty. In fact, weary of waiting to be told what to do, the fort's commander simply left the keys with a nearby American and departed. After that, settlement grew, but slowly. In 1804 a visitor found a cluster of seven families on the Chickasawhay, just to the west in Mississippi, and most of the other Americans on the Tombigbee. Sixty families made up the Tensaw community, "much the most opulent and respectable settlement in the country," while another 140 families stretched on up the Tombigbee to Saint Stephens and beyond. The same visitor declared that "the present inhabitants (with few exceptions) are illiterate, wild and savage, of depraved morals, unworthy of public confidence or private esteem; litigious, disunited, and knowing each other, universally distrustful of each other." The population seemed a mix of descendants of the early French settlers, Loyalist fugitives from the Revolution a quarter century before, later arrivals who seem to have been on the run from justice in the organized states, and more recent settlers actually trying to make a new start.[9]

An emissary of President Jefferson feared that left to themselves these people would never develop into anything but a fringe of bandits and public liabilities. They must be encouraged, he said, toward "industrious habits, increase of population, and the introduction of regular society."[10] It would take until after the War of 1812, however, for the spread of newcomers really to swell these initial settlements into genuine towns and villages, bringing with them the civilizing influences of "regular society." The same was true of the settlements that spread up the Alabama River. Only the Mobile area produced a real town in the early days, and that remained Spanish until 1813. Meanwhile, settlement and the beginnings of community were most sparse of all far to the north in the hill country below the Tennessee River.[11] This was the country Crockett looked over in 1816, where even relatively few Indians lived and probably no white man actually settled before 1800. In or about 1815 a few men crossed the Tennessee and moved a few dozen miles into north central Alabama to "light" at what came to be called Bearmeat Cabin, and by the end of that year settlement exploded. Richard Breckinridge rode through the next year and found two mills operating in one valley, another under construction, a small store, and the rude origins of village life. Jones Valley boasted a settlement, though no village names as yet. In a few years Huntsville became a town, as did Mud Town, Guntersville, Brooksville, and others, all of them small and isolated but providing the concentration of people from which sprang frontier society.[12]

After that towns jumped from the soil of Alabama at a rate faster than almost anywhere else in the country, many as a result of speculation by unscrupulous promoters who did not hesitate to stretch the truth and conceal the unpleasant. One Alabamian even set the mood to crude verse.

> *What own a city! you exclaim,*
> *Yes own the spot, that's just the same,*
> *On which the place must stand;*
> *For if on maps its once laid down,*
> *It is as genuine a town,*
> *As any in the land.*

"Town-making, now is quite a trade," the bard went on, even giving a recipe for starting a frontier community. One should choose a bluff above a navigable river, a spot of natural and scenic beauty, with clear, sweet air. If a sandbar impeded actual passage on the river, one need not broadcast the fact, and if no one had ever visited the spot before, then none could gainsay any claims made by the speculator:

> *'Tis when the rage is at its height.*
> *That knowing ones will quit the site,*
> *Whilst those that stop behind,*
> *Of this desertion can't complain,*
> *For what they lose in wealth they gain*
> *In knowledge of mankind.*

Alabama town builders advertised their new communities in the eastern press, and from such beginnings sprang Florence, Athens, Demopolis, and more. Florence and Bainbridge actually competed with each other for population and investment as they stood separated only by the Tennessee River. Backers of the former advertised the width of its streets, the size of its half-acre lots, each one on a corner, and the plots set aside for a college, courthouse, market, and other public buildings, even a female academy. Promoters sold at least 284 lots and raised $226,000, and the settlers came in immediately. The story repeated elsewhere, including Cahaba, which advertised itself successfully as a potential state capital, and for a few years actually did house the legislature.[13]

Much the same experience took place in neighboring Mississippi during the speculation boom after the war with Britain, though not to the same extent because so much of the territory by then was already coming to settlement. Indeed, by 1830, as Alabama's "paper towns" became realities, many of Mississippi's early communities were already languishing as the shift from the Trace and other overland routes to steamboat traffic left some villages isolated, while movement to closer markets or better soil caused the abandonment of others. With Natchez such a thriving town by then, other places in Adams County, like Kingston, sixteen miles away, no longer had a reason for being and soon expired. The same happened to Selsertown, Uniontown, Greenville, and more on the Trace, and to Leflore. Hamburg was laid out as a town in 1826, in Hinds County not far from Jackson, but in two years it was gone, having been set on ground too marshy to support homes.[14]

When a few families first built their cabins into a "settlement," it often meant simply that they were within relatively easy reach of one another, if not actually in eyesight or earshot. During the War of 1812, and afterward as the Creek became increasingly hostile, such settlements clustered close by forts to which the settlers could withdraw speedily for protection. During times of hostilities, however, a fort could become dreadfully uncomfortable, and some families returned to their homes during the day to work the fields, then gathered at one house for the night, repeating the process each day but always staying at a different home in order to mislead any lurking Indians.[15] Such experiences encouraged the feelings of mutual support and bond that led to a spirit of community. It also helped that in many of these settlements the immigrants had come together from some other community, bringing with them intact the friendships and trust that cemented a society.

In a few years, and once the region entered the territorial stage, people formed counties and little settlements vied to become county seats, though in the more isolated areas there may have been but a single contender for the honor. Still, designation as a seat ensured for the time being that a place, be it a rural inn or just a settler's cabin, would grow into a town. Business, law, mail, and a host of the other trappings of community naturally gravitated to such a place. On the other hand, among the paper towns created by speculators, there was no guarantee at all. In fact, several future "cities" saw all their lots sold during the speculating frenzy of the second decade of the nineteenth century, but then languished as not a single house went up. Promoters engaged in considerable competition to get a county seat for their offspring. Tullahoma and Pittsburg were both laid out in northern Mississippi, with nothing more than the width of a street to separate them. Pittsburg opened the bidding for hegemony by securing the post office and a newspaper, but Tullahoma fought back by hiring the publisher away from its rival, then reportedly stole into Pittsburg at night and dragged the post office building across the line. So heated did the rivalry become that each village posted signs on the dividing street warning the citizens of the other not to trespass. The warfare only ceased when the two towns became one, taking the name "Granada."[16]

One thing that most of the larger and more successful new towns had in common was the driving force of one or more prominent early settlers, either men of vision, luck, or determination—and all of them with a keen eye for opportunity. English was first spoken by a genuine settler in the Natchez district, a man named Richard Thomson, who obtained a land grant in 1767 near Saint Catherine Creek south of Fort Panmure. He built a home, planted crops, raised livestock, and showed that it could be done successfully, leading to a handful of subsequent grant applications from other English-speaking colonists. Moreover, Thomson showed his intent to stay by leaving his family back in South Carolina for two years while he established himself and got in his crops. This was no speculative venture or intermediate stop. Unfortunately, he returned from fetching his wife and children to find that the Indians had raided the fort in his absence, and destroyed his home and crops. But Thomson stayed on and rebuilt, impressing a visitor as "one of the best settlers here." He died young, unable to realize the full potential of his perseverance, but he served as a beacon to attract others. His widow stayed on and remarried, and his seven children grew up in Natchez, founding families of their own, a part of the early nucleus of the future community.[17]

Frontier women, too, were vital to the beginnings of rough society. When Anthony Hutchins fled Natchez in 1781 after his part in the brief rebellion, he left his wife Anne behind. She had already shown her spirit in 1778, when Willing's raid saw Willing himself come to her door to demand her gold and silver. She refused, he aimed a pistol at her, and she stood defying him to shoot. Willing backed down. Her son John said of her that "she was a woman of high mettle and was not to be discouraged." When her husband fled, she told her children their situation and exhorted them to help her in running the farm on their own. When Anthony Hutchins returned a few years later, he found the plantation thriving.[18]

The exceptionally fortunate frontier community attracted someone of special note, a man or woman who could so elevate the place as to make a major contribution to the establishment and flourishing of a settlement on its way to becoming a town. The Scotsman William Dunbar, of the Forest, probably did as much for Natchez as any other citizen in the settlement's early history. "This land offers all the human spirit can desire," Dunbar proclaimed when he moved to Natchez in 1792, then he set about proving it. Forty-two when he arrived, he brought with him perhaps the only English university education in the territory. He wanted to try new ideas of scientific planting, settling first in Louisiana in time for the Willing expedition to plunder his plantation and nearly destroy his house. The next year the Spanish finished the job, since he was a Briton and they were allied with the Americans. Undeterred, he rebuilt, worked hard, served his new Spanish governors, learned to be a surveyor, and in a few years regained his prosperity. He also spent his few idle hours in scientific study. Experiments filled every room of his house. Friends often saw him wandering the fields and woods looking for interesting specimens. And when not buried in his fields or his books, he traveled constantly to New Orleans on business and brought back guests to entertain at his home.

He continued this lifestyle when he moved to Natchez and built the first Forest house. He had made himself a man of note in the territory, the kind to whom others came for advice and counsel, a lightning rod for what intellectual activity flourished in the district. He brought books and eastern newspapers and exotic imported consumer goods to the village on the bluff, all of which encouraged and nurtured community. His planter peers regarded him as their leading man of agriculture. And he was in exactly the right place at the right time for his prescience in steering his own fields toward cotton, and later in designing the cotton press. Soon his intellect and achievements attracted the notice even of Jefferson, whose fast friend and longtime correspondent he became. He wrote and published scientific articles, served in the territorial legislature, and invented the cottonseed oil industry—several decades too early to make it profitable. He also helped found schools and humanitarian endeavors, and spent eleven thousand dollars of his own to bring recently invented smallpox serum from Philadelphia, and then himself used a syringe to inoculate thousands of Mississippians. This was the kind of man who built communities by contributing to almost every facet of public life. Much of what Natchez and the lesser towns of the Southwest became, they owed to the impetus derived from these original civic-minded citizens who, though always primarily serving their own ends, also advanced their societies in the offing.[19]

William Dunbar's Natchez, of course, was the jewel of the Southwest, though it looked a rough-cut gem in its early years. A visitor in 1776 stated that the district enjoyed "the most fertile, beautiful healthy and variegated Lands in this province, or perhaps on the whole Continent of America."[20] Twenty years later when Francis Baily arrived under the bluff after his eventful trip down the river, he saw more than just the land. A village had grown, though still not much of a genuine town. Eighty or ninety houses sprawled over a considerable area on the high ground, and even though actual streets were laid out, so much space intervened between the cabins that it looked more like each house had a small plantation around it. They were frame dwellings for the most part, showing already an evolution from the first stage of rude log cabins and dogtrots, but at the same time Baily also noted that the villagers had not yet developed any real sense of neatness and order, civic pride, that impelled them to keep their houses and grounds clean and neat. Some of the homes—and ones inhabited by people with some claim to prominence—exhibited barely more than the rudiments of comfort, with not a chair to sit on or a table to dine at, and a bed made of rough boards nailed together with some blankets carelessly thrown over a mattress to sleep on. Other homes showed more attention, and some modest expenditure on better furnishings, but still they exhibited a plainness "without any of those luxuries which decorate even the cottages of our English farmers." Clearly living in Natchez did not yet carry with it any sense of obligation to show either taste or wealth.[21]

But Baily did find a hospitality in Natchez that betokened the beginnings of some community feeling. There being no public buildings for civic meetings and social gatherings as yet, most homes opened themselves generously to friends in order to provide some society, and at the two or three operating taverns Baily got food and lodging for a dollar a day. He also found there a billiard table, one of the few but important catalysts to bring people together and stimulate conversation and association—the building blocks of community. Indeed, despite his reservations at its plainness, Baily found Natchez very desirable in 1797. "I think this an excellent place for a person to settle in," he wrote, "if he can persuade himself to give up the advantages of refined society." Yet he found interesting and amusing company while there.[22]

Progress in forming the town by the river was slow but steady in the immediate years that followed. In October 1803 the townspeople held a lottery to raise $1,875, a considerable sum, to build a public market house and to dig wells and cisterns. They also wanted to buy a fire engine, for as the town grew, the wooden houses sprouted closer together, with the ever-present danger of a fire in one spreading to its neighbors.[23] Still the climate worked against the village in the minds of some. Edward Turner suggested moving the federal land office from Washington to Natchez, but then in early 1804 changed his mind. "None of us are willing to spend the *Summer* in Natchez," he told his superiors, though "in the winter it would be agreeable to us to be there."[24]

Nevertheless the growth continued. Christian Schultz visited in the spring of 1808 and saw a scene far different from that witnessed by Baily a decade before. The bank under the hill appeared to be lined with boats for nearly a mile, token of the thriving business being done in goods coming downriver and cotton going on to New Orleans. Some three hundred or more houses now topped the bluff, and no longer did Natchez look like a scattered collection of plantations. It had all the appearances of a growing city. Mercantile establishments flourished, and at least one of them actively imported luxury goods from England for the new wealthy of the community. Two weekly newspapers brought citizens local, territorial, and limited national news. A number of small hotels took in guests with considerably more comfort than the old taverns, and though they did not exhibit quite the refinement that Schultz saw in some of the homes, still he confessed that "they afford no trifling luxury."

The town streets remained unpaved dirt as yet, and where no sidewalks stood, walking in the rainy season was a steady battle with mud. Yet the new public market and the several stores offered a good quantity and variety of meats and produce, and already the citizens seemed to have made something of a division among their number, the planters, the wealthy, and the professional classes living on the bluff, while the laboring people, especially those given to less than genteel ways, settled on the bank called Under-the-Hill. Still, Natchez could not hide the fact that it was a frontier town, and not a few of the doorways on the streets, even when freshly painted in the most fashionable colors, exhibited the skins of wildcats and other animals recently shot only miles from town. Of the people themselves, Schultz remarked happily that the women were attractive and friendly and the men straightforward. "The ladies in general are extremely delicate," he noted, "and excite the warmest sensations in the beholder." As for the men, they passed their time in three occupations: making love, play, and money. "The inhabitants seemed to indulge themselves in all the ease and luxury of the east," he concluded.[25]

Fortescue Cuming visited at about the same time and found that Natchez reminded him of towns in the West Indies. Many of the houses sported balconies and piazzas, and even some of the stores showed adornment. The mixture of breeds and races, from blacks to mulattoes, enhanced the impression, especially when he found several of the small shops run by men with French and Spanish accents. At the market house he heard a babble of tongues and dialects among the vendors, and he encountered even more Under-the-Hill. Unlike Schultz, Cuming encountered the streets during the rainy season, and found many of them impassable. Natchez was not yet ready to be regarded as a genuine city, he thought, yet he conceded that as "the principal emporium" for the trade of the Mississippi territory it stood as a place of considerable importance. He noted the number of new houses in the town, and remarked even more on the fine plantation homes of Governor Sargent, Dunbar, George Poindexter, and others, as he rode along the main road south of town. Interspersed along the way he saw "some tasty cottages," evidencing that not all the refinements of the area were limited to town houses and planter mansions. Everywhere he went he met with gracious hospitality. A mere stop at a plantation to ask for some fodder for his animal inevitably led to a dinner invitation and a long chat with his host, and perhaps an amble through his garden to inspect the latest imported plantings.[26]

By now a single crop for one of those planters could yield forty thousand dollars before expenses. No wonder some visitors concluded that "they live in the style of eastern luxury." With the population of the Natchez district approaching ten thousand now, about half of them in and around the town itself, and with the expanding businesses of the town offering an increasingly wide variety of consumer goods, demand was such that prices on everything but venison and game escalated in the boom time. Even labor did not come cheap as everyone tried his hand at making his fortune.[27]

As the War of 1812 broke out, Natchez was an incorporated city with a public square boasting a city hall, a jail, the market, a firehouse, a public water cistern, and the customary public whipping post for blacks and a pillory for offending whites. Two years later a volunteer fire company organized itself despite the immediate setback of having the fire hall burn down at the same time. City officials managed the market by appointing a manager who let the stalls for a rent, made certain that the quality of the goods sold was acceptable, and even fixed the prices asked for produce. At the same time, as the houses continued to go up and more and more streets were laid out, the city erected a powder magazine, built a ferry across the Mississippi, and established a cemetery for planting the dead and a nursery for growing chinaberry trees that the city fathers then gave to citizens to encourage uniform plantings along the streets. Sargent's Code of 1799, the first body of American law for the territory, considered poor relief and provided that the indigent and impoverished should be identified to receive care, from food and clothing to medical care and, in the last instance, burial. Later law established poorhouses, though most relief work was left to the individual counties.[28] From 1803 onward a major share of the revenues raised in Natchez went to poor relief and welfare, and in 1805 they incorporated the Natchez Hospital to serve both the people of the city as well as itinerant paupers and the ever-present Kaintucks coming down the river. All this the city financed by taxation including property taxes, a levy on carriages and wagons, a tax on slave sales, and a tonnage tax on boats at the landing, as well as a quarter for every crewman aboard them. Tavern operators paid a license fee, and entertainers of all kinds handed over a payment before they could put on their show or exhibition. During its first fourteen years after incorporation, the city took in more than seventeen hundred dollars annually and enjoyed an average surplus of nearly five hundred after expenses. Only with the growth of a base like this could a community begin to spend the money that turned a frontier settlement into a city.[29]

The coming of the second war with Britain put a severe strain on Natchez's fortunes, as it did on those of every American community. Many of the town's sons went off to join the volunteer companies that helped defend New Orleans and the Mississippi Valley not only from the British but also from marauding Creek in Alabama. Yet the war also stimulated the growth of the community, for uncountable men from Kentucky and Tennessee who came south to fight liked what they saw of the Southwest while there and returned after the peace to make new homes. During the boom and bust years that followed with the land speculators and the Great Migration, Natchez seemed largely immune, because there was always the cotton and always the market for it abroad. For Natchez and its people, the second and third decades of the nineteenth century were not so much a time of prosperity or depression as simply one of more or less prosperity.

By 1817 the continued growth in the town and its wealth showed in the increasing number of neat houses with their galleries for taking the evening breezes, and the widespread reputation of their owners for hospitality and indulgence. Visitors found that, as one put it, "learning begins to receive attention," though another at the same time thought Mississippians had as yet little interest in literature and the arts. Still, leading citizens subscribed enough funds to charter their first college, even while devoting themselves to their chief interest, the accumulation of wealth. "The inhabitants of Natchez," wrote a visitor in 1818, "live in ease and affluence." Why should they not? That is what they came into the wilderness in hope of finding—opportunity—and for those who prospered by their risk, hard work, or simple good fortune, there was no modesty at displaying their success or enjoying it.[30] The people of Natchez themselves reveled in their prosperity and growth. "It is truly gratifying to witness the improvements which have been made and are still progressing in this city," a Natchez editor wrote in 1818. Their streets bettered and would soon be graveled, and more and more spacious homes went up, though the price of an average house had now doubled to $860, for which the builder might wait months or even years to get paid.[31] The new Bank of Mississippi was capitalized at three million dollars, symbolic of the wealth of the city and the territory.[32]

While Natchez reflected the concentrated growth and success of the Southwest in these years, communities sprouted and thrived elsewhere in their smaller way. Just below Natchez in Wilkinson County the village of Woodville appeared around 1805, settled by pioneers from Georgia and South Carolina. To it, among others, moved Samuel Davis and his wife Jane, along with most of their ten children, including the tenth and last still clinging to his mother's apron, young Jefferson.[33] Far to the east grew Mobile and Saint Stephens. By 1816 Mobile rivaled Natchez in size, with twenty or more stores, and many of its finer homes of elegant brick. In 1816 alone six dry goods shops, a lumberyard, and a hardware store opened their doors, as this city, too, prospered on the trade in lumber, cotton, rice, and other goods that came and went through its bay. Saint Stephens was not much smaller, with 250 houses, a school, fifteen stores, and a newspaper.[34] The citizens of these and other towns and villages showed much the same varied national and racial complexion as those of Natchez, with the added spice of a number of refugees from Napoleon's high command following his defeat at Waterloo and subsequent exile. In the modest home of one former general a visitor found a supper prepared by a French cook and accompanied by the best imported wines. Moreover, on his walls hung the colors of France, and all about the rooms were strewn campaign trophies and mementos, including pistols and daggers and captured flags of other nations. On a rough cedar pedestal in the center of one of his bedrooms sat a bust of the emperor himself—in all, a small piece of the French Empire in the New World.[35]

A man on horseback paid six and one-half cents for the ferry across Saint Catherine Creek to get from Natchez to its smaller neighboring community Washington.[36] The genesis of the village went back to John Foster in 1798, when he set aside a parcel of his plantation six miles north of Natchez in hope that it might become a town. Two years later, as the territorial legislature voted to select a new site for its capital, Foster's plot had been surveyed and laid out ready to become a community, and so the politicians chose it for their new home, making the act official on February 1, 1802. Subscriptions raised money for putting up the new public buildings in a place that promoters believed would be healthier than the riverside, the federal government established Turner there to open the land office, and the town was in business.

Almost at once the opportunists and the power seekers flocked to Washington. The territory's second newspaper opened there in 1813. The territory's first college got its charter almost as soon as the embryonic village became the capital, Adams County moved its seat there from Natchez, and every aspiring lawyer and merchant now looked not to Natchez but to this upstart community artificially created to be a capital. An immediate rivalry and animosity arose between the neighboring communities and did not abate for two decades, until eventually the capital moved on in 1822. Yet while it briefly throve, Washington became everything that the new American ideal expected of a town. It housed learning in Jefferson College. It encouraged the press with the *Washington Republican*. Its business grew, and its religious community did no less so, with Methodist and other churches opening their doors. Men of letters and science like Benjamin L. C. Wailes, noted geologist and agriculturalist, made it their home; as did John Monette, physician and historian, and briefly the naturalist John J. Audubon.[37]

When the first federal officials arrived in 1803, they found Washington an "indifferent looking little place in which scarcely one house was finished." Yet three years later it boasted a vigorous social life as the great and near-great of the territory gathered where the power resided. By 1808 there were three hotels, as well as three taverns, a Masonic lodge, bathhouses, thirty houses, a store, an apothecary, and a jail. Yet it was still a pitifully small capital, with barely three hundred citizens, who struggled all the more—thanks to their limited numbers—to make a society for themselves.

At every opportunity they gave public dinners in honor of some visiting dignitary, whether it be the Marquis de Lafayette or General Andrew Jackson fresh from his triumph over the British. By 1815, when Jackson came, Washington numbered one thousand inhabitants—the largest it would get before its eventual decline—and all the efforts at town beautification and expansion made in Natchez were mirrored there. Meanwhile, the legislature never quite got around to voting funds for building a capitol, and instead they met for years in a rented house, lending the insecurity of impermanence to Washingtonians' grasp on fame and power. Yet it was there in 1807 that the territorial superior court held the treason trial of Aaron Burr, once Jefferson's vice president and now accused of plotting to separate part of the Southwest from the United States by armed uprising. And when a wealthy woman decided to donate funds to establish the South's first college for women, it was here in Washington that she chose to locate her female academy.[38]

Yet Washington did not last, for unlike Natchez, it lacked the trade and the river to keep it alive and healthy. Once the legislature moved on to Jackson in the 1820s, this little town on the old Trace immediately began a slow decline, evidence of how fragile even the most seemingly blessed community could be on the southwestern frontier. Nevertheless, despite its brief rivalry with Natchez, it shared much more in common than not with its neighbor, for in both towns— indeed, throughout the Southwest—the same kinds of society flourished, and men and women sought the same entertainments and took the same paths to add some variety to what would otherwise have been, even for the wealthy, largely a life of toil and tedium.

John Perkins made the long float down the river in 1800 and soon prospered sufficiently that he built the first brick dwelling in Natchez. Yet his next four years there proved to be the most unhappy of his life, not because of the danger of malaria or the rough and wild nature of the country in which he lived. Rather, he missed a genuine society, a social life something like the one he left behind.[39] He hardly stood alone in that, and yet he and other newcomers did not idly wait for a society to find them. Making do with what they had, they improvised a flourishing local culture for themselves.

Naturally people called on their neighbors when they could, and there began the rudiments of southwestern society. People went to visit on foot, walking several miles sometimes, and in the early days they did not let the traveling time pass without putting it to use. Women in the country filled their aprons with raw cotton and picked the seeds from it as they walked.[40] In Natchez men and women alike gathered beside a cool spring near Saint Catherine Creek, and there under the shade of the trees they drank the waters or picnicked while buying wine and liquor from a vendor.[41] For the men society could start with something as mundane as a haircut. In 1803, as Perkins languished for society, barbering cost $1.50 a month for a shave, and then as always men gathered at the barber's and shared conversation, jokes, and politics while awaiting their turn in the chair.[42] At least a few of the taverns had a billiard table, and there, too, amid the pungent aroma of tobacco and whiskey, men met to pass some idle time with company. At twelve and one-half cents a game, the tables provided a cheap respite from their loneliness.[43] Even down at Stirling and Gillaspie's smithy the men could meet and talk while having their horses shod or a plow blade repaired. When Natchez held the capital and county seat, the visits of the lawyers on court days always brought fresh men and news into town, and often when they took their lodgings at an inn or boardinghouse, they took it on themselves to invite locals to join them for dinner and pleasantry.[44]

The Natchez City Tavern offered another opportunity for a gathering place in its "Coffee Room," which featured newspapers from around the United States, many of them brought over the Trace by the mail riders, and no more than a week old if from Nashville, and two weeks if published on the East Coast.[45] Once a newspaper began publication in the town, people gathered in its office where they could also find sheets from other parts of the country to peruse and discuss.[46] And of course men and women gathered at the inns without needing an excuse, to dine with friends or share a few glasses of beer or cider. A midday dinner cost fifty cents, being the big meal of the day, while a lighter supper ran thirty-seven and one-half cents in Washington's Mansion House Hotel, and similar prices ruled elsewhere.[47] Moreover, understanding the need of people for some society, and expecting to be repaid eventually, innkeepers actually put the meal expense on a running bill, and some even made small loans of cash to their patrons as well. If tongues were tight, the innkeeper loosened reticent lips with whiskey at twenty-five cents a quart, and that soon got people talking.[48]

To be sure, tavern manners were not usually very refined. Men in the South—and many women, too—gave little pause while the food actually sat on the table. With scarcely a word passed in conversation, diners ravaged the platters, consuming a whole meal in a quarter of an hour, and with little attention to courtesies. They reached in front of one another to be first at the best bits of meat and cooled their coffee by pouring it in saucers—if they had them—then slurping it from the dish. They ate, thought one observer, as if it were to be their last meal. Through it all, one often heard nothing but the sounds of the forks scraping the plates, the diners coughing, and the men blowing their noses. In Mobile a visitor thought she saw sixty people eat their entire dinner in twenty minutes, and she swore that no one bothered to chew. When done, a diner might very likely just bolt from the table, even if another were in the middle of telling an interesting story. The whiskey jug beckoned, and talk could go on there at leisure. Unfortunately, no matter where he was, at table or bar, the man of the Southwest very likely kept a plug of tobacco in his mouth, taking it out only to eat his food. Otherwise, he squirted a near-constant stream of expectorant on the floors and carpets, over the walls, and all too often even on the dresses of ladies who inadvertently got in the way.[49]

Inevitably the settlers wanted more. Perkins lamented "the lack of the society of refined and congenial ladies," as he put it. Indeed, Natchez at the turn of the 1800s was not a great place for a bachelor. He could find no unmarried women, and the wives of the town seemed too occupied with running their homes, or else too weary of cleaning tobacco juice from their skirts, to spare time for society. That, of course, changed dramatically as cotton and trade and slaves brought wealth and leisure. In the early years after 1800, the people of the town held public "balls" at the market house, city hall, or one of the taverns, and these drew people from the surrounding plantations as well.[50] A visitor at one of these gatherings always found a welcome, and many who just happened to be passing through on the river found themselves received with unfeigned hospitality. "We all had repeated and pressing solicitations to return," wrote one visitor as early as 1801, and not surprisingly.[51] An outside visitor brought fresh news and a fresh face to the little dances, and more than one left with a genuine feeling of regret.

Thomas Rodney came into town in August 1804 to visit an old acquaintance, but found all the ladies of the house a few blocks down the street. When they heard of his arrival, they insisted that he join them, and when he did he found one of the small Natchez balls in sway. He met "Ten or a dozen of the finest Ladies of the City and Territory," and found them playing chess, and then singing and dancing to the music of a piano or other instruments. Later they all—both the married women and the young single girls—walked him to his inn by the light of a lantern. "I mention this merely as a Trait of the Cheerful and pleasant Manners of the place," Rodney wrote his brother.[52]

These so-called "assembly" dances became one of Natchez's best-known features in the early years, and not to be missed. When Dr. John Bedford arrived in 1807 after his downriver trip, he stayed as a guest at the home of Ferdinand Claiborne, one of the town's most famous hosts. On March 6 Claiborne treated him to a sumptuous dinner in the company of several other local doctors and men of importance. First came a course of salad and meats, followed by sweetmeats, and finished with pastry, apples, cheese, and more. Throughout the meal they all drank Madeira in copious quantity. Indeed, Bedford felt nearly drunk and excused himself afterward to walk off his light head by a stroll around the town, "viewing the scenery as attentively and correctly as our deranged faculties would permit until somewhat restored." He returned to his host's to learn that there would be a dance at 8 P.M. "Having a wish to see a collection of the most genteel and respectable persons, males and females, of the Territory, presuming this to be the most favorable place and time, presuming on what I knew of their place and its customs," Bedford resolved to accept an invitation. Men of the town took turns acting as hosts or "managers," and the host for the night introduced Bedford to some forty men and about fifteen women.

With such an imbalance in the sexes, the men had to draw numbers for partners. Walking into an adjoining room Bedford saw "a red-headed, hump-shouldered, hard looking fellow, resembling the baboon tribe," standing on a stair with a handful of tickets and a cluster of men crowding about him trying to grab them. Some walked away beaming, while others—those drawing numbers higher than fifteen, looked glum and sullen. Bedford grabbed his own ticket, and delighted to find he had number ten. When the young lady with the same number was called, the manager introduced Bedford by misstating her name and ignoring his entirely. Once past that social gaffe, Bedford and his partner "flirted through the dance, with all the gracefulness and activity" he could muster. That done, he seated his partner and went off to have coffee with some of the other men, as different males now came forward with their numbers. The conversation went on until midnight, when a meal was brought out, the ladies dining first. Then, without a word from the manager, the men "flocked like hungry shoats to a stye." And thus eating and dancing they continued until nearly four in the morning.[53]

For those like Perkins who did not or could not dance, often a card game flourished during the revels, and separate card parties were held in the evenings. They played whist or loo—both variants of bridge—and sometimes added a little zest to the gaming with very modest wagers.[54] To encourage more to get to their feet, however, a Mrs. Giedraen opened her own dancing school in the Planter's Hotel in 1813, leaving Natchez's men no excuse to eschew the balls.[55] For others, singing offered an agreeable means of getting together. One genial traveler arriving at the end of 1822 was in town no more than a few days before he joined local society by attending a meeting designed to form a singing association. Only five men attended, but they were enough to appoint a committee to draft a constitution and by-laws, and with a couple of women present they finished their evening in songs. Indeed, music seemed prevalent in Natchez. As one of the committeemen dined at McAully's boardinghouse near the market, he found that his host could play four different instruments for the entertainment of his guests, while McAully himself helped with drafting the constitution for the Natchez Harmonical Society. Every one of the better homes seemed to have a piano and a daughter who could play it to accompany song. The daughter of a Colonel Taylor played both piano and guitar and gave lessons as well, while as an accomplished member of the Harmonical Society she lamented only Natchez's lack of a good bass voice.[56]

Inevitably the need for society showed itself in the beginnings of fraternal groups that spread westward from the more settled parts of the United States. None did so earlier or more successfully than the Freemasons. By 1801 Natchez hosted Harmony Lodge Number 7, which met, like many another civic group, in Colonel Yerby's Assembly Room.[57] Andrew Jackson Lodge started in 1816. Masonry started in neighboring Alabama in September 1811 with Madison Lodge Number 21 at future Huntsville. Two years later another lodge opened in Mobile, both of them, like the Harmony and other Mississippi lodges, operating under the management of the grand master of Kentucky until the states' own grand lodges incorporated. By 1830 Alabama alone would host thirty-one new lodges.[58] Still, an egalitarian side of the frontiersmen left him slightly suspicious of secret societies—or jealous of not qualifying for admission—and when an anti-Masonic wave spread through the nation in the late 1820s, membership in the Southwest, especially in Alabama, declined dramatically.[59] Volunteer military companies also attracted men, more for their social advantages than from any substantial martial spirit (except in time of danger). The Natchez Rifle Corps and the Adams County Dragoons organized before the second war with England, and both continued long after the peace. They chiefly paraded on public holidays, put on benefits, and seemingly bestowed titles like major and colonel on everyone. The Natchez Fencibles formed after the war, and more would follow, all serving an important role in the social life of the community, especially its leading families.[60] Very early in its history Natchez embraced the theater as well, with a flourishing Theatrical Association staging plays shortly after 1800.

Outdoor sport gave the people of the territory some more active recreation and society, and nothing appealed to them as much as racing. As far back as 1783 the people of Natchez had held horse races on a quarter-mile stretch of land Under-the-Hill, and there they continued for many years. Early visitors decried the gambling and cavorting that went on at the track, but of course it was only the spillover from the taverns nearby below the bluff. Riders mounted their animals at the foot of the hill and rode straight toward the river to the finish, assuming that they could rein in their horses in time not to plunge into the muddy water. Indians often rode races, too, but not liking the prospect of a dunking, they rode in the opposite direction, with a less watery but certainly more abrupt conclusion awaiting them at the wall of the bluff if they went too far.[61]

In 1794 organizers established a subscription to fund prizes for stake races at Fleetfield, just outside the town, and a decade later, in 1807, the Mississippi Jockey Club formed itself at Washington to manage racing more systematically.[62] The club oversaw the clearing and management of new tracks, set the rules of racing, and in time even involved itself in breeding and showing horses. Initially the owners themselves generally rode their animals, but as the sport became increasingly refined, and the owners more and more wealthy, slave men replaced the whites as jockeys. They held their racing seasons fall and spring, with the purses to be made up of the entrance fees paid by horse owners. A winning animal could take fifty or even one hundred dollars, and by 1815 horses ran for five hundred and more. An 1821 race saw a sweepstakes of three thousand dollars dangled before the entrants. As more money and more refinement entered the sport, the old track was soon abandoned for ones on higher ground, the most popular being at the toll bridge over the Saint Catherine, which in time became known as the Pharsalia Race Course, the most famous in Mississippi.[63]

Race day originally consisted of two "heats," the same horses running in both and only racing again in case of a tie. Then they went to three heats. The running spread over successive days, with three-mile heats on the first, two-mile runs on the second, and one-mile sprints on the third, and all or most of the horses running in every race. Speed certainly counted, but endurance mattered most by the end of the series. Soon tracks spread throughout the territory, including one at Grindstone Ford on the old Trace. All of them took the rules of the Natchez club for their model, and by 1830 at least six such clubs flourished in Mississippi alone.[64] Horses with names like Paddy Carey, Blucher, and Brushy Mountain vied for the prizes funded by the sixty-dollar entry fees paid, fees that rose as high as two hundred dollars in the 1820s and clearly reflected that the sport had become more and more the province of the aristocrats, what the Natchez press called "the Fancy."[65]

Race day could be the most exciting event of the year for those who attended. In December 1828 the Saint Catherine course hosted the fall sweepstakes featuring, among others, a race meeting for four colts named Red Rover, Paul Pry, Stockholder, and George Washington, each of them locally bred. Three of the jockeys rode in variations of red caps and jackets, with white trousers, while Paul Pry's rider affected a silk-and-velvet cap and plaid silk jacket, white pants and red boots. Despite his jockey's somewhat garish outfit, Paul Pry was an early favorite, and interest in the race attracted a large crowd despite the inclement day.

One of those brought for the fun by the competition was a rakish-looking fellow, his overcoat thrown back across his shoulders, his thumbs stuck cockily into his vest, his hat perched at a jaunty angle, and his boots sporting massive spurs. He wore enormous whiskers, declared himself to be a major of some sort, and impressed most present as what they called a "Georgia-man"—meaning something of an overbearing blowhard. With undisguised bombast he yelled that he would back Paul Pry against the field. When a seemingly unknowing little Dutchman essayed to bet his own horse and equipment that Red Rover would win, the major took the bet gladly and confided to others in a stage whisper: "I've got the d——d puden [pudding] mouth s—— of a b—— I reckon."

The first heat commenced when the starter yelled "Go!" the favorite taking an early lead. The major loudly proclaimed that the foolish Dutchman would soon be riding shank's mare home from the track, but the fellow just responded by betting his coat against the major's that Rover would take home the prize money. The Georgian responded that he would take any bet, and the Dutchman even spoke of putting his shirt on the race, but when he reached out to jostle the major's shirt in jest, the ruffled front proved to be a dickey and the whole thing came off in his hand. Suddenly all parties ignored the race as onlookers wondered if a fight would ensue.

But then Rover passed Paul Pry, and so did Stockholder, the two leaders staying at a dead heat for the rest of the run. The owners of Paul Pry and Washington were sufficiently disgusted that they took their animals out of the competition, and the second and third heats went to the handsome gray, Red Rover. And the major's horse and coat went to the Dutchman. As he rode them back to Natchez, he passed the Georgian, now on foot, and offered him a ride on what had been until lately his own horse. "Go to h——l you d——d sour crout rascal," shot back the major. The winner only laughed and trotted off, splashing the major with mud from his own horse's heels.[66]

Other spectator sports came to the towns and villages from time to time, none more unusual than a brainstorm of Gideon Lincecum's. Plagued like so many of these frontier characters with an inability to stick with one calling for long, and a chronic shortage of money, he wandered in the woods alone for two months or more one year, trying to find inspiration for something to make his fortune after a venture at storekeeping failed. Finally he conceived the idea of forming a team of ballplayers among the Choctaw and taking them on the road to play exhibition games and perform their ancestral war dances. On November 28, 1829, Lincecum met with an Indian named Fulahooma, who announced that he had found some players for him. Gideon's delight turned to gloom when he reached a field to find four hundred young men, all expecting to make the team and none seeing why they could not all travel with him. All he could do was propose what he called a "draft," selecting one out of ten by drawing lots. In fact he wrote the names of the men he actually wanted on pieces of paper and mixed them with 365 blank pieces. His deception worked, and for the next several months he took his traveling team throughout the territory, and even north to Tennessee, but he never made a profit, and so—like all frontiersmen—turned to something else to find his opportunity.[67]

Happily for the people of the territory, and especially Natchez, traveling shows and entertainments came up and down the river during the spring and fall seasons, providing considerably varied amusements. They could be as simple as an artist who prepared silhouettes called "Physiognotraces" for fifty cents apiece.[68] Visiting musical performers and groups appeared at Colonel Yerby's and elsewhere, sometimes exhibiting exotic wild animals from Africa and India. At Texada's Tavern in 1808 a Canadian brought his display of wax figurines, along with doing his own bird imitations and juggling and balancing demonstrations.[69] Some people staged fights between animals or showed trained bears. Others brought fireworks or dazzled with feats of ventriloquism. Not a few used sleight of hand and trickery, and sometimes they were embarrassingly found out, as with the artist who boasted that if someone in the crowd would fire his pistol, he would catch the bullet on the end of his knife. On one occasion when a visitor pulled the trigger of the pistol, it failed to go off, but by then the artist was already holding up his knife with a bullet stuck to its point.[70]

Rougher sports were there for those so inclined. Besides the bloody exhibitions of bearbaiting and wolf torturing that appealed to the Under-the-Hill crowd, men sometimes played a foolish Tennessee game called "snick-a-snack," in which they simply sat around a table and started hitting each other on the head, shoulders, and hands with their knives, the game continuing until someone said he had had enough "enjoyment." The gander pull was easier on the men, but tough on the geese, who found themselves stripped of their head and neck feathers, greased, and then tied to a rope that allowed them only a few feet of movement. A whole gang of horsemen then rode by again and again, reaching low from their saddles to try to grab the head and yank it off. More dangerous to the participants were mock battles held at night, in which the men threw lighted firebrands at one another. For more pacific throwing they hurled tomahawks at targets and heaved heavy stones with one hand to see who could attain the greatest distance. Then there was "flinging the rail," in which they literally threw a fence rail through the air like a spear. They even devised a game of "push-pin," which two men simply played on the crown of a hat with straight pins.[71]

With boredom and isolation a constant companion on the southwestern frontier, men and women had no choice but to look to their own devices to find amusement and an excuse to spend time together at leisure. Even shopping became a pastime, especially in Natchez, with its growing collection of stores. Putting up a new shop, with all the necessary shelves and counters, could cost a merchant eleven hundred dollars or more by 1819.[72] Then there was the cost of the stock. Even at wholesale prices Benjamin Smith spent twenty-five thousand for the goods he brought to his Natchez store, "and a handsomer assortment never was," he boasted. "I have got something of everything," he proclaimed, and expected to be amazed if he could not "screw" enough money out of the citizens to make a profit.[73] Another merchant in Greenville, Mississippi, in 1824 noted that, among other things, his stock included tea, tape, candles, cigars, jewelry, fabrics, clothing, shoes, wine, door locks, whiskey, socks, spurs, hats, cutlery, paper, soap, almanacs, flints and lead, screws and nails, lampblack, artificial flowers, baskets, trunks, inkstands, spectacles, lead pencils, ginger, wafers, china, tools of all description, playing cards, tinware, ovens, kettles, gun locks, butter molds, beaver hats, and silver toothpicks.[74]

That the people of the territory found such stores logical places both to gather and to shop is reflected in the variety of the goods sold and the sales figures themselves. The Greenville store averaged $1,000.00 a month in sales during 1826. A Natchez mercantile establishment in 1830 took inventory to find $6,308.00 worth of stock on hand, while another merchant with stores in both Natchez and Washington recorded net sales in 1824 of $30,000.00, and the next year did $37,000.00 of business in January alone.[75]

For the woman of means, even in little Natchez the trip to emporiums with such a wide and varied array of goods provided considerable diversion. Writing paper that cost thirty-eight cents a quire gave her something to keep her in touch with friends and family in the East, and ink powder at a quarter for a "paper" needed only to be mixed with water to allow her to write. She could beautify her home with a new dining table for $20.00, then set it with cutlery, a dozen glass tumblers, china bowls, and more for another $13.64. A cloth for the table was another $3.00, and a looking glass for the wall commanded $1.25.[76] When she went out to visit or to shop, she walked under a $6.00 parasol and wore clothing of handsome calico, linens, muslin, black bombazine, cambric, and more. Turtle-shell combs held her hair, and morocco leather shoes at $2.25 the pair shod her feet. If she made her own clothing, her favorite merchant sold her silk thread for twelve and one-half cents a skein; and a paper of pins—which her husband might use for a game as well—cost seventy-five cents.[77] Outfitting her husband could require $2.50 for a pair of pantaloons and $4.00 for a tailored coat, though a really handsome frock coat went as high as $10.00. His socks cost fifty cents a pair; a cloak $17.00 or more; and a razor, shaving brush, and cake of soap a dollar all told. A silver watch in his pocket set him back $10.00 at least, and a bundle of a dozen cigars ran a penny per smoke. Considering that some men went through a dozen "segarros" every day, the pleasure provided by smoking was no paltry expense.[78]

Every trip to the stores offered something to take home to the table, too. Stephen Minor's store offered pound cake, candy, and the somewhat more exotic "macaroney." Burbridge and Smith provided spices in abundance, including whole nutmegs and loaf sugar, and gunpowder tea, along with their customary stock of china and fancy fabrics. Clark and Wren's establishment sold lard, flour, bacon, prepared biscuits, corn by the barrel, claret by the bottle, pickled herring, hams, pickles, raisins, and the like, and even over-the-counter drinks of "grog" at fifty-six and one-quarter cents a mug.[79]

Moreover, to compete for all this trade, and to offer the people of the territory as much opportunity as possible to gather in the stores, the businessmen stayed open every day of the year but Christmas and New Year's. Even Christmas Eve found the storekeeper open for business and doing a brisker trade than usual, thanks to the next day's holiday, especially in gift items like shoes, whiskey, socks, gloves, bonnets, and toothbrushes. Even on July 4 he stayed at his counter. For his trouble he got paid much of the time in cotton or else did not get paid at all. Clark and Wren may have been pleased with the $6,000.00 worth of stock on their shelves in August 1830, but the $1,725.12 in unpaid accounts receivable on their books were no comfort. Virtually all customers ran accounts at the stores and then paid occasionally as hard currency came to hand or when they could no longer walk into the shop without embarrassment.[80]

It was a small reward to the merchants, who sometimes went to considerable trouble to bring goods to them. In 1822 just getting a barrel of white flour to Montgomery, Alabama, required first taking the wheat from Washington County, Virginia, to a mill on the Holston River in east Tennessee. Then the flour was floated 150 miles downriver to the Hiwassee, then ten miles up another tributary to Hildebrand's Landing. A twelve-mile portage from there got it to the Connussawga, where it boarded a flatboat to go down to the Coosa, and from there finally to Montgomery. Leaving February 20, the flour could arrive on April 27, yet this was still faster than shipping it by boat down the Atlantic to the Gulf of Mexico and then—in the days before steamboats—poling it by flatboat up the Alabama from Mobile.[81] And after all that trouble, and despite the brisk sales at some establishments in the territory, many could not stay in business. "There was not one man in the country with money enough to buy a barrel of flour," said Anthony Hutchins's son John of the early days. They had to take contributions from several and then divide that barrel accordingly, which made importing some items rather risky.[82] Charles Dencker found that even in New Orleans he could not make his wine-and-spirits shop turn a profit. He moved to Natchez to "see if I can not do better," and there he did, partly by playing on the less refined palates of the Mississippians. He shipped in cheap dry Malaga wine by the barrel and then put it up in bottles himself to sell at inflated prices.[83]

And if lagging sales and closures did not attest to the occasional lack of business and society at the stores, the evident boredom of the clerks certainly did. More than one found himself with so little to do that he daydreamed and idled away the hours by composing doggerel to fill the endsheets and back pages of the ledgers that should have been recording sales. They doodled and drew pictures, practiced their lettering, and made up the occasional poem. "Let Sighs and Streaming tears resume their course," wrote one of Stirling and Gillaspie's workers in 1820, "and My sad eyes be there eternal source."[84]

One kind of occasion brought the whole population, regardless of social station or refinement, together in these frontier communities. They all loved holidays, especially the children. "No restraints were laid on our sports," recalled one, "except the injunction to 'keep out of mischief.'"[85] Christmas, New Year's, and the rest never failed to turn out everyone. During the War of 1812, news of a victory like the Battle of Lake Erie saw Natchez erupt in illuminations, bell ringing, and the firing of musket and cannon volleys. The Fourth of July, of course, opened with gun salutes at dawn, an obligatory oration or reading of the Declaration of Independence, and then at 2 P.M. a banquet at one of the neighboring springs.[86]

They observed Christmas in the usual way but also made an event of Easter. Grindstone Ford on the Trace proved a popular spot before the sacred morning, and there the celebrants gathered for a sunrise service to sit on pine straw to protect themselves from the heavy dews. They came from all around on foot, on horseback, and by carriage and farm wagon. Everyone brought breakfast and dinner for their families, and all dressed according to his or her means. Women appeared in tartans and plaids, while the "Fancy" came in their silks and satins. Bonnets covered every female head, and every head was bowed at ten o'clock, when the morning service was preached. The minister for the day might well appear in a scarlet coat with silver adornments and a tricorne, but before he addressed the throng he changed to somber black. After the services and dinner the people frolicked at dances and games, many staying over to continue their play on Monday, and as the women did their jigs, the men tried curling by skimming heavy stones over the straw.[87]

Yet nothing brought the people together like the religious holidays, especially those connected with the end of the year. As far back as 1704 the French in Mobile commenced what they called the Société de la Saint Louis, celebrating Saint Louis' day on August 25. It continued until 1842. Meanwhile, building on that precedent, in 1711 the French in New Orleans organized the Boeuf Gras Society to meet every year on Shrove Tuesday. They mounted a huge bull's head on a cart and pulled it down the Rue Royale and Rue Dauphin with a team of oxen. Ahead of and behind the cart masked revelers marched and danced along with the society members. After a change in rule the Spanish created the Mystic Society in 1793 and added a Twelfth Night march to the tradition. They dressed in white and carried torches. Pushing a cart bearing a statue of the Virgin, they danced and drank along the way. Inevitably the citizens gathered each year in greater and greater numbers to watch the festival, and small outlying communities began to copy the tradition until it spread through several southwestern communities.[88]

Then, in 1830, along came Michael Krafft, already known as a character in Mobile. On Christmas Eve the year before he showed up at an eggnog party in a red flannel shirt and wearing a cutlass. Now, several weeks before New Year's Eve, the cockeyed cotton broker got a sailor's "monkey" jacket and cap from a ship in port and went out on the town. Having drunk more than enough, he walked down to James Hall's hardware store, stole a rake, tied cowbells to its tines, then slung it over his shoulder, and began to march through the city, singing and jingling. People aroused from their slumbers came outdoors and started to follow him, and as Krafft looked back at his fellow revelers, he dubbed them the "Cowbellion de Rakin Society" and announced that they would march again on December 31. When that evening came, Krafft and his friends dined and drank until they were ready, then set off on a march, this time to Partridge's hardware, where they took rakes and hoes and cowbells and repeated the performance, marching and ringing through the night, drinking more at every stop, and gathering fifty or more fellow partyers dressed in grotesque costumes. When Shrove Tuesday came, people resurrected the revel, and Mardi Gras, southwestern style, was born.[89]

And so the people living at what once had been the edge of the wilderness made their culture. They borrowed from the French and Spaniards and British and Indians, and added their own American spice to the mix, to build a sense of community based on living, eating, working, and playing together. By that last day of 1830, when Krafft and his band of miscreants marched the old year out, community had spread throughout the old territory, with only the remaining Indian lands not yet settled and under increasing pressure to open to white civilization. Both ends of the Trace that brought American culture north to south and back again now flourished, and if New Orleans and Natchez at one end captured all the grandeur, still rural Tennessee at the other could boast a surprising degree of development. In Williamson County alone there were by now 64 teachers, 23 merchants, 24 doctors, 14 lawyers, 13 clergymen, 11 grocers, and 9 innkeepers. At least 58 carpenters worked at erecting the houses that were the building blocks of community, and every other trade essential to comfort and necessity flourished, from chair makers to carriage makers, from glovers to hatters, from distillers and dyers and millers to gunsmiths, tobacconists, and printers.[90]

And if some communities came and went, and others, created like Washington, could not outlast time passing them by, yet others were born only to flourish. When the Mississippi capital left Natchez's little neighboring village, it went on northeast, up the Trace to the Pearl River, where Louis Le Fleur once ran his stand. In 1822 the legislature declared that the new capital would be Jackson. Actually, in typical egalitarian frontier fashion, they decided to locate themselves in the exact geographical center of the state as it was then constituted. Unfortunately, that would have put them in a swamp "accessible only by canoe." They made an adjustment and moved it to nearby Le Fleur's Bluff, though one wag complained that the shift constituted "a serious abandonment of principle."[91] Far more serious complaints came from those who first saw the new capital, for there was nothing to it. A year before there had been only one of Le Fleur's old cabins. But by March 1823, when a traveler on the Trace came by, he saw nearly a dozen log cabins and as many new frame homes, with one of brick and another projected to be built. He found three taverns, two stores, two printers, a weekly newspaper called the *Pearl River Gazette*, and the new state house, a substantial brick edifice sixty feet wide and thirty-five deep. "The mechanics are very busy on all sides," he observed, and all the talk was of more new houses to go up in the year ahead. As in so many other places in the territory tied to the old Trace, the men and women had come, and where they stopped a community arose. "We may truly say that there is a city springing up in the midst of the forest," concluded this one visitor, "as if it were by enchantment."[92]

7

The Road to God

"This whole region, it is true," said Timothy Flint in 1826, "wears an aspect of irreligion; but we must not thence infer, that we do not often see the semblance and the counterfeit of religion. . . . There is no country where bigotry and enthusiasm are seen in forms of more glaring absurdity, and, at the same time, more arrogant assumption."[1] But Flint's jaundiced view came from observing too many of the extreme fringes of what passed for piety in the Southwest. Most others would have disagreed with him. "We are in fact a 'church going people,'" a Natchez newspaper boasted in 1828.[2]

Yet it was not always so. In 1800 John Hall complained after riding through the territory that, bad as was the absence of educators, "the case is no better respecting religious instructors." He found but one Episcopalian minister, one Methodist, and two Baptists in the whole region along the Trace, most of them illiterate.[3] Four years later a settler on the Tombigbee in the Alabama country lamented that "as to churches or houses of worship, or any means of communicating moral principles, to the mass of the people, they are as utterly unknown as among our Chactaw neighbors."[4]

In fact religion, that essential component of all frontier communities, came very early to the region. Priests arrived with the first Spanish explorer, Hernando de Soto, in 1540–41, and of course Marquette was himself a priest when he came down the Mississippi in 1673. Nine years later another Catholic father came with the French explorer La Salle, and on March 29, 1682, he performed the first mass in Mississippi not far from Natchez. Iberville and Bienville started the first last-

131

ing settlement in 1699 near Biloxi, and Père Paul Du Ru established the first regular services there, even while the early missionaries went into the southern wilderness to bring the god of the Europeans to the Indians, including the ill-starred Natchez.[5] On February 1, 1700, Du Ru baptized his first Indian child, with Iberville acting as godfather.[6] A few years later a settler named Huber moved to Natchez with his family and slaves to grow tobacco, and with him he took what one called "a troup of clerics."[7]

At first the Catholics' chief—indeed, only—concern was conversion and baptism of the natives, and in the first decades of the eighteenth century they sent several of their number out into the unknown regions. Many secured souls for the church. Many more lost their lives, and after the Fort Rosalie massacre in 1729, their missionary activity dwindled, especially as authorities back in France had to concentrate their efforts elsewhere in the world during the continuing conflict with England. Several of the priests themselves died in the Indian attacks. Then, with the downfall of their order in the internal politics of the French church, the Jesuits, the original priests in the territory, found themselves ordered back to France. They left as criminals, and their chapels were razed to the ground. Thus when the commandant of Fort Rosalie's forgotten garrison married Marie Deverges on April 26, 1753, there was a priest in Natchez to perform the ceremony and to minister to the tiny community of no more than a dozen white families. But fifteen years later, when a daughter, Henriette Marie, was born to the commandant in December 1768, there was no longer a Jesuit there to do the baptism. Consequently by 1763 the missionary effort in the Southwest ended a complete failure. In that same year the colony passed into British hands.[8]

Catholic activity did not cease, of course, but it found little encouragement from the British, who still had anti-Catholic laws on their books, though these were little enforced. Outposts like Natchez and any remaining missionaries overlooked by the Jesuit purge simply got along by being too remote to notice. Meanwhile the influx of new grantees from Britain and the American colonies ensured that Protestantism became and would remain the dominant belief in most of the territory outside the old established communities like New Orleans and Mobile. Happily for the Catholics, political affairs far beyond their line of sight saw the territory pass from Britain to the Catholic king of Spain in 1781, and once more their religion was not only accepted but encouraged.

Interestingly enough, when Spain took over, it chose to reassert its religion by sending four Irish priests to the colony. The policy made sense. The inhabitants, especially after the British settlement years, predominantly spoke English. English-speaking priests made the most sense, therefore, and that meant Irishmen. The Spanish governor in New Orleans established two parishes, one at Natchez and the other at Cole's Creek, while officials back in Spain launched a search for their priests. They settled on William Savage, Michael Lamport, Gregory White, and Constantine Mackenna, paid each a salary of $480—which they would hardly have an opportunity to spend in the wilderness— and sent them on their way in April 1787. All but Lamport went to Natchez, and he wound up near Mobile.

The Spaniards made a considerable show of tolerance as governors of the region. They made no interference with their Protestant subjects, allowing them the free practice of their religion in their homes, but mandating that the only churches were to be those run by the Irish priests. It was an enlightened policy for its time, and the priests themselves flourished, leading Spain to send six more in 1792. Besides ministering to their own flocks, they soon undertook to perform the marriages and baptisms of Protestants as well, a sign that Spain hoped eventually to convert all of its subjects to the one faith, but many Anglo settlers refused to cooperate, especially after a few itinerant Protestant preachers came down the Trace or the river.

Indeed, by 1795, as some of the Irishmen died, and with the rapid immigration of more and more Americans, Governor Gayoso in Natchez fretted that the Catholics were on the verge of being overwhelmed. There was little Spain could do by that time, however. Moreover, some of the remaining priests offered problems. One left the calling in 1799 after squabbling with the church. Another, Gregory White, though well liked, took to appearing for the mass too drunk to conduct the service. And when a would-be matrimonial couple stood outside his door for too long waiting for him to perform the services, one of Gayoso's aides found the padre passed out drunk on the floor.

Best loved of them all was John Brady, who came to Natchez in 1795. Despite the dignity of his priestly orders, Brady's Irish temperament could not stay submerged, and he entered into the frontier fun as well as any Protestant, shooting at a mark with the best, and besting most with his horsemanship. Of them all, Savage exerted the greatest influence, however, though his strong will often brought him into conflict with the civil authority, Gayoso. He dedicated the new Church of Our Savior of the World in 1791, and quickly attracted as many Protestants as Catholics, thanks to his powerful preaching. Not a few actually made the conversion that Spain so ardently desired, though for some it may have been more a political than a spiritual move. Alas, he lived only two years after starting his work, and his successor began almost at once to alienate the Protestant faction by attacking the few non-Catholic clergy who had come to Natchez by then. When Gayoso finally evacuated in 1798, it fell to this man, Francis Lennan, to collect the church possessions from Cole's Creek and Natchez and take them south to what was still for a time Spanish West Florida.[9]

When the priests left, several of the Catholics went with them to Mobile or New Orleans. Scarcely a dozen families of the faith remained in Natchez itself, with not many more scattered through the rest of the territory. The year after Gayoso left, the Catholics still living in Natchez sent a request to their former bishop asking that he send them a priest and promising to raise a handsome income of eight hundred dollars for him from their own resources, but none came, and not even in 1801, when one would-be parishioner offered free room and board in his home for a priest.[10] By 1807, when Fortescue Cuming visited Natchez, he found Our Savior of the World's building falling apart in decay, and during the next three decades, the Catholics of Mississippi saw very few priests, and for periods of years none at all.[11]

Protestant denominations stood poised to overwhelm the Church of Rome even before the Spanish finally evacuated the territory, thanks to the influx of settlers during the British years. The tide began in 1773, when Amos Ogden financed a new settlement by selling some nineteen thousand acres of his land in the East, bringing with him to his new colony on the Homochitto River two brothers, Samuel and Richard Swayze, who emigrated from New Jersey to Adams County.[12] Both were Congregationalists, and Samuel a practicing minister; not surprisingly he established a meeting house to which other Congregationalist settlers flocked. That was fine during the British years, but once the Spanish took over, Swayze's church barely survived, and when he died in 1784, his church went with him, leaving the Congregationalists to fend for themselves or await the coming of some other Protestant clergy.[13]

It proved not too long a wait, and when they came, they came to stay, though their beginnings saw no little turmoil. Baptists came among the many American and British immigrants during the 1770s and 1780s, and apparently as early as 1780 some Baptists may have met informally in their rude frontier homes without benefit of clergy.[14] Quite certainly, however, in October 1791 a group of seven Baptists met at the home of Mary Stampley about eighteen miles northeast of Natchez and organized the Church of Jesus Christ on Cole's Creek. They elected Richard Curtis their minister and began the intermittent practice of their religion until 1795, when Father Lennan managed to have Curtis threatened with deportation if he continued to hold services and perform marriages in spite of the Spanish edicts. In fact, Curtis fled to avoid being sent to a Mexican silver mine, waiting in South Carolina until 1796 when the news that Spain would cede Mississippi to the United States made it safe for him to return, even though Gayoso and his garrison still occupied Natchez. He came back without molestation and took up the pulpit once more, there to stay until he died in 1811.[15]

After the Spaniards left, the Baptists multiplied rapidly. By 1800 four churches operated in Mississippi, and two more opened in the next six years. In 1807 they formed the Mississippi Baptist Association and went ahead with the work of spreading their faith. Wherever half a dozen or more Baptist families came together to worship, another congregation formed. All their churches went up at the lower end of the Trace and its contiguous counties, however, for they could not penetrate the northern reaches of the territory—and later state—so long as the Chickasaw and Choctaw lands remained inviolate. Most emigrated from Georgia and South Carolina, and by 1830 they had so spread their numbers that they subdivided the Mississippi Association twice to achieve better administration of the growing flock.[16]

In neighboring Alabama the Baptists first came in the person of David Cooper, who arrived in the Tensaw vicinity in 1802 and soon established the first of many churches that tried against heavy odds on this frontier to "soften and refine the people," as Albert Pickett recalled in 1851, "and to banish much sin and vice from the worst region that ministers ever entered."[17] They helped establish the Mississippi Bible Society in 1812.[18] Later, in 1816, they created their first association, which six years later boasted seventeen churches and 555 members. Like Baptist congregations everywhere, the members of these frontier churches devoted themselves to simple piety, a rigid observance of the Sabbath, and something of a fixation on watching one another's behavior, reporting any infraction of the rules to the church for proper action. In 1826 alone the Alabama association excommunicated ten of its members for breaches of piety. Even their ministers did not stand above scrutiny, especially over the always-troublesome matters of doctrine. Associations warned their congregations against a host of heresies and constantly argued among themselves as to which was the true way. Sadly, the schisms and disputes that so divided the Protestant denominations in the Old World and the East found their way to the Southwest in the minds and Bibles of the immigrants.[19]

Richard Curtis was not to be the only Protestant to suffer persecution from Father Lennan. Adam Cloud came to Natchez to bring the

Episcopalian faith to the frontier, and almost immediately fell afoul of the Spanish authorities. Arriving in 1792, he ignored the strictures against Protestant preaching, and three years later Gayoso arrested him and sent him to New Orleans to be tried. There his judges gave him the choice of going on to Spain or Cuba for trial—in a distinctly hostile environment—or else leaving the territory. Cloud prudently decided to go, returning to South Carolina, whence he had come. But, like Curtis, he came back, only not until 1816, when he settled near Greenville and founded Christ Church, the first Episcopal ministry in the territory. Ironically his only ordination came from the Methodists, and he seems never to have taken genuine Episcopal orders. But here on this frontier men as often as not assumed the mantle of the Lord merely by declaring themselves to be ministers. Some years later, in 1826, the Protestant Episcopal Diocese of Mississippi was finally organized, with only four parishes and five clergy, a modest start for a denomination that would never really compete with the Baptists and others.[20]

While all the first Protestant ministers in the territory certainly brought conviction and zeal to their labors, none of them thus far brought any official sanction from their organizations back in the East. It remained for the Methodists of South Carolina to accredit the first genuine minister to Mississippi, when, in 1799 they sent Tobias Gibson to investigate the new territory and report on its likelihood as an outpost of the faith. Gibson made the typical journey, overland to Nashville, down the Cumberland to the Ohio, and then on to the Mississippi and thence to Natchez, where he arrived in April. Almost at once he made a circuit of the several towns and villages in the vicinity and selected infant Washington for his first church, which he started with a congregation of four men and four women. Significantly, he also included two slaves in the meeting.

By 1802 Gibson could report that he encompassed eighty-five whites and the same two blacks in his circuit, and each year he rode up the Trace to Tennessee or Kentucky to attend the Western Methodist Conference on their behalf. Gibson's success encouraged the South Carolina Methodists to send the Reverend Moses Floyd to assist him, and in 1803 two more ministers joined them. It proved a daunting routine for these wilderness preachers. They rode almost constantly up and down the Trace, off to the settlements to the east, and only completed a full circuit of their territory once every four to six weeks, often preaching every day. The rigors proved too much for Gibson, who died in 1804, and his passing seriously jeopardized Methodism in the territory for a time. Floyd found a wife whom he married without her parents' consent, which put him in bad stead with the elders. And besides he wanted to move, while another of the preachers fell gravely ill, and the other also wanted to give up his circuit riding. Membership began to dwindle.

The general conference that met in Kentucky in 1804, however, decided not to be deterred by the gloomy prospect in the aftermath of Gibson's death. Instead it appointed two new ministers to take up the itinerant life of the Methodist preacher and sent them south. Along the way they met the charismatic Lorenzo Dow, who took his appointment not from others but from himself, and together they brought Methodism back to the Natchez area. It was a grueling job. "This is the worst country on the continent to get our traveling plan in successful operation," wrote the Reverend Learner Blackman as they got started. He and the other ministers wore themselves out, fell ill, and had no one to spell them when they could not keep appointments for preaching. Worse, he did not find a uniform piety among the different classes in the Southwest. The poor seemed too ignorant to educate in religious matters. The blacks sometimes appeared eager but were dreadfully wicked. And the rich planters "are so rich they are above religion." They preferred their sumptuous living and fine raiment. "I am awfully afraid many of them will never awake to a proper sense of their condition till they see scorching flames all around them burn."[21]

Lurking dangers awaited the Methodists on their constant journeys up and down the Trace, and along its byways leading to the settlements. Occasional bandits threatened to waylay them, and the landscape itself offered more obstacles than any preacher in the settled East had to face. Blackman nearly drowned once at Grindstone Ford as he crossed Bayou Pierre, and concluded from that and other experiences that "Satan had much to do in trying to afflict, drown or otherwise kill the preachers who came to the Territory." Yet the fruits of the peripatetic Methodists were great, by their lights. Francis Asbury himself, the great organizer of the church in America, came to Williamson County, Tennessee, at the northern reach of the Trace, in 1812, and was well pleased with their work. That same year the Tennessee Conference, which had assumed jurisdiction from South Carolina, stepped aside for the formation of the Mississippi Methodist Conference, with membership of 1,067 whites and 240 blacks, a healthy beginning, especially considering that Methodists in general still excited suspicion among many.[22]

At about this time the eastern press observed that "it is indeed true that the Southern and Western States are infested with these fanatics, but we believe the nuisance is decreasing."[23] The persuasiveness and fervor of those itinerants proved the easterners wrong. Numbers continued to grow steadily as they converted believers from a host of other doctrines. People on this frontier could wander rather casually from one faith to another, depending on which had the nearest minister or offered the least line of resistance to glory. In one family the father called himself "a highland or dry-footed Baptist," meaning that he did not believe in total immersion during the baptism. The mother professed Methodism but went to the Baptist church to keep her husband happy. Their son Thomas Griffin had no well-developed feelings until 1808, when he heard one of the itinerants preach. Originally he went to the meeting to taunt the preacher and spread the prevailing rumor that Methodists were false prophets. But when he heard one of them sing a hymn, his flesh trembled. He stayed not to taunt but to listen, even though the camp meeting went on for several days. He went home a convert, bent on heeding the call to preach himself, and he started with his father, no easy task. Yet the elder Griffin gave in eventually, and his son went on to travel to Natchez at the instance of the South Carolina Conference. He went with three others. One would give up and go back east. Another wore himself out on the circuit and died of tuberculosis. The third fell in a swamp one winter and froze to death. Bringing the gospel—of any denomination—called for as much stamina and fortitude as it did piety.[24]

The Presbyterians did not stand far behind the Methodists and Baptists in taking their brand of the word along the dark paths of the old Trace. Indeed, they actually arrived alongside the Methodists when the Reverend Joseph Bullen came from New York in 1799, but his only charge was to act as missionary to the Chickasaw, and he made no attempt to establish his church among the white settlements. That had to wait until the following year, when the Presbyterian General Assembly sent James Hall to Mississippi. He it was who traveled the Trace and other roads and wrote down a "Brief History of the *Mississippi Territory*" as an assessment of the church's prospects there after eight months' investigation. Hall and two others met with Bullen when they passed through Chickasaw country on the Trace, and then passed on to travel hundreds of miles to all of the settlements in the lower territory scouting possible members of future congregations. Here and there they set up places for preaching as forerunners of churches to come at Grindstone Ford, Bayou Pierre, Washington, Natchez, and more. Then they rode back up the Trace once more to make their reports.[25]

Soon after Hall returned to North Carolina, Bullen finished his mission among the Indians and moved to embryonic Uniontown, north of Natchez. By settling there he became the first permanent Presbyterian minister in the territory, and the little Bethel church that he built of logs was thus the first of its denomination in the Southwest when he opened its door in 1804. Bullen preached his gospel there for the next twenty-one years, until his death in 1825, meanwhile taking his message to Natchez and other communities from time to time. In 1816 he helped organize the first Presbytery of Mississippi and acted as its first head, or moderator.

Other permanent Presbyterians followed Bullen. James Smylie came around 1805 to settle in Washington, where he soon organized another church, the territory's third. At the same time, committed to education, he opened a small classical academy, then in 1811 moved south to Amite County, organizing more churches there and across the line in Louisiana until he died in 1853. He it was who rode alone up the Trace in 1814 to a meeting of the Tennessee Presbytery to get them to petition the regional synod in Kentucky to grant Mississippi its own presbytery. For years afterward he served as its secretary.[26]

More followed Smylie, as the Presbyterians applied arguably the best organization to the effort of bringing God to the wilderness. Jacob Rickhow came around 1809 to Natchez, and soon moved on to the "piney woods" country to the east along the Pearl. "You saw him in all his glory," one of his flock wrote of the traveling minister. "In the hot days of August, he was mounted on his grey mare, with solemn pace traversing those long stretches through the piney woods, and with his reproving frown, curbing those young blades that accompanied him. . . . He had the true spirit of a pioneer preacher." After him came William Montgomery, who traveled with Hall ten years before. He settled in Washington, first as an educator, but in 1814 returned to the ministry as pastor of several churches in the vicinity. These Presbyterians had their peculiarities. Rickhow regarded the Sabbath as so holy that he refused to say a blessing over any meal that had been cooked that same day, the work of preparation being a violation of the Sabbath. And Montgomery, an enthusiastic leader of camp meetings, so enjoyed them that when one of his was not going on, he attended the Methodists' and worked just as hard for theirs.[27]

Natchez itself finally got a Presbyterian church in 1817, after a lottery organized to raise five thousand dollars for its construction.[28] Back in 1800 Hall had found some interest in forming one there, but as others observed, the wealthy class simply had other uses for their money and other things on their minds. Some did set a cornerstone in 1812, and three years later the building was largely completed, but it could not be paid for until the lottery, or formally organized. When the congregation did form itself in 1817, it had only nine members, and another nine soon joined, but with eighteen in all in its first days, the Natchez Presbyterian Church, at an expense of five thousand dollars, had to be the costliest house of worship per capita in the territory.[29]

Like all the denominations, the Presbyterians had their share of factional differences and "heresies." When a minister in a church at the other end of the Trace was rumored to be preaching "Campbellite" sophistries to his congregation, a friend sought to advise him of what was being said so that he might "take such a course as his fruitful mind might direct," yet protesting at the same time his own desire to avoid involvement in "as unpleasant a business as some times grow out of these religious controversies."[30] Similar imbroglios swept through the southern part of the Southwest as well, reflecting the turmoil in the mother church. Presbyterians went through this as a result of the great religious revival that swept most of the United States, starting in 1797 and continuing through its zenith in 1800. The heavy demands for more ministers to serve the vast new flock put severe strains on the Presbyteries in Kentucky and Tennessee, and in the latter's ten ministers there was an even split between those who supported the revival and those who opposed it on doctrinal grounds. By 1805 the split between them proved fatal, and the Cumberland Presbytery dissolved. The Anti-Revivalists attached themselves to the Kentucky, or Transylvania, Presbytery. The Revivalists had nowhere to go but determined to remain together, to continue to preach their fervent message. Finally, in 1810, they formed the Cumberland Presbytery once more, but on their own terms, creating a denomination to be called the Cumberland Presbyterian Church, regardless of where its disciples formed their flocks. It grew rapidly, thanks to the residual enthusiasm from the great revival, and like splinter groups from most religions, it saw its best opportunity for survival and flourishing in the sparsely settled new territories. Inevitably it moved south into northern and middle Alabama, along with the settlers who took the Alabama fever, and soon they demanded formal houses of worship. Just which minister first came to them, or when or even where, is lost, but by 1807 the Cumberland Council was ordering a minister to northern Alabama's first real settlement at Hunt's Spring, later Huntsville. The next year there came another, and then another. They began to ride circuit like their Methodist brethren, and to hold camp meetings, Alabama's first being put on by the Reverend Robert Donnell around 1813, with many more to follow. Indeed Donnell seemingly single-handedly spread Cumberland Presbyterianism throughout his territory, founding one church after another. One of his successors, John Morgan, rode a circuit that took him four hundred miles to complete before he had visited all the settlements and isolated country cabins where his flock dwelled and gathered to hear him preach. Wherever a band of "Cumberlands" settled, they soon sent out a request for a minister of their own, one petition alone containing five hundred names. Donnell or Morgan or one of their peers had to go and see to each new congregation.

The Cumberland Presbyterians took a special hold in Alabama, and by 1819 were already preparing to send missions to the Indians to expand their flock among what one called "the tawny sons of the woods." By now their circuits were as wide as any ridden by the Methodists, perhaps wider. In 1821 the Reverend R. D. King and Daniel Patton arrived in Jones Valley in northern Alabama and started to "seek out a people to preach to." They lost no time in forming their circuit, yet found very little encouragement at first, though they rode for six weeks from Jones Valley to Tuscaloosa, then south to Cahaba, then to the eastern border of the territory at Pleasant Hill, on to Selma on the Alabama River, and then north again to Saint Clair. There Patton finally found enough people to make what he called "my first preach." He stood beside a whiskey barrel, set his Bible and prayer book atop the keg, and held forth. King recalled that none of these settlers had seen a Cumberland Presbyterian before they came. "What they heard of us was from our enemies; so we had to fight our way against prejudice and opposition." [31]

Indeed, the opposition to his group reached far and wide, the most substantial religious schism to stir the Southwest. During one of his passes through Cahaba, the state legislature then meeting there asked King to preach to them. There being yet no church, they had him come to the state house itself, as did the other three denominations already represented in the town. Thus each minister had the use of the hall one Sunday a month. On the day appointed for King's first sermon, he was on his way to town when the local Anti-Revivalist Presbyterian preacher went racing past him, and on King's arrival at the state house he found his rival already speaking in full sway even though this was not his Sunday. Then the interloper began a harangue against the Cumberland Presbyterians, their ignorance, and the danger of listening to them. The sergeant at arms of the legislature offered to evict the fellow, but King declined, then commenced his own appointed sermon to a packed house. Apparently the other Presbyterian proved his own worst enemy, for when he came again the following Sunday at the scheduled time for his own service, there was no one in the chamber to listen but his wife.[32]

The Cumberland Presbyterians never took the hold in Mississippi that they did in Alabama, not even forming their first Presbytery until 1832.[33] The difference reflected in part the social and economic lines along with the church divided itself here on the frontier, as elsewhere in the nation. The wealthier or more refined the settler, the less likely he or she was to identify with one of the more fundamental or revivalist churches. The Episcopal church, while small in numbers, almost from the first attracted the landed aristocrats, just as it did in greater numbers east of the Appalachians. Many among the few Roman Catholics remaining were also prosperous, and so, too, the mainline Presbyterians. However, the more remote, the more uneducated, the more impecunious the potential parishioner, the more likely he was to identify with the Baptists or the Methodists or the Cumberland Presbyterians, as well as other smaller sects. In part this may have been because of a cultural heritage that these peoples, mostly Celtic, brought with them from their former homes. A strong Calvinist streak ran through much of the plain folk of the South, exported from across the Atlantic when they emigrated. The uncomplicated message offered by the Baptists, the emotional terms in which it came across, and the uncompromising Almighty they represented, appealed to people living at the edge of civilization. Moreover, the Methodists and the rest were the only denominations that actively took their religion out to the settlements, to the farmer toiling in his remote canebrakes and the hunter buried deep in the impenetrable forests. These preachers did not wait for a flock to find them. True evangelists, they spread their message at the risk of their lives. Often in the places where they took it, theirs was the only message available. Its simple, unsophisticated dogma exactly suited the tastes and needs of a simple and unsophisticated backwoods people: Believe in Jesus. Be baptized. Be saved.[34]

Besides the orthodox denominations, the great unsettled expanse of frontier America naturally attracted more exotic and unconventional sects that found the crowded East and North unsuitable ground for planting their new dogmas. Many moved to the Old Northwest to start their communities in Indiana and Illinois, but not a few came to the Southwest as well. Quakers established a monthly meeting a few miles south of Natchez in 1811. The Disciples of Christ settled on the Mississippi north of Natchez in the early 1830s and saw some spread elsewhere in the state, as did a splinter group from Asbury's church, calling itself the Methodist Protestant Church. Most did not last long before their small numbers worked against them. Having few brethren with whom to associate and worship, they generally gravitated to one of the more conventional faiths, usually the Methodists or Baptists.[35]

Though few of them encountered quite the fate of "the Pilgrims," theirs was not an entirely atypical experience either. The group started in Canada sometime after 1810, motivated by a growing dissatisfaction with all the established churches. They sought a perfect society, and believed they would find it in the Southwest. Selling all their possessions, the small band began to move south, and when passing through Vermont picked up a charismatic leader who styled himself the Prophet, though others thought him a Cromwellian compound of hypocrite and enthusiast. As they passed through New York, their utopian dream helped swell their number to fifty or more and even saw them forming an alliance of sorts with the Shakers for a time, until their practices came into conflict. The Pilgrims eschewed cleanliness and neatness, thinking somehow to reach God by wearing their clothes unwashed until they disintegrated. The more patched and greasy they looked, the less worldly the wearers, and thus the closer to the Almighty. "They made it a point," said Timothy Flint, who encountered them, "to be as ragged and dirty as might be." They may also have practiced a bit of polygyny, whereas the Shakers rejected sex entirely even between husband and wife, let alone with multiple mates.

Not surprisingly the two sects parted less than amicably, and the Pilgrims, carrying their doctrine of filth, promiscuity, and indolence, continued on the road to the New Jerusalem they expected to find in the Southwest. Finally they floated down the Mississippi to New Madrid and there tried to establish themselves on an island in the river. The Prophet ruled them in everything. Every night he had visions that told him what they should do on the following day. They ate mush and milk by sipping it through hollow cane straws from a common trough. They did a variety of penances imposed by the Prophet, from fasting to standing for three or four days without rest. Though still ragged and dirty, they now began to adorn their ragged clothes with stripes denoting each individual's standing within the cult. Then they marched through the settlements, single file, chanting their monotonous song, "Praise God! Praise God! Repent, fast, pray." Invited into homes, they refused to eat the most savory dishes and instead stood motionless as statues, chanting their song and inspiring adults and children alike with a mixture of fear, disgust, and wonder. Their behavior had in it, said Flint, "something imposing to a people, like those of the West, strongly governed by feelings and impressions."

Yet, like most cults, they had within themselves the seeds of their own destruction. The Prophet refused to allow any of the flock to leave, and those who lost their faith or their interest he kept under restraint, though a few did escape. After some time on Pilgrim Island, the malnutrition, the filth of their lifestyle, and the climate itself took a toll, and when people died, the Prophet had a vision that they should not be buried but left to rot on the shores of the island. Travelers passing down the Mississippi on their broadhorns saw the bleaching bones as they floated past. Indignation spread in New Madrid when people heard that the Pilgrims' children were being starved, and the local sheriff and others took a boatload of food to them and held the Prophet and others at bay with swords while the youngsters ate.

Finally, through death and increasing desertion, only the Prophet, two of his wives, and three children remained. Passing Kaintucks, hearing that they had money, robbed them at one point of what was believed to be several thousand dollars kept as proceeds of the sale of their belongings back in Canada, but which remained unspent since they had no use for worldly things. In the end, sickly and destitute, the Prophet took his tiny band south to the mouth of the Arkansas River, just opposite Mississippi. They went in the summer during the fever season, the Prophet declaring that "suffering was a part of their plan." Soon the Prophet himself was too ill even to talk to visitors, and the rest took on the dull, listless aspect that betokened mental and emotional exhaustion. After Flint left them they were heard from no more. "This history of the delusion and destruction of between thirty and forty people, most of them honest and sincere, left a deep and melancholy impression of the universal empire of bigotry," said Flint, "and its fatal influences in all ages and countries." Soon afterward another wild-eyed visionary came down the river preaching largely the same message, and determined that by descending the Mississippi he should reach Asia and find Jerusalem. A large audience turned out to hear him when he preached, some for inspiration and many no doubt just for entertainment. It depressed Flint, who lamented, "Let none think that the age of fanaticism has gone by."[36]

The variety among the ministers and their messages could be innumerable, all reflecting the enduring desire to find perfection, as well as a tendency to think that whatever dogma the believer had, it was not quite the best. "I believe it is the Nature of man never to be satisfied for we have a great Viriety of all sects of ministers here," one backwoods Tennessean wrote as early as 1796. "Anabaptists, Antipedo baptists, Ranting baptist," and something he called "Hell Redemptioners" all vied for souls, "so that we have no need of no more soarts minister hear."[37] Nothing so stimulated—or symbolized—this vitality of variety, and what appeared to some to be a resort to fanaticism, quite like the camp meeting, "those great parades and sacramental seasons, those extraordinary exercises of falling down, rolling, shouting, jerking, dancing, barking," as one Baptist recalled.[38]

A mid-nineteenth-century map by the Natchez scientist B. L C. Wailes, showing the
Old Southwest as it appeared when it was the British province of West Florida.
(Natchez Trace Collection, Center for American History, University of Texas)

Natchez and Fort Rosalie as they appeared in the early 1700s. *(David G. Sansing, Sim C. Callon, and Carolyn Vance Smith,* Natchez: An Illustrated History, *1992)*

How the immigrants reached the wilderness: A flatboat on the Mississippi. *(Samuel A. Drake,* The Making of the Great West, *1851)*

An imaginative depiction of the
great New Madrid earthquake,
which forever changed the face
of the Southwest. *(Henry Howe,*
The Great West, *1851)*

The keelboat, early and colorful commercial transportation down the rivers, and laboriously back up them. (Harper's New Monthly Magazine, *1855)*

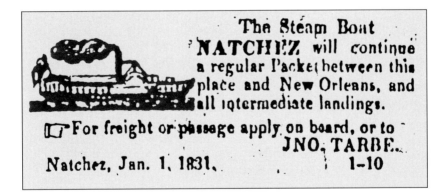

The coming of the steamboat changed transportation dramatically, and the history of the wilderness with it. (*Natchez,* Mississippi Free Trader)

The stagecoach connected the few
cities and frontier communities
with mail and passenger service by
the 1820s. *(Basil Hall,* Forty Etchings from Sketches Made with the
Camera Lucida in North America
in 1827 and 1828, *1829)*

Wealth came to the region in cotton once it could be ginned quickly
and baled, as shown here at a cotton press. *(Library of Congress)*

As keelboats brought more and
more consumer goods into the Southwest, retailers advertised "Groceries
and Liquors, of the best quality."
(Pittsburgh Directory of 1819)

The coming of steam attracted many an entrepreneur to invest in the region's own vessels to free them of dependence on Northern shippers. The Natchez Steam Boat Company issued shares at $10 each. *(Natchez Trace Collection, Center for American History, University of Texas)*

Natchez Steam Boat Company.

NO. 44

THESE ARE TO CERTIFY, That *~~~* do — hold and *~~~* entitled to *Fifty* — Shares in the Stock of the President, Directors and Company of the " NATCHEZ STEAM BOAT COMPANY," from No. *633* to No. *682* inclusive; and hath paid thereon the sum of *Ten* — Dollars, on each Share.—The further sum of *Fifteen* — Dollars on each Share remains to be paid on or before the *1st* day of *January* next; and the further sum of *Seventy five dolls.* on each Share remains to be paid at such periods thereafter as shall be prescribed by the President and Directors, due notice whereof shall be publicly given; and on payment of the said installments on the days respectively limited, each Share shall be entitled to an equal proportion of the quarterly or half yearly dividend that may be declared by the President and Directors.—No transfer to take effect, until entered on the books of the Company, on the return of this Certificate.

Natchez, *tenth* day of *~~~* 1818

The beginnings of rough frontier community: Basil Hall sketched the new little town of Columbus, Georgia, in 1828. *(Basil Hall,* Forty Etchings from Sketches made with the Camera Lucida in North America in 1827 and 1828, *1829)*

Part of the glue that held family and community together—the pioneer woman. A silhouette of Ann Hutchins, wife of the fiery and erratic Anthony Hutchins. *(Courtesy of Dorothy Breckinridge)*

Frolic was where they found it, and Natchez had many gay ballroom parties like this one, sketched in 1830 by Charles A. Le Sueur. *(Scharff Collection, Natchez Historical Society)*

Slavery played a small but important domestic role, as with this servant grinding corn in a "hominy block." *(Library of Congress)*

A crude early woodcut of Jefferson College in Washington, Mississippi, showed the region's burgeoning attempts to address education. *(Mississippi Department of Archives and History, Jackson)*

John James Audubon, briefly a teacher at Elizabeth Female Academy in Washington and later a tutor elsewhere in the region. (*Mississippi Department of Archives and History, Jackson*)

The camp meeting—part circus, part revival, part hysteria—brought religion to the scattered peoples along the Trace. *(New-York Historical Society)*

The quaint, eccentric man of God, Lorenzo Dow, who covered the Trace time after time in search of souls. *(Library of Congress)*

Lorenzo's long-suffering and equally eccentric wife, Peggy Dow. *(Peggy Dow, Vicissitudes; or the Journey of Life)*

A center for sin: Natchez Under-the-Hill, sketched by a visiting Frenchman in 1817. *(Scharff Collection, Natchez Historical Society)*

Idle time demanded sport, and horse racing early became a passion with the Natcheans. (Mississippi Herald and Natchez City Gazette)

Crime and violence, though their prevalence was greatly exaggerated, still lurked along the wilderness roads, as in this woodcut of highwayman Joseph Hare robbing travelers on the Federal Road. *(New York Public Library)*

Lurid stories made a criminal hero of the almost pathetic John Murrell, shown here disposing of one of his fictitious victims. *(Virgil Stewart,* A History of the Detection, Conviction, Life and Designs of John A. Murel, the Great Western Land Pirate, *1835)*

The archetypal frontier character and hero, David Crockett of Tennessee, half legend, half reality, a perpetual opportunist. *(Tennessee Historical Society, Knoxville)*

A fictitious Crockett exploit, showing the character of the rowdy frontiersmen at their "fun." (Crockett Almanac, *1841)*

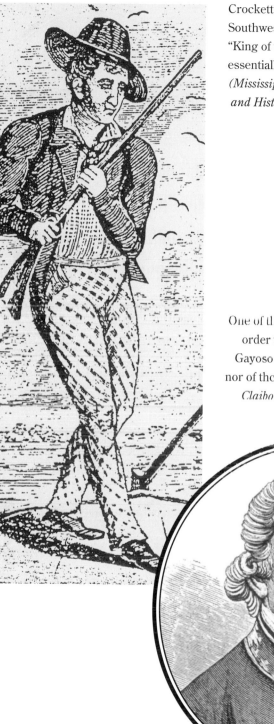

Crockett's rival for status as premier Southwestern folk hero was Mike Fink, "King of the Rivermen," a bold, brutal, essentially irresponsible roustabout. *(Mississippi Department of Archives and History, Jackson)*

One of the first to attempt to bring true order to the raw wilderness, Manuel Gayoso de Lemos, last Spanish governor of the Natchez territory. *(John F. H. Claiborne, Mississippi as a Province, Territory and State, 1880)*

David Holmes, early governor of the Mississippi Territory, and friend of Jefferson, who helped spread Jeffersonian politics to the frontier. *(John F. H. Claiborne,* Mississippi as a Province, Territory and State, *1880)*

Greenwood Le Fleur, mixed-breed Choctaw leader who agreed to the Treaty of Dancing Rabbit Creek, which ensured the removal of his people west of the Mississippi. *(John F. H. Claiborne,* Mississippi as a Province, Territory and State, *1880)*

The rough frontiersman made president by the Old Southwest. Andrew Jackson as his countrymen saw him in 1817. *(John Reid and John Henry Eaton,* The Life of Andrew Jackson, *1817)*

The camp meeting came about when the circuit rider gathered enough prospects to form an audience and then persuaded them to come. The established churches also put them on from time to time, especially during periods of revival like the great movement of 1799–1803. People attended out of a host of impulses, partly religious, partly social. After all, any gathering that brought several score—perhaps hundreds—of settlers together offered a welcome break from the routine of daily labor. A farmer and his family might not be able to give themselves a rest because of a holiday other than Christmas, but an assembly doing the Lord's work gave an acceptable excuse to leave the fields for a few days, especially since it brought them together with others for some brief society and community. Everyone took food for themselves and to share. Those with musical instruments carried them along. All ages and sexes gathered beside a creek or river, or in a rude schoolhouse as at Elyton, Alabama, for its first camp meeting in 1824. Those who could slept under tents or in their wagons or simply beneath the stars.[39]

All day long, day after day, the preachers exhorted, as Rev. King did at Goshen Church in 1810, on the northern fringe of the Trace country in Tennessee. Just ten years earlier, in Kentucky, the first camp meeting ever had been held, and now King's Cumberland Presbyterians, like the Methodists and Baptists and others, adopted the inspiring assembly wholeheartedly. Those that encouraged their organizers became yearly events, with people traveling two and three "sleeps" to get there, and at Goshen the ritual became so entrenched that men built special cabins to house the annual visitors. The meetings themselves, however, took place out of doors, or under arbors to shade worshipers from the sun.

Beforehand the host families held "preparation day," when the men and boys hauled wagons loaded with straw to the site, cleared the meeting area, and perhaps erected pews from the nearby church, if there was one. Their women meanwhile baked the special bread used for the sacrament, prepared the wine, and polished their best pewter service for the ceremonies. Then, of course, they attended to the more social needs of the affair. "No better food or richer could be produced," recalled one who spent his boyhood near the Goshen meeting. "Baked ham, fried chicken, and a choice lamb, which was saved to kill for the August meeting. Cakes, pies, sweet pickles, salt-rising bread."

On the appointed day the people gathered in the morning, and around eleven o'clock the preacher in his black coat strode to the pulpit, Bible in one hand and a pitcher of water in the other. He prayed. They sang. He prayed again. They read a text. And then the sermon commenced. "As the sermon progressed the solemnity grew oppressive," said one witness to its majesty:

> The mighty power of God rested like a weight upon the people. Men almost held their breath. The preacher felt it as well as the others. By and by the solemnity grew so great that even the preacher's tongue was silent. He stood for a moment with looks of unutterable awe, and then went down from the pulpit and started to the woods. When he had gone about a hundred yards, he turned abruptly back, and entered the pulpit. There was no longer any look of awe, but a holy rapturous light on his face, and he resumed his sermon with a thrilling power which swept everything before it.

When he finished, he read again the text for the day, and the audience replied with hearty amens. Then came the communion.

That was only the first sermon. On into the afternoon they would go, more preachers rising to speak, the sermonizing often broken only by meals and hymns. Soon the converted began to come forward, announcing that they saw the light of the Lord and desired baptism. Forty, fifty, eighty, a hundred or more might seek the rite, most of them being led to the riverbank for complete immersion in the soul-cleansing waters of the stream.[40] Even as late as 1833, long after the great revival, the camp meeting held on as a part of backwoods culture and belief. In Maryville, Tennessee, on the fringe of the Appalachians, revival meetings took place every day of the week, with sermons three times a day.[41]

Some, caught in the enthusiasm, inspiration, or consuming revelation of the event, were left speechless. Instead they manifested the presence of the spirit in bizarre and often alarming ways that moved some witnesses and disturbed others. During the 1824 Elyton meeting, one man noted that in addition to a number of conversions "I saw two or three persons having 'jerks.'"[42] The more conservative and staid denominations, like the Catholics and Episcopalians, looked askance at such actions, regarding them as more properly the province of the Methodists and Presbyterians and some of their splinter groups, like the "New Lights" and the "Schismatics."

"These strange expressions of zeal," wrote a Baptist, "which have made so much noise abroad, came in at the close of the revival, and were in the judgment of many, the chaff of the work." The Methodists seemed to accept such convulsions as genuine, but the Anti-Revivalist Presbyterians strongly opposed them. They could not stop the frenzy, however. At one grand meeting of several thousand, spectators believed—no doubt with some exaggeration—that eight hundred people fell down in writhing. Then there was the "rolling exercise," in which the spirit moved a person to fall down violently, rolling over and over across the ground like a log. "The rolling disciples often met with mud in their way," observed a skeptical witness, "and got up from their devotions in a sorrowful plight." Others danced, even though their preachers condemned dance itself as sinful, and defended themselves by citing David's dancing before the Ark of the Covenant.

But nothing so characterized the revival phenomenon as the "jerks." It started with a backward-forward, then side-to-side jolting of the head. The subject tried to stop it but could not, and the harder he tried, the more he twitched and staggered. Soon it spread to the rest of his body, and before long he cast himself about uncontrollably in every direction, ran into trees, flopped to the ground, and hopped around, head and limbs jerking violently "as if they must inevitably fly asunder." Spectators marveled that the celebrants did not injure themselves, and undoubtedly some did. Women's kerchiefs and other headgear inevitably flew off unnoticed.

"There was something altogether unaccountable in this jerking exercise," wrote one. Initially only people suffering a serious religious conversion seemed to fall prey to it, but in time they communicated it to others. In one instance a Presbyterian of the Anti-Revivalist school felt concern that the jerking had seized a neighboring congregation and went to try to save them from the hysteria. But when he talked with the afflicted, he himself began to convulse, and then when he went back to his own congregation, he seemingly spread the phenomenon to them as well. Some thought that the worst sinners were most likely to be affected, and some of the wicked were heard to curse and damn the convulsions even as they writhed. A man about to enjoy a whiskey at his tavern suddenly found his hand tossing the drink over his head. Another gambling at poker uncontrollably flung his cards from the table. Yet sober observers among the Baptists, anyhow, maintained that the jerks proved to be a curse rather than a blessing. "None were benefitted by them," complained one. "They left sinners without reformation, and Christians without advantage." When a jerker suddenly commenced his convulsions in the church of a Baptist minister in West Tennessee, the preacher shouted loudly: "In the name of the Lord, I command all unclean spirits to leave this place." The jerker fell still and silent, confirmation in the minds of many that, rather than being holy, the jerks were the dances of the devil. Some continued jerking periodically long after the great revival itself waned, and one skeptic wrote years later, "I know not as they have got over jerking yet."

Then there were the "barks." Seized by the spirit, the victim crouched on all fours like a dog or a wolf, crawled about the ground, growled, snarled and snapped his jaws, and barked and howled continuously. Sometimes they jerked while at it, combining both common forms of possession, yet many suspected the barking, at least, to be nothing more than an affectation. One parson heard a whole crowd of people on their way to a meeting "barking like a flock of spaniels" in rehearsal. When they reached the camp, however, one after another seemingly took up the barks spontaneously, rushed about howling and foaming, and severely disturbed the peace of mind—and just the peace—of their more sober brethren. While mature clerics could see that some truly seemed possessed by a captivating force while in their throes, they concluded, like one Baptist divine, that "dancing, barking, rolling, shouting, and so on, were undoubtedly, for the most part, works of choice and imitation, which were hypocritically played off by a set of deluded, mistaken people." Ministers who condemned such behavior seemed to be troubled by it very little in their congregations. Those who condoned or encouraged the manifestations saw a consequent rise in their incidence.[43]

In the face of these peculiarities it is no wonder that eastern observers looked askance at both the people who practiced such eruptions, and at the clergy who encouraged or at least condoned them. "Holy Willies," one skeptic called the Presbyterians.[44] Yet less than a decade after the waning of the great revival, natural events rekindled its flames, confirming the predictions of some that the end was near. When the great New Madrid Earthquake commenced its shocks in December 1811, people remembered the comet that had been seen in the skies a few months earlier, and saw a connection and the hand of God in both events. "It was a time of great terror to sinners," recalled a survivor. The landslides on riverbanks made people mindful of their own "back-sliding" into sin, and everywhere people flocked to churches and camp meetings, or begged the preachers of all denominations to come and save their souls. The Methodists alone experienced a massive surge of 50 percent in membership in the territory, and some preachers of other denominations were quick to capitalize on the bonanza. The Reverend James Finley happened by pure chance to be in a cabin full of rough and unrepentant frontier types when one of the great tremors hit. As the others fell to the ground in terror, he thought quickly and leaped on a table, shouting, "For the great day of His wrath is come, and who shall be able to stand?" Who could doubt that the Lord was in touch with Finley at that moment, even as he set the earth to trembling in his anger at human sin?![45]

Happily for God and man alike, the excesses of preachers and their sometimes excitable flocks lay outside the mainstream of religious life along the Trace and throughout the Southwest. The men of the cloth christened and baptized the newborn, blessed the union of the betrothed, and saw the deceased off into eternity, and therein lay the major substance of their ministries. Matrimony especially brought out the happiness in the backwoods community, as well as some of its ingenuity. Along the Tombigbee and Tensaw, in the early years before the first ministers came, young couples could not wait for the irregular and often distant visits of the circuit preacher. Instead they simply paired off and took up housekeeping together, while promising that they would observe a formal ceremony as soon as possible. One such union passed between Daniel Johnson and Elizabeth Linder in 1800. On Christmas Night they and a large party of others gathered for a frolic, and then this couple, along with several other matrimonial hopefuls, stole out of the party, boarded canoes, and paddled down the Tensaw to the Alabama, and then on to Fort Stoddert, arriving just before dawn. There they awakened the commandant, assuming that a fort's commander, like a ship's captain, had certain nuptial powers. Thanks to a free flow of holiday eggnog and hearty persuasion from the young people, the captain overcame his doubts as to his authority and finally pronounced them men and wives. "Go home!" he told them. "Behave yourselves—multiply and replenish the Tensaw country!"[46]

In many of the communities along the Trace weddings took place on Thursday evenings, several couples sometimes uniting at a time.[47] Out in the pine country the families sent for fiddlers to provide music for the dance and revels to follow, and almost everyone knew the story of the couple who said their vows and then commenced the party afterward, with the fiddler yet to appear. As they drank a "horn" or two of whiskey, and then another, the young people ranged around the rooms in the house gradually settled into chairs or on the floor, still waiting. Then came the supper, adding the soporific of bulging stomachs to the spirits already imbibed. Someone yawned, the bride dozed, and a hardy few of the young men actually tried dancing a little "pigeon wing" without music, but the fiddler's absence proved by now an embarrassment. "A wedding without the fiddler was scarcely considered legal," complained a Mississippian. In the end they went out looking for the fellow, but on the way they came to an abandoned house near which they heard an infernal howling of wolves. At first the sound of the animals made the more superstitious—or more inebriated—

think that the devil lay within. Then they heard coming from inside the building a brisk, saucy music. Some feared that Old Scratch himself was in there amusing himself and refused to go farther. Finally the layman who performed the wedding strode forward, resolutely reciting the only godly words he could think of to ward off the Evil One—"Dearly Beloved," and so on. But his recitation of the matrimonial ceremony only made the wolves howl the louder and the devilish fiddling the more frenzied. Finally the men all broke in terror, rode back to the rest of their friends, and spent the rest of the night praying for protection. Only daylight got a few to ride back to the scene of the night's horror, and there in the rafters of the old house they found, not Satan, but old John the Fiddler, still clinging to his perch to avoid the wolves and fiddling to keep himself awake.[48]

Most weddings, however, went off without such complications. "Your Marriage pre-sented a pleasant scene," the Reverend Thomas Rodney wrote to William Dunbar's daughter after he bound her in matrimony at Washington in 1805. "The Ladies appeared, I will not say, like a band of Sirens, but like a Choir of Seraphs just descended from above. Their Music and Charms were Enchanting and spread blissful pleasure around." He lamented that the Forest had not been fully decorated with flowers throughout, that it might the more resemble the Garden of Eden where Adam and Eve joined hands and lives, but still the occasion was joyous. Nevertheless he reminded all the young ladies present that "tho they appeared like a Choir of Cherubims and perhaps hereafter may be such, yet that at present they ar Mortals and are only sent here a while to beautify adorn and replenish the Earth—Therefore I wish them all happy Matches and as soon as they please."[49]

Of course, everyone hoped for "happy Matches," pairings like that between the rising young Andrew Jackson and Rachael Donelson, who married near Natchez, then traveled up the Trace on their honeymoon return to Tennessee. But some unions commenced ill starred, and others inevitably went sour despite all that gods and men could do. When that happened, like as not, it was the wife who suffered the greater burden, for hers was the duty to obey and endure in what was undeniably a man's world. In 1801 Joseph Willis of Natchez published the intransigence of his wife, Sarah, in the local press and warned all that because of her "disobedience and ill conduct" he would not honor any debts incurred by her.

Furthermore, he admonished any and all not to give her aid or to assist her in leaving the territory until "she would again be a dutiful wife."[50] A few years later, while selling his Natchez tavern, after their matrimonial disagreements became public, John Walton forbade anyone from "harboring or supporting in any shape" his wife, Phalby.[51] And when man and wife reached a complete impasse, divorce, though difficult, remained a final option. John and Sarah Burns divorced in 1806 thanks to "unhappy differences." He gave her a settlement of a mare, a colt and saddle, their household furniture, beds and bedclothes, and a yearly income of "three sous," though the value of the French money by then was arguable, and in any case it was little enough to live on. He took their son, and she their two daughters, and he acknowledged thereafter her right to live apart from him.[52] Similar articles of separation passed between Phillip Brill and his wife, Mary, by which he awarded her a part of his estate "for her future support and maintenance." That done, Brill notified Natchez publicly that henceforth he accepted no responsibility for any debts "which she may contract on my account whatever."[53]

Thanks to the general paucity of ordained ministers, people stood little on ceremony when it came to choosing officiating clergy at their weddings and funerals. If Methodists could not find one of their own when needed, a Baptist would do, or even a Presbyterian. In fact, despite their doctrinal differences and their frequent virulent diatribes against one another's heresies, most of the denominations cooperated in some degree. Washington hosted in 1817 a "Religious Convention of Christian Denominations," dedicated to working together to improve public morals, regardless of creed. Some churches formed loose partnerships with local Masonic lodges to build mutual meetinghouses, and when one congregation could no longer maintain a school's funding, it sometimes turned it over to another faith better prepared to do so. Baptists and Presbyterians let Methodists use their meetinghouses when they did not have their own, and occasionally a prominent member of one church lent his organizational skills to the founding of another of a different denomination. But none would have been foolish enough to mistake such interdisciplinary generosity for a relaxation of internal adherence to dogma. The Methodist who strayed could expect swift and public judgment. Drinking, drunkenness, profanity, adultery, and a number of other transgressions, including marrying outside the faith, all could lead to excommunication. When a man named Abram stood accused of adultery, his argument before his judges, that "he believed, there was none of the male members of Antioch Church, but what was guilty of the same act," did him little good. Ministers did not stand above judgment either. Theodore Clapp, Presbyterian pastor in

New Orleans, found himself charged with heresy when he questioned church orthodoxy, and after a grueling trial his order deposed him humiliatingly.[54]

As a rule these conservative Christians did not welcome change, in whatever manner it came. Methodist ministers continued to wear eighteenth-century clerical garb well into the 1820s and later, despite its becoming radically out of fashion. Use of musical instruments in services to accompany the hymns also met with some resistance. While the Episcopal church in Natchez proudly installed a new organ in 1827, essaying to present Handel's *Messiah* that Easter, the Methodists continued even through the 1830s to regard any instrument as a threat to the "spirituality" of singing. In one church the only thing the pastor would allow was a tuning fork to give his people their starting pitch.[55] Then there was the matter of preachers straying outside their calling. On this frontier men invariably talked politics when they gathered, and men of the cloth were, after all, men too. "Preachers are still citizens," argued one observer. "I do not deny their right, in common with others, to discuss politics."[56] Yet not all felt quite so tolerant, thinking that a holy man should be above temporal concerns. William Winans declared that when his friend and fellow preacher Roswell Valentine took up politics he "lost much of his religious integrity, if he did not make 'shipwreck of faith and good conscience.'" Indeed, Winans asserted sadly, "How few Christians there are that can involve themselves in political pursuits, and maintain their integrity as Christians." They were interesting thoughts from a minister who himself identified with the Whig party and made a bid for Congress only a few years before he wrote this.[57]

Spreading the message always presented a challenge, and few could look hopefully to the bizarre expedient used by one preacher in young Montgomery, Alabama, when he caught goats, stuck religious tracts on each horn, and then drove them out into the town streets.[58] All these servants of the same God sought to expand their flocks, and but only for the Catholics, they sent men rather than goats out into the wilderness to carry the word. Some outside groups sent agents occasionally, as with the American Bible Society, which kept a man on horseback up and down the Trace almost constantly.[59] But evangelism of this sort was chiefly the domain of the Methodists and the Presbyterians.

None excelled William Winans, the second Methodist missionary in the Southwest, who came in 1810 with serious apprehensions about his success. From what he heard, he expected the inhabitants to be "a mongrel race, compounded of French, Spanish and Negro, with a slight sprinkling of Anglo-Saxon ruffians and outlaws," he recalled, "illiterate and profligate." The climate itself was reported to be a killer, and Winans accepted his assignment, as he said, with "little expectation of living through so protracted a residence in such a region of pestilence and death." He left his home in Kentucky in tears.[60]

On November 23 Winans and a companion departed Nashville on the Trace, bound for Natchez. Their trip was a tale of one mishap after another, lost horses, cheating stand keepers, and cold nights without a campfire. Yet Winans preached his first sermon at Folsom's stand, with the Folsoms and their slaves in silent but respectful attendance. After twenty-seven days on the Trace, Winans finally emerged from the Choctaw country and at last encountered white settlements, and happily his first hosts proved to be Methodists. When he reached Port Gibson on Bayou Pierre, he stayed some days with another family and promptly fell in love. Only with reluctance did he tear himself from the young lady when he remembered why he had come. He set off to Clark's Creek to conduct his first real meeting, and then on New Year's Day, 1811, began to ride the wide circuit assigned him. Almost every day he preached, or if not preaching he rode to his next meeting. He encountered a number of the local preachers, most of them self-appointed, many illiterate. Thus he found the frequent meetings at which several of them preached most helpful, for the ignorant among them learned from those like himself with some education. Equally to the point, the announcement of several men holding forth brought a larger crowd to attend. "This was an important point," he said, "in a country where grown-up persons were to be found who never heard a Gospel-Sermon." It was easier to move men and women when they stood in large crowds and could be influenced by mass emotion than it was to persuade them one by one. "Sympathy and example have great influence, whether for good or evil, in moving the minds of men," Winans observed, and anything that would "most successfully conduce to the accomplishment of these purposes must be not only unblamable but laudable." It was a neat rationalization to excuse Winans's use of crowd psychology, a use made by every circuit preacher in the Southwest if he had the ability.

But evangelizing at such meetings on the circuit carried with it pitfalls, and Winans saw them. Seeing their power over the crowds, and especially witnessing the effects that exaggerated behavior and hyperbolic oratory could have, he observed some preachers getting carried away with "extraordinary display" and noted that some came to rely almost exclusively on such demonstrations, abandoning the old Methodist principles of calm discussion, sober prayer meetings, and humility.[61]

It was the beginning of forty-seven years that Winans would spend preaching in the Southwest, a time of service unsurpassed by any of the other messengers of the gospel who came down the Trace. At first he found "small and cadaverous" congregations at his stops, some communities seemingly ravaged by the seasonal fevers or "the murderous system of medical practice." He baptized and christened. He performed his first marriage, noting that the lady involved enjoyed just about the most infinitesimal quotient of beauty of "any Lady whom I ever served in the character of a Bride." Making matters worse, her marriage license had been obtained in Mississippi, but on the day of the ceremony bad weather made her fearful to cross the rough great river from her home on the Louisiana side. Winans steadfastly refused to perform the ceremony at her home, which would have been unlawful, and in the end they settled for the expedient of putting bride, groom, and parson in a boat and paddling across the torrent into the partial shelter of a bayou, where Winans made them man and wife, all standing in the boat rendered motionless by the bridal party's holding one another with one hand and holding willow branches overhanging from the bank with the other.

Like many a sincere man of the cloth, Winans faced a time of self-doubt early in his circuit days: "The word failed to take hold in the heart of my hearers," he lamented. He questioned his penchant for humor. He wondered if his frequent infatuation with young women distracted his full attention from his mission. In the end he concluded during a camp meeting that he simply was not "sufficiently spiritual nor sufficiently zealous in the good cause, of glorifying God, in saving souls." No one seemed moved by his preaching for a day or two. But then on Sunday night the men and women at the meeting divided and went off into the forest to pray and "wrestle with God" on their own. Soon a cry came from the women's group, and the men rushed over to them through the trees to discover that somehow a revelation had come to the ladies. They had shouted for joy. Winans gained twenty-five conversions that night, and regained as well his self-confidence. In the weeks that followed he seemed to stimulate more "awakenings." Indeed he became so exhilarated by his success that he worked and preached incessantly until midnight and beyond and nearly died of exhaustion and fever.[62]

If few could match Winans's years of dedicated service, others, like the Presbyterian evangelist Henry Bryson, certainly tried. In December 1826 the Presbytery of South Carolina sent him off into the wilderness to preach to Alabama, and he came, as did so many others, by way of Tennessee, then south through Jones Valley and on down toward Selma. The journey alone almost defeated him. "I feel considerably depressed in spirits," he wrote in his diary one night. "O the fortitude, perseverance, and resignation that a missionary of the cross of Christ needs. Had not God given them many great and exceeding precious promises for to rely on they would certainly shrink back from the undertaking."[63]

But he did not shrink, and his resolution held. Showing the kind of tolerance that characterized most frontier preachers, he traveled in company with a Baptist for a time and spoke to a group of Cumberland Presbyterians near Chattanooga. It was nearly New Year's when he finally reached the first appointed stop on his circuit, Fayetteville, Tennessee, only a handful of miles above the Alabama line. In the coldest weather he ever experienced, he preached day after day. Equally disconcerting, having no home of his own, he was taken away every night to lodge by a different member of the local congregation. Then he had a tooth pulled and spent several days more visiting before January 29, when the congregation gathered to see him off across the Alabama line to start his mission.

His first experience hardly proved encouraging. The second day out he preached at Ditto's Landing on the Tennessee "to almost the empty walls." "There are a great number of people here in this little town," he found, "but they are a most desperately wicked, disapated people." While he preached indoors, he heard some of the townspeople standing outside talking loudly, even swearing. "I thought it was high time for me to be traveling." Happily, the next night out in Blountsville he found a polite, attentive group of listeners and felt his confidence somewhat restored.

Bryson's were the experiences common to all circuit riders. Like Winans, he nearly lost his life more than once just in swimming his horse across swollen creeks in the rainy season. He sat up all night shivering in the wet and cold beside a puny campfire, or accepted the charity of any who would let him lodge for the night. To buy what he needed he had to depend on what listeners at his sermons chose to give him—if anything. More than once, after a day's preaching, he wrote in his diary that he left with "nothing for my labours." During the months that followed he rode the entire length of Alabama, finally crossing the Chattahoochee into southern Georgia, and then on to West Florida. "There are not many who care about religion of any kind," was his conclusion of much of the ground he covered.[64]

The experience of the missionaries sent to the Indian nations could be just as frustrating, and added to that was the uncertainty that the natives really understood what was happening when they agreed to be baptized and accept the white man's god. Joseph Bullen took the word of Presbyterianism into the Chickasaw country in 1799 and remained there almost continuously for the next four years, chiefly in the vicinity of Tupelo on the old Trace. He seemed ill suited to the task in some ways. An acquaintance described him as "a man of great simplicity of manners, and wonderfully ignorant of all established modes." Indeed, Bullen seemed to annoy some people with incessant curiosity about their lives and affairs, and when one wearied of the interrogation and started to question Bullen in turn, he discovered from the missionary's answers that Bullen had led "a life as little chequered by incident as can be conceived."[65]

When Bullen preached listeners found him sincere but undynamic, "more 'a son of consolation than a son of thunder.'" Perhaps that is partially why his mission failed. More to the point, the Presbyterians and Bullen tried to deal with the Chickasaw as they would have with whites. Laboriously Bullen talked dogma and doctrine to the Indians. Worse, he did not speak their language, and so worked through an interpreter. And he failed utterly to grasp not only the mind-set of the Chickasaw themselves but also the psychology of aboriginal peoples in general. Religion meant something to them, to be sure, but it did not stand alone in their culture. It was a part of it, and to convince them that the white man's god was a better one than theirs, he needed to persuade them that the white man's life in general was superior: Lead them to adopt the ways and practices of western civilization, and they would naturally tend to adopt its religious life as well. Bullen never understood that, nor did most of the other early missionaries who tried to convert these men of the forests.[66]

Bullen found the Chickasaw "poor but kind" when he reached Long Town, one of their larger villages beside the Trace. Soon he met with Levi Colbert and told him of his mission, and in fact started the work of conversion by trying to explain to him the story of Genesis. It proved slow going. "Close application does not consist with their indolent habits," Bullen mused. Moreover, noting with naive hypocrisy that they did everything from mounting a horse to writing in ways opposite to the whites', he concluded that "they are a left-handed people," meaning more than just which hand they favored. Another obstacle met him when Malcolm McGee, his interpreter, proved to be utterly ignorant of the Scriptures, and Bullen had first to instruct him before he could even begin to translate for the Chickasaw what the missionary said. At that, McGee said Bullen really ought to see John McIntosh at Tockshish. He would exert more influence with the Indians. So Bullen went to McIntosh, only to find that he thought the idea of converting the red men ridiculous. "God is able to make them good Christians," Bullen replied. "We wish for the honour of being workers together with God."

McIntosh at length agreed to translate for Bullen, and soon a fair number of Chickasaw came to Tockshish out of curiosity to hear the wonderful stories that Bullen related from the testaments. In the main they seemed impressed, but when they raised simple questions such as why a god that did only good would make bad things like the rattlesnakes that bit them, or the terrible thunder and lightning that destroyed trees and even men, Bullen's response—with the catchall rationalization that men could hardly understand the Almighty's mysterious workings—left them unsatisfied and bewildered.

Still Bullen, in his innocence, thought that he was making great progress. "It was a happy season," he wrote after only a few weeks with the Chickasaw. "The parade of a royal palace would be nothing to it." But almost the day after he wrote those words, he began to feel discouragement. He wanted to talk with the whole Chickasaw nation, or all its leaders, perhaps thinking that, as with the conversion of Constantine, if he could win over all the chiefs, their people would automatically follow. "We even think of leaving the nation," he confessed.

Thereafter it proceeded thus. One day Bullen felt optimistic and the next the opposite. Finally on June 27 he got his big meeting with the people of a chief named Wolf's Friend. They seemed attentive—Bullen always found his listeners attentive, though he mistook interest and politeness for the beginnings of spiritual awakening. He found a rude awakening of his own when he took his message on to the Cherokee in the northeast of the territory, and discovered that they scarcely even pretended to listen to him.[67]

Later missionaries would have much more success than Bullen, when they established schools and brought new tools and farming techniques, essentially converting the Indian way of life and not just its religion. The missions came in time to be not just itinerant preachers but whole establishments, placed by the indulgence of the Chickasaw and Choctaw chiefs on Indian lands. Missionaries would live in large log homes, with small libraries for use in teaching the children English reading and writing. Storage sheds nearby held the produce that the whites themselves raised, and that their pupils and converts brought them as gifts, and not far off sat the schoolhouse itself, the most powerful weapon in the missionary's arsenal.[68]

Of all the men who mounted their horses and set off down the Trace to bring God to red men and white alike, none was more colorful or better remembered than the eccentric Methodist Lorenzo Dow. In fact, he covered virtually all of the territory of the United States in his peripatetic life, from New England to the Louisiana Territory, but his journeys through the Old Southwest left an especially indelible impression. He called himself "Cosmopolite," thanks to all the ground he covered, but others not infrequently referred to him as "Crazy Dow." He wore a long black coat, let his beard grow wild and untrimmed, and allowed his hair to match. He approached his camp meetings with not a scruple. The concerns of Winans and others about what was proper in the service of the Lord troubled him not one whit. At some of his meetings he paid slave boys to hide in the trees and start screaming on cue when he wanted his sermon to raise emotions.[69] One year he would preach under a specific tree, then announce that a year hence, to the day, he would speak again under that very same timber—and he did. When asked his age he invariably gave it not in years from the date of his birth, but from the day of his accepting Methodism. On September 3, 1804, he married an equally peculiar woman, Peggy, and then the very next morning left her for an eight-month trip through the Mississippi Territory.

"I went to the Natchez country where I found religion low," said Dow, "and had hard times, but thought this country one day would be the garden of America."[70] Everywhere he preached he saw potential, and unlike others was content to wait for his seeds to grow. "The fruit I expect to see at a future day," he would say. His prudence in not expecting immediate results showed itself in Natchez. On a visit in 1803 he encountered almost total indifference, leading him to conclude glumly that there were not three Christians in the place. But on his return in November 1804, he arrived coincidentally just as a newspaper editor was about to print a burlesque of Dow that had appeared in some of the eastern press. It ran in the same issue as a notice inserted by Dow announcing his forthcoming camp meeting. The result of the juxtaposition brought out the curious by scores for three successive Sundays and some weekdays besides. "Give the devil rope enough and he will hang himself," concluded Dow.[71] The devil meant a lot to Lorenzo Dow. Sometimes when planning a camp meeting, he actually announced at the top of his lungs that he had just received the latest bulletins from Hades and would make them public in his exhortation. That got a crowd.[72]

Considering the oddity of the man, it is interesting that he was not a great believer in the "jerks" and some of the other violent manifestations of revival feeling, yet he tolerated them and felt that there might be some divine presence connected with them. At a camp meeting in late November he asked if any backsliders stood in the crowd, and several came forward and fell to their knees in tears. Immediately the rest of the congregation went into a panic. "We had a cry and shout," he said, "it was a weeping tender time." Dow maintained that this sign of repentance angered the devil, as did the success of his four-day meeting, and when he garnered fifty or more conversions for his efforts, he concluded: "The wilderness begins to bud and blossom as the rose, and the barren land becomes a fruitful field."[73]

Peggy came to join him during one of his later missions in 1812. She failed to impress as he did, even the charitable Winans declaring her intellect "barely respectable" and tainted by "a small portion of fanaticism and superstition."[74] Peggy herself admitted on her arrival at a stand on the Trace that "those that professed religion seemed not to take much notice of me." She could not manage her little money and lived with relatives that were even worse at economy, and so amassed considerable debt that Lorenzo had to find a way to repay.[75] Worse, she seemed to attract attention from one of Dow's partners, Roswell Valentine, that the latter's wife found offensive enough to charge her husband with infidelity. In the end Valentine shipped his spouse off to her family back in North Carolina and saw no more of her.[76]

Eventually the Dows settled in the territory on a piece of canebrake where they built a log cabin, but Lorenzo could never stay put for long. Once again he left Peggy for several months while he wandered off in search of souls and some means of making a living. Time after time he came back to her, often appointing a camp meeting for the place and hour of their reunion. At one point Dow went into business with two partners in a mill a few miles from Port Gibson. Winans met him there and felt almost disappointed that the "celebrated and eccentric" preacher had stayed put, as he said, "long enough to sink down, in public estimation, to the ordinary standard of respectable humanity." Dow seemed somehow diminished in the greatness that had made him famous, and in fact, after associating with him for a time, Winans concluded that Dow, "but for his eccentricity, would never have been estimated above mediocrity."[77]

Perhaps not. But in this territory an eccentric man or a peculiar woman could stand out and still be accepted, especially outside Natchez and its more conventional society. And if that man and woman were on the business of the Almighty, then their peculiarities might not be eccentric at all, but rather yet another of the myriad signs that surrounded simple Christians in an era of seeming wonders.

8

The Road to Knowledge

David Crockett liked to quip that he feared neither man nor beast but felt a mortal dread of being granted an honorary degree from Harvard College. Perhaps so. The certain fact is that he enjoyed more education than most men of his time in the Southwest, and that was precious little. "All my misfortunes growed out of my want of learning," he concluded around 1803. "I had never been to school but four days." Though already about seventeen years old, Crockett hired himself out to a schoolteacher who gave him lessons four days a week in return for work on two others. "At it I went, learning and working back and forwards, until I had been with him nigh on to six months," Crockett recalled. He learned to read in some degree, to write at least his name and soon more, and memorized multiplication tables "in the three first rules," or times three. "And this was all the schooling I ever had in my life."[1]

It was more than most got, and when the territory at either end of the Trace first came to be settled, there was no education at all beyond what the early missionaries sought to provide, and theirs leaned exclusively toward instruction in the Scriptures and dogma. By 1799, after the United States finally took complete control of the Southwest, not a single school, public or private, existed within its bounds. That same year some of the citizens of Natchez petitioned Congress to help them in inaugurating a seminary, primarily for training ministers, but also with it a school for educating their young.[2] Nothing happened, unfortunately, and a year later, when John Hall passed through the territory, he concluded that "the state of the territory is indeed deplorable for

160

want of literary instructors." He blamed this lack for the immorality that he saw in Natchez and elsewhere, especially in that, genuine English teachers being almost impossible to obtain, the few tutors who advertised themselves proved often to be charlatans of "such vitiated habits" that they did more harm than good and failed to last. "It would, undoubtedly have salutary effect, should a number of men, well qualified for the business, and of established moral characters, remove to the territory," he concluded. But that was easier said than accomplished.[3]

The wealthy, of course, hired tutors, who instructed their children, and usually only theirs, but this hardly assured any uniform kind of learning. Indeed, often it bought only mayhem. Thomas Griffin declared after spending some time in Natchez that the kind of tutor he found there was a deist run out of North Carolina for stealing hogs, and later to be found "in that celebrated school of all forms of vice, known as 'Natchez under the hill,'" from which, evicted, he went on to announce himself a schoolteacher.[4] Even more disturbing was a Joseph Lloyd, who in 1808 tutored the children of former Governor Sargent, among others. One day when the master of the house was out, Lloyd and a dancing master and a music teacher, all got roaring drunk and instead of educating the children, spent the afternoon on a spree.[5]

Beginning in 1801 when David Ker, an Irish Presbyterian minister, opened a public "female school," small private academies gradually started to appear in Natchez, but most failed to last. Meanwhile Congress finally authorized the sale of public land in each township in the territory to raise money to support schools, but little came of the effort at first.[6] The situation stood just as bad in the Alabama lands, and in 1805 when one man complained that "neither youth nor age has any instruction or any consolation here," he could have been speaking for virtually the whole Southwest except New Orleans. "They are born amidst the clouds of ignorance, and die without having the ear gladdened with the cheering light of revelation. Our schools are few and ill supported."[7]

In fact by 1805 only Louisiana had taken real steps to establish public academies at state expense.[8] For the Mississippi and Alabama lands it was still up to the people themselves, and often the churches. Three years later the Reverend James Smylie opened his "Washington Academy" to give boys a classical education at Washington, and Jacob Rickhow inaugurated his at Natchez. During the next decade more than a dozen others opened their doors—or, more accurately, they opened the doors of the inns and taverns where they held their classes in fundamental reading, writing, and arithmetic. Most failed for want of patronage, and considering the haphazard educational opportunities available by 1817, the editor of the city's *Washington Republican and Natchez Intelligencer* must have been speaking hyperbolically when he wrote that "the spot on which we stand, snatched from the rude dominion of the untutored savage and prowling tiger" could now boast a rapid development of learning.[9] Mostly it could boast of illiteracy, even among some of its leading citizens.

Throughout the Southwest education, or such of it as there was, often stood barely a step ahead of raw ignorance. Anyone could set himself up as a teacher, and often just about anyone did. Gideon Lincecum's father put him in a "school" run by a man named Young Gill, at a cost of seven dollars per year. The schooling lasted only five months before the spirit in the elder Lincecum's feet told him to go, and he answered the call once more. Before he left, Gideon learned the alphabet and not much more. Gill's teaching methods were not particularly sophisticated either. "Mind your book," he yelled at the commencement of a lesson. Immediately the students began reciting from their primers in no order and certainly no unison, and Lincecum, considerably behind all the others, merely sat in shamed silence as they talked. After awhile, however, Lincecum could boast of being able to spell "words of four letters," and found himself able to stand and recite almost as often as the rest. He applied himself at home at night studying two-syllable words to spell the following day, especially after his father got him one of Noah Webster's spellers.

Pride swelled young Lincecum's bosom when he proved himself sufficiently to Gill to be told to bring ink and paper to school. The master set aside a place on a writing table and told the boy that it should be his, that henceforth he was to keep his paper, pen, and ink on that spot, and there they would remain, unmolested. Every day when the time came to practice writing, Gideon and the others sat on a split log bench before that table—itself just a thick plank standing on wooden legs— and wrote and stared out the gap in the log wall in front of them, dreaming instead of the outdoors and its freedom.

The pupils appeared at the schoolhouse an hour after dawn every morning, and the first one there—they were all boys, of course— recited his lesson, then the next to arrive, and so on. Gill himself arrived soon thereafter and shouted, "Come, First," ordering the first to arrive to repeat his lesson for the teacher. There they stayed at it until an hour before sundown, when all went home, weary and numbed by the raw rote method of learning. Still Lincecum learned to read "very well," by Gill's pronouncement, during his five months in the log school.

His arithmetic advanced even farther than Crockett's, for Gideon could cipher to twice the rule of three, and his handwriting was legible. He carried Webster's book in his head memorized in its entirety, and even clung to a few poems that Gill gave him to remember. By the lights of his peers, Gideon Lincecum was an educated man.[10]

Naturally that qualified him to become a schoolteacher himself, just as he later became a doctor for a time. In 1816, after another move with his father, of course, Lincecum learned that the schoolboys in a local "academy" had risen up and thrown their schoolmaster into the river, and then abused him sufficiently that he quit his job and left the community. As their fathers despaired of finding another teacher who could manage the rascals, Lincecum allowed that perhaps he could. Certainly he needed the work, and when others offered to pay him ten dollars a head for forty pupils for the next nine months, he could hardly believe his luck, even though the fathers did prudently stipulate that payment would be due at the end of the term. "It struck me at once that this would be a more profitable employment than hunting and fishing," he recalled, and that was all the thought he gave the matter before accepting.

The curriculum looked easy enough, just reading, writing, and elementary math—about everything that Lincecum knew—but when he appeared at the schoolhouse on the appointed day, the new "master" discovered forty-five pupils including fifteen adult males, five of them married, five more adult women, and the balance children of all ages. The school committee of five men also awaited his coming, and now they sat and watched silently as Lincecum examined the primers in the hands of his students and then assigned them their first lessons. "We feel well pleased at your method of setting your classes to work," announced one of the elders as they rose to leave. "You see what you have before you," he said, and wished Lincecum luck. Then he was on his own.

Gideon Lincecum's description of his mixed bag of pupils would have fit almost any frontier school. "These children had been born and raised to the age I found them among the cows and drunken cowdrivers of the outer borders of the State, and they were positively the coarsest specimens of the human family I had ever seen." They laughed and talked incessantly during the lessons. During their recess to play outdoors, Lincecum had constantly to run from one group to another at the anguished cry of some victim of teasing, while the older boys started half a dozen fights, most of them actually during school time. At the end of just an hour of recess, he called them back into the house despite their complaints and hinted to one of the older boys that he had a scheme that would make this a model school and that he wanted his help.

That, of course, was bound to keep them buzzing during the afternoon's lessons as they speculated on what he had in mind. From time to time he shouted, "Mind your books" at them, just as Young Gill had at him years before, but these "outrageous ruffians, rollicking young women, and naughty children" paid little heed. Now and then he called one to the front of the class to recite a lesson. And for the balance of the week the school continued in this desultory fashion, Lincecum meanwhile often letting them shout and rant while he buried his head in a constitution he was drafting for the students to "govern" themselves. Friday afternoon, one of the boys impudently asked, "what's up now, hoss?" and he told them. While the class listened—for a change—he read them their rules of government.

They should have a court, and Lincecum, as "sheriff," would bring before it for judgment those charged with infractions. It seemed a great lark to the pupils, but turned more solemn when, after they voted on and approved the document, the teacher made each of them sign it, he writing the names of those who could not do so for themselves. "This is a big thing," one married fellow announced. "We never had such sort of doings afore in these diggings." Next he supervised the nomination and election of the judge and other officials. "We succeeded in bungling out the officers," he recalled, then he read them the document once more, saying further that it should be read each day at noon to remind them of their laws, and that on Fridays they should hold court.

Lincecum believed the attitude of the students appeared changed the very next Monday when they arrived at school. "The effects of having put their names to the constitution on their general behavior was very visible." For the balance of the week talking in class stayed at a minimum, and not one fight erupted. Friday afternoon came, and the students gathered after their recess in anticipation of "court" day. The felons brought before them were a dangerous lot. Stephen Herd threw a little girl's bonnet into the creek. Elijah Scatterwhite—a juror, as it happened—had "run over" a little boy on the playground. Herd came forward first after the jury was selected. Consultation with counsel accomplished little for him. Being a grown man, he felt little apprehension of punishment, and when the verdict of "guilty" came out he did not flinch when the jury assessed him three lashes with a hickory stick. His grin quickly changed, however, when Sheriff Lincecum administered them with a new-cut rod, well laid on "with all the force I possessed." Herd walked away in tears, the homespun waistcoat on his backside frayed in ribbons.

Thus Scatterwhite came up suitably sobered for his trial, and so that Herd should not entirely miss all the day's fun, Lincecum gave him Scatterwhite's place on the jury. Having seen real punishment inflicted, Scatterwhite and his counsel deliberated long and thoughtfully before presenting their case, and the jury looked forward gleefully to passing verdict, having seen what Herd got. Yet it was Herd who talked reason to them, pointing out that if they, out of pure fun, started passing down harsh sentences on every little infraction like his own, they would all soon fall to spiteful resentments and be fighting and squabbling once again. He persuaded them to find Scatterwhite guilty, but not with malice aforethought. They sentenced him to pay a fine of three dozen goose quills. Herd would be the first and last to draw corporal punishment, and thereafter—until Lincecum got the wanderlust and left once more with his father—this little Southwest school actually accomplished something, and the parents gladly paid the "sheriff" every dollar they owed at the end of the term. Herd, incidentally, went on to become a lawyer.[11]

It was no mean feat making the students behave out of fear of each other. Generally the master relied simply on whatever terror he could instill in them himself, and most relied heavily on the rod. "Our time was wasted," one Tennessean recalled of much of his frontier schooling, "but, between learning and thrashing," they absorbed something.[12] Besides the rudiments, masters also taught their students to make their own pens from quills, prepare inks from lampblack or even berries, and then draw the rule lines for their own lesson books. In some rural areas the teachers also had to accommodate what they taught to the whims or beliefs of the parents. Certainly all teachers had to steer clear of religious controversy, or else, if in a predominantly Methodist or Presbyterian or Baptist community, tailor what little they said of the relations of man and God to the prevailing orthodoxy. A few masters, at least, prudently realized that knowledge was not immutable. One parent asking a prospective candidate whether the world was round or flat, got the reply that "I do not know for sure, but I am prepared to teach it either way." Obviously the fellow wanted the job.[13]

As often as not, school first commenced with no place to teach it, leading to the daytime use of a tavern room or one side of a settler's dogtrot. In time the community met with axes and mauls and spent two or three days felling trees and erecting a log schoolhouse. At the leading edge of settlement they were called "forest schools" because of being literally on the verge of the wilderness. The older communities with a few years behind them were more likely to locate their schools on an abandoned piece of worn-out farmland. Whole generations of Southwestern pupils would years later look back on attending such "old field" schools.[14] Mary Welsh recalled her Alabama school as "one of the rudest of rude cabins; dirt floor with not even all the 'grubs' taken up, split log, backless benches, open to the roof. Across one side and one end holes were bored into the logs, long pegs driven into them, and planks laid across for a writing desk. The crack above it was widened to give us light." The description would have fit the school where Lincecum learned, or almost any other early schoolhouse.[15] Children sat on split log benches, all made in one height regardless of the varying sizes of the pupils.

Masters showed little sophistication in dividing their classes. At first no grades existed. There were simply groups for the bigger boys, the smaller boys, and "the girls." All of them could feel the master's wrath for an infraction. Most relied on the rod, but at least one inventive—if cruel—teacher used his own suspenders to hang and nearly strangle a boy until he promised better behavior. The dunce cap could make a child an object of derision, and seating him on the "laugh block" achieved the same result. Teachers forced pupils to stand for hours or kneel indefinitely or stand on one foot on a block of ice in winter. Parents for the most part supported such punishments, and one school in infant Tuscaloosa actually acquired the unenviable title, "Thrashing Machine."[16]

The teaching itself was as idiosyncratic as the men and the times. Most schools only ran full-time during the winter months, the boys—the bulk of the pupils—being needed on the farm spring, summer, and fall for the planting and harvesting. Thereafter only one or two days a week, or a few weeks in summer, were all the schooling children could get. They learned, as Lincecum did, by pure mindless repetition, aloud, over and over. No wonder these frontier centers of learning were sometimes called "blab" schools, for all day long there came through the chinks in the logs an incessant babble. Their materials were few, especially the books. They worked from titles like *The Boston Reading Lessons for Primary Schools*, *The American First Class Book*, and J. Pierpont's *The National Reader*. Many of them were simple compilations of extracts from the Psalms and Ecclesiastes, some anecdotes about animals, a passage or two from a British encyclopedia, Ben Franklin's story of his arrival in Philadelphia from his *Autobiography*, a newspaper article or two, and some writings by Washington Irving and the popular historian Jared Sparks. Reading aloud such lessons as "the wickedness of abusing a horse," a student presumably learned a moral lesson while sharpening his vocabulary and pronunciation. "Every thing low, in thought or language, I have studiously endeavored to avoid," wrote the editor of one popular text. He sought, rather, to include "sublime, devotional thought" in his text, "for, when high thoughts and divine philosophy are clothed in simple language, the mind of a child easily apprehends them, and is capable of feeling the power."[17] As evidence that many of the teachers finding employment were not far ahead of their pupils, most of the lesson books, especially those with math problems, came with "keys" that provided the solutions even to simple sums, for the use of the masters. A man might thus show his students the right answer, even if he could not explain quite how it was achieved.[18]

"Our progress was necessarily slow," Mary Welsh confessed, "but the little we acquired was thorough and it was a lifetime possession." At least they got a two-hour noontime recess for their meal and some play, and at the end of the day some masters dangled a reward for attentiveness by having the students spell aloud, those who got words right being allowed to leave before those who misspelled.[19] The students, in turn, seemingly exacted a measure of revenge on the teacher around Christmastime by "turning" him out, a ceremony in which they literally occupied the schoolhouse before he arrived and barricaded themselves inside, refusing to allow him entrance. Anything could ensue, from the teacher meekly going home to his breaking down the door, and depending on what happened, the episode could end with him thrown into a nearby—and ice-cold—winter creek, or gathered with the students over a picnic dinner of fruits and cider. The whole thing generally proved to be a charade, gotten up between master and pupils, in order to get them a few days' holiday at the end of the year and release him from a week or so of dealing with them.[20]

One step above the "old field" schools were the private academies that began to appear after 1800, most of them opened by itinerant teachers who saw potential in settling in fixed and more affluent communities like Natchez, Washington, Port Gibson, and the like. Almost every year saw one or two new ones commence operation in Natchez especially, though in time the planters became suspicious of them after seeing so many close with a school year incomplete, and tuition already paid. The Natchez Academy opened in 1817, offering among other things instruction in French, music, and painting. The year before the newly formed Female Charitable Society undertook to educate the orphaned and the children of the poor by making a subscription that raised more than twelve hundred dollars for providing a schoolroom and hiring Dr. Benjamin Davis at five hundred dollars per annum.[21] That November this new "Lancastrian Academy" announced lessons in the classics, and instruction in the "Lancastrian" method of having older pupils teach the younger. Soon thereafter Dr. Samuel Caswell was taking in students. Fees ranged widely, from twenty-four dollars for the August–June term at Caswell's, to as high as fifty dollars per quarter at one run at the opposite end of the Trace, but that also included board.[22]

In such communities the substantially elevated quality of academy education created a demand for good teachers, the schools often advertising in neighboring towns to lure away their instructors.[23] Early in 1817 Richard Pearse opened his Natchez academy and within three months had eighty students, paying an average of fifteen dollars each per quarter. More pupils came in continually, some of them traveling quite a distance from the countryside. Each bought his own books from Pearse, and many other academy operators also provided laundry services and even advanced money to their boarding students, all of it going on the bill, of course.[24] A visitor to Natchez, noting the success of Pearse and others, wrote in April 1817 that "one year ago there was not a proper school-teacher in the place; now nearly all our children are under the care of well qualified *pious* instructors."[25]

The academy system spread up the Trace and through much of the Southwest. Madison Academy opened at Port Gibson in 1809, its founders including old stand operators like Cobun and Brashears, and by 1825 the Flower Hill Academy was offering mathematics and surveying. In 1819 and 1820 a host of schools opened in Claiborne County, suddenly bringing to the children of the territory Greek, Latin, French, rhetoric, philosophy, and even bookkeeping—something of passing interest to Mississippi's future planter elite. By 1830 John Cobb taught orthography, reading, writing, math, grammar, ancient and modern geography, philosophy, astronomy, and a host of other disciplines for twenty-four dollars a year.[26] At Columbus, Mississippi, the Franklin Academy proposed to admit boys *and* girls in 1821. In Hinds County, where the new capital at Jackson enjoyed its building boom, the Hampstead Academy commenced operating in 1826, it, too, proposing to educate females as well as males.[27]

Far to the north the Woodward Academy opened in 1809 in Maury County, Tennessee, not far from the Trace, and later to be known as the Old Male Brick Academy, ample evidence that *it* did not intend to admit girls.[28] And along the Harpeth in Williamson County, the Harpeth Union Male Academy opened in the early 1800s.[29] Young James Maury attended an earlier Harpeth Academy in 1810, and found his teachers there "supplied with a store of erudition" that left him with little he remembered other than excellent handwriting. He got six months of Latin that he found "wanting in euphonism and melody," but in time he could read Erasmus. What he derived most from academy education, however, was awe for the oratorical skills of the preceptor, Gideon Blackburn. He never heard a man "gifted with superior eloquence," Maury remembered years afterward. "His action was graceful and commanding, his language pure, classical and copious." As Blackburn drummed their Latin and Greek, their grammar, logic, rhetoric, natural and ethical philosophy, geography, geometry, and astronomy into the students, he seemed at times to "rise above himself and soar beyond the limits of human conception." Maury got his twenty dollars' worth and more each year. "From the time of my fellowship in Harpeth Academy, I was a better student," he said. "I began to appreciate the value of an education and entertained a pride of scholarship."[30] By 1822 the academy was expanding to 100 students.[31] And in Alabama, so often behind events in Mississippi thanks to its isolation and smaller population, young Madison County began devoting the income from fines and forfeitures to support a school, while Baldwin County designated ferry rents for its pupils.[32]

Most of the academies, of course, depended entirely on the owner-operator, and theirs was a haphazard existence at best. The forest and old field schools generally provided a house for the master, or else the parents boarded him at nominal or no cost. But the man who commenced an academy was an entrepreneur, solely responsible for his own support, and should his pupils drop out, fail to pay, should they not buy their books from him, or run up high bills for food and laundering that went unpaid, he bore the results. James Smylie left his first academy at Washington and moved on to Port Gibson in 1815, hoping to do better there. He arranged for rooming at a local woman's boardinghouse for those pupils needing it, and also to provide—through her—board for which the students would pay. Unfortunately he proved to be less than precise in his own correspondence, and in contracting with her he specified that he would provide bacon for the boys at four dollars per hundredweight. In fact he meant to say pork, which cost considerably less. Somehow the students saw the contract and demanded that they get bacon, and all his arguments about the confusion meant nothing to them. In the end all the pupils boarding with the woman left, "& so my school terminated," he lamented. Only two local students remained with him. He would do his best with them, but they were already talking about riding to another master seven miles distant.[33]

While most thoughts of education extended only to the young

boys who would one day become the husbands, fathers, community leaders, and major planters, the academy concept did haltingly extend itself to girls as well. A Mrs. Berreut opened her "Boarding School for Young Ladies" in 1810, and charged pupils according to the curriculum they chose—nine dollars for English, nine for French, eight for embroidery, and so on—with a charge of forty-five dollars for the boarding itself.[34] The next year "Madam Florian's Seminary for Young Ladies" cost eighty dollars a quarter for reading, writing, arithmetic, French, English, Italian, geography, history, and needlework. An extra fifteen dollars for each subject could add drawing, piano, harp, singing, and dancing to a girl's list.[35] At the other end of the Trace in Williamson County, Tennessee, its first "Female Academy" opened in 1822.[36]

Some communities, and especially among the less wealthy Alabamians, used lotteries to raise money to commence their own academies. Washington Academy's was the first, authorized in 1811 for an anticipated five thousand dollars, but the tickets never sold and three years later it remained unbuilt. Green Academy in Madison County raised its four thousand dollars by lottery and went into operation; then in 1818 the Saint Stephens Academy—probably a revival of the Washington Academy project—finally opened. Thereafter the legislature granted charters to a groundswell of such schools: one in 1820, two in 1821, two more in 1823. Between 1825 and 1831, another twenty-seven such schools gained legislative approval, some of them getting as well a head-start gift of five hundred dollars from the lawmakers.[37]

Yet until 1819 such charters and occasional gifts were about all that territorial and then state government did to foster education. When Mississippi framed its state constitution, all it said about public education was that "religion, morality, and knowledge, being necessary to good government, the preservation of liberty, and the happiness of mankind, schools, and the means of education, shall for ever be encouraged in this state." That was fine, but nowhere in the document did the framers say or imply that the state itself had a responsibility to provide that learning or to raise a cent for its maintenance. And this was in spite of congressional policy for some years that when a new state was admitted from the older territories, one-sixteenth of every section of government land—that is, a sixteenth of a square mile—was to be turned over to the state to be used in some fashion to support education.[38]

Now, for a change, it was Alabama, so often behind, that took the lead. In July 1819 delegates to its constitutional convention at Huntsville specifically asserted that "schools, and the means of education, shall forever be encouraged in this State." That, too, was fine, and word for word from the Mississippi Constitution.[39] But then the framers went on to require their future legislature to take advantage of the sixteenth-section lands, administer them wisely "for the promotion of the arts, literature, and science," and even to found a state university. Later that same year, by then a state, Alabama enacted legislation to organize its public schools. Each county should secure agents to contract with teachers and provide schoolhouses "when and wheresoever they may think proper." The proceeds of leases of the sixteenth-section lands were to carry the expense.[40]

The lease system did not prove effectual at first, and the next year the legislature, trying to modify its original policy, only made it worse. Yet the lawmakers kept at it, and after a few years of tinkering, finally emerged in 1823 with a new law that created actual school districts, with elected trustees, charged to do the teacher hiring either at an annual sum or else on a fee-per-pupil basis, to buy books and stationery, and to choose those poor and orphaned children who were to be admitted without fee. The unstated goal was to make some form of education available to all regardless of ability to pay.[41] Moreover the legislature now required courts in each county to oversee appointing school commissioners charged to lease the public lands at auction every ten years, rather than handing the leases to friends at favorable rates, as had been the practice.

Good as this sounded, it hardly created a system of public education. What it did was provide funds to educate the indigent, but otherwise all students paid a subscription. Not only was it not, therefore, "free" public schooling, but some counties lagged severely behind others even in opening schools. The first school township did not incorporate until 1825, in fact. But Mobile County went far beyond the legislature on its own the following year when it instituted the first true system of public education in the Southwest. On January 10, 1826, the legislature authorized the county's commissioners to establish and regulate schools, and to fund them not only from the sixteenth-section lands but also from fines and forfeitures, court fees, and a variety of local taxes. Still the commissioners did not actually start free public schools. Rather, they used the additional funds to support the private academies already operating. But it was a start, for Alabama had tacitly assumed that free public education was, or could be, a public responsibility.[42]

Just two years after Alabama's constitution, Mississippi's Governor George Poindexter made his state's first tentative step in the same direction when he called for the creation of a "literary fund" for educating poor children and orphans, and that it be supported from tax revenues. But as in Alabama, the frontier notion of one man's taxes paying to teach another man's son seemed to violate some guarded ethic of self-reliance, and Poindexter's plan failed in the end, with what little revenue he raised being refunded to the counties.[43]

But if they failed primary education, the legislators in these territories that became states paid early attention to the needs of higher learning. Indeed, even before Natchez had a single boys' school, Governor William C. C. Claiborne declared on May 4, 1802, that the Mississippi Territory needed "a System of Public Education." "A *People* involved in mental darkness, become fit subjects for despotic sway," he went on, "but when informed of *their Rights*, they will never fail to cause them to be respected." He asked the legislature to extend its attention to the education of their youth, and especially to the establishment of "A Seminary of Learning." He meant a college.[44]

That very same month the territorial legislature acted on Claiborne's request and passed "An act to establish a College in Mississippi Territory." Furthermore, to honor the president of the United States, they decreed that it should be called Jefferson College. Unfortunately that is all they did. No one said anything about where the money was to come from. They left that to the trustees, a board of the leading men of Natchez, including Claiborne himself, Dunbar, Hutchins, Ker, Daniel Burnet, and more. They met in January 1803, made Governor Claiborne president of the group, and then sent a vague request to Congress for help. At the same time the trustees issued to the people of the territory at large—which meant chiefly Natchez—a memorandum announcing that "a place of public education is to be created at a considerable expense without any public funds." Consequently they asked for private donations and pointed out to parents the advantage of being able to educate their sons locally rather than send them to the East, or even abroad.[45]

While waiting hopefully for the donations to come in, Dunbar and others organized the customary lottery to raise up to ten thousand dollars. When the trustees next met on the Trace at Selsertown, Dunbar reported a plan for selling two thousand tickets at five dollars each, though in proposing to award a total of ten thousand in prizes while keeping only 15 percent of the awards for the college, they would raise but fifteen hundred dollars. Undaunted by this, and the fact that response to the appeal for donations proved sorely disappointing, the trustees went on to approve a location near Greenville, on the Trace, but when they next met at the new site, they quickly changed their minds, and instead accepted the gift of some ground just off the Trace at Washington. Now at least they had a campus, and Congress finally answered their appeal by giving them some government plots in Natchez and a substantial parcel elsewhere. From these lands the college should be able to realize income to get started. Unfortunately people already lived on that large parcel, and Natchez itself claimed the buildings already erected on the town lots, and in the end Congress regranted all the land away from the college. Meanwhile ticket sales to the lottery were so poor that the trustees had to cancel it. And when they announced an academy in Washington to be designed as a first step in preparing students for the college to come, no pupils applied. The path to knowledge, it seemed, was not to be an easy one.[46]

For more than five years the idea of the college languished, the trustees not even bothering to meet between 1805 and 1810. Reverend Smylie, meanwhile, opened his Washington Academy on their grounds and put up some frame buildings to house his school. He had a board of trustees, and in 1810 his board met with that of Jefferson College and the two agreed to merge, the college taking over Smylie's buildings and the funds he had raised from a subscription of his own. Equipped with this, meager as it was, the trustees believed that they could at last commence operations in a modest way. On January 1, 1811, Jefferson College finally opened its doors.

Of course it needed a teacher. Advertisements went out to the press in some of the northern and eastern states, and soon David Holmes, one of the trustees, was dealing with applications. One came from Charles Norton, who announced his competence in Latin and Greek, Euclid, navigation, trigonometry, surveying, geography, and natural philosophy.[47] Seemingly that was enough for Holmes. Norton became at once principal teacher and overseer of the buildings and grounds, and perhaps everything else as well.[48] No one fooled himself: Jefferson College was not a "college" yet. At best, with its pitiful buildings and tiny staff, it could do little better than act as an intermediary school between the academies and the full-fledged college to come. The board set tuition at two dollars per month during the first semester, and three a month for the second, and both rates doubled between 1813 and 1814, while board in Washington cost students twelve dollars a month.[49] That basic tuition covered reading, writing, English grammar, and basic mathematics. The other electives—all reflecting Norton's background—cost three dollars each for geography, Euclid's "Elements of Moral Philosophy," astronomy, natural philosophy, Greek, and Latin. He could also add bookkeeping for those who wanted it.[50]

While Norton no doubt exhausted himself trying to teach every-thing, the trustees kept working doggedly to raise more money, and gradually they enjoyed the success that previously eluded them. They went to court, and eventually back to Congress itself, to recover title to the lots in Natchez they had lost, and in the end they got them. They also got title to the township of land Congress had granted, but it was on the faraway Tombigbee and would not produce income until 1818. Then in 1816 Mississippi's legislature finally did something more than talk about education, passing an appropriation of a thousand dollars per year for six years. This, at least, was enough to expand the existing academy, and the next year they hired a Kentuckian to come take charge of the school.[51] They also revised their fees to seven dollars per quarter for the "three R's" and combined Latin, Greek, algebra, geogra-phy, rhetoric, logic, geometry, and trigonometry into a set package at $12.50. Another $15.00 also got the pupil geometry, philosophy, astron-omy, history, and belles lettres.[52]

The result of all this was that, finally, by 1817 Jefferson College began offering a few courses in keeping with the notion of higher edu-cation, and that same year the trustees gave out the last contract for the construction of its permanent buildings. They wanted an initial structure forty-eight feet deep and seventy wide as "a House of Tuition," estimating that it would take at least two hundred thousand bricks. They started the east wing first, then commenced the west wing the following spring. A year later the trustees at last commenced finishing off the interior of the hollow shell.[53] When Thomas Nuttall passed through Washington in January 1819, he observed that "although we perceive but little attention paid to science or literature in this territory, it does not by any means appear to be destitute of public patronage, as there is a very handsome endowment in lands appropri-ated by the state for the building and support of a college." Jefferson College's problems, he was told, were almost over.[54]

He spoke too soon. Assuming that the college's Tombigbee land would soar in value after the great immigration to Alabama com-menced, the trustees borrowed nine thousand dollars on it to complete their construction, and accepted another four-thousand-dollar loan from the legislature. But then the land boom went bust, the trustees found their land almost worthless, and they had to take on personally the debts they had incurred for the college. More problems ensued. The president of the institution came under fire from an interdenomi-national meeting of territorial clergy in 1818. They accused him of holding "unorthodox" views on religion and condemned both him and Jefferson. The trustees replaced him with the Reverend R. F. N. Smith, but then Smith resigned in 1821 when the money from the loans was gone and he could not be paid. Thereafter things only got worse. Enrollments lagged, and the frequent changes of instructors meant curriculum could not be maintained. In 1825 the legislature tried to sue for recovery of the four-thousand-dollar loan; then the next year Natchez brought up again the issue of those town lots taken away years before. The trustees and the selectmen of the city met to try to effect a compromise on what they termed "that old, and expensive law suit, 'Jefferson College, vs. the City of Natchez.'" In the end the college agreed to put the lots up for sale at the end of 1827, but as usual, it availed the school little.[55]

Many of the people of Natchez—and certainly some of the long-suffering trustees—were heartily sick of Jefferson College by now. Governor Poindexter, once seemingly so friendly to higher education, complained that the school was nothing but "an empty dome with pensioned preceptors," while others charged that its tuition was too high, it had no scientific equipment, and it lacked a first-rate president.[56] Most embarrassing of all, even the publishers of almanacs in the state, which would receive a distribution nationally, lashed out at the college. William Willeford's *Mississippi & Louisiana Almanac* in 1827 complimented the school's nice brick building as being "calculated for every purpose of Education, but unfortunately, very little, *if any*, individual or public benefits, have as yet, resulted from the institution."[57]

The college could not take much more. In 1829 the long-suffering trustees talked with the legislature about turning their charter over to the state, which now showed some interest in starting a state university. But examination of the charter itself revealed that, by its terms, it could not be transferred. Left with no alternative but closing the place, the trustees decided to make one more try. They reorganized it somewhat along the lines of the U.S. Military Academy, included military instruction with the rest of the curriculum, somehow hired new instructors, and opened their doors once more in December 1829. At last Jefferson College started to grow.[58] Its library expanded to include the major eastern periodicals like the *Knickerbocker Magazine*, and even some of the great British journals such as *Blackwood's* and the *Edinburgh Review*. The enrollment expanded that first year from 98 to over 150, thanks largely to the attraction of military instruction, and meanwhile the school became the center of social and intellectual life in Washington, and a magnet even to the elite of Natchez.[59] Instructors were being paid up to a thousand dollars per annum, and the naysayers of years gone by seemed at last put in their place. Yet the college never entirely escaped its early financial straits. In 1832 the trustees were still trying to sell the Tombigbee grant, now nearly thirty years old, and a year later they raised yet again the perennial matter of a "float"—a lottery to keep the school in business.[60]

Even while poor Jefferson struggled, another, farther-reaching educational experiment took place right in Washington. Jefferson College, of course, opened its doors only to young men. In fact, throughout the nation as a whole, and certainly in the South, higher education was limited to males. Elizabeth Roach of Washington did not approve. Born a Quaker in Pennsylvania, she later adopted Methodism, married well, and when widowed found herself possessed of some fortune. Aged about sixty, withered and emaciated, she foolishly married a fellow thirty years her junior who loved her until she gave him seventy thousand dollars. Then he disappeared.[61] A woman of learning herself, she decided to do something more useful with part of what remained of her wealth, and early in 1818 she gave to the Mississippi Methodist Conference some grounds and buildings in Washington that she owned, with the stipulation that they were to be used for a college for young women. (Not long after founding the school, she left Mississippi and returned to Pennsylvania.) Its trustees chartered it with the legislature the next year, calling it the Elizabeth Female Academy in honor of the benefactor, and adding to their charter the significant proviso that "no religious test or opinion shall be required by the by-laws of the institution of the pupils admitted." They had seen what religious intolerance did to neighboring Jefferson College.[62]

The trustees wasted no time, thanks in part to having a campus and instruction rooms already in place. They announced the school in October 1818, and actually commenced classes on November 12, with Chilion B. Stiles as president. Indeed, the only interesting restriction applied to staff was that the president must be thirty or older if married, and fifty or above if single: Elizabeth Roach, understandably, felt a hearty distrust of single young men.[63]

If tolerant, Elizabeth Academy nonetheless established stringent standards. While Chilion ran the school, the young ladies were to be ruled by Jane Sanderson, a governess required to be "pious, learned, and of grave and dignified deportment." She oversaw order, discipline, and instruction, as well as watching the behavior of the students. While Chilion won the affections of all, Sanderson lived subject to frequent depression and appeared stern and forbidding to the students. But then, college was not supposed to be fun. In Caroline M. Thayer's class the girls convened in a common room every morning at dawn and again at 8 o'clock in the evening for prayer. Then came instruction from 9 A.M. until noon, then from 2 P.M. for another three hours. During

May, June, and July, however, classes began an hour earlier in the morning, though they then got a three-hour recess. The girls could not have "ceremonious visits," meaning male callers. They wore plain dresses and bonnets. Beads, jewelry, artificial flowers, feathers, "or any superfluous decoration" were forbidden. Miss Thayer did not even allow them to have curls in their hair, and furthermore forbade them to attend balls, dances, the theater, or any other festivity.

The faculty announced that they wanted their curriculum and methods to address "understanding without oppressing the memory," meaning essentially that they relied on discussion and explanation more than rote memorization for learning.[64] The classes offered at the academy actually put poor Jefferson to shame at the time. They included chemistry, natural philosophy, moral philosophy, botany, Latin, Aesop, Virgil, history, Caesar, "Evidences of Christianity," and more. Those who completed got a parchment diploma naming them *Domina Scientiarum*—roughly "mistress of knowledge," a degree she probably invented—and if they took honors in their studies, they could stay an additional year with no tuition to pursue graduate study in science, "polite literature, and ornamental studies." Of course, they all got religious and Bible studies. Mrs. Caroline Thayer came to the school in 1825 as governess, and after her arrival its fortunes advanced greatly. Winans visited the Academy in 1826 and found her "a woman of middle size, coarse features, some of the stiffness of yankee manners, but of an intelligent and pleasant expression." The new president, the Reverend John Burrus, went farther to say "Mrs. Thayer is a most extraordinary woman; I have never seen such a teacher." Indeed, the accolades for Thayer came from all sides, and not long after the editor of the Natchez *Southern Galaxy* attended the examinations of her classes, he actually began publishing poetry and "polite" literary expressions from some of her students.[65]

The most prominent politicians and businessmen sat in on the academy's examinations and attended its commencements, an audience that would have intimidated the fainthearted—and often did. Girls were known to pass out from tension, or else keep themselves from swooning by sniffing sachets of hartshorn, a natural ammonia made from antlers. Still the academy conferred degrees on six young women in 1829. Until that time its student body annually ran from twenty-eight to sixty-three girls, and a surprising number of them—sometimes a third of the whole—received honors for their studies. Proud of her achievements with her girls, Thayer declared her belief that these young women of the Southwest could now "aspire to the dignity of intellectual beings."[66]

Like Jefferson College, the academy's fortunes fluctuated, and especially after the capital moved on to Jackson, several yellow fever epidemics, and the gradual shift of population away from Natchez, pupils became fewer and fewer.

Yet the experiment in female education that Elizabeth Roach started found good ground in the Southwest. The Athens Female Academy opened its doors in the northern Alabama town of the same name in 1822, after a benefactor donated land with the stipulation that the townspeople would build a school there and hire a teacher. It would be Alabama's first such school, to be followed four years later by the Tuscumbia Female Academy, and then Sims' Female Academy in Tuscaloosa in 1829.[67] Meanwhile, at Russellville, the Franklin Academy opened with both male and female instruction, but with the students rigidly segregated.[68] The Athens Academy, Presbyterian in outlook but, like Elizabeth, nondenominational, drew its principals from Baptist and Methodist faiths as well. In 1834 Rebecca Hobbs became probably the first female college principal in the nation, but after only two years she and the trustees argued over some unknown matter relating to her gender and she resigned. Under the management of Hobbs and others the academy added new buildings, including a music room and a laboratory where "Chemical and Philosophical apparatus" allowed the girls to do a few experiments.[69] Just as Alabama, starting later than Mississippi, often seemed to catch up and then surpass its neighbor, so in women's education it built on the Elizabeth Academy precedent and continued to expand its colleges for ladies on into the 1830s. Already, as that decade dawned, the people of Livingston began to talk of an academy of their own.[70] Moreover, by 1830 virtually all the states formed out of the old Southwest came to realize that young women needed to have their own schools, that they would get nothing more than rudiments at the old field grammars, and that women—while indisputably not the equal of men—still could profit from learning.[71]

Alabama led the way, for a change, in 1820, when the legislature chartered the University of Alabama at Tuscaloosa. In April 1822 real work actually got started, though it moved slowly. Five years later trustees selected the site, and building started the following year. Finally on April 17, 1831, some fifty-two students walked through its doors for the first day of classes.[72] Meanwhile Mississippi turned its attention to starting a state college as well. The Hampstead Academy opened at Clinton in January 1827, with a meager student body of thirty, both boys and girls, segregated by sex. The next month the legislature changed Hampstead's charter and called it Mississippi Academy instead, apparently with the future intention of endowing it with the proceeds from the state's sixteenth-section lands. They further gave the school five thousand dollars, and by 1830 two new buildings went up, one for girls and one for boys, and at the same time the legislature once more changed its name, this time to Mississippi College. It also granted the college the right to award degrees, and two years later Mississippi graduated its first two recipients, both young women.[73] Trustees gave the young ladies gold medals with their diplomas, and the examiners regarded the performance of these women as "a triumphant refutation of their supposed incapacity of high scientific attainments."[74]

Despite its high hopes and the legislature's evident intent, Mississippi College never did become the anticipated official state "seminary." Legislative dithering, state politics, and the perennial scarcity of money for educational pursuits were to blame, along with the shift in settlement to the north, and a consequent demand of those people to have the seminary in their region. A decade later they would have their way, and Mississippi College passed to the Methodists, and then the Presbyterians. In 1830, meanwhile, the Presbyterians were already founding their own college at Rodney, intended at first to train men for the ministry. They chose the rural location because they felt it would keep their students away from the health and moral dangers of the cities like Natchez, "far removed from the minglings of sectarian interests which tend to compromise the interest of true piety." Their new Oakland College started that same year with sixty-five pupils, all of them in grammar or preparatory school, and a mere five freshmen and two sophomores at the college level. It held its first commencement in 1833, and granted its first bachelor's degree. Moreover, despite the years of struggle of Jefferson College, and Mississippi College to follow, and the Elizabeth Female Academy, this degree from Oakland was the first actual B.A. to be granted in the state of Mississippi. It could not have been more fitting than that it should go to the man who had worked for a quarter century to elevate education in the state, including his role in the origins of Jefferson College—James M. Smylie.[75]

The Methodists opened their La Grange College in Alabama at the same time, and it, too, like Oakland, sought to provide a "monastic" life for its students, as far from the cares and temptations of daily life as possible.[76] In fact, during the last years of the 1820s and advancing into the decade to follow, more and more schools of higher education started their tortuous rise to operation. In Mississippi the legislature incorporated some twenty-nine schools and "literary societies" between 1817 and 1832, and in the last years especially the pace accelerated. More and more now Mississippians and Alabamians thought of educating their college-age children locally rather than sending them to the North and East. The increasingly strident cry of those opposed to slavery and advocating its abolition seemed to be taking over at Harvard and Yale and elsewhere. These planters had no desire to send their children there to have their minds polluted by nonsense spouted by the enemies of the South and its way of life.[77] Moreover, after decades of treating education backhandedly, the people of the Southwest by then felt a measure of resentment that colleges elsewhere should think themselves superior to what could be provided right there in Mississippi, Alabama, and Louisiana. "That our children are the better of a temporary exile at the north, to breathe a Hyperborean air, catch the impression of northern manners, and receive their finish at the northern institutions, combined with the established belief, that we of the south, cannot maintain any plan for home education, are among the stronger and most ruinous prejudices of our State," one Mississippi journalist complained.[78]

And so, though at times and in places slow to come to the notion, the southwesterners were determined by 1830 to educate their own. As far back as 1817 the Presbyterian Daniel Smith had spoken optimistically of the growth of learning and its institutions in Natchez and its environs. "This is an object on which my heart has been very much set," he wrote then. "The effects I doubt not will be happy." Sadly admitting the possibility that the parents of the day, the rough pioneers and settlers who came to take hold of the land, might be *"irreclaimable"* where education was concerned, he looked to the future. "They will not live always," he mused, "and the children will I have reason to believe come forward into their places with different sentiments & feelings."[79] And so they might.

9

The Road to Enlightenment

In 1812 Moses Fisk wrote to a relative that, though his home in the Southwest was a wild place, still "there is room, prospects, salubrity Here. 'pleased with a rattle', I may found an academy. True, I want Yankey society. Will they come, or visit they not? A clergyman, a preceptor, a printer, &c, &c, &c, are wanted. They should be *live* people; *folks* of energy; happiness their object, wealth as a mean, *webbed* together; a constellation, a city on an eminence. Two or three such *formed* institutions here might benefit others as well as themselves. Will people come, I say, or will they not?"[1]

Of course, by the time Fisk wrote, some such men were already in the Southwest, or else on their way. The clergy were there, and so were the educators. But he wanted more. Most of all, behind his words lay a plea for knowledge, a thirst keenly felt by Fisk and his fellows in this great expanse so far removed from the rest of the United States and the world. They craved to know as much as they could, and lamented that for so much of what they could know in those days, they had to depend almost exclusively upon outside sources.

In the first days, of course, they had nothing but the mails, and thus the Natchez Trace. The letters came few in number, and with frustrating infrequency. That first schedule on the post road only brought a rider from Nashville twice a month, making Saturday afternoon something of an event on the bluff as people looked off toward Washington and the Trace for a sign of the mail rider on his lathered horse.[2] Even when the rider came, there were aggravations. The Postmaster General in Washington ordered when the mails started that they be carried

181

in a portmanteau with a lock, but almost at once problems arose. While not a single rider was lost on the way, sometimes not all of their letters made it with them. It seems that at first the rider from Nashville, on reaching the relay point at McIntosh's, was in the habit of taking his letters out of his portmanteau, and exchanging them with those brought by the rider coming up from Natchez. In the exchange letters could get mixed and sent back where they came from, or else lost entirely. After a few months Habersham directed that the riders not open the containers at all, but simply exchange them whole.[3]

That solved the problem of loss, but still the mail did not come often enough. By 1803 Washington received more and more communications urging it to increase either the speed or else the frequency of delivery. The threat of conflict with Spain over the Southwest added to the urgency, as did the negotiations for the purchase of the Louisiana Territory, so Washington obliged by increasing the mails to once a week and requiring riders to cover fifty miles a day. Now they would leave Nashville on a Monday evening and reach Natchez on Tuesday, eight days later, at 6 P.M.[4]

The increased frequency also helped deal with the growing volume of mail. By 1804 so many people in the territory subscribed to eastern newspapers, large and sometimes bulky sheets that took up much space in the portmanteaus, that there could not be room for everything on some runs. The postmaster general directed that they obtain larger saddlebags, to be kept secure with chain and lock, and that the rider carry two, one labeled "letter mail" and the other "Newspaper mail." Even that did not completely solve the problem of volume until eight months later, in July 1805, when Washington directed that riders now take with them a second "led" horse to carry additional bags.[5]

Yet security remained an issue. When a rider was some eighteen hours late in arriving, the concern spread all the way back to Washington. So did the chagrin when careless riders opened their bags and allowed people to copy letters. When customers paid two cents or more for local mail along the route, and as much as seventy-five cents to send something the length of the Trace, they expected it to arrive intact and on time.[6] By 1815 the postmaster general was conducting experiments with oiled deerskin pouches and oiled linen bags, testing to see which was more waterproof, since the riders always ran the risk of a ducking as they crossed streams. He also ordered all letters wrapped tightly in packets to prevent them rubbing together during the long ride, defacing addressees' names. Still there came the complaints of newspapers and journals not received, and inevitably the government began to experiment in 1819 with sending mail by steamboat during the months when ice posed no danger on the rivers.[7] Yet as late as 1820 would-be recipients in Natchez still grumbled from time to time of a letter being a month overdue, or of mail being held up in the New Orleans post office for weeks when sent via the Atlantic route. So much did the literate people of the territory crave news that they never admitted to anything like satisfaction, no matter the improvements made in Washington, Nashville, along the Trace, or in Natchez itself. "The management of letters keeps pace with that of all other offices here," complained a disgruntled wine merchant.[8]

Even more than the letters from relatives and business associates, the reading people of the Southwest devoured newspapers. As early as 1804 Trace mail riders began to find that the volume of newspapers being mailed to Natchez grew so great that they could not carry it all on one ride, and had to leave some for subsequent runs.[9] Inevitably when the papers arrived they were weeks—perhaps a month or more—out of date. They came too infrequently, and of course they contained nothing of territorial or local news.

Someone had to start the territory's own press, and the avidity with which Mississippians craved news is evidenced in the fact that the first local newspaper appeared even before the post road started bringing the eastern sheets on a regular basis. Andrew Marschalk had served in the Continental Army during the Revolution and remained in uniform afterward. Soldiering was only an adopted trade, however, for his real profession had been printing, and while still serving in the army in 1790 he made a trip to London and brought back a small mahogany press. For the next six years he lent it to a friend, but when superiors ordered him to the Southwest in 1796, he regained his press and brought it with him.

He also brought a small font of type, not sufficient for printing more than a single sheet, perhaps, and once established near Walnut Hills with his command, he experimented with the press by setting and printing a popular ballad called "The Galley Slave." When the news-hungry leaders of Natchez heard that there was an operating press in the territory, they begged Marschalk to bring it to the city on the bluff. Instead, he used his small press as a model and himself built a much larger one capable of printing a full foolscap sheet, approximately thirteen and one-half by seventeen inches. In 1798, when Congress organized the Mississippi Territory, the territorial legislature engaged Marschalk's new press for printing its laws. Very soon thereafter he sold the press to Ben Stokes of Natchez, who dreamed of bigger things.[10]

In the summer of 1799 Stokes printed his first issue of the *Mississippi Gazette*. "We intend to make it our study to render the gazette a vehicle of useful and pleasing information," he announced. Inviting the citizenry to submit to him essays that did not contain "immoral, indecent matter" for him to publish, he promised that in time Natchez would have "as large a paper as any published in the Western country." Unfortunately, his subscription price of six dollars a year was simply too high for the trade to bear, and he failed after only a year or two.[11]

Others did not wait for Stokes to fail before they sought to capitalize on the hunger for news. In the spring of 1800 a Baltimore man brought a new press to Natchez and commenced publishing his short-lived *Green's Impartial Observer*.[12] When Green failed, his press passed to James Ferrall, who moved it to the home of George Cochran, opposite Brooke's Tavern. There, even while advertising in his own sheet for printing apprentices, Ferrall started the *Intelligencer* in August 1801. He, too, asked six dollars a year, and he too would soon fail.[13] Then it became Marschalk's turn. Returning in June 1802 from a trip to Philadelphia, he acquired a press—probably Ferrall's—and started publishing his *Mississippi Herald and Natchez Gazette* on July 26. It would only last five years, but Marschalk's fiery political partisanship made it one of the best-read organs of the day, even as financial difficulty gradually forced him to reduce it in size from regular newspaper stock to the much smaller foolscap.[14] Nevertheless, Marschalk would be heard from again.

Others made their attempts. The *Constitutional Conservator* commenced in 1802, destined to fail within the year. The *Mississippi Messenger* followed in 1807, and then the *Mississippi Republican* around 1812.[15] By the time the last came along, the editors were learning something about business and priced their sheets at four dollars per year. Even with paper costing up to six dollars per ream, and printing up to seven dollars per ream when done by a contract printer, still the *Mississippi Republican* managed to stay in business through most of the decade.[16]

In the neighboring territory that became Alabama a similar minor publishing boom occurred, and with a similar history. Predictably, printing began in Mobile in 1807 with broadside and pamphlet publications not unlike Marschalk's first ballad. Then, in 1810, a federal judge for the territory named Harry Toulmin announced plans to commence publishing the *Mobile Mercury, or Tombigbee and Alabama Advertiser*. However, Toulmin seems not to have managed to put type to paper, and in the end the first actual newspaper to appear came out the following year. John B. Hood of South Carolina and Samuel Miller from Tennessee both had successful printing experience behind them with other papers. Meeting in Tennessee, they bought a press and brought it overland from Chattanooga to the Alabama River, and then downstream to Fort Stoddert, just north of what was still Spanish West Florida.[17] They put out the first issue of their four-page weekly, the *Mobile Centinel*, on May 23, 1811. If their spelling left something to be desired, so did their sense of place, since they published thirty miles north of Mobile at Fort Stoddert. In fact, they had intended at first to operate in Mobile, but at the time they started, that city still lay in Spanish hands, and would until 1813. Hence they published at Fort Stoddert until they could move to an American Mobile. Alas, even at only four dollars a year they went out of business the year before American soldiers marched into the city.[18]

Barely did Hood and Miller fail before Thomas G. Bradford, a kinsman of John Bradford, whose *Kentucky Gazette* was the first newspaper published west of the Alleghenies in 1787, established his own *Gazette* in Madison, Alabama. This second newspaper in the territory first appeared in May or June 1812 and—like the *Centinel* and most other frontier sheets—ran four pages each week. Two of them the editor gave over to advertisements, including everything from runaway slaves and horses to the latest arrivals of clothing and farm implements or the current prices of whiskey and tobacco. The local news—such as it was—consisted in the main of announcements of sales and auctions, civic meetings, the dates and times of militia musters, and lists of letters sitting uncollected at the post office. National or world news came almost verbatim from recent issues of the eastern press, and thus was not particularly timely. The editors also included poetry and "polite literature" from local people, and of course included their own commentaries on current local and political affairs, with no attempt at all to be nonpartisan.[19]

The press continued to grow in Alabama at an even faster rate than in Mississippi. James Lyon opened the Mobile *Gazette* in 1813 as soon as the city became American territory. It ran for nearly a decade before merging into the *Commercial Register*, itself founded in 1821. Meanwhile, in 1815 Thomas Eastin bought a printing press in Mount Vernon, outside Fort Stoddert, and commenced publishing *The Halcyon* at Saint Stephens on the Tombigbee. He had been in newspapers since the age of fifteen, came to the Alabama area with Andrew Jackson's army during the War of 1812, and then in late 1813 went into partnership with Marschalk at Washington, Mississippi, to issue a sheet.

The next year, as he described it himself, he left Marschalk and came to Mount Vernon, where he saw this press and its equipment literally sitting in the street. Very possibly it was the press of the defunct *Centinel*, but in any case he bought it and got out his first issue of *The Halcyon* just in time to carry an announcement of the conclusion of the Treaty of Ghent.[20]

One characteristic of these frontier entrepreneurs was that they rarely let failure subdue them for long. In Mississippi Marschalk would be associated with at least five journals in his career. Here in Alabama, Hood of the *Centinel* commenced another paper, the *Gazette*, in Huntsville in 1816. It failed, too, perhaps because it appeared only weeks before a competitor, the Huntsville *Republican,* started publishing under an editorship with better political connections. The *Republican* secured some state printing contracts that were usually the object of rabid competition between printers, and that ensured its longevity for more than a decade. Meanwhile Miller of the old *Centinel* began publishing the *Sun and Alabama Advertiser* in Blakeley, near Mobile, in 1818. Then came the *Commercial Advertiser* in Mobile, the *Alabama Courier* in Claiborne, and the Tuscaloosa *Republican* in 1819. When Cahaba became the first state capital that same year, William Allen came from Boston to open his *Press and Alabama Intelligencer.* By the end of that year, despite all the false starts and failures, Alabama had six weekly or semiweekly newspapers in operation.[21]

These publishers were almost as peripatetic as the itinerant preachers, whose paths they occasionally crossed. Between 1810 and 1820 some twenty-six men at least opened newspapers in Alabama alone. Like everyone else who came to the Southwest, they sought opportunity, and when it failed them in one town they did not hesitate to move to another to try again. They begged and schemed to get government printing, competed vigorously for local advertising, and always had their next paper in mind. Combined, they started thirty-one sheets in that decade and projected at least eight more. When they failed entirely in the territory, they moved on, founding yet more papers wherever they went. Truly, journalism could erupt on the frontier anywhere at any time, as these consummate opportunists packed their presses and their type and kept on trying.[22]

Following statehood, Alabama journalism expanded even more rapidly, and saw something of a first. Just as Alabamians took a lead in education, so now one Alabama woman, Augustina Parsons, became the first of her sex to operate a newspaper in the Southwest. In 1820 in Cahaba she opened her *Alabama Watchman*, which, though it lasted but a few months, enabled her to secure some desirable state printing contracts, attesting to her ability as a printer if not editor. Thereafter Cahaba, Florence, Tuscaloosa, Huntsville, Tuscumbia, and more all saw weekly newspapers published.[23]

After 1820 even the secondary communities began establishing their weeklies, especially with the advent of Jacksonian democracy, and the rapid—and rabid—growth of party politics. Seemingly every town of any standing had to have at least two sheets, one vehemently supporting one political ideal and the other another. The editors barred no holds in attacking not only opposing views but one another as well. Most of it was done in the spirit of good-natured partisanship, but more than once a man went too far in his editorial and found himself called to account with a whip or a cane in a chance encounter in the street, or else a challenge to meet on the dueling field. Marschalk himself would be soundly beaten with a cane by Poindexter for some of his editorial statements.[24]

At the northern end of the Trace papers like the Columbia *West ern Chronicle*, appearing in 1811 in Maury County, followed the same pattern.[25] In fact, the press exploded across much of the Southwest largely because there was so much more news to print and so many more people to read it and to place and respond to advertising. During the War of 1812, of course, the sheets were all jammed with war news, most of it out of date. Then once the war concluded and the shortages it brought abated, more presses opened. Marschalk started the Washington *Republican and Natchez Intelligencer* in 1817, and meanwhile the Natchez *Mississippi Republican* got going. By 1828, with the opening of the Jacksonian era, these editors assumed a new importance, not just as local businessmen, but as moulders of public opinion in the so-called era of the common man.

When Jackson first ran for the presidency in 1824, Mississippi journalists generally either opposed or ignored his candidacy. Nevertheless, Jackson's friends in the state assiduously set out to turn that around before his next bid four years later. In an act common to frontier journalism and politics—and reflecting the increasing combination of the two—supporters formed an association to create a newspaper in the state capitol to advance the cause of the man for whom the city was named. In 1826 they began publication of the Jackson *Mississippi Statesman*. "Let us have something home-made," its hardly impartial editor wrote in the opening issue. "It is time to awake—time that the voice of Mississippi should be read at home and abroad—time, that our own citizens should hear, from our own papers, not one but both sides." Having said that, of course, the editors proceeded to present one side, and one side only.[26]

In fact, the growing involvement of newspapers with political affairs reflected itself in the names the editors chose. From the preponderance of *Gazette* and *Intelligencer* and *Clarion* of the early days, more and more they switched to *Republican* and *Democrat*, *Whig* and *Statesman*, or *Political Synopsis*. Patriotism, too, they demonstrated in mastheads like Tuscaloosa's *Flag of the Union*, while their sense of sectional identity became more and more defined by titles like the *Southern Advocate* in Huntsville. With the dawn of the 1830s Alabama commenced a decade in which more than fifty weeklies would start publication, and almost as many sprouted in neighboring Mississippi.[27] With more newspapers, the editors tended to become more intemperate. Dugald McFarlane almost had to flee Tuscaloosa for his life after he castigated the townspeople in his *Chronicle* for their "thermaphrodite bigotry or religious haluccination."[28]

The local press reflected only a part of the southwestern hunger for information and learning. People also subscribed avidly to the sheets from elsewhere in the Union. Two years of the Lexington, Kentucky, *Western Review* cost William Hunt eight dollars, and gladly paid. Stephen Bullock took the even more remote *Virginia Gazette* at four dollars a year, and the *Virginia Patriot* at the same rate.[29] They also devoured books as they became available. John Menefee opened one of Natchez's—and the territory's—early bookstores in 1818, though books themselves were already a longtime presence in some of the town's more affluent homes. Back in 1781 John Blommart already had a library of more than 150 volumes. Anthony Hutchins repeatedly ordered books from his London cotton buyer, leaning heavily toward popular novels and scientific tomes and journals.[30] In 1811 Abijah Hunt counted in his collection at least 200 volumes estimated to be worth $658, among them works by Robert Burns, David Hume, and Jonathan Swift. By 1804 books were being shipped to order more or less regularly from New Orleans. Histories, religious works, Webster's dictionaries, medical treatises, and even cookbooks with "receipts" for the local housewives—all stood on sellers' shelves for the reading public. Almost everyone bought almanacs. At a store in Greenville more than half the customers on some days bought the new editions of the regional and farmers' almanacs.[31]

What they read reflected both the tastes of the time and merely what they could get. One planter consumed Samuel Johnson, Alexander Pope, Joseph Addison, Thomas Macaulay, and more, reflecting a decided preference for English writers. Shakespeare was to be found in many a home, of course. On the other hand, the territory's literate seemed to feel little impulse to write much on their own. Aside from occasional contributions to the newspapers, mostly essays and florid poetry, they remained content to read the works of others. In Alabama no prose for entertainment was published prior to 1830 other than some light humor, and certainly no poetry, histories, biographies, or memoirs. The first locally published novel would not appear until 1833.[32] The story would be much the same in Mississippi. A merchant named John Henderson wrote some poetry for the press, but otherwise local literary output related mostly to the sciences and was published exclusively in the East.[33]

But literature and such pursuits were a vital part of the upper level of southwestern society. "Knowledge is the lightest of all baggage," some said, and men like William Dunbar, Hutchins, Governors Claiborne and Sargent, and others agreed. These men accordingly became leaders in the effort to provide some more systematic and organized source for the enlightenment of similar active minds. In 1803 Claiborne, Dunbar, and several others formed the Mississippi Society for the Acquirement and Dissemination of Useful Knowledge. They announced its goals as "intellectual good fellowship" and "collaborative pioneering on the frontier of knowledge." The next year Dunbar purchased a chest of books from London to inaugurate their library, and also obtained a six-foot-long telescope with several magnifying powers, a chronometer, an astrolabe, a sextant, compasses, a pneumatic pump, and "1 Electrical Machine with apparatus for philosophical and medical uses," all of it costing him more than $2,250.[34] Thereafter they held meetings every Monday at 10 A.M. for discussions, to exchange books, and to hear talks prepared by their members.[35] It was to be the first learned organization of its kind in the Southwest, and one that, thanks to its members, would be hard to surpass or even match elsewhere.

More such associations followed, most aimed at the more elevated among the territory's people, but some, like the Natchez Mechanical Society, strove toward the education of the workingman in such practical sciences as chemistry and mechanics. In 1815 the territorial legislature commenced assembling its own library, primarily of legal texts, as well as encyclopedias, dictionaries, and economic and political treatises. And immediately after statehood in 1817 a crop of new learned organizations sprouted. Port Gibson started its Literary and Library Company. Wilkinson County, south of Natchez, commenced the Franklin Debating and Literary Society, and Greene County inaugurated its Library Society. In 1820 Amite County formed its Liberty Debating and Library Society, and the next year came the Pike Library Society.[36] Natchez's Debating Club also started about now, meeting in the city hall to discuss political, moral, and philosophical issues of the day.[37] The state also established a Literary Fund in 1821, something no other state seems to have handled in quite the same fashion, by designating the proceeds of some fines and the liquidation of estates that fell to the state for "the encouragement and support of education."

That same year Joseph E. Davis founded the Natchez Athenaeum, aimed, like so many of the other groups, at voluntary education of adults, chiefly males. The Athenaeum charged a ten-dollar annual fee, or it offered a lifetime membership for one hundred dollars, and declared its goals: "to lay the foundation of a Literary institution, which shall be of practical utility to the present generation, and live in after times, for the benefit of posterity . . . for extending the means of intellectual improvement to persons of all ranks and of all professions."[38] Four years later little sister Washington saw the inauguration of the Adams Athenaeum, with a membership to rival that of the original Mississippi Society. Naturalist Benjamin Wailes and Doctor John Monette, among others, lent it a special cachet, and it drew heavily from the talent that passed into and out of Jefferson College during that institution's episodic career. The Adams Athenaeum determined to start a library and reading room to contain not only prominent literary and scientific works but also as many of the popular journals and magazines of the day as possible. At its regular meetings the members intended to offer "dissertations upon useful and interesting topics" and subject them to the critiques of their fellows. President Wailes hoped that their success might outshine the other "abortive attempts at forming literary organizations," and he was not to be disappointed. Inside a month they had their Washington reading room open, and with Monette acting as chief librarian, they soon had subscriptions to some of the leading journals, such as the *North American Review, London Quarterly Review,* the *Edinburgh Philosophical Journal*, and others, including even full sets of their back issues. At monthly meetings members heard Wailes talk of the benefits of a new design for a plow, or a Jefferson College teacher lecture on scientific experiments. Despite its wonderful start, however, the Adams Athenaeum ceased its operation in less than two years.[39]

Perhaps the reason many of these groups did not last was that they could not offer a broad enough appeal. By their goals and definitions they attracted only the territory's elite and well-to-do. The workingmen and the farmers had little in common with Wailes and Dunbar. But then, in 1826, a new movement began to spread through America. The Lyceum attempted to elevate and improve the entire community by being open to everyone. Instead of studying science for its own sake, it promoted such inquiry only as it could be applied to the practicalities of daily life. Here was something for all, and Mississippians wanted it very much. In 1830 the editor of the Natchez *Southern Galaxy* noted that the state desperately needed a Lyceum, and a year later it got one. Not surprisingly it emerged at Washington, first in the pages of a magazine called *The Natchez*, and then a year later with a formal organization. In the next few years dozens would follow.[40]

The caliber of the men active in these organizations made them stand out, not only in the Southwest but in the nation as a whole. Sir William Dunbar was already a man of great note, thanks to his cotton-planting innovations. But after 1800 he dedicated himself almost entirely to scientific investigations, easily demonstrating himself to be among the most learned men of his time and place. Riders going up and down the Trace carried his letters to and from the likes of Dr. Benjamin Rush, William Bartram, and even Thomas Jefferson. A friend of the last told him that "for Science, Probity & general information [Dunbar] is the first Character in this part of the World." Jefferson took advantage of that knowledge, carrying on a steady correspondence with him for many years. It was Jefferson's suggestion that the American Philosophical Society in Philadelphia elect Dunbar a member, its first from the Southwest. "Dunbar ought to be associated to us," he told them.[41]

Indeed, it would be hard to find another man of his time so much like Jefferson himself. He studied the phenomena in the skies. He observed plant and animal life in Mississippi. He charted climatic changes. He looked at Mississippi's water through a microscope to discover new forms of microscopic life. He turned his eye to the variety of animals, fish, birds, and reptiles of the forests and savannas. Fossils, too, caught his attention. Starting shortly after his election to the society, Dunbar began publishing articles in its *Transactions*, sometimes as many as a dozen in a single year, finding himself on the same contents page with Benjamin Latrobe and Joseph Priestley. He also studied human beings, including the Choctaw and their sign language. Every day he went outdoors morning, noon, and night to take sightings and temperatures. Meanwhile he gave thought to a system of "telegraphy," a process for making artificial ice, and of course his work in vaccination against malaria. Nothing seemed to escape his interest and attention. Moreover, he spoke out as a champion of active participation in scientific inquiry and development by the federal government, advocating a national observatory, the funding of botanical expeditions of discovery, and public involvement in the dissemination of knowledge of all kinds. "Our politicians are confined within the narrow circle of the Customs & Excise," he lamented in 1802, "while literature of our present illustrious President will correct & enlarge the views of our public men, & that under his auspices & protection, Arts, Science, & Literature may take a flight, which will at length carry them beyond those European brethren as wel to as above them in the enjoyment of national liberty." Two years later Jefferson appointed Dunbar himself to one of the first nationally funded expeditions of exploration up the recently acquired Red and Arkansas Rivers in the Louisiana Territory.[42]

Dunbar was only the most illustrious of these learned men promoting enlightenment in the Southwest. The Methodist Reverend Henry Tooley produced a useful study of yellow fever, published in 1823. Henry Vose joined with Marschalk to publish the territory's first literary journal, *The Tablet*, in the late 1820s. In 1803 George Pendergrast authored a geographical study of the Mississippi, Louisiana, and West Florida Territories. More than one of Jefferson College's teachers wrote books and texts, and the works of geography and history by men like Wailes and Monette would bring them distinction in future decades.[43] By 1830 arguably no other community of its size in the nation could match the scientific and philosophical output of the thriving small city at the end of the old Trace.

In these same circles other arts flourished as well. Painting, and especially portraiture, began to appear on the walls of the finer homes by 1810. In 1817 a painter named William E. West was selling a copy of one of Raphael's "Madonna and Child" paintings through newspaper advertisements and had already painted likenesses of a number of the Natchez first families. Soon afterward Matthew Jouett, already noted as a portraitist in Kentucky, came to Natchez and found it a good field for his brushes, and so did Joseph Bush, also from Kentucky. All these men—like most portrait painters in the western states and territories—traveled almost constantly, as itinerant as the circuit riders, taking their oils wherever people would pay for them and sometimes traveling with prepainted bodies on the canvas, needing only to fill in the head of a buyer. Then, of course, there was John J. Audubon, who came in the 1820s to teach for a time at the Elizabeth Female Academy, and to paint both the city and some of its people. None of these men were true residents, and they, like their art, traveled through much of the Southwest on the Trace and then eventually left it, but behind them remained the colorful evidences of their passing on the parlor walls of the region's elite.[44]

Music and the dance also became more and more a part of the culture of high and low. Out on the farms and in the stands along the Trace, music was as rough-and-tumble as the people themselves, chiefly older Appalachian tunes brought with the immigrants and accompanied on a fiddle or harmonica in strains not much changed from their ancient Celtic antecedents. Players banged out tunes like "Possum up a Stump," "Sugar in the Gourd," and "Old Sister Phoebe," usually while others danced either in pairs or in great circles that presaged the later square dance. The dances often formed a major social event in the backwoods and could last for hours, even most of the day, fueled by food, frolic, and whiskey.[45] Those in the settled communities seeking to learn more refined dance took lessons in Natchez and Mobile and then attended balls held by groups like the Natchez Dancing Assembly.[46] From time to time traveling musical troupes took engagements in the larger towns, once they had theaters or other buildings sufficient to house an audience.

The theater especially took hold in the urban Southwest, actually showing its popularity well before places like Natchez or Mobile could truly be said to have been cities. In fact, on February 4, 1806, the very first known theatrical performance west of the Alleghenies went on at the City Tavern in Natchez, when members of a traveling troupe put on a now-forgotten play called *The Provoked Husband*. A week later they repeated it, plus a better known comedy, *A New Way to Pay Old Debts*.[47] The potential from the response to these performances was not lost on the city fathers, for in the week between the first and second shows they passed an act to regulate "public amusements," including a means of deriving a bit of tax from them.

Such early troupes did more than perform plays. They also did sleight of hand, ventriloquism, animal impersonations, and some mysteries the press described as "Thaumaturgic Experiments." But from the first it was the acting that the people most loved, and even after this first troupe moved on—not to be followed by more professionals for several years—local amateurs stepped forward to fill the void. The Natchez Theatrical Association formed in 1808 and flourished for years afterward. They secured an old hospital building abandoned by the Spanish when they left Fort Panmure, refurbished it, and presented their plays in it until 1813 when they built their own auditorium. Audubon thought it rather a poor affair, but other visitors who passed the building as they walked up the steep street from Under-the-Hill found it a "nice little theatre." In order to fund their new five-hundred-seat playhouse, the Association charged subscribers two dollars for a ticket in 1809, from three to five dollars later that same year, and then in 1813 one dollar for a ticket, and nonsubscribers two dollars when purchased the night of a performance. For that the audience got English comedies like *Point of Honor,* farces like *The Jew and Doctor*, and some twenty-five other programs over the years, almost always offered in a double feature of two plays per performance. Sadly, their playhouse burned in 1821, but in 1828 donations reflecting the interest of Natchez in the theater allowed them to erect a new brick building capable of holding an audience of seven hundred or more.[48]

The year 1817 saw the first return of a professional traveling theater company, and at the same time inaugurated several years of regular seasons by these itinerant players. That November or December the American Theatrical Commonwealth arrived in Natchez to prepare for its opening. The actors surveyed the town first and liked its looks. Unfortunately some of the people in the community mistook them at first. They came down the river on a flat and landed under the bluff. An enterprising fellow boarded their boat and, seeing their crates of costumes and props, assumed that they carried some valuable consumer goods. He wanted to buy them out on the spot, but when told by a wag in the company that all they had to sell was "live stock" and "men, women, children and dogs," he now assumed that the boat carried slaves instead. The charade went on for some time longer before Noah Ludlow took pity on the poor fellow and told him that "we are a company of comedians." They laughed all around, and then the visitor told them about the theater in town and how the citizens were most anxious to get a regular company of players to come and relieve them of the amateurs' offerings. That same evening he met with the theater's managers, and the next morning Lewis Evans, sheriff of the community but also on the theater's board, came to the company's boat. He offered them the use of the theater free of charge, whereas professional companies usually rented a house themselves and then recovered their expense from tickets. This was too good an offer to pass by. Within days the actors went to Marschalk to print handbills announcing their performances of *Honeymoon* and the farce *The Lying Valet*, and were soon on the stage.[49]

The American Theatrical Commonwealth came back the next year and the year after, with another company following them in later years. Common consensus was that the actors were not particularly good. They overacted, relied too much on histrionics, and consistently forgot their lines, making the prompter almost as much a part of the play as if he had been on stage. Moreover, the plays themselves tended toward broad farce and melodrama, with very little in the way of literary pretensions about them. In fact, drama critics soon began to write for the *Mississippi Republican* and other sheets, and they did not scruple at finding serious fault. "With mingled feelings of contempt and indignation," wrote one for the *Mississippi State Gazette*, "we witnessed the performance of Mrs. Centlivre's indecent Comedy." He suggested that the theater's managers had quite "mistaken the taste of our citizens, if they suppose that coarse and vulgar allusions, and indecent expressions, are calculated for this meridian."[50]

Other kinds of performances took place in that early theater besides plays. Lantern slide shows displayed transparencies of scenes against a white backdrop. A one-dollar admission gave the gullible a chance to thrill to the "Invisible Lady's exhibition of the occult and of consultation with spirits" in 1809, with children admitted—and terrified—at half price.[51] And some of the backstage scenes entertained the public as much as the plays, for the actors' troops often feuded among themselves in a very public fashion. In an era when the theater still carried about it some stigma held over from earlier generations, the novelty of seeing women working with men enhanced the reputation that some of the actresses already had for being "exotic," to say the least. Still, when they delivered their two or three weekly performances during a season, despite the dim lighting from candles and whale oil lamps, the crude and worn scenery, and the tired jokes in the plays, the audiences packed the theater. By 1819 the managers may have been taking in as much as seven hundred dollars or more a week, which soon induced them to enlarge the building and add some further income-producing options like boxes. Following a custom that dated back to the Elizabethans, they also put in a bar to sell drinks between the acts.

The burning of the old theater in October 1821 inaugurated a two-year theatrical hiatus in Natchez while managers tried to raise the capital to erect the new brick building. When a professional troupe returned to the city in 1823, they performed in Parker's inn, and for several years thereafter any performances took place in other public buildings or else outdoors. By 1826 a number of leading citizens finally put together a subscription to erect the new brick Main Street Theatre, progressing in a desultory fashion for two years more until James H. Caldwell, an entrepreneur who owned most of the traveling companies in the Southwest, bought into the project and then supervised its completion. They located the building on an unused cemetery not far from the center of town, and included in it a gallery where blacks, free and slave, could sit at reduced prices.[52]

Once the new house opened in 1828, theater was in Natchez to stay. Caldwell's companies came year after year, bringing actors and actresses with whom Natcheans became familiar and comfortable. In time people of national and even international repute trod the boards on the bluff. Brilliant child actress Louisa Lane would be the ancestress of Drews and Barrymores. Charles, the son of the legendary English tragedian Edmund Kean, spent more than one season here, and in 1829 two of the new lights of American theater, Junius Brutus Booth and Edwin Forrest made their Natchez debuts.[53]

The appearance of men of the caliber of Booth and Forrest finally gave the Southwest a chance to experience truly great drama, especially the works of William Shakespeare. In fact, plays by the Bard appeared at least as early as 1814, the first known being *Othello*, done by the Natchez Theatrical Association on April 15 of that year. This may have been the only amateur presentation of the great playwright's works, for the next time his words were uttered seems to have been in 1818, when the Commonwealth was in town. They did a version of *The Taming of the Shrew* in May, and then offered *Romeo and Juliet* that November. In the years that followed, Shakespearean works returned again frequently. *The Merchant of Venice* came in 1823 and twice more before the end of the decade. *The Taming of the Shrew* was also repeated two more seasons, as was *Othello*. *The Comedy of Errors* came in 1828. However, it waited until the arrival of Booth and Forrest for the most powerful of the tragedies to fill the stage on the graveyard. Booth delivered a strong *Richard III* in January 1829, and again the following month, to the universal acclaim of the local press. "Richard was himself," said one. "Whenever the points depended upon the efforts of Mr. Booth, they were effected with the power worthy this distinguished tragedian." Booth also offered his *Hamlet* in February, and then Forrest performed the same role and also *King Lear* in March.[54] Nothing in all the Southwest could match the kind of nearly world-class acting the people of Natchez chanced to see by the close of the 1820s.

By comparison to the Natchez stage, the rest of the Southwest stood considerably behind. Alabama did not see its first professional performance until December 1818, when a traveling troupe stopped in Huntsville for a ten-week engagement. They were so popular that they came back again—four years later. By May 1822 Mobile also had a semiresident company, and then two years later Noah Ludlow, having left the Commonwealth to start his own group in Nashville, moved it to Huntsville, where they performed at the Bell Tavern. Ludlow put on Alabama's first full theatrical season in Mobile, starting that Christmas Eve 1824. Thereafter he remained during the winter months and took his players on the road to Cahaba, Tuscaloosa, Montgomery, and elsewhere in the interior during the summer.[55] Meanwhile Caldwell sent one of his troupes to the opposite end of the Trace to play in Franklin and middle Tennessee through the 1820s.[56]

For these actors covering the more rural and less settled communities, professional life offered a host of vicissitudes, and some that the simple folk shared whether they liked it or not. Ludlow took his company to Montgomery in December 1827, induced by a promise that the town would support him well, though the assurance did come from the owner of the only hotel with a room large enough for presenting a play, who therefore had no small portion of self-interest in the matter. His actors made the trip overland in wagons, and their first night out begged lodging and food from a modest cotton farmer on the roadside. Almost at once the more impish of his players began to dazzle and tease their hosts, who could not tell whether they were serious or just what was happening as the actors lapsed into and out of lines from Shakespeare and the like. One fellow, assuming a wild-eyed appearance, stood two little slave boys in front of him and asked one, "Friend, what is thy name?"

"Sip, massa."

"Sip, meaning Scipio? Surnamed Africanus?"

"Yes."

"Scipio Africanus, stand farther from the presence; for, to say the truth, I like not the contiguity nor the superfluity of the perfume of thy epidermis; it partakes not of the 'Sabean odors from the spicy shores of Araby the blest'; nevertheless, I retain you as one of my hundred! But I do not like the fashion of your garments; you will say they are Persian attire,—let them be changed!"

While the other actors kept faces straight, the two terrified children and the utterly puzzled hosts simply stared in wonder. It did not help that as the troupe was leaving the next morning, another member told the hosts that the fellow was insane and they were taking him to an asylum in Philadelphia. Something over a week later, when Ludlow's people were in Montgomery and into their engagement, this same puzzled host walked up to him in the bar after a performance. He liked the show, he said, but he was rather dumbfounded at seeing one of the actors who looked a perfect double for the "crazy man" he had seen at his house. "I would be glad to see that man," said the farmer, "just to ask him if he hasn't a crazy brother."[57]

The frontier theater could be a far cry from Natchez's handsome Main Street edifice. When Ludlow opened his company in Nashville in 1817 he put them in an old warehouse used to store salt, built a rough

stage, and then put backless benches out for the audience, who sometimes sat on them without complaint through a full five-act play. Needing a large cast of extras to portray the Peruvian army in one play,
manager Sol Smith engaged twenty-four Creek Indians, complete with
their own weapons, and paid them fifty cents and a glass of whiskey
each. He gave them the spirits in advance, unfortunately, and they proceeded to stage a war dance that terrified the house and continued
even after Smith lowered the curtain.[58] One manager on the road
through Tennessee gave a performance at which he knew he had seen
more than two hundred in the audience, yet the receipts showed that
only seven people had bought tickets at the door. The rest climbed in
through windows.

These rude country people also occasionally had trouble differen-
tiating between the make-believe and the real. More than once some
buckskin-clad hero leaped from the audience onto the stage to save a
threatened heroine, and during a play in Huntsville in which a woman
and her child were depicted as starving, a fellow in the crowd jumped
to his feet and shouted, "Gentlemen, I propose we make up something
for this woman." Before he got the idea that the play was only a play, he
had thrown his pocketbook up onto the stage for her. In time, however,
backwoods audiences came to understand the concept of the drama,
and even to fancy themselves critics of a sort. They may have known
nothing of the theater, but they knew what they liked. "I don't go much
to theatricals, that's a fact," one fellow said when asked his opinion of a
tragedian's performance, "but I do think *he piled the agony up a little
too high* in that last scene."[59]

As the theater became increasingly popular, it attracted more in
the way of criticism, and not just for piling on "the agony." In Natchez
the more refined theatergoers began to complain of the vulgarity and
carnality of the farces, of the fact that women sometimes dressed in
men's clothing in order to play multiple roles, and apparently of some
actual profanity in the language. In fact, the players did not perform on
the Sabbath, which may indicate their own awareness that they over-
stepped the bounds of politeness and taste, but if so, the majority of
their audiences did not mind. The playhouse often attracted a crowd
far rougher than anything the actors portrayed, and Sheriff Evans and
his successors found more than one excuse to send police to oversee a
rowdy crowd. Men talked during the performances, shouted insults at
characters or actors they did not like, and sometimes made an inten-
tional show of striding about the hall or walking out. Some came
drunk. Others tried their aim by squirting tobacco juice at the stage.
Many just jeered. But at the same time, when an actor developed a iol-

lowing at any theater, whether in Natchez or Huntsville or Tuscaloosa, he or she could expect a great turnout on those evenings toward the end of the season when the company held a "benefit," quite literally a performance to honor that actor, and during which his or her fans threw flowers and not a little money onto the stage.[60]

Only a few years after the advent of Booth and Forrest signaled a new quality to Southwestern theater, another innovation arrived that, typically, linked the spirit of the entrepreneur with the technology at hand. In 1834 the first "floating theatre" tied up under the bluff. A man named Chapman simply built a large room atop a barge in Ohio, then boarded his actors, costumes, and props, and started the float down the rivers. At every community he passed he tied to the bank, blew a trumpet to announce his coming, and put on as many performances as the crowds justified. Then he moved on. Now he came to Natchez, and when done there he would go to New Orleans, and when he finished playing, simply sell his boat for wood and go back to Ohio by steamboat to start all over again. It was the beginning of a whole new era in entertainment for the Southwest, the modest harbinger of the palatial showboats that would for the rest of the century bring music, dance, and drama to a population ever hungry to add the arts—however unrefined at times—to their lives.[61]

⚓ **10** ⚓

The Road to Prosperity

The river led the new floating theaters to the Southwest just as it carried so much else from the very beginnings. Above all, the flowing highways—and to a lesser extent the Trace and its own tributaries—brought the means of acquiring wealth. They brought the settlers looking to capitalize on the rich and cheap new lands. They brought the slaves and the machines for the labor. They brought the raw materials of the industries that would seek to take hold in the territory. Most of all, they brought the men of vision and the prevailing sense of opportunism who risked their sweat and their capital to try to wrest a fortune from the raw frontier.

From its very outset river trade formed the foundation of frontier economy, and anyone could get into it. In 1828 young Abraham Lincoln joined a friend for his flatboat trip down the Mississippi to take a load of pork and the like to New Orleans, where they sold the boat and walked back up the Trace to Indiana. Two years later Lincoln made the trip again, first building a broadhorn on the Sangamon River in Illinois, then floating it down to New Orleans with another load of hogs.[1] Like many another frontier youth, Lincoln thus saw his first bit of the world and also experienced his initial taste of the lifeblood of the river—trade.

Back in 1801, before the steamboat, and even before the cotton industry began to boom in earnest, southwesterners saw their coming prospects. "People are beginning to turn their attention to exportation," Moses Fisk advised his son, "and our prospects are flattering."[2] Indeed they were. Every dawn brought more of the Kaintucks and their cargoes down the Mississippi, and not all of their goods went for local consumption. Flatboats like the *Independence* out of Kentucky carried pork, beef, and tallow. The *Mary* from the Tennessee River brought corn. The *Susannah* from Louisville delivered potatoes and whiskey, while the *Betsey* brought bacon. Keelboats like the *Kitty* delivered Tennessee flour and pork, and the well-named *Sweepstakes* poled downriver laden with bacon and gunpowder.[3] With a shortage of hard cash in the early days, these traders often bartered for cotton in return for their cargoes, even for such items as mustard, chocolate, Demerara rum, brandy, and English cheese.[4] They got even more of the staple when they imported black silks, satins, "jeans" fabric, Cossack boots, and cotton umbrellas and silk parasols.[5]

A typical mercantile trip started in Ohio at some point like Rossville, near Cincinnati. A trader had his prospective cargo shipped there to be loaded, and just before embarkation made final arrangements with the local commission merchant who actually entrusted the cargo to his charge. Then, if the prevailing winds did not keep the broadhorn pushed against the bank, they put off into the stream, not infrequently lashed together with two or three other flatboats. In addition to what he carried for the commission merchant, the trader might also have some of his own cargo aboard, one boatman taking what he called "an adventure of fowls," meaning chickens he hoped to sell. If the river ran high at the time, the boat could cross the small falls of the Ohio at Louisville without difficulty, and from there on to the mouth of the river the trip should be untroubled except by weather. They might even float by night, in the darkness gauging their distance from either shore by banging on the side of their boat and listening for the echo.

After a few days of traveling lashed together, the several trading boats might take to calling themselves a "squadron," and inevitably the most experienced—or overbearing—of the masters became captain of the whole. Along the way they usually stopped at "Cave in the Rock," a natural cave on the Illinois bank of the Ohio that showed its gaping fifty-yard-wide mouth to the broad stream. The traders found thousands of names of passersby carved on its walls and invariably added their own. Once out on the Mississippi, they generally made no sales stops, all their cargo being consigned either to Natchez or to New Orleans. Arrival at the former was cause for some celebration, especially if the market was running brisk. But even as late as the 1820s, the scarcity of hard cash tended to depress yields. Prices on pork, bacon, and flour ran low in such times, but the merchant had no choice. Certainly he could not take his perishable goods back up the river, and so he sold for what he could get. As a result, the state of the market exerted a considerable influence on the state of mind of the merchants themselves. After one stop in 1822 when a trader found the market dull and prices low from want of cash, it colored his whole view of Natchez itself. He left after three days of liquidating his cargo, putting behind him "little that I loved, and less that I admired, and all that I abhorred." It did not help, of course, that most of the commission houses and warehouses were situated below the bluff, cheek by jowl with the taverns and bordellos and all the seamier sides of Natchez life.[6]

Once the boatmen reached Natchez, they tied into the next industry to flourish here, cotton. When the cotton gin made that crop commercially practical and the territory found its cash crop, its economic future lay inextricably linked with the fluffy white fiber. All hinged on the performance of that first gin built in 1795. Almost immediately John Barclay built another, improved model in Natchez and submitted it to several planters for experimentation. When only partially completed, with fewer than half the "teeth" it would have for extracting seed, the machine cleaned eight pounds of raw cotton in fourteen minutes. They thus calculated that when finished and operating twelve hours a day, it would produce over a thousand pounds of cleaned cotton in a day. "It must also be observed that the machinery was very incomplete, work'd by a bad horse and none of us understood attending properly," confessed one of the examiners. Clearly a complete model run by experienced operators would work wonders.[7] Once Barclay finished his machine, another set of examiners looked it over and noted that though "the workmanship of this Machine is performed in a rude and imperfect manner," and their experiments were done on a damp morning when the cotton was soggy, still in forty-five minutes the gin cleaned a bit more than eighteen pounds of finished fiber. Better yet, the fiber passed through the teeth without being cut or damaged. "Upon the whole," they concluded, "we are of opinion, that this invention will prove of infinite utility to this Province." Barclay himself felt no modesty at what his contraption could accomplish. If a field hand could pick five hundred pounds of cotton, the old roller gins required more than a month to free it of its seeds. His machine could do that in half a day, "therefore resulting in the saving of thirty-three days to each worker employed in the cultivation of cotton." Given the number of white and black workers picking cotton in 1795, his gin would save a total of sixty-six thousand days of work in a season. At the rate of twelve and one-half cents a day for cost of labor, that meant a savings of $8,250.[8]

People in the territory needed little convincing, and soon Barclay had what he wanted, an exclusive franchise to build gins in Mississippi and a subscription raising more than $1,500 from local planters as an initial cash prize for his incentive and ingenuity. It was even proposed that every planter who used a Barclay gin should pay him $5 as a royalty. Unfortunately, the whole concept was far too simple, and in no time other entrepreneurs like David Greenleaf began designing and building variant gins of their own. Within a few years, most major planters owned their own machines and men like Barclay and other entrepreneurs found themselves left entirely out of the industry they helped to create. In 1792 the Natchez area planters produced a mere seventy-five thousand pounds of cleaned cotton. By 1800, thanks to the gins, that rose to perhaps 2 million pounds or more.[9]

Others, besides the planters themselves, certainly profited from the new gin industry. Men like Abijah Hunt, always willing to try something new, owned and operated a string of gins between Natchez and Port Gibson, and used the income from them to help acquire a 3,200-acre plantation of his own, as well as operating a retail business that imported and marketed a host of articles. An early example of an opportunist with an instinct for a "vertical," or integrated, enterprise, he grew cotton on his land, ginned it at his own gins, and then acted as a broker not only for others but also for himself, making an extra share of profit on his own cotton at every step. The notion that shrewd business sense was exclusively a Yankee trait clearly overlooked men like the enterprising Hunt.[10]

Several other planters like James Wilkins followed Hunt's lead and even opened cotton commission and brokerage houses outside the territory through which much of the Mississippi cotton passed. One of Wilkins's clerks in 1833 said that his "books are kept like the Bank books, & their transactions are almost as extensive." Just a single quarter's balance sheet that year showed more than six hundred thousand dollars on the tally.[11] And by then others were finally paying a little attention to Dunbar's early experiments with cottonseed oil, and starting to muse that this waste by-product might bring them even greater profits from their fields.[12]

Yet another by-product of cotton was industrial organization of a sort. In Claiborne County, Mississippi, one of the earliest known cooperative agricultural associations in America got its start on December 20, 1809, when some twenty-one local planters, including men with old ties to the Trace, like Coborn and Brashears, gathered to form the Planters Society. They announced their aim to be "the laudable purpose of promoting the public good and individual and public economy,"—which they of course hoped to achieve by serving their own ends. They wanted to bargain collectively for the goods and supplies they each had to import from New Orleans every year, reasoning that by combining their orders into bulk purchases, they could exact a better price. It would be some decades yet before the idea of such agricultural cooperatives took hold elsewhere in the nation, yet here it started in the minds of cotton growers with a keen eye to a profit, and to keeping every cent of it they could.[13]

Of course, there was more to industry in the Southwest than cotton, though it dwarfed all other enterprises. Small local entrepreneurs tried a host of projects to perform a useful service and derive a tidy profit. In any frontier community almost the first industry to appear was milling. While the farmers of the territory grew no appreciable wheat, still their staple grain, corn, required heavy grinding to turn it from dried kernels into cracked corn for fowl, crushed flakes for livestock, and fine meal for bread. The first mills were simple "hominy blocks," used at home with a stone by the farmwife, but very soon the growth of communities meant that there was money to be made by providing the service to others, and in quantities that the farm household would find impractical.

At first pioneer millers used a variety of crude techniques, including floating mills made from two canoes on either side of a modest waterwheel. It could be floated wherever the grain awaited, then anchored in a stream to let the current turn the wheel and grind small amounts of corn on two round stones on a "deck" between the canoes. In the absence of running water, other millers hitched horses or oxen to a round treadmill, and as they walked in harness, remaining stationary, the wheel turned beneath their feet and powered the turning of the grindstones. All these rude methods were slow, and produced meal and flour of varying and often inferior quality. Consequently, as soon as money to attempt something more ambitious became available, the real entrepreneurs located themselves beside streams that provided a good run of water year-round. Instead of locating right beside the flow, they dug mill races that diverted some of the water to their paddle wheels, usually building a dam as well in order to keep the flow steady and provide some extra impetus from the force of the backed-up water above the dam. David Crockett tried this in Tennessee, to some success at first, until his mill in Lawrence County, a few miles east of the Trace, was taken down by a sudden flood.

If well designed, the mill offered its operator additional means of exploiting the waterpower, for when there was no corn to grind, he could mount a circular saw blade to his main shaft and use it to turn trees into lumber, always a needed commodity as the frontier became more settled and people with money wanted frame homes instead of the drafty dogtrots.[14] Indeed, there were several ways to produce lumber, and where no mill was available, a few men with whipsaws could do the job, only more laboriously. The inevitable Gideon Lincecum took a hand at it between moves and practicing medicine and teaching, and typically he did so purely as a matter of capitalizing on passing opportunity. "I started out early one morning, intending to accept an offer to engage in any kind of business that might present itself to me," he recalled years later. Initially he walked toward a local doctor's house, intending to continue his less-than-stellar medical career. But along the way he encountered a fellow carrying a whipsaw over his shoulder, and who happened just to have lost his partner for the other end of the blade. Lincecum immediately suggested himself. Looking at the scrawny Gideon—perhaps still pale from all that bloodletting—the lumber man suggested that Lincecum could not stand the rigors of the work. To make planking one man stood atop a log while the other stood beneath, and they pulled and pushed at the saw the full length of the trunk to slice off each plank. It was truly backbreaking work.

Yet Lincecum did not shrink from the labor. "My money was out," he told the sawyer. "I must try to make more some way." Moreover, with a job staring him in the face, he added that he "liked the looks of *that* saw pretty well." Finally he convinced the other, and they formed a partnership, the one providing the saw and all other needed tools, and Lincecum making for him a lodging in his own home. Their very first commission came from a Yankee merchant intent on starting a store. He ordered a thousand board feet of one-inch planks to build a counter and lay a floor, and in only a few days the whipsaw completed the job, at four dollars for each hundred feet. Moreover, the storekeeper paid them another twenty dollars to put down the floor and build the counter. Then Lincecum earned another ten dollars by marking prices on all the store goods and putting them in their places in the counter. Thereafter he and his partner continued for another two months, sawing some two hundred feet of planking each day and making about eight dollars for the work before an accident forced him to leave the partnership.[15]

Those planks sawed by Lincecum and his partner bore an intimate link with another young industry struggling along in the Southwest even as the first rude lumbermen started cutting a living out of the pine forests. The boards they made into floors, counters, shutters, and doors all depended on iron for nails and hinges and more. No wonder the earliest cargoes coming down the rivers in the barges and broadhorns contained so much of the precious manufacture, and that when one house burned or was taken down, its owners salvaged their nails to reuse in the new one. Inevitably, sooner or later some enterprising character would realize that it would be cheaper and easier to make iron locally than to import it, and that therein lay a road to profit.

Early travelers on the Trace noted signs of iron ore as early as 1805, and especially on its northern reaches in Tennessee. Substantial deposits were to be found around McLish's stand on the Buffalo River, and there sometime after 1810 a man named Hed seems to have established the first iron works in the Southwest. Iron making was a crude process here on the frontier, its products limited by the means of its manufacture. Men dug the raw ore from the ground and then simply fired it until white-hot. Then they beat the glowing ore with hammers, the constant hammering gradually knocking out the impurities even as it condensed and flattened the ore itself. Under repeated heatings and even more pounding, the ore finally took shape as a nail, a door hinge, a bit of harness, a part of a gun lock. It could be worked and reworked and wore well, but by the nature of its manufacture from small bits of ore, it could not easily be made into larger items like plow blades. Unlike such iron, produced in a forge or "bloomery," more substantial wrought iron came from stone furnaces in which more sophisticated smiths mixed the ore with limestone and charcoal and then melted it completely. Drawing off the impurities that floated to the top of the molten iron, the smith poured the remainder into molds to make "pigs," and these could be reheated or melted later to be shaped into almost anything within the capabilities of the smithy's tools.[16]

In 1822 three men organized the Buffalo Iron Works near the old McLish inn, and immediately applied to the state government for 3,000 acres of timberland nearby, large supplies of firewood being essential to ironmaking. For several years they failed to make much of a success at the enterprise, but when more partners came with experience at ironmaking in Virginia, the business started to prosper. In addition to the timberland, they secured a 165-acre "ore bank," literally a deposit of iron ore where the raw stuff could be dug out of the ground just beneath the surface. The Trace ran right through the middle of the bank, and the feet of thousands had already well exposed the telltale red earth that contained the ore.

It could be a tiresome process, and it consumed raw materials in prodigious quantities. First they cut the timber into four-foot lengths and stacked some twelve cords or more end on end in a large clearing. Then they covered the whole with earth and started a fire somewhere at the bottom of the pile. For the next fortnight the wood smoldered, the earth covering preventing it from actually bursting into flame. Finally the workers uncovered the still-smoldering charcoal, let it cool, and took it to the furnace. Meanwhile, as the wood turned to charcoal, workers used picks and shovels to dig the ore from the earth, generally along the ridgelines, and sometimes right alongside the Trace itself. Rarely did the miners go more than ten or fifteen feet beneath the surface for the ore, and nothing like the later timbered and galleried mines was yet to be seen. After that backbreaking work, they then removed the soil and other impurities from the ore by hand, and followed that with a low heating that made much of the rest fall away. What remained was what they called brown hematite, an ore that contained almost 60 percent iron. From this, a furnace might produce perhaps half a ton of pig iron per day. The Buffalo Works would last nearly a century, though it only prospered intermittently. Yet it proved a harbinger of a much later industrial boom that would erupt from the iron-rich hills of central Alabama in decades ahead.[17]

The earth yielded other assets besides its iron and wood and cotton. Far to the south, territorial planters found that sugarcane flourished and learned how to turn it into sugar and molasses. Laborers cut the cane in the fields, then carried it in bundles to the crusher, where animal-drawn vertical rollers chewed tons of the cane and set the sugary sap inside to dripping into a trough. That juice, and sometimes some of the crushed cane containing still more sap, they then put in large iron kettles and boiled it for hours until what remained was molasses. Five men, working all day, could make five to ten gallons depending on the quality of the cane, and so much of the juice got into their clothes that some claimed seriously that their trousers would stand by themselves at the end of the day.[18]

Almost any industry that provided necessary consumer articles could find some modest success in the Southwest, the chief limitations being only the supply of power, raw materials, a market, and ingenuity. Mining and founding never took a firm hold in the region in the early days. By 1840 no one in Mississippi made a living at it, and even in Alabama only a single furnace made cast iron, five forges worked iron, and the whole process from ore to nail employed a mere 30 men at a capital investment of only $9,500. Just the portion of Tennessee at the head of the Trace, by contrast, employed several times that number. Alabama did have gold, but was only producing just over $60,000 worth, and also Alabamians plucked some 23,659 bushels of bituminous coal from their earth. On the other hand, Mississippi outstripped its neighbor in manufacturing. Some 274 men produced $242,225 worth of machinery in that year, equalling Tennessee, more than doubling Alabama's output, and completely dwarfing Louisiana's tiny $5,000. Still many industries remained small, and some no more than cottage industries. Mississippi's 7 gunsmiths made a mere ninety firearms and no more than 23 men were employed in producing precious metals. By contrast, nearly 700 men earned a living making bricks, testimony to the expanding demand for permanent home building materials. Meanwhile Alabama artisans made hardware and cutlery, four times as many firearms, and even cast four cannon. Textile making also occupied some men and capital, though never in anything like a challenge to the Eastern and European hegemony. Alabama had but fourteen factories and 1,502 spindles in operation. Mississippi had 53 manufacturers, but a pitiful 318 spindles limited their output. Louisiana and Tennessee produced barely any more. Leather tanneries employed a few more Mississippians, as did soap making, drug and medicine making, pottery, sugar, printing and papermaking, and more. Saw- and gristmills between the two states comprising the bulk of the Southwest totaled 1,803, the bulk of them in Alabama. But Alabama built not a single ship, though it was a major seaport state, and Mississippi built but two.

The boom in home building was manifest in the 2,391 houses erected in Mississippi, each costing an average of $491. Alabama saw only 539 go up, but they cost some $1,372 apiece, reflecting the higher cost of materials and labor. Alabama employed 882 men at construction, while Mississippi occupied three times that many. Putting all their capital investment in industry together, Mississippi and Alabama had just under $4 million involved in manufacturing.[19] Many industries were as yet embryonic. Only in 1831 did investors charter and capitalize the West Feliciana Railroad out of Woodville, though it would be the third line built in the whole nation. Twenty-two more would follow in the next decade in Mississippi, though two-thirds of them failed. In short, while the people of the Southwest had about them most of the raw materials and skills for industrial self-sufficiency, such pursuits—but for sugar and cotton cultivation and house building—remained largely unexploited opportunities. They required too much capital or too much labor, and for many, especially in Mississippi, it was simply too easy to depend solely on the fluffy bounty from the soil to provide means of buying all other necessities from the outside. As early as the 1830s some division between Mississippi and Alabama especially began to be evident, illustrated in the later observation that an Alabamian could wear cotton from Anniston and Tuscaloosa mills, pound nails made in Ashland, wear shoes from Nashville, and heat himself at a stove from Tennessee, whereas the Mississippian arose in the morning to don socks made in Massachusetts, shoes cobbled in Boston, a suit of clothes from New Hampshire, and then sat in a Chicago chair to drink Brazilian coffee on a table made by a Yankee.[20]

Part of the driving force behind Southwestern lethargy at industrial investment and development lay in the very nature of the people themselves. Men of the region in their own time would self-servingly suggest that they simply were not interested in money—greed was something for Yankees—and even Northerners came easily to believe the myth. It served different needs for both. To the Southerner a studied carelessness about making a fortune denoted a man of high culture and breeding, one who lived above such mean ambitions. To the Northerner it offered a visual proof of the basic laziness and sloth that he saw in men of the South. Yet most certainly it was a myth. These men who came down the rivers and the Trace were of the same breed who had been moving west ever since their ancestors landed on the shores of Tidewater Virginia in 1607, or stepped off their ships at Baltimore and Philadelphia a few generations later. They were opportunists all, men looking for the main chance. The only difference between them and their Northern counterparts on that score was that the Yankee found that he could prosper by staying put on his limited landscape and applying ingenuity to the abundant raw materials near at hand.

The southern settler, quite the opposite, found fewer natural industrial resources within easy grasp, but an inestimably greater availability of land, and much of it more suitable for cultivation than that in New England. Quite naturally, then, these men over the generations developed an instinct for finding their wealth in the soil. The fact that agriculture may have *looked* to be a more indolent way of making a living to some Yankees did not make it any less backbreaking than building ships or weaving textiles. And if some small planter minority did live a life of lazy freedom from toil, it was only because they had already done something that their own mythmakers denied: They had shown more than enough interest in making money to amass sufficient fortune to free themselves from labor—chiefly by buying it from others. Even Timothy Flint, usually a keen observer of the life of the Southwest, misread what he saw when he observed that these people were reckless of the value of money, more so than any others he had ever seen.[21] Some would even go so far as to say that understanding things like stocks and corporations, and using money to make money, were concepts beyond the ken of these seemingly elevated and altruistic people of the Southwest. A chorus of voices from those who participated in the frantic Yazoo and Mississippi land speculations, or who formed the Natchez Steam Boat Company, or manufactured their own improved cotton gins, or maneuvered and schemed to influence the location of county seats and state capitals—all those men and a host of others in the Southwest would have shouted "nonsense" in unison. Those who could make fortunes made them. Those who could not tried another line of work or moved, like the Lincecums, to another locality. Southerners and northerners alike, seeing this apparent propensity to keep moving, mistook it for some innate wanderlust and an indifference to penury in preference to commitment and responsibility. Yet the truth lay in exactly the opposite direction. If there was one lesson to be learned from the whole history of the settlement of the southern half of the continent, it was that the first men in one generation to reach the newest edge of the wilderness became the landed aristocrats, the wealthy and the influential, of the next. Those who came after them often scrambled for smaller and smaller shares of what remained, and having before them so visibly the example of the planter lords, decided instead to try again by moving farther west. The Lincecums and the others, far from being indifferent to or careless of wealth, anxiously chased it all across the South from the Alleghenies to the Mississippi.

Places like Natchez and Mobile and Washington especially put the lie to the notion of southwestern indifference to money. Natchez in time would come to house more millionaires per capita than any other city in the United States. Washington throve on the business opportunity provided by being briefly the capital, and when the legislature moved on, the town started its slow death. Jackson became almost overnight a growing magnet for business and speculation, while Mobile and the rivers filling its bay, along with the Mississippi, saw the constant flow of commercial wealth into and out of the territory. Certainly the river cities like Natchez were atypical of the rest of the interior, most of all for their greater range of ideas, their worldliness, their excesses, and their tolerance, but that is precisely because they were peopled by men dedicated to trade and fortune, and the rivers simply afforded them a better opportunity than did inland routes like the old Trace or the Federal Road.

Nothing better revealed the southwesterners' fixation on their ambitions of fortune—within the limitations of their means of acquiring it—than the early appearance of institutions to manage money. Hard cash clattered about the territory from its earliest days, and always in smaller supply than the inhabitants wished. Moreover, a confusion of old Spanish and French coins—doubloons, pistareens, picayunes, *sous,* and more—sometimes made issues of exchange and purchase a nightmare, especially when paper cotton-gin receipts fluttered into the mix

along with the scrip of state and local banks from the East, and the few
U.S. dollars that came in after 1798.[22] No system existed to ensure an
equitable handling of all this, and men often settled the value of goods
or a debt not on some fixed basis, but rather on individual negotiation
based on the desirability of the particular form of currency about to
change hands. Gold specie often brought discounted prices on goods
because it was in high demand. Paper currency, on the other hand, was
often itself discounted from face value in exchanges.

Moreover, in the earliest territorial days there was no place to
keep money in any quantity other than some home strongbox, vulnera-
ble to bandits or thieving servants. Consequently people of fortune
kept their wealth in real property instead—land, slaves, livestock,
buildings—all of it just as actively involved in producing even more
wealth as if it had been money in a bank earning interest. Merchants'
wealth often lay in the sizable accounts due them from their customers,
debts that in time could be redeemed by seizure of property if not paid.
Yet outsiders looking on this scarcity of hard cash and high rate of debt
mistook them as signs of financial indifference or ineptitude. In fact
they only showed that the Southwest was not yet ready for a more
sophisticated monetary system.

The first attempt at banking came before statehood, in 1809 when
Francis Martin, Ferdinand Claiborne, Abijah Hunt, Winthrop Sargent,
Samuel Postlethwaite, and others secured from the territorial legislature a twenty-five-year charter for the Bank of the Mississippi, with a
capitalization of a half million dollars to be realized from sale of five
thousand shares of stock at one hundred dollars each. As soon as the
first fifty thousand dollars was raised, the bank went into operation in
Natchez, even as the directors continued selling more shares. The
bank was empowered to print and issue paper currency backed by its
capitalization and deposits. It could issue loans at no more than six percent annual interest, and could pay its stockholders twice-yearly divi-
dends out of its profits. At the same time, if recklessness led to a circu-
lation of paper money more than three times greater than the actual
current capital from investors, the law required the directors themselves to make up the difference.[23]

When the bank opened its doors in Natchez, the traditional system of finance began to take hold in the territory, as the institution
placed itself as an intermediary between savers and borrowers, making
a small profit from both. Further, it imposed the beginnings of financial
stability on the community, since its own privately printed banknotes
became a standard medium of currency against which all the others

were to be measured. Better yet, the bank's currency soon gave to consumers—especially the big purchasers like large planters—an option they had not enjoyed previously. In former times people often paid their bills to one creditor by signing over—at a discount—notes due them from another. The discount was negotiated largely on the basis of the presumed ability of the latter to pay. Besides limiting the value of goods that a purchaser thus obtained, it also limited the options of the seller for his own purchases, since he was most likely to obtain his payment in goods rather than cash. If William Dunbar bought some books and paid for them with a note due him from merchants Clarke and Wren, the bookseller could only use that note to obtain goods from those merchants, even if others in town sold the same goods at lower prices. Or, if the note was a personal one from some other planter, the bookseller had to shop around to find a merchant who would accept the note for credit, usually at a hefty discount, and still the poor bookseller did not necessarily have a chance to buy his own goods at the best prices. But once the bank opened, it at first agreed to discount such notes, essentially making itself surety for final payment in case of default. Backed by the bank, the bookseller could now use his bill from Dunbar to buy anything, from anyone. Better yet, as the bank issued its own paper currency, buyers and sellers alike no longer had to worry about the reliability of some third-party debtor. Once people accepted the soundness of the bank, sellers took its currency without question and at face value. Moreover, with the cumbersome system of discounting on the wane, the extra markup that retailers inevitably added into purchase prices to allow for what they could lose in discounting disappeared. That, combined with an enhanced ability for buyers to shop for the best price, spurred more competitive pricing and a brisker trade.[24]

In its first years of operation the bank looked small, and *was* small by eastern measures, but it showed promise from the first. At the time of its incorporation in December 1809, only $44,000 in stock had been sold, and of that just $6,250 was actually paid for in hard cash or other immediately negotiable assets like bills of exchange due on major northern and eastern banks. That left the bank with just $37,750 in assets, being entirely composed of the amount remaining due on the shares sold thus far. The situation remained unchanged the next year, with the bank essentially unable to function since it had not yet reached its $50,000 minimum capitalization. But in 1811 share sales at last passed the mark, and at the same time most of the original investors finally paid for their shares in full. On June 10, 1811, the bank took in its first deposits. Suddenly it had $36,000 in liquid assets and a big jump in share sales due in years to come. Now it was in business. Its first loans went out, most for only six-month periods, though usually renewable automatically upon application. By 1814 the bank had assets of nearly $150,000 and liquid assets nearly the same, and actual capital in hand of more than $100,000. A frontier financial institution had come into being, and in a region where supposedly no one cared about money and profits.[25]

It was a very difficult time for a bank to get started anywhere in the United States and its territories, for just then the country was nearing the end of its second war with Great Britain. Throughout the country one bank after another suspended payment of the hard currency that backed its paper money on demand. Fears of counterfeiting by enemy agents who used their bogus bills to deplete American specie and bankrupt the struggling nation led almost every bank to hoard its gold and silver, in spite of public protests. The Bank of the Mississippi finally did so only in the last month of the war, and after almost every other American bank announced suspensions, and then only after its primary supplier of coin in New Orleans halted its own specie payments. Far from being a sign of weakness, the suspension came at a time when the bank enjoyed considerable strength. Still the territorial legislature had to respond to complaints, and its investigation revealed only sound banking policy, resulting in a complete exoneration from any stigma of bad management. When the war ended the bank resumed honoring its notes for specie.[26]

In the four years that followed, the cotton boom that came with peace saw the bank's assets quintuple to nearly $2 million, a phenomenal growth reflecting the kind of wealth being built in the territory. Moreover, the bank still charged only 6 percent interest, while similar institutions elsewhere in the nation levied up to twice that from customers. When Congress divided Mississippi from the territory to make it a state, a new constitution had to address the issue of banking again. While no one argued forcibly against the policy of private banking— which prevailed throughout the nation—still some felt that the state ought to have some involvement in bank finance and operation, and now reserved to itself the right—but not the obligation—to subscribe for itself up to one-fourth of any new bank's shares, with concomitant representation on its board of directors. Also before the new state legislature would be the matter of how many banks there should be. Hoping to preempt the appearance of rivals, Postlethwaite, president of the Bank of the Mississippi, proposed that his institution open branch offices wherever population could support them. His bank would provide all the banking services needed statewide, including those for the state government itself, and in return he asked for a promise that the legislature not charter any competitive institutions until 1841. While he or the other private directors would continue to manage the bank's operations, they would allow the state to purchase shares and have representation on the board.[27]

Postlethwaite—backed by the record of the bank and by the general prosperity that followed the war in the territory—proved persuasive. In 1818 the new state legislature rechartered the institution as the Bank of the State of Mississippi and authorized it to extend its capitalization to up to $3 million. The new bank could open offices for discount and deposit wherever it chose, but the legislature mandated that branches open in Port Gibson and Woodville specifically, and also in Marion County. And the state guaranteed the bank a monopoly for twenty-three years.[28]

The new institution flourished even more than its predecessor, thanks to expansion, the state's involvement, and the continuing boom that Mississippi enjoyed. By 1824 deposits in the Natchez, Woodville, and Port Gibson branches totaled nearly $279,000. The whole operation had $400,000 in its own currency notes circulating, and outstanding loans raised total assets to $1,612,595.[29] Moreover, it enjoyed an enviable reputation for fairness. The directors held its operations above politics and factions, ran itself conservatively and participated in no speculations or special favors to individual industries. As a result, during its years of operation under its several presidents, it never encountered a single substantial complaint that resulted in action against it either by the territorial or state legislatures.[30]

But it did have enemies. The rapid spread of population during the 1820s saw the growth of new cotton counties to the east, outside the river counties that made up the old Natchez district. These newly wealthy planters in the old "piney woods" regions resented the monopoly enjoyed by the bank, and began to exert more and more pressure on the legislature to abrogate the 1818 charter. Moreover, they believed that the bank favored Natchez area planters with its loans, and apparently the frontier counties did suffer some stunting of their development from inability to get loans and from the glaring absence of a branch to serve them. While the overwhelming majority of planters along the Mississippi were at most twenty miles from the nearest branch office, piney woods planters could find themselves a hundred miles or more distant. By 1830, when the population of the newer counties outstripped the old, their voice in Jackson proved decisive. Despite its promise of unchallenged operation until the end of December 1840, the legislature annulled its charter to pave the way for new banks that would, in turn, open the door for new investors to create and control their own regional finances.[31]

Banking took a new and dangerous direction in February 1830 with the chartering of the Planters Bank of Mississippi. It, too, was headquartered in Natchez, but the charter required it to operate seven branches in the new eastern counties, and the legislature—in a blatantly political move reflecting the power of the eastern counties now—committed to fund not just a fourth of its capitalization, but two-thirds of the $3 million to be raised. To get that kind of money, the Planters Bank had to look to outside investment, commencing a decade of attempts to capitalize Mississippi banks by selling stock elsewhere. They had to do so to provide the greatly expanding demands for credit from the new counties. So did the new Agricultural Bank of Natchez, as the Bank of the State of Mississippi restyled itself. But when ensuing national financial travails beset the economy in a few years, credit collapsed drastically, and most of the banks eventually failed. Perhaps the directors of the first bank foresaw this, for—unwilling to follow the lead of the Planters Bank—they closed their doors in 1831 of their own accord with fully balanced books, all debts paid, and all investors including the state repaid with interest.[32]

Few of its competitors would see such an end. Speculation, reckless printing of bank notes, irresponsible investment in railroad schemes that never saw a single tie laid, all swallowed millions in capital from the banks and their investors, and the state foolishly got involved by taking out loans to invest in its own banks. When the crash came in 1837, brought about largely by the political machinations that now penetrated every corner of American life even here in the Southwest, the banks and their economy collapsed together.[33]

Still, prior to the great Panic of 1837, and especially during the 1820s, no state in the Union enjoyed such a rapid growth of population and prosperity as Mississippi, with Alabama, as usual, not far behind. Not surprisingly, federal, state, and local government could not view all that financial gain without deeming some portion of it due to maintain the civil authorities and their operations. Among the several provisions in the first set of laws drafted for the territory in 1798, Sargent's Code, were those for raising tax revenues. When each county submitted an estimate of its needed expenditures for the year, the governor then apportioned that amount out to the communities comprising the county. Commissioners there assessed property values and assigned taxes based on everything from income-producing properties like ferries and taverns to boats, oxen, horses, and of course slaves. The code determined the value of property not by its sales potential but based on the income it could produce. Officials left tax collection to the county sheriff, and the code thus enacted remained in effect without change until 1815. There were no territorial taxes, only local levies as apportioned by the governor. However, in that year the legislature enacted its first territorial tax, and on the same kinds of property and basis as the county taxes. Evaluators rated land chiefly on its relative proximity to Natchez and the Mississippi, acreage in the city being assessed as high as twelve dollars per acre, while land fourteen or more miles distant could rate as low as two dollars. A building in town owed taxes at the rate of two mills, or two-tenths of a cent, per dollar of assessed valuation, while store merchandise and investments like bank stock brought two and one-half mills. Slave owners paid fifty cents for each black male, and paid sixty-two and one-half cents for themselves. Slave traders paid a $5.00 per head tax on every Negro brought into the territory for sale, and men who rode about the countryside paid $1.25 for the privilege of sitting in a carriage. No one liked the system, but it did raise revenue.

Cities like Natchez imposed their own additional taxes, including $6 for wagons, fees on boat tonnage, slave sales, and more. Then there were the license fees paid by traveling shows and performers. Tavern owners paid their $20 a year, and vendors in the city market paid $10 annually. As city, county, and territorial then state demands rose, assessors found more items to tax, like silver tableware, musical instruments, guns, watches and clocks, and even "assets" like outstanding notes due.[34] It all became increasingly more capricious—or so it seemed. By the time statehood approached, taxpayers in the western counties along the Mississippi were on the verge of revolt. They could see that the population was starting to shift to the piney woods counties. Once those people gained control of the legislature, they could enact whatever new taxes they liked and enforce them on the wealthier Natchez region, whose counties were already paying three-fourths of the taxes for the entire territory by 1815.[35]

Indeed, as 1817 and statehood approached for the first of the old Trace territories to be carved from the Southwest, the cost and the burden of prosperity became more and more manifest. They had come for opportunity. They began their planting and launched their industries, built their fortunes, and even commenced their rude financial systems, largely independent of men and events elsewhere in the nation, and with relatively little interference from the political gorgon. But expanding population meant statehood, and that meant a struggle for power, as the newcomers inevitably sought to take rule for themselves and the old established planter society fought just as much to hold on. Meanwhile, events far to the east and north could not pass indefinitely without involving the Southwest in their turmoils. Young America was advancing into a turbulent adolescence, and no part of the new nation could escape its impact. There was a cost for success—a tax to be demanded far in excess of the levies on silver watches and livestock and men. They were all political animals, and what beliefs and prejudices they did not bring with them when they came to the territory in search of elusive fortune the peculiar exigencies of the land and one another soon created.

⟨ 11 ⟩

The Road to Rule

Soon after he arrived in the territory, Andrew Ellicott complained to Sir William Dunbar of "the refactory disposition of Natcheens." He found them, he lamented, "as difficult a people to govern as Moses did the Children of Israel."[1] It was to be a refrain commonly heard in the years ahead. In 1800 David Ker observed that the inhabitants were so secluded from regular intercourse with the rest of the United States that they lacked "even the common means of political information." Men knew little of the affairs or issues of government. Instead "party zeal without knowledge has gone greater lengths here than I ever saw it elsewhere."[2] Several years later Fortescue Cuming saw it even further developed. "The curse of party pervades this territory," he said in 1808. "Any opinion of a publick character, would not fail to offend one or the other party."[3]

Any people and any region that had served so many masters in so short a time as the early settlers of the Mississippi Territory were bound to find themselves riddled with conflicting loyalties and opinions, an amalgam of all the fealties they had paid and the bargains they made to survive the changing regimes. In May 1797, before the first territorial governor arrived from the United States, General James Wilkinson warned Captain Guion that Natchez itself was "an extensive, opulent, and polished community, agitated by a variety of political interests and opinions." He knew what he was saying, all the more when he predicted that once the Spanish left for good the "Natcheens," as Ellicott called them, would "find themselves without laws or magistrates,

218

and the bonds of society being dissolved, more or less irregularities may ensue." Indeed, they had already.[4]

In its earliest days under the French the divisive image of politics did not appear in the Southwest. After all, rule lay solely with the king in France, and his emissaries in the New World. And of course, with God in the presence of the clergy. Both rules were absolute, and if there was a clash, it came between the two or within them, but always across the ocean. All that Mississippians saw were the latter-day evidences of battles fought far away. They had no say, and virtually no involvement, when the French gave them and their territory to Britain in 1763 at the end of the Seven Years' War. Only then did the seeds of future political battles see planting at Natchez, as the British began granting choice lands to their own, and one of them, Anthony Hutchins, late of His Majesty's Forces, came to stake his claim to prominence. In 1772 he took office as justice of the peace, the territory's first English-speaking officeholder. One admirer called him "a man of marked characteristics, courageous, active, of restless and indomitable spirit."[5] Another would in time use almost exactly the same words, yet phrase them as a condemnation when he referred to Hutchins as "a man of unlimited ambition, of an active, restless and discontented spirit."[6] Opinions of men, like the men themselves, differed as the fences dividing them grew higher.

Then came the American Revolution, the Willing expedition, and Natchez at last was dragged directly into the public affairs of the growing nation to the east. Now began the changing of sides and the bending with the prevailing breezes that would characterize so many of the territory's leading men. Their will to survive inadvertently made passive politicians of them, but a few like Hutchins, taken prisoner by Willing and seeing his plantation sacked, felt the stirrings of future, more active participation. Willing's backers, of course, eventually had to flee the territory, and those remaining paid overwhelming allegiance to England, but not wholeheartedly. They had seen themselves left to Willing's mercy, experienced the neglect by West Florida authorities that allowed the outrages suffered by Hutchins. Wisely the British decided to give Natchez four delegate seats in the provincial assembly that met in Pensacola. They thought that perhaps this move would still the grumbling. It did not.

Within only months Hutchins, now an activist, led a small rebellion against the unpopular commandant sent to Fort Panmure and soon saw him replaced, but only in time for the Spaniards to move into the territory. Then came John Blommart's abortive plot, in which Hutchins again assumed considerable prominence and exerted his influence to defeat the American sympathizers and keep Natchez briefly British. Events passed with dizzying speed, and when the Spaniards again took control, and this time in strength, Hutchins and others fled as far as South Carolina. Then, in 1783, Britain formally ceded the territory to Spain, and for the next fifteen years, chiefly under Gayoso, the territory enjoyed a Spanish peace.

Gayoso had no desire to see factions and parties arise in his domain. After all, he, like the French, served an absolute monarch. There were to be no parties if he could help it. Instead, he turned to the leading men who remained, men like Dunbar, and included them in a new *cabildo,* or council, he created to help him administer justice. Their powers were very limited, and in no way political, but Gayoso added to their reputations as men of note by appointing them, which would lend them influence in any future efforts at self-government.

Meanwhile Natchez remained politically quiet. The only overt expression of opinion on the larger matters of men and nations then agitating the Atlantic world was the publication of the first book written in the territory, John Henderson's *Paine Detected, or The Unreasonableness of Paine's Age of Reason.* When it appeared in 1797 it attacked the Enlightenment views of Thomas Paine, but then, being published in a colony tightly controlled by a European monarchy, it could hardly have done otherwise.[7]

Yet Spanish policy also inadvertently helped to create the discord and faction it sought to prevent. Predictably in this region of opportunists with sights set more clearly on fortune than loyalty, the issue was one of money. When Spain stopped buying district tobacco at inflated prices, the resulting slump in the region left many of the planters heavily in debt to local merchants and unable to pay. The merchants complained loudly against the planters. The planters accused the merchants of charging outrageous prices and exorbitant interest on their debt. In response the Spanish authorities decreed a three-year moratorium on planter debt and set an interest ceiling of 5 percent, both of which outraged the creditors, even though the law also required planters to pay one-third of their debts in each of those three years in order to clear the books. But with tobacco prices down—and cotton still in the future as a cash crop—at the end of the first year they could not pay. Hutchins himself complained to Gayoso that the merchants were in confederacy against them. With tobacco out of the picture, the merchants had halved the market prices paid for the other crops the planters grew. As a result it would take them twice as much produce now—or twice as long—to repay their debts. "Matters will drift from bad to worse," Hutchins warned. "The time is not very far distant *when the planter must destroy the merchant, or the merchant must destroy the planter.*" All the merchants did was respond to the lament that their going rates of purchase were capricious, by posting those rates publicly—but they were still half what they had been.

The controversy never in fact ended. Authorities gave the planters additional stays of payment, and the merchants continued to pay too little for what they bought from the growers, meanwhile charging double the allowed interest in spite of Spanish decree. At the same time, both added renewed promises of loyalty to the King to their pleas for justice, and typical of Natcheans, both meant it only so long as the king served their interests.[8]

Then came the wake of the Revolution, the influx of hundreds of Americans from the East, and increasing pressure on the slender Spanish hold on the province. When Spain and France went to war in 1793, sudden threats seemed to appear from French sympathizers up the Mississippi. In fact, during those years a host of small alarms came and went, most tied to discontent upriver over Spanish control of the Mississippi trade, and the adventuring desire of professional schemers like Wilkinson, who took Spanish pay as a spy even while holding a commission as brigadier general in the new U.S. Army. Then came the Treaty of San Lorenzo and Spain's formal yielding of the territory to the United States in 1795. Yet Gayoso did not leave. Indeed, he hoped that the treaty would be abrogated. Better yet, a schemer himself, he expected that Kentucky and other western territories of the United States might be persuaded to separate themselves from the Union and perhaps form some league with Spain, especially since Wilkinson constantly urged that such could be the case.

Only by early 1797 did authorities in New Orleans finally yield their hopes and order Gayoso to begin preparations for evacuating the Natchez district. Then Ellicott arrived to oversee the turnover to the United States. Gayoso sent his Pennsylvania-born Captain Stephen Minor to try to keep Ellicott out of Natchez, unsuccessfully as it happened, but Minor did thereafter act as go-between and aided in stretching out the process of turnover. Gayoso delayed and refused to leave, citing a number of excuses, some real, and others transparent. Ellicott just kept demanding that the Spaniards leave and appealed to the people of Natchez to rise in his support. Gayoso tried to undercut that by buying planter loyalty with yet another moratorium on debt payments to merchants, which only succeeded in driving some of the latter to the American camp. Soon Ellicott became very friendly indeed with many of the merchants, which only served to alienate Hutchins and the

planters. As a result, by the middle of 1797 there were not just two parties in Natchez but a host of factions all governed by self-interest, forming and then unforming coalitions as it suited their ends. Daniel Clark
led the merchants, yet he retained close ties to Gayoso and the Spanish. Hutchins led the planters, who were now forgetting their promises
of fealty made just two years before, and forgetting, too, the relief
afforded them by the repeated Spanish stays on debt payment. Then
there were the indigent and adventurers, mostly recent arrivals from
the East, pressing for free land and expecting to get it from an American Natchez. On the other side sat men like Minor, recipients of considerable bounty from their Spanish masters over the years, and grateful and loyal in return despite their own American origins.[9] Hutchins,
for instance, was now pro-American but anti-Ellicott.[10]

Finally in June some three hundred men assembled in open
rebellion, aroused by Gayoso's arrest of one of their friends for inciting
riot. Nothing happened, as Ellicott strained to keep violence from
erupting, and Gayoso finally met with Ellicott and others to find a
means of keeping peace. Hutchins had earlier tried to persuade Ellicott
to capture Gayoso and his garrison and send them to the Chickasaw
country, but no one would join him in the plan. Now at this meeting
Hutchins suddenly turned conciliatory and pressed for moderation.
Gayoso saw clearly enough that Hutchins, having seen the character of
the mob gathered to rebel, feared that they would become like Willing's crowd and start plundering indiscriminately, which meant that
Hutchins's own property could get involved.[11]

The meeting produced only a temporary and uneasy peace.
Hutchins became chairman of a committee to maintain order in the
community, and with Gayoso so weak and virtually barricaded in his
fort, Hutchins's group became Natchez's effective rulers. But later that
summer the temporary committee was replaced by a permanent one
chosen by general election, and this time Ellicott had time to politick
heavily for his merchant associates, who carried the day and turned
out Hutchins and his fellow planters on the old board. Not surprisingly
Hutchins screamed fraud. He went to the meeting room of the newly
styled Permanent Committee, stamped on the floor, and shouted that
"they were dissolved, and they were accordingly dissolved." The
Cromwellian performance only amused the merchants, and then
Hutchins actually went to Gayoso for sympathy and support. Ellicott
derisively called the eighty-year-old Hutchins "Squeaking Tony, long
and bony," but the old man was a potent force. Soon he managed to
stage another election, and this time the planters once more won the
day. But the merchant-controlled committee refused to yield its man-

date, with the result that both committees now met and attempted to impose their vision of order on the community. Happily, accustomed to blowing with the wind, Natchez managed to bend to both groups without incident for awhile, but Hutchins was not done yet.

By now he detested Ellicott and publicly charged him with sexual misconduct, which hardly seemed likely given the hypochondriac Ellicott's morbid fear of poison ivy that kept him mostly locked in his house. Hutchins and his rump committee drafted a petition to Congress outlining Ellicott's mismanagement—to their way of thinking—of the Natchez situation, and demanding that he be recalled and replaced. On November 20 Hutchins gave it to Daniel Burnet, along with three hundred dollars in payment for his trouble and expenses, and sent him off on the Trace toward Nashville, his eventual destination being the capital, then in Philadelphia. Unfortunately Hutchins and his confederates could not keep their mouths shut, and word of their intent leaked throughout Natchez and certainly to Ellicott and the other committee. Playing both sides for safety as usual, Hutchins had already sent another copy to Spain's envoy to the United States, but Spanish officials intercepted it in New Orleans, with the result that Gayoso and Ellicott already knew its contents. Having achieved an uneasy truce, all they needed was for Philadelphia to insert a new player on the field. Consequently, when Burnet set out on the Trace he got only a few miles. No doubt he went armed, for there had already been rumors that he might be robbed. But at Coles Creek, near the house of Thomas Calvet, Silas Payne and James Truly surprised him and at gunpoint relieved him of his packet of letters, including the memorial.[12]

Hutchins and friends screamed foul play and accused Ellicott of hiring the two thieves, and since the document finally turned up in Ellicott's possession, they were probably right. Gayoso had been transferred to New Orleans by then, leaving Minor in command at Natchez, and he immediately instituted a thorough search for the paper and its purloiners. Hutchins himself knew soon enough who they were, since Burnet recognized both, and the old schemer ordered two men loyal to his committee to arrest Payne and kept him bound until he gave his parole not to leave the district.[13] Since Payne had been a past employee of Ellicott's, the responsibility seemed even more to rest on the American commissioner. Minor finally found the paper in Ellicott's house and returned it to Hutchins, then gathered depositions and evidence for a trial, but in the end allowed the matter to drop. "Generally speaking the People are getting heartily tired of all party business," he told Gayoso just a few days after Payne's release, "and American politicks is now becoming an old thing." Indeed, the increasing silliness of affairs left him exasperated. "God send a speedy determination of things," he added, "otherwise they will all run mad, with memorials, certificates, circular letters, &ca."[14] No sooner did Hutchins recover his memo, in fact, than he sent Burnet on his way once more, this time sending along a man well acquainted with the Trace and able to act as bodyguard. Burnet got across Coles Creek and all the way to the Tennessee without mishap, where he dismissed his companion and made his way at last to Philadelphia.[15]

Hutchins could have saved himself the effort. Congress would not replace Ellicott. Meanwhile rumors floated in Natchez that politics was about to extend to its ultimate extreme in a plot to assassinate Hutchins, whose family promptly issued a warning that "Mr. Ellicott may be the next victim, for retaliation will have no bounds when once begun." The fortuitous arrival of Captain Guion and his soldiers finally brought some order, though thanks only to the intimidating presence of his muskets. He tried to reason with the contending factions, but found them so frustrating that he finally turned a deaf ear to their endless backbiting and bickering. He simply kept the peace until the Spaniards finally evacuated on March 30, 1798. That, at last, relieved Ellicott of his divisive role in Natchez and freed him to start his boundary survey. Unfortunately the men assigned to help him run the line included Burnet, Minor, and a number of others from all sides in the recent imbroglios. As a result the job took far longer than it should have, as Ellicott complained that all his surveyors wanted to do was "talk politics."[16]

If they thought that talking politics would cease when the government sent a new territorial governor that fall, the Natcheans proved sadly mistaken, for no sooner did Winthrop Sargent arrive than the old factions realigned and renewed their battle. The faces and names were the same; only the issues had changed. Sargent almost immediately identified himself with the more influential merchants and creditors, which immediately put him on the wrong side of Hutchins and the planter debtors. Worse, the new governor showed an apparent contempt for the lowly farmers and laborers, preferring the company of the wealthy instead. As a result the anticipated relief from partisan politics never came. Sargent, like President John Adams who appointed him, was a Federalist, a man out of sympathy with the egalitarian ideas being booted about by Thomas Jefferson. He naturally gravitated toward the economic and social elite. Arrayed against him were, in the words of a friend who warned him, "parties headed by men of perverseness and cunning." That meant Hutchins, of course, and others like Cato West and Thomas Green, both of them related to Hutchins's family. These men soon aligned themselves with the Jeffersonians to become Sargent's opposition. The new governor made the mistake of consulting with Ellicott as to good men to receive appointments in his administration, which also alienated the old Hutchins faction. But then Sargent actually offered high appointments to some seven of the opposition, all of them related to Hutchins either by blood or marriage. All but two declined because Hutchins himself was not offered a position. "He ought to have been in some high office," complained Clark, "to be kept quiet."[17]

Instead, West, Green, and of course Hutchins plotted against the governor and tried to undermine him with a host of legal actions, protests, circular letters, and memorials, all aimed at persuading Congress to remove him when it reconvened. Sargent helped their cause by his arbitrary and autocratic manner, and after a mere fifteen months in office, his measures attracted so much public outcry that even close supporters like Dunbar and Clark resigned from the positions he had given them, fearing as Clark said that "we shall acquire a character which will deter even a Kentucky man to adventure among us."[18]

Sargent, of course, did not get the message that defections even from his own ranks conveyed. The Hutchins people, now effectively led by West and Green, enlisted powerful support in Congress for the creation of an elected legislature to act as a curb on gubernatorial excess, and in May 1800 a bill passed and was signed by the president. Moreover, in response to complaints from Natchez—and in an effort to embarrass the ruling Federalists—Jeffersonian Republicans in Congress began an investigation of Sargent himself. Suddenly the Mississippi Territory became a political tool for the ends of men a thousand miles to the east. In the Southwest itself, when Sargent held the election for legislative delegates, his opponents won an overwhelming majority, even old Hutchins taking a seat. Posing as champions of the common yeomanry, Hutchins and the rest answered to no more egalitarian imperatives than did Sargent. They, too, were men of the elite, property owners. But Sargent's predilection for the trappings of aristocracy made it convenient for them to attack him on the democratic issues of Jeffersonianism. Nevertheless, they did not at all complain at the distinctly undemocratic requirement that a man own at least fifty acres to be eligible to vote. After all, many of their old enemies the merchants and creditors, being town dwellers, owned no property at all, and therefore could not vote. Democracy, it seemed, was as much convenience as conviction.

All at once the opposition took control of Sargent's legislative functions as governor and began to threaten his remaining powers, while his supporters struggled to undo the damage done by petitioning Congress to dissolve the new legislature. The Federalists were fighting a losing battle, however, not only in the territory but in the nation as a whole. Jeffersonian democracy was on the march, and ambitious adherents in Congress rejected an exoneration from the committee investigating Sargent and continued the probe. Then in March 1801 Jefferson himself took office as President, and almost at once replaced Sargent with William C. C. Claiborne. Party politics had been triumphant, and the strange amalgam of factions and interests that made up the Jeffersonians in Mississippi could at last revel in their ascendancy. Yet they remained apart from the party in the rest of the United States, unconcerned with national events in preference to the world as they knew it in Mississippi. Still, sensitive as always to the road that offered them the easiest path, they realized that it lay in their interest to be cooperative with the Jefferson administration. At the same time, one of the chief old divisions between men in the Southwest was breaking down. With the coming of the cotton gin and cotton's rise to preeminence, a new cash crop offered to all land owners the chance to escape their debt to the merchants. When that happened, realignments began to take place as new issues arose to supplant the old ones.[19]

With the Mississippi Territory once under secure management within the United States, Mississippians could start the work of local self-government as well. In March 1803 the new legislature incorporated Natchez as the first city in the territory, and gave it far-reaching authority considerably beyond that of most American communities, almost to what John Monette called "the despotism of monarchy." The reason was simple. This was still a raw frontier. The nearest American town of any comparable size lay more than four hundred miles away. Natchez—like all of the lesser communities slowly appearing along the Trace and its tributary roads—must look chiefly to itself for law and order.

The legislature authorized a Common Council to rule the city. The assembly itself appointed the mayor, city clerk, marshal, and three aldermen, and the townspeople elected each year their treasurer, assessor, collector, and half a dozen aldermen's assistants. Furthermore all of them but the marshal and the assistant aldermen were vested with the powers of justices of the peace. The mayor ran the council and selected its subcommittees, and in meetings themselves rules approximating those of Congress prevailed. While paid very small incomes for their service, the members of the council had to watch against the exactions their own regulations could cost—one dollar for missing a meeting, and five dollars for missing one without just cause. Law was to be dispensed by a Mayor's Court, consisting of himself, the clerk, and the aldermen, and its jurisdiction extended to all civil matters not involving more than one hundred dollars, and criminal cases that did not go beyond the misdemeanor stage, or involve penalties exceeding thirty days in jail, a fifty-dollar fine or thirty-nine lashes. The court also licensed attorneys to practice in the city, and granted tavern licenses. It soon acquired a reputation for arbitrariness that led to repeated public outcry, and eventually a grand jury investigation for being a "public grievance."

Cities ran on paperwork just as much as nations, and Natchez was no exception. The council had to order quills, sand for drying ink, powdered ink and bottles to mix it in, blank and ruled ledger books, and reams of paper. A leatherbound blank ledger book could cost $18.00 from the binder's in Philadelphia, and quills some $2.00 a dozen. When Edward Turner established his land office in 1804, it cost him $317.25 to lay in twenty-three blank books, a ream of folio paper, four reams of foolscap, six reams of letter-size paper, a dozen papers of black ink powder and a dozen of red, four quires of blotting paper, three hundred quills, and a bottle of "gum elastic" to use as glue.[20] Yet a clerk could use all that, for the council required that everything be recorded, and when it added the incentive of twenty-five cents for each one hundred words that he inscribed, the clerk's transcriptions became wonderfully detailed.

The marshal also had extensive duties, and not just once seem ingly in keeping with his title. He had to capture and dispose of stray dogs and sell licenses to dog owners. Moreover, when horses died in the streets, he had to remove them, all of which brought him an extra fee, of course. The council, and the Board of Selectmen that succeeded it after a revision in the charter in 1809, also contracted with local printers to publish its proceedings and public announcements. Most noteworthy among the printers used was the pioneering Marschalk, who also held a seat on the council for three years before his contentiousness got him ousted.

For the better part, the city rulers in Natchez did an effective job of governing the only substantial community in the territory. They were well-to-do middle-class merchants and professionals, yet avowedly Jeffersonian in politics. None of the mayors came from the great names or established aristocratic families of the region. Samuel Brooks was a tradesman. John Shaw was a printer. Turner, of course, was a lawyer in addition to being federal land agent at one time. Among the twenty leading land and slaveholders in Adams County, not one ever served in the city government, despite many of them maintaining town homes in addition to their plantation dwellings. And while the old creditor class dominated political affairs in Natchez—and in the territory as a rule—the old planter-debtor faction continued to rule the economy of the community thanks to its new cotton wealth. The antagonisms that had spiced territorial politics before and during its American period, also played on a smaller stage in the city workings of Natchez, but the merchants never saw a serious challenge to their control. Ironically an outside threat eventually brought the two factions together, at least within the city. In the rivalry with Washington, and later Greenville, for the territorial capital and county seat, both classes in Natchez had the same stake. Moreover, in the years after 1810, as the population shift transferred power increasingly to the eastern regions of the territory, both nabobs and nobodies in Natchez found common cause by identifying a common foe—the piney woods people. In 1817, when statehood finally came, the planters and the merchants of Natchez joined forces in spite of their other differences to exert influence that brought the capital back to their city. And after that, as newer threats appeared on the national stage, they found it easier and easier to forget the old animosities in the need to take a common stand.[21]

Meanwhile territorial and national politics swirled all around them. Inhabitants prayed that Claiborne would have more sense and better judgment than Sargent. "At least his fate will teach him more prudence," David Ker predicted. As for the people of the territory, "the oppressions of the Spanish government & even of our first territorial government has served to inflame the love of Republicanism among these & they want only a little experience to become good American citizens."[22] As it happened, they had quite a bit of experience ahead of them, but few ventured to estimate just how much they learned about Republicanism from it all.

The victorious Republicans under Governor Claiborne first vented their resentment of largely Federalist Natchez by taking away from it both the territorial capital and the Adams county seat and giving them to nearby Washington, which became a Republican stronghold. Then the legislature awarded the first charter for a college to Washington, naming it for their leader Jefferson. In symbolic gestures they also renamed Pickering County to be Jefferson and then sliced off half of Adams County—named for the Federalist ex-president—and created Wilkinson, in honor of their more than tarnished hero and sometime conspirator. Green, Hutchins, Ker, Shaw, Turner, and others dominated the new Mississippi Republican Society, which ran the party in the territory, and with them stood Marschalk and his *Mississippi Herald* as well as another paper.

Very soon, however, cracks in the thin wall holding them together began to appear. West wanted the capital moved to Greenville on the old Trace, and Turner backed him. Claiborne wanted it left in Washington. Marschalk broke with the society to stand by Claiborne, while the *Mississippi Messenger* supported West's faction. The next year, 1803, Claiborne left—gladly—to assume another territorial governorship, and West succeeded him for several months but remained unable to budge the capital. Then the Republicans feuded among themselves over the location of Jefferson College, Hutchins, West, and others pressing again for Greenville, where most had personal interests that would have been served by locating the capital and other cultural centers there. Foiled, all Hutchins could do was impede the college's legislative financing, postponing its opening for several years. And when Robert Williams came in 1805 as Jefferson's new governor, the Hutchins crowd immediately took a dislike to him because they had wanted West confirmed permanently as governor. Though a fellow Republican, Williams soon found himself under fire from those who should have been his friends, and this time not just Hutchins, West, and their crowd. A new internal opposition arose in Washington, headed by George Poindexter and Cowles Mead, Ferdinand Claiborne, and others. Rather quickly they left the Hutchins Republicans in the shade, while in Natchez yet another splinter faction of disgruntled Republicans joined with a few Federalists actually to support Governor Williams.[23]

Into the middle of this sailed—quite literally—one of the country's most famous men, and at the moment certainly its most wanted fugitive. Aaron Burr attracted the attention of the nation first for his bravery in the war with Britain, and then by his rapid rise in New York politics, and then in the vice presidency after narrowly losing the presidency to Jefferson. In 1804 he killed Alexander Hamilton in a fair duel that still led to partisan accusations of murder, and two indictments. Then, after leaving the vice presidency in early 1805, he began a new venture, still shrouded in mystery and controversy. Accusers and later legend would say that he intended to foment a rebellion along the Mississippi, probably to separate the new Louisiana Territory from the United States and set himself up as its regent. If so, it was a fantastical scheme, and one in which the ever-scheming Wilkinson played a role, and on both sides as it happened. More likely Burr intended nothing quite so ambitious. He did have eyes on taking Mexico away from its Spanish overlords, and wanted for himself to establish a basis for making his fortune on the rich prairies of what would later become Texas. Like all the rest who came down the Trace and the river, he was an opportunist. Only he thought on a much grander scale.[24]

When Burr started to raise men and money and put them on a flotilla to sail down the Ohio and Mississippi, authorities all across the frontier reacted in near panic. Orders went out from Washington, D.C., that he should be apprehended. Governor Williams was absent when Burr's expedition approached the territory, and Cato West temporarily held power. He called out the small militia and prepared to stop Burr, whose flotilla pushed ashore just above Natchez on January 10, 1807. Burr knew Natchez, having been handsomely entertained there on a visit the year before, during which he supposedly met with Stephen Minor and confided to him his plans for the Mexican adventure.[25] Afterward he rode back up the Trace to Nashville. Now as he came ashore and went to the home of a nearby judge, he found awaiting him a four-day-old copy of the *Mississippi Messenger*, carrying the announcement that the governor had ordered his arrest, and publishing several documents supposedly attesting to his guilt, including one from his supposed friend Wilkinson.

Apparently Burr immediately abandoned his planned expedition to Texas and Mexico and decided instead to clear his name first. Making no attempt to get away, he sailed his flotilla a few miles farther south and waited there while the Mississippi militia mustered and marched. He sent a letter to Territorial Secretary Cowles Mead pleading his innocence, and then dispatched emissaries to the militia commander marching against him. A few days later Burr himself met with the officer, and though he may have expressed an intent to resist any interference from the military, he promised to surrender himself at any time to the civil authorities. Mead soon arranged a meeting at Thomas Calvet's house on Coles Creek, and there Burr agreed to surrender himself and his men. The Mississippians took him to Washington, where they bound him over on five thousand dollars' bail until a grand jury could convene in a few weeks. That done, Burr simply awaited the jury and spent his leisure renewing old acquaintances in Natchez, being wined and dined once more, and if local legend is to be believed, even wooed and proposed to—unsuccessfully—a local lady.[26]

Politics entered into the confused and exaggerated episode when Burr—a Federalist—engaged a local Federalist to act as his attorney and accepted bail money from another. On February 2 the jury met at Washington. Poindexter, attorney general and a member of the ruling clique of Republicans, startled everyone by moving for a dismissal because the Natchez court possessed no jurisdiction in the matter. Perhaps so, but more likely he sought to shift the burden of trying such a prominent Federalist elsewhere to avoid the inevitable political fallout. But his motion lost. Nevertheless, the jury did decide not to indict Burr and let him quietly slip away with the aid of other quite-delighted Federalists who did not mind the forfeiture of his bond.[27]

While the whole episode had little national significance, and Burr later did stand trial and was acquitted in the East, its repercussions in the Southwest were considerable. Having had the man in their grasp and let him get away, the Republicans attracted open ridicule from their Federalist opponents, all the more because the divisions within their own relatively new coalition showed so badly. On his return Governor Williams dismissed Mead and Claiborne from their posts for their handling of the affair and soon began replacing some other Republicans in his administration with Federalists, despite his own leanings. While the remnant of his party feuded within itself, Williams only made things worse by what now appeared to be friendly leanings toward Burr. Where did he stand, asked his people, for or against Burr? And what sort of Republican was he? Confusion seemed to reign everywhere, and the Federalist-dominated city of Natchez watched in glee, a disgruntled Republican lamenting at the time that they "seem to feel a secret pleasure in the present order of things in this Territory; which they cannot conceal frequently declaring." Suddenly men who seemingly despised Williams before he took office, now stood as his most staunch friends "after having measured his talents in the hollow of their hands" spat Republican Walter Leake. Now the Federalists showered the governor with flattery and civilities, and he seemed not to have the strength or courage to withstand them.[28] Fortescue Cuming, visiting at the time, simply observed that "I forbear mentioning my opinion of the governor."[29]

Jefferson soon replaced Williams with Governor David Holmes, a well-liked man who managed to conciliate all the ingredients in the political stew out here. In part events made his task easier, for no sooner did the Burr fiasco settle than the growing controversy with Great Britain led to embargoes that severely hurt the territorial economy, and then followed the second war with the old mother country. Such things largely diverted the attention of Federalists and Republicans alike from their internal differences, and under Holmes's temperate management a measure of partisan tranquility settled over the territory. Certainly it helped as well that some of the most outspoken partisan spokesmen like Hutchins, Green, and even Dunbar finally died of old age, leadership passing to a newer generation. Almost everyone liked Holmes, an engaging mixture of elements. He was utterly helpless at anything mechanical or requiring coordination, unable even to ride a horse or drive a carriage without mishap. Stories of his sense of humor and cordiality reached every corner of the territory. His courage seemed unquestionable, as did his sense of justice. Even his slaves received inordinately gentle treatment, and when one ran away, Holmes said he should not be pursued. "It was natural in him to get away from such a tiresome life with me," Holmes explained. "Let him run Sir."[30]

But even Holmes's bonhomie could not stay the inevitable rise of politics again when the unifying influence of the War of 1812 ceased with the end of the conflict. Yet now the rising antagonisms stemmed not so much from party as geography. During the past decade more and more settlers had poured into the territory, and more and more of those had settled in its eastern reaches, in future Alabama. With sales of public lands slow and inefficient, thousands simply squatted and started clearing plantations. Steadily they began to pressure the territorial delegate to Congress, Poindexter, to press for acceptance of their established property lines at two dollars per acre. Poindexter was sympathetic, but not the Federalists, who saw the growing eastern counties' population as an added threat to their already minority status in the old Natchez region.[31] Western Republicans, too, saw a threat, in that the influx of potential Republicans in the piney woods region could shift the center of power away from them.

For years the ruling politicians in Natchez and Washington looked forward to statehood—but only one state, comprising the entire territory from the Georgia line to the Mississippi, and from Tennessee down to the boundaries of Louisiana and West Florida. Seeing themselves ignored by the dominant Natchez-Washington powers, the early settlers in the piney woods argued for two states instead, but their arguments met only silence. After the War of 1812, however, the surge of people into the eastern counties being formed put a different complexion on affairs. With the population center shifting ever eastward, it now seemed possible to men along the Mississippi that if only one state were formed, they would not be its leaders, while the new Alabamians suddenly rather liked the idea of a single state. And while their roles thus reversed, other Southerners in Congress saw larger issues. To maintain their own parity of representation in the Senate, they needed more Southern states, and that argued for carving the Mississippi Territory in two.[32]

Meanwhile the old and seemingly inevitable local squabbles came out once more and now began to erupt in violence. "It is a fact well known to those who have visited that country that party feeling is unusually strong and vindictive," said the Natchez *Mississippi Republican* in July 1815, "and that no public man, however pure and upright his motives and conduct may be, escapes the shafts of calumny."[33] George Poindexter, one of the leaders behind the separate statehood movement, offered a case in point. "There was nothing romantic, picturesque or imaginative about Poindexter," wrote one who knew him, "neither fanciful nor classical, but a strictly logical, demonstrative, matter-of-fact man." He was more often to be found in taverns or the courthouse than in refined society, and possessed a directness of speech and a volume of temper that often put him in difficulty. In 1803, within months of his arrival at Natchez, he narrowly avoided a fight over a newspaper article; two years later almost precipitated a duel with a fellow lawyer; and then in 1811 actually did fight with Federalist Abijah Hunt. They went to the West Bank of the Mississippi, and there Hunt took a mortal wound. The controversy over whether Poindexter fired before the signal was given would last for years and involve him in yet more arguments. Indeed, one of the Claibornes recalled that "his life, at this period, was a perpetual embroilment." Within months of killing Hunt he nearly came to pistols with Minor, and when he left Congress to assume a territorial judgeship, the political attacks on him only intensified.[34]

"Parties in the Territory of that day were personal rather than political," recalled one Mississippian, and the fragmented Republican support for Williams and Holmes, and the Federalist support given to both as well, suggests that he was right. More evidence lay in the newspaperman Marschalk, an avowed Jeffersonian, and certainly willing to proclaim his loyalties in the name of his Washington sheet the *Republican*. Nevertheless he detested Poindexter from some personal animus that spilled over into politics, and vilified him in an issue of his paper, then sent several copies across the street into Poindexter's courtroom even as it was in session, placing one copy on the judge's bench. Poindexter arrested him and charged him with contempt and then soon thereafter sued for libel, winning the case and a large judgment. Marschalk was a born controversialist himself, having been censured by the Natchez Common Council, of which he was a member, in 1806, and later feuding with Mead and others. He refused to take his conviction meekly and only stepped up his attacks on Poindexter in the *Republican*. The judge's response was to storm across the street to the newspaper office in the first week of March 1815, and there in the doorway to grab Marschalk and beat him almost senseless with a walking cane. Thereafter, upon Marschalk's complaint, Poindexter was arrested by the sheriff, and as judge signed his own writ of *habeas corpus*.[35]

While awaiting the outcome of the Marschalk affair—which never really ended—Poindexter then engaged in a fistfight on the streets of Natchez with Thomas Percy, ostensibly a Federalist opponent, but also a man whom Poindexter suspected of seducing his wife. Then when Percy's brother-in-law accused Poindexter of cowardice in the Battle of New Orleans earlier that year, the judge challenged him to a duel. When the man refused, Poindexter published a condemnation in the Natchez press, accusing the man of "dastardly equivocation," and pronouncing him a *"Calumniating Liar* and a *Pusillanimous Coward."*[36]

Thus proceeded the career of just one of the politicians in whose hands lay the issue of statehood. Poindexter made a number of enemies in the years when Natchez still resisted division of the territory and he led the effort successfully. Nevertheless, in 1816 when a memorial went to Congress from Natchez proposing statehood for just the eastern half of the territory, Poindexter like others argued in its favor. Congress also received a memorial from territorial legislators representing the piney woods section, and they argued for making but a single state. Each group contained both Federalists and Republicans, and each acted purely from local interest rather than party loyalty. Congress predictably chose to favor the Natchez plan. On March 1, 1817, President James Madison signed the act that enabled the western half of the territory to select a convention, frame a constitution, and apply for admission as a state.

In April electioneering for delegates to the convention commenced, and almost immediately men noticed no real party alignment in the canvassing. Rather, two factions emerged, those favoring application for statehood, and those who wanted the coming convention to opt for remaining in a territorial condition. The statehood forces came overwhelmingly from Republicans and Federalists in the western counties, all tied to the Natchez nucleus. Those opposing statehood came from both parties as well, and lived chiefly in the counties along the newly designated dividing line with Alabama. Their economic and trading interests linked them much more closely with commerce on the Tombigbee than the Mississippi. In the new state being proposed, they feared they would be forgotten just as much as they were in the existing territory, dominated as it was by the westerners. They wanted either to see the new dividing line moved farther east to include the Tombigbee, so they would have their own base within the state, or else they wanted the line moved to the west, excluding them from the new state and leaving them in the Alabama territory.[37]

In the election some forty-eight delegates were chosen, two-thirds of them from the seven wealthy plantation counties of the old Natchez district, and just sixteen from the remaining seven newer counties to the east. All but one of them gathered in the Methodist church built by Lorenzo Dow in Washington on July 7, 1817, to begin what would become six weeks of debates. They chose Governor Holmes, an elected delegate from Adams County, as their president, and on the very next day those of the eastern bloc made their move. When they arrived they felt they had only a dozen votes in favor of delaying statehood. Within hours half a dozen others came over to their side, and then they began spreading rumors that the Natchez district men were not sincere in their promise to support moving the capital to a more central part of the new state in order to secure the support of delegates from Hinds County, where Jackson would one day stand. At best they hoped to defeat any proposal for statehood. Failing that, they hoped they might postpone the convention for several months, which would give them time to gain more votes. As soon as the convention met on July 8, Cato West offered a resolution that they should not at that time form a state government. Holmes immediately ruled it out of order, and then they debated for two days a motion from Edward Turner that it *was* expedient to go ahead with state making. Support for the eastern counties began to erode, and when a motion by Poindexter to postpone action until the next March failed—he hoped to make the state larger by moving the boundary east—Turner's resolution passed overwhelmingly and they got on with the business of making a constitution.

Poindexter headed the constitutional committee, and despite the number of Republicans in the convention, they produced the most conservative state constitution that would be seen among any subsequent states to join the Union. It reflected not their supposed Republican principles but their ideals as men of property, supported by the conservative Federalists among them. The eastern county men wanted universal male suffrage; the western men put through a taxpaying qualification, which effectively excluded propertyless men from voting. Easterners wanted to elect their state judges rather than see them appointed. They did not want officeholding to be conditional on owning property, and they certainly opposed legislative apportionment based on property holding rather than straight population. They lost on every issue, and also failed to get into the constitution a provision for amendment.[38]

While the draft constitution went through debate, the eastern delegates saw themselves steadily being reduced to insignificance in any future government. As a last desperate measure, they moved that Turner's motion stating the expediency of forming a state at all should be reconsidered. In effect, they proposed that the convention dissolve and go home. A number of delegates from Wilkinson and Jefferson Counties joined with them, out of causes including the desire for a larger boundary and a resistance to moving the capital. The debate was tense and the vote tight, so close on July 15 that it ended in a tie, which by the rules of the convention meant the motion lost. It would be the last real resistance from the eastern bloc.

On August 15 the convention concluded debating the constitution and signed it, as well as adopting an entreaty to the president asking that he disallow any Indian claims to land in the new state, which would effectively disown the Choctaw and Chickasaw and open all their tribal lands to settlement and exploitation. Another petition to Congress made a last attempt to get the eastern boundary of the new state moved in order to include Mobile and the Tombigbee lands. Neither would be adopted in Washington, D.C. Once the convention approved its own constitution, there was nothing more to be done. They made no provision to submit it to popular referendum. Instead, under its provisions, Mississippians chose a new legislature that fall and elected their future congressmen, and then the state assembly chose their two senators to go to Washington. That done, it remained only for the new president, James Monroe, to sign a bill on December 10 admitting the newly designated state of Mississippi to the Union.[39]

Less than two years later, the people of the remainder of the Old Southwest got their own state. Alabama followed largely the same path into the Union as Mississippi, achieving statehood in 1819, with its capital at Huntsville and a host of internal political divisions of its own, chiefly centered on the geographic and economic dominance of Mobile and the Alabama and Tombigbee River communities. Yet constitution making did not leave a majority of the inhabitants or the legislators of either state pleased for long. In fifteen years Mississippi would revise its document, and—under pressure from all the immigrants coming to the state—its conservative elements, reflecting chiefly the concerns and interests of the landed aristocracy, were almost all cast aside.[40]

Not surprisingly a great proportion of the men who took part in framing charters and then ruling the territory and its subsequent states came from the same profession. New frontiers always attracted a lot of lawyers, in part for the land but more because where there was land, there was always a lot of legal work to be done with surveys, deeds, and disputed claims. Moreover, just as the first planters to arrive usually emerged with the greatest fortunes from the soil, so the initial men of the bar generally assumed prominence in the cities to come, and could themselves end up with considerable plantations of their own.

The profession had its expenses, of course. A small law library out on the frontier could cost four hundred dollars and had to be ordered from the East.[41] To offset those costs, the lawyer went to court on behalf of merchants with bad creditors, settled estates, prepared writs of seizure, like that of the keelboat *Maria* and her cargo to recover debts, and charged fees in the area of fifteen dollars, which they then often had trouble collecting themselves.[42] And naturally they faced the inevitable complaints about those fees, in one case of which the aggrieved debtor protested his as "not only utterly inadmissable but extravagent & unreasonable in itself beyond all bearing."[43] They formed the Mississippi Bar Association at Natchez in May 1821, headed by Edward Turner, who knew about as much about the land title business and other frontier litigation as anyone. They agreed on set schedules of fees—from five dollars for verbal advice to fifty for handling slander suits—in the hope that this might end the complaining, but of course it never did.[44]

In part because they had trouble getting paid, and also because their profession naturally put them in an adversarial position with other attorneys, these men of the bar often stayed only a few months before moving on to find better prospects or to escape the fallout of some duel or altercation. In Barbour County, Alabama, R. M. "Three Legged Willie" Williamson arrived to start practice in 1823 and remained but a year before he killed another lawyer in a duel. His name came from a peculiar deformity that kept one leg permanently bent at the knee. In order to walk he had to strap on a wooden one, and he used it after the killing to get out of the county and the state.[45]

A lawyer who worked hard could do well. "My business was limited to my deserts," recalled James Maury of Port Gibson, "but such was my economy that the termination of each year left me a shade more affluent than I was at the beginning." Unfortunately lawyers, like everyone else, could succumb to boredom during lulls in the profession, as well as to the freedom of behavior encouraged on the frontier. In Maury's circle among the bar "many of them were addicted to gambling or drunkenness, or both, which shortened their lives and speedily replaced them by a new set."[46]

Sooner or later those who could stay put and sober tried to get a judgeship, either elective or appointed. In the territorial days, the appointments lay with the president, whom the settlers bombarded with recommendations of their favorites in such quaint terms as "a grate judge of law," and "a Law Carracter."[47] There were also other appointive positions—territorial clerk- and secretaryships, land sales agents, and more, all of them heavily political in cast. When Henry Hitchcock left his law office at Saint Stephens to become territorial secretary of Alabama in 1818, the job brought an annual salary of twelve hundred dollars. Yet he knew of the dangerous waters of political patronage. "One misstep would cast me to the bottom," he confessed. "I feel now more sensibly the responsibility a man is under to his own character and the danger there is of destroying it."[48]

When the population formed counties, more positions opened. The ever-enterprising Gideon Lincecum found himself in Monroe County, Mississippi, when statehood came, and "cut off from the law." The legislature appointed him chief justice of the peace for the new county and told him to organize its offices and officers. They also made him chairman of the school commissioners. "Everybody wanted office," he lamented, and he soon found himself swamped, "holding the courts, appointing the officers, surveying the town lots, appointing and regulating school commissioners at town, and all the other school sections in the county, procuring teachers, engaging workmen for the academies and opening the mail six times a week." No wonder that when some associates suggested electing him to the legislature, which might mean even more work, Lincecum moved away yet again "to avoid such a dilemma."[49]

When friends suggested to Hitchcock that they send him to Congress, he also declined, fearing that his inexperience "would place me in a situation which might render me if not ridiculous at least unpleasant."[50] But not everyone tried to avoid the "dilemma" of elective office. George Gaines's friends in Clark and Marengo Counties, Alabama, came to him in the 1820s and asked him to be a candidate for the state senate. He consented reluctantly because "I owed it to my friends." Of course, in the political ethics of the time, "reluctance" was a prerequisite in an elected official. Any man who evidenced ambition seemed untrustworthy in those egalitarian days. The office sought the man, not the reverse—or so they liked to pretend. But once the campaigning started, these candidates fought with remarkable vigor for positions they supposedly did not want.[51]

Public campaigning took on a distinctive character in the Southwest in the decade immediately following statehood, when more and more offices became open, and it reflected the temper of the people. "It is hard to explain the place filled by political concerns in the life of an American," Alexis de Tocqueville wrote after visiting the country during this time. "To take a hand in the government of society and to talk about it is his most important business." For everyone it became entertainment, even for the women attending the political debates. "An American does not know how to converse, but he argues; he does not talk, but expatiates. He always speaks to you as if addressing a meeting, and if he happens to get excited, he will say 'Gentlemen' when addressing an audience of one."[52]

When candidates met on the hustings, the public gathered at their church and camp meeting grounds, or simply in clearings or on courthouse steps. Since they often had nothing more for a stand or podium than a tree stump, the whole process of campaigning soon came to be called "taking the stump," and so it remained regardless of venue. Picnics and barbecues followed in train, vendors sold whiskey—often the candidates bought it for the crowd to win votes—and the whole business assumed a carnival atmosphere, frontier entertainment at its best. Very quickly, too, the aspiring candidates learned to play to their crowds. In the era of the "common man" that followed Jefferson into the presidency, office seekers tailored their approach to the mass of newly arrived and entranchised landowners. "No politician now should venture to be eloquent," a Mississippian wrote after a visit to the piney woods country. "Rhetoric is fatal to success."[53] In no time at all polished lawyers from Natchez or Mobile learned to speak in the frontier vernacular when necessary. Some even changed their clothes from city broadcloth to country homespun or buckskins.

No one understood this better than David Crockett of Tennessee. In 1821 he sought a seat in the legislature, "a bran-fire new business to me," he confessed. "It now became necessary that I should tell the people something about the government, and an eternal sight of other things that I knowed nothing more about than I did about Latin," he recalled disingenuously. When people suggested issues to discuss, Crockett instead joined a hunting party and won votes by bringing back a load of squirrels for the stump-meeting stew. When he did make a speech—"a business I was as ignorant of as an outlandish negro"—he told his audience that he had never even seen a public document and did not know there were such things, despite having signed many of them some years before as a town commissioner. Unable to discuss the actual issues of the campaign, Crockett also recognized that his audiences were in any event more interested in politics for entertainment than for substance. Consequently he compared himself to a man found knocking on a barrel, explaining that he knew there had been some cider in it a little while earlier but he couldn't seem to get it out now. Crockett said there had been a little bit of a speech in him, but now he could not seem to find it. Instead he told them stories and jokes and concluded by saying his throat was dry and led them all to the liquor table, leaving his competitor without an audience. As the frustrated candidate spoke, Crockett continued his anecdotes over the jug, as he would do again and again. When he followed others who did bore the audience with a lot of genuine political debate, he knew well enough to eschew politics and just tell a couple of stories. The audiences loved him and elected him again and again.[54]

The ways in which men got their votes were as varied as the characters seeking them. Gaines won his seat in the legislature in part due to his Scots ancestry. "There are nineteen boys who always vote with me," said a sympathetic Scotsman in his district, "and we'll give him every one of them."[55] Others quite literally bought votes, and in Natchez an embryonic political machine called the Junto largely dominated voting between the coming of statehood and 1830. They catered to the rising sentiment for the common man and so-called Jacksonian democracy, even though many of their leaders were the wealthy and landed, who only used the current vogue to attain and retain power. They were, said one critic, "understrappers and hirelings, . . . Jacksonians and great intriguers."[56]

In fact this new surge of democracy had a profound effect on the states at the end of the Trace. In the early 1820s the growth of population in the less affluent eastern counties of Mississippi led to the movement to shift the capital, and even after it relocated in Jackson, attempts to move it elsewhere such as Clinton, Vicksburg, Port Gibson, Madisonville, Centreville, Gallatin, Monticello, Westville, and more reflected the continuing desire of the yeomanry to bring it closer to their center.[57] At the end of the decade they would succeed in redrafting the constitution, and before then they had their say on the national stage by their votes in two crucial elections.

When Andrew Jackson ran for the presidency at the head of the new Democratic party in 1824, he inherited the mantle of Jefferson, though the two men themselves could not have presented a greater contrast. Jackson was a western man, a resident of Nashville at the upper end of the Trace, a frequent traveler on the old road, a military hero of a war with the British and others against the Indians, a man who rose from nothing and thereby represented the unrealized aspirations of all the rude frontiersmen. Predictably Alabama stood squarely behind him in 1824, giving him 70 percent of its vote. Mississippi did even better, Jackson carrying every one of the state's counties.[58]

Nevertheless Jackson lost that first bid, but when he returned again in 1828, Alabama did even better with nearly 90 percent of its vote, and in Mississippi Jackson repeated his 1824 performance. Throughout the Southwest, newspapers appeared devoted to promoting Jacksonian ideals and candidates, linking the region with the groundswell across the South and throughout much of the nation that this time swept Old Hickory into office.[59]

With the election of Jackson the Southwest finally joined the political mainstream of American life, and itself began its rise to national prominence as the men Jackson brought to Washington, and whom Alabamians and Mississippians elected to Congress, made their presence felt. Yet it also signaled the disappearance of the Southwest as a distinct political region, for now its interests no longer stood out independently. By 1828, and especially with Jackson's reelection four years later, the territory found itself linked inextricably with its neighboring states to the east and north. Now its interests were southern interests, or Mississippi Valley interests. Instead of being a distant wilderness crying out to be heard by someone—anyone—its voice now joined a chorus of others shouting in unison in advocacy not of local issues, but regional, and even national concerns. By 1830 people no longer spoke of the Old Southwest but only of the South itself. It was one of the costs of coming of age in American politics.

12

The Road to Ruin

"These old Pioneers had hardships, privations, disappointments, and dangers to contend with of which the present generation can have no conception," a survivor wrote some years later. "And furthermore, the system of morals, was not so refined then as now, especially in the backwoods, as we used to call the frontiers, so that allowances should be made for their aberations."[1] If anyone of the era wanted to go in search of those "aberations," the Southwest offered such a spectator an unrivaled theater of observation.

As usual, Natchez set the tone and was at the same time a hyperbolic example of the kinds of excesses that gave the whole frontier its reputation. No traveler down the Trace or the river failed to note the character of the place or, more particularly, of the soon-to-be infamous Under-the-Hill. "It is well known to be the resort of dissipation," Henry Ker reported in 1808. "Here is the bold-faced strumpet full of blasphemies, who looks upon the virtuous part of her sex with contempts and hatred; every house is a grocery, containing gambling, music and dancing, fornicators, &c."[2] A decade later Bradbury thought much the same. "There is not, perhaps, in the world a more dissipated place," he complained.[3]

Few disagreed. By 1830 J. H. Ingraham called Natchez the "nucleus of vice," a "moral sty" where "fashionably dressed young men, smoking or lounging, tawdrily arrayed, highly rouged females, sailors, Kentucky boatmen, negroes, mulattoes, pigs, dogs, and dirty children" cluttered the streets and sidewalks.[4] A Methodist evangelist quite understandably painted the horrors of the place in even more vivid colors, calling the Under-the-Hill scene "that celebrated school of every grade of licentiousness." Viewing its saloons and bordellos and gaming tables, he believed that these "haunts of hydra-headed vice were inhabited by the most degraded and lawless men and women, whose sole object seemed to be to beguile, entrap and ruin their heedless victims." Time after time, he lamented, innocent youth went down to the landing out of curiosity and "'the lust of the eye,' which led him by an easy and rapid process to the indulgence of 'the lust of the flesh,' and soon honor was in the dust, his money in the hands of strangers." From there he found no way to return: "His feet went down to death, and his steps took hold on hell."[5]

Indeed, the resemblance to a netherworldish place occurred to many. "This part of the town is without a single exception the most licentious spot I ever saw," a visitor wrote in 1815, and seven years later another commented that Under-the-Hill "the Prince of Darkness is, I believe, the only acknowledged superior—It is without exception, the most infamous place I ever saw—where villainy, hardened by long impunity, triumphs in one day."[6]

Universally men blamed the river and the Kaintucks who came down its broad course, making Natchez their first real stop, and Natchez Under-the-Hill their neighborhood. As far back as 1800 James Hall commented with some understatement: "It cannot be supposed the most of those, who are employed as boatmen, are the most regular livers." They lived on their boats at the wharf or else slept in the dram shops and the brothels, even in the streets.[7] While some of the locals thought them not such bad men, boasting that "the Kentucky boys stand no chance with us," most thought them demons incarnate.[8] "Thoughtless as sailors or soldiers," a Natchez jury said of them in 1800, "and as fond of whiskey." In their characteristic striped pants and checked shirts, they strode about the landing and the town impressing more respectable citizens as a "lawless race, for whom a semi-barbarous life had charms, which the refinement of civilization could not dispel."[9]

When they arrived they got their pay, and a crewman's wage of fifty dollars for a month's work could go a long way in buying all manner of fun and mischief.[10] No sooner did they tie up at the bank and lash down their broadhorns and keelboats, than they took their pay and leaped onto the muddy shore to "raise the wind," as they put it. Most never made it to the streets of the civilized city on the bluff. All that they wanted they could find here at the riverbank. Still, the townspeople counted themselves lucky if the boatmen did not become overboisterous during the ensuing night's revels, for, from the moment they stepped ashore, they gave themselves up to "all the luxuries and dissipations" to be found Under-the-Hill.[11] When their money ran out or their boats moved on, they departed, "unclean, or with the seeds of disorder and desease about them."[12]

Not that these men were not colorful or entertaining to the landbound settlers who observed them. Their attire, their swaggering walk, and their upstream accents all made them objects of curiosity. Tall and lean, bronzed a deep brown by their outdoor profession, they stood silently gazing on all as if waiting for something to happen. When some spark set them in motion, however, they seemed frenzied, turning into a roaring, swinging menace to any within reach. Then, once the fury abated, they could settle with remarkable speed into their former aplomb.[13] Their speech positively fascinated all who heard them, for the river man quickly evolved a cant all his own. He did not just act quickly, he moved "quicker nor an alligator can chaw a puppy." If speechless, he said he was "dumb as a dead nigger in a mud-hole." When he went into town and got into trouble—as he usually did—he got himself into an "everlastin' fix," and as a result had to shout to his mates to "start your trotters" to beat a hasty retreat. Those who survived usually found themselves the morning after feeling so poor and thin they had to "lean up agin a saplin' to cuss," while any who transgressed the law enough to find themselves hanged were "choked to death like a catfish on a sandbank."[14]

Most of all, these men captured the attention of the locals with their incredibly rich boast, a form raised almost to a high art. It appeared usually as prelude to a fight, and such scuffles were daily occurrences Under-the-Hill. "It was an appetite," wrote one who knew them, "and, like pressing hunger, had to be appeased." It could start with one issuing a broadcast challenge to all, and in a way unmistakable. He shook himself from his slumber or staring, rolled his sleeves up beyond his elbows, then strode to the bow of his boat or stood atop a stump on shore.

"I'm from the Lightning Forks of Roaring River," he shouted. "I'm *all* man, save what is wild cat and extra lightning. I'm as hard to run against as a cypress snag—I never back water. Look at me—a small specimen—harmless as an angle-worm—a remote circumstance—a mere yearling. Cock-a-doodle-doo! I did hold down a bufferlo bull, and tar off his scalp with my teeth, but I can't do it now—I'm too powerful weak, *I am*. I'm the man that, single-handed, towed the broad-horn over a sand-bar—the identical infant who girdled a hickory by smiling at the bark, and if any one denies it, let him make his will and pay the expenses of a funeral. I'm the genuine article, tough as bull's hide, keen as a rifle. I can out-swim, out-swar, out-jump, out-drink, and keep soberer than any man at Catfish bend. I'm painfully ferochus—I'm spiling for some one to whip me—if there's a creeter in this diggin' that wants to be disappointed in trying to do it, let him yell—whoop-hurra!"[15]

Sooner or later some other boaster took the bait, and then the two continued with a dialogue of brag and challenge. In 1808 Christian Schultz overheard two Kaintucks working themselves up to a fight.

"I am a man; I am a horse; I am a team," said the first. "I can whip any man *in all Kentucky*, by G——d."

"I am an alligator," came the response: "half man, half horse; can whip any *on the Mississippi* by G——d."

"I am a man; have the best horse, best dog, best gun, and handsomest wife in all Kentucky, by G——d," retorted the first.

"I am a Mississippi snapping turtle," said the other, "have bear's claws, alligator's teeth, and the devil's tail; can whip *any man*, by G——d." That finally did it, and the two began their fight, which stopped only after half an hour, much blood, and "when the alligator was fairly vanquished by the horse."[16]

Inevitably liquor preceded such boasts, and almost all the brawling on the frontier, whether among boatmen or any other men. Natchez alone had at least twenty-five dram shops as early as 1803, most of them Under-the-Hill. The number throughout the Southwest and along the Trace must have run in the hundreds from an early day. Drinking was widespread among men, and even among some women, and alcoholism itself ran rampant. People drank at any time and for any reason, from relaxation to medication, and they generally took their whiskey straight.[17] Some tavern keepers like John Walton found business so good that they opened more than one, and he kept houses both Under-the-Hill and atop the bluff, valuing the business as high as five thousand dollars in 1803.[18] Visitors from abroad found that to behave like "good Americans" while in the territory they had to be "high-spirited drinkers."[19] As for the locals, their intake could seem astounding. In 1811 John Alstone boarded a few days at a Claiborne County tavern and drank seven glasses of gin "sling" on March 4, a pint of whiskey and a quart of cider two days later, and on one exceptionally thirsty occasion put down three pints of whiskey and three quarts of cider.[20] Lawyer Francis Wood of Natchez came repeatedly to Stephen Bullock's store for whiskey, cider, brandy, and more, buying it by the bottle, the pint, and even the "tot" when he was in a hurry.[21] Naturally some proprietors experimented with concoctions, many of them if not deadly, at least very hazardous to well-being. At the Mansion House in Natchez barkeeper George Vennigerholtz served a variety of mint julep that earned him fame all along the river, and some others mixed them even without the ubiquitous whiskey. One version involved a glass tumbler filled to the brim with cracked ice kept buried in the ground from the winter freezes. The mixer sifted sugar over the ice, then laid three fresh mint leaves on top, and over it all poured equal parts of cognac, Jamaica rum, and port. The effect of a few of them must have been lethal.[22]

How much more must this have been the case for travelers like one pair of men on a stage who had juleps at ten of its stops during a seventeen-hour journey! Yet they could not stay away. On one of the steamboats gliding up the river a man with a fresh stab wound drank incessantly and explained that "if my arm should drop off, I must have my corn, I tell ye." A visiting Briton concluded: "An Englishman could not drink as the Americans do; it would destroy him."[23] Taverns could be the scene of so much "riot and dissipation" that more sober travelers could not concentrate even to write a letter.[24] A log tavern in Marion, Alabama, advertised itself with a sign that surely mystified all but a few of its patrons with the Latin phrase *Dum Vivimus, Vivimus,* by which the proprietor meant, "While we live, let us live it up."[25]

Many lived it up until they died. The Natchez newspapers contained several notices of citizens for whom liquor proved fatal. Some fell drunk from their horses and broke their necks. A lawyer hanged himself in remorse after his wife died, neglected by her hard-drinking husband. Others simply poisoned themselves with alcohol.[26] Meanwhile, those who merely became habitual drunks posed a considerable problem for community authorities. As soon as villages became large enough to frame city codes, they drafted regulations banning public drunkenness and accompanied them with fines or sentences of a few nights in the jail. On the less genteel frontier, as at Marion, citizens dealt with the matter in other ways. Inebriates who gave offense on the streets were grabbed and marched to a local brickyard, there to be thrown unceremoniously into a clay hole three feet deep in mud and water. The ducking could go on and on until the soggy villain appeared sober.[27] Sadly, the fondness for drink spread rapidly among the Choctaw and Chickasaw as well, visitors often seeing them nodding on some Natchez street or peddling a few paltry items to get money for whiskey.[28] In 1808 a small band of about forty of them formed a rude "orchestra" and performed at the riverbank for every arriving flatboat and keelboat. Playing their rude cane instruments, they sang native songs in return for whiskey money.[29]

• • •

A distressing concomitant to the drinking, especially among the boat-men, was the traffic with prostitutes. "Almost all the Kentucky men stop here on the way to Orleans," noted Bradbury, "and as they now consider all the dangers and difficulties of their voyage as past, they feel the same inclination to dissipation as sailors who have been long out of port, and generally remain here a day or two to indulge it."[30] A dozen or more shabby brothels crowded the sides of Under-the-Hill's archly named Maiden Lane. Boatmen could step directly off their ves-sels and onto the street, walking up to the first one that came to hand. Inside these filthy cribs they usually found black and mulatto slave women purchased and brought here specially for the purpose, "capable of business" as advertisements for them stated. A few Indian women also worked with them, and here and there even a white girl, generally driven to the trade by alcoholism or abandonment by her husband.[31]

Often as not the boatmen went into the village to find their women, then brought them back aboard their vessels for a night's rev elry. Christian Schultz reboarded his flatboat one morning to find "exactly one quarter of a dozen of the copper-coloured votaries of the Cyprian queen, who it seems had undertaken to enliven the idle hours of our Canadian crew."[32] Natchez's citizens tried from time to time to clean up Under-the-Hill, and in 1816 actually succeeded in evicting most of the prostitutes, shipping them downriver or to the other side. The move discomfited more than just the working women. "Fair Poll adieu," wrote one of their better clients. "With thee sweet Jenny goes, and Moll, and Bet, and Nell, and Rach, and Rose. Lost o'er the watery way compell'd to roam. Concordia's banks receive their wand'ring feet," he continued, "Concordia's crops supply them beds' of rest, Con-cordia's bachelors are supremely bless'd."[33]

The third element of the unholy trinity of vice in the territory—as everywhere else—was gaming. In 1825 William Hall stepped ashore at the landing and decided to see for himself what made Under-the-Hill so storied on the rest of the frontier. Walking up a street, he turned into the first open door. It proved to be a tavern, well lit, with a pair of pros-titutes dancing to the music of two violins, a clarinet, and a drum, while a black boy wearing a turban beat incessantly at a tambourine. One of the dancers approached Hall and asked him to dance, while suddenly other gaudily dressed women approached the boatmen clustered around the room and pulled them to the floor. When Hall declined, his Cyprian responded "then d——n you, treat me," and he bought her a drink. As soon as a whiskey occupied her attention, Hall slipped into the next room, and there he found a roulette wheel surrounded by anxious bettors, and other tables dealing faro, the players betting on the order of appearance of cards turned from the top of the deck.

The men sat with piles of silver coin or paper scrip before them, while some used bone or ivory chips. All spoke incessantly as the wheel spun and the cards floated to their hands. Mostly they swore. The winners kept quiet. In one corner the owner fought to eject a drunk with five hundred dollars in his hand who insisted that he wanted to bet it and double his money or lose it all. The man appearing to be the landlord refused to let him place a bet, but the drunk insisted. Finally the proprietor, seeing Hall, asked him if he would do him a favor by winning the fellow's money and then giving it back to him when he sobered. "If you don't," said the man, "some gambler will, and keep it." Hall agreed.

The drunk showed Hall three cards, then put them facedown on a counter, betting his five hundred dollars that after they were shuffled and spread out once more, Hall would not be able to pick a card and name it. Then as the dealer turned his back to take a drink, another approached Hall and picked up a card, showed it, then carefully turned up one corner so that Hall could identify it even when it was facedown again. At the last minute, however, the drunk asked to shuffle the cards once more. When Hall then picked the card with the bent corner and said it would be the nine of diamonds, his heart sank when it proved to be instead a jack of clubs. Instantly the drunk became sober, the stranger handed over Hall's money in a flash, and the chastened Hall left the establishment while the winner behind him shouted that it had all been fair.[34]

Men gambled on everything, whether cards, dice, or pitching coins at a wall, and cheating and shilling by sharps such as those who gulled Hall ran rampant. While Natchez city authorities allowed gambling to continue on the bluff, where men played at more genteel and honest games, they repeatedly attempted to ban it Under-the-Hill, but with little effect.[35] Billiards, "rowley powley," *rouge et noir* (probably a relative of roulette), faro, and others all found themselves forbidden, and all flourished. Indeed, as early as 1806 one Natchean complained that gambling "is too general in your city, for its welfare."[36] In time people in the city blamed almost all of the vices of the town on the gamblers, an attitude that spread up and down the river in years to come. Communities enacted wholesale evictions of gamblers, along with prostitutes, and a few miscreants even lost their lives when they resisted, but the plague never disappeared. They simply moved on to another community, and then they or others slowly returned.

• • •

One of the chief complaints about the combination of drinking, women, and gambling was that it so often led to brawls and eventually killings. "The gentlemen on board passed their time at cards & backgammon, and frequently had disputes about the game," a steamboat passenger observed in 1826. "One day they abused one another violently, and two of them struck & threw chairs at one another."[37] Joseph Cowell, aboard the *Helen McGregor* in 1829, found that cardplaying provided the chief amusement, and though he did not play, he liked to watch. One evening he sat with a friend who played a game involving trumps with another. His friend won for some time until an apparent onlooker sat next to him. At first unbeknownst to the player, the spectator began putting his hand on the table with a finger extended for each trump card in the man's hand. It was an obvious signal to the other player. Nonchalantly Cowell's friend pulled out his hunting knife and began cleaning his fingernails. When he received his next hand from the dealer, he found one trump in it, and the man next to him extended one digit on the table. Quick as lightning, the victim brought his knife down and severed the finger.

"Hallo! stranger, what are you about?" shouted the man. "You have cut off one of my fingers."

"I know it," said the player, "and if I had had more trumps, you would have had less fingers."

It was not uncommon on the steamboats for a man to stay behind at a poker table when some commotion drew all the other players outside for a moment. Hurriedly he "put up" or "stocked" the deck, giving every man at the table a seemingly winning hand, and himself one that just barely beat them all. It guaranteed not only a win but high-stakes betting.[38]

Drinking especially led to foolish pranks that often got out of hand. In Marion the local courthouse became the object of derision of a group called the "boys," who liked to gather at a nearby tavern. When in their cups, they devised methods of vandalizing the structure. One night they knocked away the wooden blocks underpinning one corner, which allowed the building to settle at a crooked angle. More notorious was their "circus raid," in which, heavily under the influence, the boys went by night to the camp ground of a traveling carnival and pushed all the wagons into a ravine, breaking them up and allowing the wild animals to escape.[39]

It was but a short step from pranks to violence. As early as 1798 a Natchez citizen complained to Andrew Ellicott of a "bachanalian fracas" in town during which one man split the skull of another with a sword.[40]

That same month another told Ellicott of a "hard fought" fistfight he had with Daniel Hickey. He sprained his right hand and dislocated his left thumb, but had the satisfaction of blacking and closing both of Hickey's eyes.[41] Bent and broken thumbs were a common occurrence, as no holds were barred, and especially among the boatmen the gouging out of eyes and biting off of ears were accepted practice. In Radfordsville, Alabama, in 1827, a Fourth of July celebration turned ugly when, without provocation, a drunken man walked up behind a patron in a store and assaulted him, biting away a piece of his right ear in the process.[42]

At the upper end of the Trace in Williamson County, Tennessee, a man saw the look of blood in the eye of a onetime friend who repeatedly sought an excuse to start a quarrel, from complaining of having to return a borrowed saddle to imagining that he had been insulted over making corn whiskey for his family. The man simply wanted to fight, and that was that. Then he complained that the innocent party hurt his hand when they shook as friends. The other apologized, said he could not fight, and suggested they take a drink and act as friends. Soon, however, the peacemaker heard that his antagonist and friends intended to come and kill him. "This news somewhat alarmed me," he confessed. He got up and left, but then heard his nemesis and others coming after him. In a panic the fellow ran into a dark house to hide, but the others, drunk, came in after him. When they failed to find him, they went back outside and waited by his horse, and when he approached, thinking he had eluded danger, there they were. He tried to run back to the house, but in an instant they were on him. "The licks and kicks soon put me down," he confessed. "They continued to beat and stomp my breast and head til they were tired, when they would rest and begin again." Miraculously the man survived.[43]

Sometimes men did not live through a brawl, however. In 1819 Banks Finch worked as a hand on the keelboat *Fort Massac*. Everyone knew him as a "very overbearing, troublesome man, and particularly so when intoxicated," said his mate Otha Batman. Finch drank incessantly when he could get it, even aboard ship when working, with the result that his masters ordered that passengers inside the "cabin" should not have whiskey for fear Finch would get it. When Finch went to the passengers to ask them for drinks, they refused, and he developed an unnatural enmity toward them and began threatening them with whipping. Then, in port, Finch went ashore and bought a jug of his own and came back spitting vituperation at captain and passengers alike. He quit on the spot, took his wages, and then followed the boat. When the passengers came ashore that evening, he appeared and began issuing threats that he intended to beat one of them—whom did not matter. Finally fighting started, and Finch grappled first with the captain and then with his lieutenant, who finally drew a dirk and stabbed Finch repeatedly and fatally.[44]

Dislike of law officers could also precipitate a scuffle. At the little community of Severe Beat, on Alabama's Cahaba River, several local boys gathered at a grocery and grog shop to drink and compete at shooting for a beef when the local sheriff appeared, intent on serving a writ. As the officer tried to do his duty, the rowdies grabbed him and threw him under the grocery, which stood just a foot or more above the ground. There they kept him, and would do so until he agreed to go back where he came from and never trouble them again. One of their number, a fellow called Red Fox, kept the sheriff there for two full days until he fell ill from gorging on whiskey and salt mackerel, and vomited it through a crack in the floorboards, all over the sheriff's pants. Meanwhile the other boys danced gleefully around their sick friend. Confined in his dank prison, choking with dust, sick from the foul mess spilling on him from above, and terrified by the sound of the singing and dancing overhead, the officer yielded and gave his pledge.[45]

Ministers, too, were fair game for the sons of Bacchus. The Methodist Thomas Griffin went Under-the-Hill in 1814 to attempt to preach, not knowing that a small mob of boatmen awaited his coming intent on mayhem. When finally he was warned, other Kaintucks told him to come ahead, that they would guarantee his safety. He selected a house directly between two noisy saloons that had parties in full swing, and as he approached heard swaggering boatmen threaten to pelt him with bricks if he tried to preach. Still Griffin held his meeting, and when singing of a hymn attracted the attention of the revelers, some of the Kaintucks actually threatened their boisterous brethren with harm if they did not leave the Methodist alone. "Say just what you please," one of them told Griffin. "You are not to be hurt here to-night."[46] Ministers were not always to be so lucky.

Indeed, the boatmen disliked nothing so much as do-gooders, which included those living in the city on top of the bluff who tried to clean up Under-the-Hill from time to time. "Generally they expended their animal prowess among themselves," recalled one Mississippian, "but they would occasionally break through the acknowledged boundaries of their own district, and carry the devoted city, so beautifully situated, by storm."[47] In 1807 the Natchez press complained of rioting in the city streets, especially when a mob of boatmen came up and rampaged, resulting in the death of a Spaniard. A visit Under-the-Hill by regular townspeople could be just as dangerous, as in 1814 when a Fourth of July dinner there was crashed by drunken Kaintucks angry at not being invited to a frolic in their own midst. They brought clubs and dirks with them, and a general melee commenced that left several with wounds, and a number of the rioters carried off to the city jail. Worst of all, perhaps, was the three-day riot Under-the-Hill in May 1817, when the Kaintucks took over the landing entirely, fighting with each other and with townspeople and officials. Only when they found a cannon aimed at them from atop the bluff, and militia forming to assault, did the rowdies finally give up.[48]

"Taking possession of the streets, with equal impunity they rode over the law and every physical obstruction," lamented a resident. "Having gratified their humors, drank up, or otherwise destroyed, all the whiskey in their reach, with yells and war-whoops, that fairly wakened the aborigines sleeping beneath the walls of Fort Rosalie, they would retreat down the winding road that leads to the plateau 'under the hill,' most likely to meet with a number of their own set and engage in a pitched battle."[49]

Nothing was better calculated to ignite the ferocious anger of the boatmen, or indeed any other man on the frontier, than some real or imagined slight or insult. It could be completely anonymous, as when a man at the steering sweep of a broadhorn coming down the river saw a fellow ashore start jumping up and down and "by a series of ridiculous and indecent antics" attempting to outrage a party of women and children aboard the boat. The man at the oar shook his fist at first, but the clown just renewed his obscene gestures, whereupon the other man dropped his oar and picked up his rifle. A small puff of smoke appeared first, and a second or two later people ashore heard a dull crack, then saw the clown no longer jumping but holding his hand to his abdomen. He staggered a pace or two, then fell dying.[50]

No one could walk away from insult. It was a part of the rude frontier ethic, an outgrowth partly of the lawlessness of the region and the necessity for a man to make his own justice in a place where official retribution could be a hundred miles distant, as well as the need for a man to be respected in order to survive amid rough-and-tumble wilderness competition. When Andrew Jackson left his home to emigrate to the land at the north end of the Trace, his mother admonished him: "You are going to a new country, and among a rough people; you will have to depend on yourself and cut your own way through the world. Never tell a lie," she went on, "nor take what is not your own, nor sue anybody for slander or assault and battery. *Always settle them cases yourself!*"[51]

And thus men did settle "them cases." The instinct to resent insult, to accept a fight on the spot, and to take it to the foe was instilled in them at an early age. Young Jefferson Davis was not much more than ten years old when his family lived at Woodville in Wilkinson County. One day hunting with a friend named Bob Irion, Davis ran out of shot for his rifle, and Irion exhausted his powder. When the first asked the other for the loan of some shot, Irion refused and made faces and jeered at him instead. Rather than give him shot, said Irion, he had a mind to shoot him some, and made as if to raise his rifle. At once Davis pulled out a pocketknife, opened the blade, and ran it down his barrel on top of a powder charge. Pointing the weapon, he said, "Now, sir, I'm ready for you; I dare you to shoot." Happily they gave up their foolishness and became friends once more, but Davis had shown the kind of temper expected of a man in the Southwest.[52]

Indeed, it was unthinkable for a man to accept an insult, much less a beating, without quick and forceful response. Discussing a rumor that a Tennessean had meekly submitted when an assailant pointed a pistol at him and tied his hands, a friend dismissed the charge entirely. "No one who ever knew Claveland would believe that any danger would terrify him into such degradation." He would more likely have said "fire and be d——d," said his defender. "He would rather have died than submitted."[53]

Insult and offense could be avenged in many ways, often depending on the nature of the original injury. Anthony Campbell, a onetime Natchez magistrate, rode into the city in September 1826 little apprehending any difficulty, when suddenly a large man named John Irwin walked up to him and began to rain lashes upon him with a whip. When Campbell fell to the ground, Irwin just continued, then beat him with his fists and the whip handle on the head and body. "For God's sake, don't murder me!" Campbell shouted, but Irwin just kept hammering at him. "By God," he said, "I'll murder and eat you, you ought to have been killed ten years ago!" Even as he kept hitting the prostrate man, Irwin bent down, took Campbell's left ear in his teeth, then tore it off, chewed, and swallowed. His anger sated, he walked away, probably going Under-the-Hill to a waiting boat. No one was ever charged, but some suspected that Irwin's act was retribution for Campbell's many attacks on the gamblers, prostitutes, and saloon keepers in past years.[54] Even old slights and grievances could not go unavenged.

In fact, vengeance seemed an acceptable excuse for all manner of behavior on the frontier. Harmon Blennerhasset, onetime collaborator with Burr in whatever scheme he concocted for Mexico and the Southwest, lived a wild life at his plantation, La Cache, not far from Port Gib-

son. His carousals were famous, given as he was to singing and dancing, and his wife reputedly could play the violin and drink whiskey with
the best of men. But Blennerhasset was also a violent man. When one
visitor got into a difficulty with him and tried to leave the plantation,
the host shot him as he climbed over a fence. Another neighbor nearly
killed Blennerhasset with an ax, and then, in February 1818, Blennerhasset and one of his sons appeared after dark at the home of neighbor
John Hays, called him outside, and at once jumped him, beating him
nearly to death. Several days earlier Hays had appeared at Blennerhasset's cotton gin with some friends and forcibly took several bales of cotton apparently due him in payment of some debt. The next day he
came back for more, and when Blennerhasset threatened him anew,
Hays pounced on him and threatened to cut off his ears "and do him
some private bodily harm." Blennerhasset and son both fired at Hays
but failed to hit him, and that is apparently when they decided to finish
the affair later by night.[55]

In the worst extreme, men took justice into their own hands and
dealt out death in return for the worst offenses. Jack Pitchlyn was a
Choctaw of some note in Lowndes County, Mississippi, and well
thought of except when he drank, which was too often. Once while
drunk he killed his own half-brother Silas, and from that time onward
seemed to know that he would himself sooner or later be killed in retribution. At first he went into hiding, and then made his way to Cotton
Gin Port in the Chickasaw country, always mindful that he would be
followed. One night, with Garland Lincecum, he walked out of his hotel
after supper. Unseen behind him were his half-brother's avengers, and
when he and Lincecum parted briefly, they stepped out of the shadows
and shot him. "I am a man and a warrior," Pitchlyn shouted as they
fired, attempting to draw his own pistol even as he fell lifeless. Frontier
vengeance was swift and brutal.[56]

Men of more refined manners or more calculating temper chose
another form of redressing grievances. Dueling in the Southwest went
back at least to the days of the Spaniards, who generally took their disputes to a sand bar on the west bank of the Mississippi for settlement.
As a result, well before the territory became part of America a resort
to pistols or swords here became known as going "over the river."[57] It
happened with sometimes startling regularity, often the result of a
deadly mixture of too much alcohol and too highly developed a sense
of pride and honor. Only cowards could tolerate an insult, said the code
of behavior that led to dueling, and a visiting Englishman in 1823 noted
that when affront was given among these frontier men, "they must

fight, kill or be killed."[58] So prevalent did this become as a means of settling disputes that in 1799 the territorial legislature defined as murder any killing as a result of a duel, and then, in November 1804, enacted a law prohibiting dueling, making it a felony to give or accept a challenge. If men went ahead and fought, they came liable to a thousand-dollar fine and a year in jail if no one was hurt. When a fatality occurred, all parties were to be charged with murder. In 1819 the new state legislature adopted the same law, then strengthened it three years later, but it never acted anymore to curtail the practice in the Southwest than did similar laws elsewhere in the southern states.[59] No jury of peers would convict a man who killed another in a fair fight.

In spite of the laws, many of the most prominent men engaged in duels. Poindexter, Hunt, Holmes, Governor Claiborne, Cowles Mead, and others all went "over the river" at least once, and Poindexter's shoes scarcely dried between trips. State law even defined the kinds of words that could not be exchanged between men—including "poltroon," "dastard," and "white livered coward"—but that did not keep men from using them. They dueled over anything, including even the selection of a site for Mississippi's permanent capital. Newspaper editors seemed constantly to be involved, thanks to their intemperate editorials, and lawyers and politicians accounted for most of the rest. Even Attorney General Richard Stockton of Mississippi was charged in 1827 with being involved in two duels, though as chief law officer of the state, it was his sworn duty to prevent them. Not long thereafter he would himself be killed in yet another personal affray of honor.[60]

In fact, it was only with great difficulty that personal feuds among prominent men were kept off the dueling ground. Andrew Jackson and Silas Dinsmoor, an Indian agent, carried on a long and bitter controversy growing out of nothing more than Dinsmoor's attempt to enforce an edict requiring passports for those traveling through Choctaw country. Their controversy stopped short of pistols at dawn, but Jackson engaged in other duels, and killed at least one man who indirectly insulted his wife.[61]

Any man refusing a challenge could be publicly ridiculed as a coward unless he showed that his challenger was not a gentleman— that is, not sufficiently refined to be considered an equal. In 1830 Michael Kenan of Dallas County, Alabama, offered an insult to William R. King, who would one day be Franklin Pierce's vice president. King drew his sword cane and slapped the blade across Kenan's chest but refused to accept the lesser man's challenge.[62] Still, more were accepted than refused. Sam Houston, congressman from Tennessee, went to the dueling field in 1826, in spite of deep misgivings about the whole business. He and his antagonist advanced toward each other with pistols and fired when about five yards apart. Houston emerged unhurt, but William White went down with a bullet in the groin.

"I am a dead man," White declared.

"White, my dear fellow," said Houston, grasping both his hands, "I am sorry for you."

"I do not blame you. I have no bad feelings against you," responded White. "We ought never to have fought."[63]

Such scenes of remorse and forgiveness were common, as the wounding of a man seemed usually to remove all the rancor in both antagonists. But all the blood and death did nothing to stop the practice itself. Natchez saw an epidemic of dueling in the four years following the meeting of Samuel Wells and Dr. Thomas Maddox in 1827. They went across the river to the sandbar and exchanged two rounds of shots, neither injuring the other. At this they agreed that honor was satisfied, shook hands, and they and their seconds walked toward the woods onshore to share a toddy. Suddenly three men emerged from the woods and came running toward them, one of them being the famous adventurer James Bowie. A companion of his shouted at one of the seconds in the duel that this would be a good time to settle a difference of their own, but as Bowie and the other two drew their pistols, it became evident that this would be no duel fought by the rules. The second drew his own pistol and shot his assailant in the chest. Then, with another, he fired at Bowie and missed, then drew yet another pistol and shot the other of the three. Bowie then drew his famous knife and rushed at the man. With only an empty pistol in his hand, he struck Bowie over the head with it. The blow sent Bowie to his knees, but he arose, scuffled with Maddox, and then faced others of the seconds just coming back from the woods. Within moments Bowie killed one of them and wounded another. Finally, with two men dead or dying and two others, including Bowie, wounded, the battle subsided. Later called the "sand bar fight," it revealed how slender was the line between fair dueling according to a code of ethics and rough-and-tumble brawling with no rules and no holds barred.[64]

It was no wonder that this southwestern frontier acquired a reputation throughout the United States for licentiousness and violence. Both lay just beneath the surface, and Under-the-Hill in Natchez they were in fact all too evident. By 1830, however, Natchez had at least managed to clean out much of the lawless and rough element, who just moved on to other river cities like Vicksburg or Memphis. All the things they represented—the drinking, gambling, whoring, and brawling—were elements that made up a safety valve for the pressures accumulated in living at the edge of the wilderness. Nothing happened in Natchez that did not happen at the loneliest stand on the Trace—it simply happened more often and more publicly. Vice did not hold sway in the Southwest. For every brawling Bowie or drunken Mike Fink, there were thousands of settlers and planters, tradesmen and merchants, who lived lives as free from misadventure as if they lived in New York or Boston.

Yet if living at the edge of civilization offers some excuse for a certain excess in their temperament, if "allowances should be made for their aberations," as the old pioneer said, still there were others who went beyond the edge. In the dark shadows of the Trace, the dense thickets of the piney woods, and the murky backstreets of Natchez, there were some who recognized no limits of behavior, and no rule at all but their own.

❧ 13 ❧

The Road to Law and Order

Thanks to the wildness of some of its inhabitants, and more to that of men who simply passed through, the Trace and the territory it traversed came to enjoy an unsavory reputation both within its own borders and in the world at large. While Timothy Flint found these people of the backwoods generally "amiable and virtuous," others who saw only the river or Natchez thought differently. Timothy Dwight pronounced the region "a grand reservoir for the scum of the Atlantic states," while Thaddeus Harris averred that "sloth and independence are prominent traits in their character; to indulge the former is their principal enjoyment, and to protect the latter their chief ambition."[1]

As early as 1805 Natchez, and especially the landing below the bluff, acquired an image of bawdiness and lawlessness that spread through the nation. Travelers who came wrote narratives on their return to the East, and spread lurid and exaggerated tales. Easterners believed those stories for the most part, since they fitted preconceived notions of life on the frontier generally, and in time Natchez came to symbolize in their minds the very worst excesses at the edge of the wilderness. Stories of the dreadful crimes committed along the Trace especially captured imaginations and gave rise to a genuine market for such tales, always the surest guarantee that more accounts—and more exaggerated ones—would be forthcoming, whether true or not. The rude facts of frontier crime in the Southwest quickly became legend, and that legend fed on itself until even many of the inhabitants began to accept their own myth as defining who they were.[2]

Of genuine excesses, those going beyond the ordinary misdemeanors of drinking, prostitution, gambling, and fighting—of which those practicing were usually the only victims—genuine crime did emerge in the Southwest, just as it always did wherever and whenever men moved into a new region, and if it did not live up to the lurid reputation that later spread, still it was real enough, and a perennial problem. The Spaniards met with it first, and found the challenge of bending the rough mix of Frenchmen, Spaniards, Irishmen, Germans, Britons, and Americans to obedience of their laws to be no mean feat. In such a vast area, with such a meager force as Spain had at its command, even the promulgation—much less the enforcement—of their laws posed a problem. In 1769 a Spanish governor in New Orleans, with the unlikely name of Captain-General Alejandro O'Reilly, issued a forty-four-page digest of laws for the colony and established a cabildo to act as court and council under his jurisdiction. There he would deal with civil and criminal cases from throughout the province after the commandants of frontier posts like Fort Panmure had arrested the accused and taken statements from all the parties involved.[3]

In the Natchez district there were eventually twelve administrative subdistricts, and in each of these the commander at Fort Panmure stationed two justices to assist in maintaining order, while to act as policemen he had no one but his own pitifully few soldiers. Understandably many petty criminals slipped through his fingers, while probably even more crimes of all sorts went unpunished merely because they went unnoticed and unreported. But that there was crime none could deny. Especially with the American Revolution and the influx of refugees, a number of unsavory types found in the dense woods and distant locations the kind of hiding they sought. Very quickly some of them started counterfeiting Spanish scrip, virtually undermining the worth of local currency. Others of a more active bent took up residence within the Choctaw lands—or actually with the Choctaw themselves—and used them as a base for launching small cattle-stealing raids, petty robbery, and even murders. There was little the Spaniards could do to stop them. Policing soldiers were too few and lacked horses, and frontier communications were so slow that the perpetrators had disappeared into their backwoods fastnesses before the frail arm of the law began to reach after them.

When the Spaniards attempted to apprehend malefactors, they called on local planters to raise an informal militia to assist. In August 1786 a James Armstrong and two of his sons, a black slave, James and John Lovel, and George Blair formed themselves into a gang at Armstrong's plantation north of Coles Creek and swept toward Natchez. They stopped at four houses, and in each terrified the inhabitants while robbing them of everything movable, including clothes, horses and saddles, firearms, and more. Then they rode back to Armstrong's, apparently unafraid of pursuit. When word reached Don Carlos de Grand-Pré, the commander at Natchez, he sent a circular to dozens of local citizens commanding them to enlist in parties of twenty or more "and pursue these Public Robbers without delay until taken dead or alive." He advised them to move on different roads, and lay ambushes at places where they thought the Armstrong gang might pass in returning from its nighttime "expeditions."

In the end there were two such parties, led by William Broccus and Samuel Gibson, and though they started on different paths, they accidentally met at Coles Creek and agreed to move together. After about nine miles they saw the tracks of a number of horses leading in the direction of Armstrong's plantation and followed until within five hundred yards of the house. Here Gibson's posse dismounted and crept through the fields to within two hundred yards, when they saw Armstrong leaning against a fence watching his wife milking a cow. At once Armstrong saw them and raced for the house while they started to advance and called on him to surrender. The pursuers split in two to surround the building, as Armstrong shouted back defiantly that he would surrender "with his rifle," meaning that he intended to resist. He also called to his sons and other gang members inside to get ready to fight, then appeared at a front window with his rifle in hand and yelled at the posse to "come and try it." He quickly saw that he would be surrounded, however, and he and the rest climbed out a back window to run. The others got there first, though, and when Armstrong tried to fire his rifle, Gibson ordered his men to let loose a volley. Armstrong fell dead at once, and his son James took a mortal wound, though the rest escaped, to be followed by Broccus's riders. After recovering all the stolen property, Gibson took the wounded Armstrong boy and the rest of the family back to Fort Panmure to report on the course of justice.[4]

Armstrong's activities were ample evidence of what an earlier observer had called "the ungovernable Spirit of these new Settlers, many being the Back Inhabitants of the other Provinces; without Education, without Religion, or Principles fit for the Bond of Society. Magistracy alone unaided, can administer little Justice amongst Offenders, without the Aid of a Stronger Power; untill which event Happens, every Licentiousness, and disorder, must go unpunished."[5] This was evident enough to Gayoso when he took over as governor at Natchez, and in short order he began strenuous efforts to exert the force of law. In

1791, responding to a dramatic increase in robbery, he sent two of his *alguaciles*, or justices, to apprehend two suspects. They got their men, but in the course of the arrest one of the miscreants shot and killed a justice, then escaped.

That was enough for Gayoso. By decree he enlisted thirty of the town's men into a mounted police for a term of six months, promising them a dollar a day plus rations and two hundred acres of land at the end of their term. Their first act was to trail and apprehend the killer. After that they swooped down on the Natchez counterfeiters and within a few months proved so effective that Gayoso thought the mere mention of their name sent would-be troublemakers fleeing from the district. Even after the men mustered out, they remained amenable to public service, and later helped form a militia that performed much the same functions.[6]

Most of the transgressions confronting Gayoso or any local commander were those against property, especially livestock. Cattle theft and horse stealing provided a steady stream of complaints, the latter especially being by Kaintucks facing the long walk back up the Trace and deciding to make their journey a bit more pleasant by taking a local planter's horse along for company. "It is extremely difficult to halt the introduction of persons of low character," Gayoso complained, "not only vagabonds, but those who live from nothing else than robbing Cattle." In part in reaction to this the Spanish governor in New Orleans published in 1793 and 1794 extensive regulations on the management and keeping of livestock, and more to the point governing how they could be sold. They regulated branding procedures to prevent counterfeit branding of another's animals, and prohibited people not resident in the territory from taking possession of strays—the most common way of stealing while maintaining innocence. He also forbade killing cattle in open pastures, where rustlers most often did so. Instead, cattle were to be slaughtered only in accepted places or in the planter's own yard. He also decreed that unbranded cattle under a certain age were not to be killed, another favorite practice among "the various frauds and damages that occur in this Government." Violators would be fined twenty pesos and serve a month in jail.[7] It was a start, but only the presence of his mounted police could help ensure obedience, and cattle and horses and pigs continued to disappear anyhow, thanks to the ability of the rustlers to escape into the wilderness. In time slave stealing would also become a problem, while some con artists sold a slave's services on the Natchez market, took the payment in advance, and then sent the black across the river and sold him again in a different jurisdiction. Gayoso tried to institute a curb by requiring that a full chain of title be presented with any slave offered on the block, but abuses continued nevertheless.

Then there were the crimes of violence. Gayoso tried to combat murder and homicide with a ban on knives and other personal weapons made of iron and steel, but offenders got around him by fashioning dirks and knives out of hardwood and used them almost as effectively as the real thing. And he could hardly restrict the possession of firearms, so necessary to feeding a family and preserving life against wild beasts. Too many of them were put to other uses, some in outright murders and more in spontaneous arguments over cards or women. In 1797 one Natchez man shot his own son-in-law during an argument over a slave. Sadder still was the tragedy on Saint Catherine Creek. There lived a man named Condy, "who was of that wild and roving disposition so common among frontier people," recalled George Willey. He came to believe that his beautiful wife had cuckolded him with a Spanish officer, and in a rage took his straight razor and slit her throat. In his passion he then took his three children, one by one, and slit their throats and laid them out on his cabin floor next to his dead wife. Then he lay down beside them, took his pistol, and put it to his head. Settlers from nearby came into the cabin the next day to see the entire family lying dead.[8]

Another impediment to maintaining order was that, once a crime occurred, Gayoso at first had no place to incarcerate the miscreants. Though something like jails had been built in Natchez and the other subdistricts by the 1790s, they remained flimsy things, and more often the worst criminals Gayoso put in the stockade at Fort Panmure along with his soldiers, which did nothing to please the latter. Gayoso commissioned plans for a sturdy new prison, but when the cost estimate came in at five thousand dollars, his superiors demurred.[9] And even apprehending a known criminal who was within sight of the soldiers or civilian police on the very streets of Natchez could be a problem, much less getting him inside the inadequate jail. The Spaniards still recognized the medieval right of sanctuary, the prohibition of military or civil officials from crossing the threshold of a church to pursue a felon. While sanctuary did not apply to all crimes in the Southwest, still it prevailed enough that Anglo residents in Spanish Natchez became accustomed to the sight of some shivering Spaniard, exhausted from his pursuit, standing in front of the church door with his finger through the keyhole. So long as that one part of him was "inside" the holy building, he was safe.[10]

Despite all the problems Gayoso and the others faced, the

Spaniards generally kept a lid on the worst sorts of crime, and if cattle and horse stealing remained a constant hazard of frontier living, still outright personal violence and mayhem stayed in the background, thanks in part to the simple scarcity of people. "The commission of crime was not greater than in frontier settlements of our own countrymen," said one American resident, "and indeed all of bad reputation which Natchez ever acquired, was after it came into the hands of Americans."[11]

When Winthrop Sargent arrived to act as governor at the American takeover, he found a frontier isolated, populated largely with the chaff of the East, debtors, fugitives, and indolent wanderers, as well as the ambitious and scheming like Hutchins and Ellicott. Indeed, friends warned Sargent against "the fugitives from justice & all the lawless characters which have taken refuge in that country," calling them "wild beasts," and suggesting that they would cringe at the approach of true law and justice. Sargent spent only a little time in the territory before he agreed that the condition of justice was "truly deplorable." In his domain he found "the most Abandoned Vilians who have escaped from the Chains and Prisons of Spain and been convicted of the Blackest of Crimes." "You will see camels as frequently in the eyes of needles as you will meet honest men in Natchez," lamented Lewis Evans, and Daniel Clark told the new governor that in order to maintain order "in this infant country we must not be very nice."[12] Of course, there was a great deal of hypocrisy attendant on these complaints. Clark was the same fellow who boasted to Ellicott of beating up Daniel Hickey, and Ellicott himself drank more than most, cavorted indecently with local girls, and maintained a mistress for his son.

Sargent's first difficulty lay in finding sufficient judges to administer such law as he had. Legislation provided for three men to be appointed to the territorial bench, any two of whom could at once form a court of common law. Peter Bruin, Daniel Tilton, and William McGuire brought a mixed bag of qualifications. Only the last had any real legal experience, yet McGuire turned around and left just two months after reaching the territory. Tilton brought a Harvard degree with him, but he never practiced law, had no law books for reference, and found the territory so terrifying that he stayed only two years. Bruin, at least, already lived in Natchez, so it held no terrors for him. He lacked education, drank too frequently and too much, and eventually resigned after ten years to avoid impeachment. As a result it was almost impossible for any two of these three to meet even briefly to make laws or constitute a court, and singly their background proved so limited and narrow that they gave Sargent little real help in establishing and maintaining law.[13]

In this judicial vacuum Sargent took over and enacted unilaterally his own set of laws. Called Sargent's Code, it took effect in February 1799 with the first nine of some forty-six eventual sections. By them Sargent established the several lesser courts within the territory and their judgeships. More importantly, he imbued his judges with seemingly dictatorial local powers. A judge could put a suspect in jail indefinitely, and if he actually saw a crime committed, could immediately sentence the offender without trial. Sargent also set the qualifications of members of the territorial supreme court, at the same time vesting them with almost life-and-death power. When it came to dealing with specific crime, Sargent showed his agreement with the advice not to be "very nice." The code specified what constituted several crimes, and assigned their punishments. Perjury brought a fine of up to sixty dollars, a whipping of up to thirty-nine lashes, standing in the pillory for up to two hours, and banishment from ever again testifying in a territorial court. Arsonists forfeited all their property, suffered the same whipping and pillorying, and served up to three years in jail. Hanging awaited murderers, and those guilty of treason would swing from the same gallows, along with having all their property seized by the state. Indeed, in all his assessed punishments, Sargent proved to be excessive even by frontier standards, and some of his penances violated the Constitution and would have to be changed. In the main, however, he stuck by his code in the face of considerable opposition and outcry. This was a rugged frontier, he argued, and it required tough measures to keep men in line.[14]

At the same time Sargent decreed that every county should build a strong jail, along with stocks, whipping posts, a pillory, and of course a gallows. Within those jails men and women were to be kept apart, though he thoughtfully provided that married couples might stay together. (They would most likely be in the separate chamber prescribed for debtors.) To fill these jails with offenders, Sargent created and filled positions of sheriff, coroner, and more, though from the point of view of some, he might have saved his time. Most of the counties found building jails so expensive that they never got them completed, which meant that the judges used a sparing hand in passing down sentences for imprisonment, having no place to send the convicts. As a further arm of the law, Sargent's Code also created a territorial militia. He drew considerable fire for his provision that he appoint all officers, for the American militia tradition specified that men elected their own leaders, but the governor stuck by his code and won his point. Equally disturbing to the frontier people was Sargent's smug attempt to insert government into their daily lives and behavior. He required liquor sellers to pay for licenses from the territory and pay fees to the local courts. Marrying couples had to buy licenses first, and whereas itinerant preachers generally charged just seventy-five cents, Sargent now wanted the territory to receive eight dollars, a very considerable sum for poor woodsmen and farmers. At the other end of the matrimonial scale, he decreed that only the legislature could take action to grant divorces, further interfering in the private lives of his people.

Sargent revealed in his code his own considerable fears for internal security and safety. He provided stiff penalties and confiscations for aliens suspected of treason. He proposed harsh measures to control the movements and limited freedoms of slaves, and harsher punishments if they broke the law. He also addressed the issue of liquor sales to Indians, and the potential for mayhem that could result.[15]

When a territorial legislature came into being in 1800, Sargent no longer ruled single-handedly, and his code began to wane in importance and impact as successive judges and legislators eroded its stern measures. Fortunately in 1803 Thomas Rodney, a genuine man of the bench, came to take a judgeship, and the next year Harry Toulmin arrived. Rodney served the western counties and Toulmin the eastern, and together they brought some real dignity at last to the territorial courts. In the ensuing years Congress and the president subdivided their domains into smaller judgeships, appointing more and more qualified men in the process. Unfortunately, since there was as yet only an embryonic body of territorial law, these men often administered justice in their courts based on the laws they had known in the states they came from, the result being at best a seemingly capricious inconsistency.

The new judges who came to these county courts found sometimes an alarming state of things. Ephraim Kirby took the judgeship in Washington County in 1804 and immediately formed a dislike for the inhabitants, saying they were "illiterate, wild and savage, of depraved morals, unworthy of public confidence or private esteem, litigious, disunited, and knowing each other, universally distrustful of each other." He disliked the magistrates and thought the lesser judges imbeciles and the militia incompetent.[16] Perhaps fortunately, given his attitude, Kirby died soon after arriving, and Toulmin took over for him, himself attacking the same "ascendancy which the most abandoned men, have obtained among us" as had his predecessor. Indeed, Toulmin encountered at least one assassination threat, and perhaps one actual attempt, as he attacked the "reigning villainy" of men in the Tombigbee region who resented law and sought by any means to help themselves to the land of others, even by planning attacks on Spanish Mobile.[17]

Throughout the territorial stage, and on into statehood, justice from the bench was only as good as the men sitting there, and with alarming frequency the gavel lay in the hands of drinkers, schemers, politically motivated opportunists, and worse. More than one judge would be evicted for his misconduct, and the Toulmins and the Kirbys were a happy exception. Cognizant of this, perhaps, the legislatures enacted very severe penalties—just as harsh as Sargent's—for major infractions, thinking that punishment could be a deterrent even if the judges were not. Murder, rape, slave stealing, robbery, burglary, counterfeiting, and incitement of rebellion in slaves could all send a man to the gallows. Anything less cost at least some blood at the whipping post, fines, cropping of ears or branding, and fines. They also made adultery and fornication crimes, as well as gambling, dueling, and even indulging in a number of pastimes on the Sabbath.[18]

Certainly the people of the Southwest offered enough in the way of transgressions to keep the judges busy. In the main, four basic categories of crime sent offenders before the bench: drunkenness, prostitution, gambling, and acts of violence including robbery and fighting.[19] In 1799, as Sargent's Code was in full sway, Natchez saw two men charged with murder and eight indictments for assault, as well as one for forgery. The numbers of assaults—mostly tavern brawls—reflected the fact that there were twenty-eight inns then under license in the community.[20] Two decades later, in the first blush of statehood, the two years commencing in January 1817 saw one case of murder, eleven of assault and battery, four of counterfeiting, three of theft, four of larceny, one of horse theft, one of "nuisance," one of slave stealing, and seventeen cases of runaway blacks. A slave who fired a gun in Natchez received a four-dollar fine and an hour in the stocks. Two runaway slave women received ten lashes each when caught. Another slave absent from his plantation without a proper pass incurred the same ten stripes, and so did a black who simply sold some butter without permission. Plato, a slave of high spirit, incurred twenty lashes for "rioting, drinking & noisy conduct, stripping to fight &c on Sunday."[21] The Natchez newspapers carried numerous advertisements like the one reporting the theft of a suit of clothes with "purl" buttons, with a hundred-dollar reward promised for catching the thief, or a ten-dollar reward for bringing back a runaway slave.[22] Nevertheless, by 1830 most of the criminal cases in the Southwest were assaults, and quite a number of them were defended on the basis of chivalry—that is, duels or fights growing out of affronts to dignity or honor.[23]

Naturally in a region inhabited by so many who came for opportunity, and for whom that opportunity meant land, crimes of real property were common. People squatted illegally on government land and refused, often violently, to leave. Soldiers evicted some, burning their homes to prevent their return. Other squatters assembled in intimidating groups at public land-sale days and used every effort to frighten prospective buyers away from bidding for the parcels already settled by these lawbreakers. Occasionally squatters even promised to murder anyone who bought the land on which they squatted, and on a few occasions the government land agents held their sales outside the territory in order to avoid the intimidation. Governor Robert Williams himself, after leaving office, attacked a land agent who refused to sell him land on the same terms as sold to others.[24] It all offered additional fields for the lawyers to plow. "They keep me tightly at work here I assure you," Francis Martin wrote a friend in 1811. "There is not a day in the year that the court does not sit somewhere in the territory."[25]

No precautions—not Sargent's threatening code, not competent judges, not even the militia—could prevent much of the violence inevitable on any frontier scene. These were ambitious, undisciplined, volatile men and women in large part, with tempers that could not be governed and characters that sometimes scrupled short of the law. Some were only petty thieves. During an Easter celebration at Grindstone Ford on the Trace, the Reverend James Thomson preached a rousing sermon, then asked those attending to contribute to the collection plate. The men did so in the main, but the women present noticeably kept their purses closed. They all stayed over that night, but some noted that Thomson did not join them at the supper table. The next day he had disappeared, and so had most of the money in the ladies' purses.[26] When Rachel Hartley tried to secure the estate of her late husband, Jacob, his mother charged her with not being legally the man's wife, of not treating him properly during his last illness, and then with poisoning him. Worse, she said Rachel also poisoned Jacob's brother and his two sisters. A doctor attending the dying people testified that they appeared to have been poisoned, but then afterward also admitted that Jacob's mother paid him a hundred dollars to say so. Others called Rachel a witch who killed another man with a spell. Investigation never fully sifted fact from fiction, but almost everyone seemed to be guilty of something, and all over Jacob's estate.[27]

Worse things happened. In July 1827 in Perry County, Alabama, a Mr. McNeily accused a neighbor's slave of stealing some clothing. Unsatisfied with any explanation, McNeily and his brother accosted the black one day as he drove his master's wagon. As they threatened to attack him, the slave pulled a knife and stabbed McNeily fatally. He was arrested almost immediately and taken before a justice, who delayed passing judgment even while a threatening crowd of seventy or eighty angry whites gathered outside. Then the justice stepped down from his official duty and took his place as head of the mob, decreeing that the slave should be executed by being burned to death. The crowd tied the poor man to a tree, piled pitch-laden pine knots at his feet, and set the torch, despite the protests of a pitiful few men of sense and civilization standing nearby. Soon the slave was ashes, and despite the decision of an inquest that the perpetrators should be charged, they never came to justice. In fact, much frontier violence took slaves as its victim, since they could hardly defend themselves. Sometimes they deserved their fate, as with Harry, who tried to rape a white girl. Harry was hanged. But then there was Isabel, who was whipped to death by her owner, William H. Jones. A jury sent him to prison for ten years.[28]

Frontier crime and punishment posed serious problems for all concerned. There were never enough law officers to police the wide expanse. Worse, when they took suspects into custody, they often could not keep them. Sheriff William Brooks of Adams County sorrowfully complained that his jail was so inadequate that one prisoner escaped, and others could at will. Summer heat and spring rain, not to mention winter cold, swept through the shoddy building. He could not afford to feed his prisoners, and they had no money to support themselves. Meanwhile, so long as the Spaniards still held onto their West Florida province, lawbreakers in the Mississippi and Alabama lands could easily commit some depredation, then escape across the border leaving lawmen no opportunity to pursue.[29]

Not surprisingly, when the official law could not act to apprehend or keep offenders, citizens sometimes took a hand at it themselves. They formed vigilance committees and in the absence of law itself, made law of their own. Alabama especially saw them flourish in the remote northern counties, where almost every band of regulators came to be called "Slicks" after a mythical leader, Captain Slick. "Captain Slick and his Company were *tolerated*," one Alabamian said, out of pure necessity, but even the law-abiding citizens regarded them with some fear. In Jackson County, for instance, local authorities were "powerless" to deal with the lawbreakers in their midst. In such a circumstance, "Slick's law" was all they could turn to.

The Slicks struck by night, swiftly, without warning, and brutally. For lesser offenses their favorite punishment was to drag the presumed offender from his bed, tie him outside to a tree, and then whip or beat him until he was semiconscious. William Hall, for instance, heard a band of Slicks ride up to his house on a Sunday in 1831 and demand that he come out. His wife slammed the door, but they battered it in and then attacked both husband and wife. While she suffered a broken thumb, Hall found himself dragged some two miles into a swamp, where they gave him a kangaroo trial, convicted him, and administered fifty lashes. His crime had been counterfeiting, and he seems to have been guilty. It was a transgression officially punishable by death, which allowed the Slicks to argue that their brand of justice in such cases was more lenient. Moreover, because so many of the counterfeiters and other offenders in these remote counties were reputed to have accomplices everywhere, Slicks despaired of seeing impartial juries empaneled in the regular courtrooms. They thought their justice was more genuinely unbiased, more truly blind—and blind they were, though often to innocence and due process. Further, when men like Hall went to court themselves to charge the Slicks with assault and battery or any other crime, the same situation obtained. The Slicks, too, had many friends. Impartial juries to try them could be just as hard to find, and prosecutors, attorneys, jurors, and plaintiffs alike also had to contend with fear of clandestine reprisal should a Slick be convicted or even indicted.[30]

The Slicks did not use only the whip. A company in Perry County, led by the sheriff, David Chandler, as it happened, devised "Chandler's Coach" for offenders. They put a man inside a large hogshead or barrel, drove wooden pegs through the sides for him to hold onto, and then turned the barrel on its side and rolled him for whatever distance his crime seemed to warrant. Often the Slicks put a drunk in the hogshead and set it rolling down a hill, believing that at the end of the ride the man would emerge sober.[31]

As happened sometimes on the undisciplined frontier, a few of the men leading the Slicks were themselves nothing better than brutes, drunk on their little bit of power, and anxious to abuse it to satisfy nothing more than their own meanness. On the Alabama fringes of the Creek nation one group of regulators answered the command of a man so ready with punishment that they called him "Captain Whips." He struck some as more ape than man, a character of "indescribable ugliness" who carried a teamster's whip and used it brutally on any who offended him. Finally the people of the district themselves banded around a disgusted minister to subdue the Slicks—ironically, gathering as vigilantes to put down the vigilantes who supposedly kept the peace.[32]

By 1830 virtually every community on the Mississippi and most of those in the interior had some kind of vigilante or regulator body to assist—and sometimes thwart—the established authorities in maintaining law and order. It made sense in the main. After all, when thirty or forty Kaintucks took it into their heads to climb the bluff and go on a spree in town, the city police were hardly numerous enough to contain them. Beyond the "regularly" constituted vigilantes, however, townspeople sometimes arose spontaneously in mobs either to exact initial justice or else to set aright what they took to be miscarriages at the bench. Since mobs were generally composed of the poor and ignorant, there may also have been a tinge of class resentment behind their actions, especially when they involved more affluent offenders.[33]

James Foster of Natchez came from one of the better families and was himself a reasonably prosperous planter when he married. Unaccountably, only a few months after the ceremony—perhaps under the influence of drink—he brutally beat his young bride to death outside their house one day. He enlisted the help of some of his slaves to clean the body and help him bury it, but rumors got out and soon the law came to disinter the woman, and on seeing the evidence that she had been beaten, the sheriff arrested Foster and charged him with murder. One delay after another postponed the trial, and when finally it came the sheriff neglected to swear into office the deputy who summoned the jurors. That of course meant that the jurors themselves were not properly empowered, and on discovering this the judge threw out the whole case as a mistrial.

The result incensed the townspeople, including even some of the lawyers and leading men, but especially the lowly, who suspected that Foster evaded justice thanks to his social position, and that the sheriff intentionally failed to swear the deputy. They may already have been banded into a loose group called the "Lynchers," but if not, they formed it then, and the moment Foster stepped from the courthouse a free man, they seized him, bound his arms, and blindfolded his eyes. With no pretense at formality, they shoved and dragged him to a ravine near town, with quite an audience following. "His clothes were torn from his back," said a gambler nicknamed "Thimblerig," who happened to be in town, "his head partially scalped, they next bound him to a tree; each Lyncher was supplied with a cow skin, and they took turns at the flogging until the flesh hung in ribands from his body." That done, others poured hot tar over his head and every inch of his lacerated flesh, then emptied a sack of feathers on him. Clothed only in his feathers and a sad pair of trousers, Foster was paraded through the streets with a drummer playing behind him.[34] "We had seen Foster but an hour or two previously, in the prisoner's box, apparently in perfect health, and one of the finest looking men in the country," wrote an editor of the *Courier* who witnessed the affair. "It was a horrid sight to see him as we afterwards saw him; pale and trembling, the blood trickling down his neck; the tar and feathers making his appearance that of a monster. So far from recognizing Foster, we could scarcely realize that he was a man. The mob believed that he was a monster at heart, and were determined that his external appearance should correspond with the inner man."[35] The Lynchers took him back to the prison, intending to brand his forehead and cut off his ears a little later, but two friends helped him escape, not to be seen again in Natchez.

"Sights of this kind are by no means infrequent," Thimblerig told a friend. He had also seen a gambler caught at cheating flogged nearly to death, tarred and feathered, then set adrift in a canoe at night on the Mississippi with nothing but a paddle. "This is what we call Lynching in Natchez," he said.[36] Indeed, frustrated by the ease with which many felons escaped justice, and the equal frequency of jailbreaks like Foster's, even some of the best citizens argued in favor of the Lynchers and Slicks and their brand of law. "To resort to the laws for protection, seems to be worse than useless," complained an editor weary of seeing malefactors escape justice. "But one mode and only one suggests itself to us of getting rid of them—and that is not to trouble our courts or juries with them." "They ought to be hunted down as wild beasts," he continued, "and their carcasses left as food for the buzzards." Some communities heeded the call. In western Tennessee, aroused by a robbery of a flatboat, citizens gathered to clear out a nest of thieves that preyed on river traffic. The Lynchers swept into one rude village, arrested several men, and burned their houses. Another group of fifty or more approached the same village by water, then swooped through the interior indiscriminately arresting. With more than twenty suspects under guard, they turned them all over to a local sheriff and judge, who immediately released all but seven for want of evidence. Even then, the sheriff took several of those freed to a tree and whipped them. In a measure of the nature of justice from several points of view on the frontier, the sheriff freed one man named Geno when he offered to inform on others. But when Geno later returned to his criminal friends, they tied him to a tree and whipped him for informing. Geno himself then later whipped a man from Tennessee in retribution against the regulators who started the chain of violence that left his back scarred.[37]

• • •

Both in rumor and in part in fact, criminals in the Southwest seemed to band together in gangs, forming virtual small communities that mingled with some of the squatters and others at the ill-defined edge of civilization, often just inside the borders of the Indian lands. Given the chaotic state of the banking system, a perhaps unsurprising number of them chose counterfeiting as a profession and linked themselves with horse thieves and slave stealers. All three "professions" needed to be conducted at long range from their haunts, and in some ways each could complement the other.[38] Perhaps best known of these mobile gangs were the Kempers and their confederates, who lived near Pinckneyville, close to the Spanish West Florida line. Counting on the uneasy truce between America and Spain, they raided with impunity across the border into Spanish territory, then rode back to their village with little fear of being brought to justice by territorial authorities. Wisely they contented themselves with not stealing American cattle and horses, and when they did raid fellow Yankees, it was only the Horton gang, their rivals in crime.[39]

In time rumors of great robber confederacies spread through the region, fueled by the natural propensity for mythmaking of the frontier, and based on a smattering of fact. As early as 1802 Governor Claiborne tried to deal with a gang of boat robbers that operated on the Mississippi. Their habit was to raid a flat or broadhorn, then disappear across the line into Spanish West Florida to avoid apprehension. In time the governor came to believe that the perpetrators were the infamous Samuel Mason gang. While rumors and myths of pirates and highwaymen flourished throughout the territory, the Mason bunch were far more than frontier legend. They were all too real.

Samuel Mason came with a villainous pedigree. Born in 1739, probably in Pennsylvania, he lived on the fringes of civilization, and on the same edge of the law. By 1788 he was telling friends that he always expected "an advantage" in dealing with anyone, and generally made his own regardless of statute. In 1794 he may have killed a tavernkeeper, and not long afterward he found his locality no longer conducive to his way of living.[40] He shifted first to Cave in Rock on the Ohio, and there opened what purported to be a store for passing boatmen. Instead he sometimes robbed them and, if legend is to be believed, left them for dead while he and his associates took their boats down to Natchez and New Orleans for sale. Inevitably much fancy soon attached itself to Mason. In time, *every* robbery and murder on the river was done by him, and the mere sight of buzzards circling over some patch of woods or muddy river bank led watchers to murmur, "Another murder has been committed by Mason and his gang."[41]

If Mason did not do all that was attributed to him, still he did enough. When Cave in Rock became too hot for him, he moved to the Trace in 1801 and began preying on travelers, settling near Walnut Hills and keeping the eyes above his hooked Roman nose alert for any signs of a northbound rider carrying the profits of a downriver voyage about him. His gang included his brother John—sometimes identified as his son—his sons Thomas and Mango, an Irishman named Thomas Setton, a brutal fellow named Wiley "Little" Harpe, and half a dozen others, enough so that Mason could keep watchers posted in Natchez, Bayou Pierre, and even as far north as New Madrid. With the men in their company were a number of women and at least three children, forming a virtual criminal community. In time Mason came more and more to rely on waylaying northbound Trace traffic, since it was easier than attacking boats and saved him the trouble of selling their cargoes. Now he could concentrate just on relieving men of the proceeds in cash.[42]

Mason's depredations—and the other crimes commonly attributed to him—sent Claiborne into a fury. "While these Sons of Rapine and Murder are permitted to Rove at large," he complained, "we may expect daily to hear of *outrages* upon the Lives & properties of our fellow Citizens." Claiborne told Colonel Daniel Burnet that "these men must be arrested," and offered a reward of two thousand dollars.[43] Over and over again Claiborne sent militia out along the Trace to apprehend the gang, but time after time they returned empty-handed.[44]

Mason and his men hid in the canebrakes or other dark spots along the Trace to wait for their victims to approach. Then they suddenly leaped out, leveled their rifles and pistols, and demanded that the quarry "stand by." Despite legend, it remains to be established that the gang unquestionably murdered anyone on the Trace. At best, two killings and a possible third are specifically linked with them, but by and large they remained content with their booty.[45] Trace post rider John Swaney frequently encountered Mason as he rode over the road with his mail sacks. Mason always greeted him amiably, and even inquired curiously what was being said about him in Natchez and Nashville. "He often told me not to be afraid of him," Swaney recalled, "as he was after money and not letters, and that he did not wish to hurt any one, but money he must have."[46] In time northbound men leaving Natchez sewed their money into the lining of their clothes or inside rawhide bundles in hopes of concealing it from robber eyes. But

Mason's associates living in and around Natchez all too often detected such subterfuges and sent word ahead to the others lurking in the shadows on the Trace.[47]

Within a few months of Mason's arrival in the territory word of the scourge reached even back to the nation's capital. "The road passing through the Indian Country from Nashville to Natchez has for sometime past been infested with a gange of Bantitti," one official complained. Jefferson himself paid attention to the problem, leading to his order to post troops along the road at intervals, and a separate reward of four hundred for the capture of any bandit caught working the Trace. He also recommended that travelers form themselves into caravans for safety until the Masons and their kind were hunted down.[48] Meanwhile genuine murders did occur, despite caravans and rewards and the pitiful efforts of the few militia, and even the Slicks and Lynchers, who seldom strayed far from their homes. In August 1803 a Major Brashear of Kentucky left Natchez after a successful business trip with at least two thousand dollars in gold in his saddlebags. He got as far as Kegg Spring, near the Duck River, having picked up along the way a companion named Tranium. Brashear chose his company rather badly, for Tranium already had an unenviable reputation, with a cropped left ear that betokened either violent brawling or else some penalty exacted by a jury or Slick company in his past. A few days later Brashear's body was found at Kegg Spring, his horse and his money and Tranium gone forever.[49] A few weeks later Natchez newspapers carried the sorry story of a flatboat coming from Maysville, Kentucky, reported *"robbed and sunk"* near Walnut Hills, its flour, whiskey, bacon, two oarsmen, two slaves, and cash from recent sales all missing.[50] It was all taken to be Mason and his gang at work.

Adding salt to the wound was the inability of authorities to bring the felons to justice. On one occasion some of the Natchez Lynchers formed a party and rode up the Trace to the Pearl River, where they found evidence that the villains might be in the vicinity. Before going on the men rested themselves and their horses, and two of them bathed in the river, then swam to the other side. Much to their surprise, they found Mason and others waiting for them. At the same time that the robbers scooped up the swimmers, the men on the opposite bank saw what happened but could do nothing when Mason yelled across that his hostages would be killed should they make any attempt to molest him. Moreover, Mason ordered them to stack their arms and ammunition on the river bank and then withdraw while his men crossed and collected the booty. With the weapons in his hands,

Mason let the hostages go free and disappeared into the wilderness he knew so well.[51]

Even when the law did take Mason, it could not hold him. In January 1803 he and part of his band rented a house at Little Prairie, Missouri, not far from New Madrid. Spanish authorities still governing in that region swooped in and arrested him and most of his gang and put them in the New Madrid jail, confiscating some $7,163 in banknotes in the process. The local commander put them on trial, but then decided to send them downriver to New Orleans for sentencing. There the governor, in turn, determined to hand them over to Claiborne, since Mason's crimes had mostly been committed in the Mississippi Territory. But during a storm on the river, as a sloop carried the criminals back up the river, someone managed to get a gun and shoot the vessel's captain, and Mason and the rest escaped. Claiborne fumed, and it did not help that when Natchez authorities had brother John Mason in their jail, others of the gang boldly came into town and broke him out.[52]

Finally, however, Claiborne's reward seems to have borne fruit. One of Mason's victims passing through the Trace country happened to have a copy of the governor's reward proclamation on him, and Mason relieved him of it and found it rather amusing, if not flattering. Two of his men saw it in another light, however. Mason had just recently exchanged harsh words with them, and now the reward added the possibility of profit to their motive of resentment. One evening when John Sutton and James May were alone with Mason, and when he may have been asleep, one of them buried a tomahawk in his skull, and the two of them then severed his head. They put it in a sack and took it to Greenville on the Trace, to present it to a judge of the circuit court and claim Claiborne's reward of two thousand dollars. Many people in the town and from the neighboring country flocked to the office to view the grisly relic, and to attest to its being Mason for sure, though some claimed that it was not the robber. Almost certainly it was Mason, for he never again surfaced. Unfortunately for his killers, some in the crowd also recognized them, especially Sutton, who turned out to be Wiley Harpe. The two were arrested, tried, and subsequently hanged, not for murdering Mason but another of the gang's victims, waylaid on the Trace two months before.[53]

The end of Mason signaled the end of his gang, and to some extent brought a conclusion to the depredations of highwaymen along the Trace and in the Southwest generally, at least from organized bands of brigands. The worst of the danger spread between the limited span from 1802–5, and even then scarcely half a dozen genuine murders took place on the road.[54] Robberies were more frequent, and even their number came to be exaggerated at the time and in later years. Typically, as a trader rode northward, perhaps with a mail rider for company and security, he would see one or two horsemen following them at some distance on the Trace. The men might be followed for hours without molestation, either because the followers meant no harm, or else because they wanted to wait for the best time and place to strike. In the dark a trader could take refuge in the woods hoping to elude his pursuers, or else find safety with some Choctaw or Chickasaw, who harbored a considerable dislike for criminals of all classes and rarely if ever failed to give aid to their quarry. But when hunter and hunted did come face to face, results could be swift. Mail rider Swaney and a companion rode south toward Natchez one morning and just came around the end of a fallen tree that blocked the road when they saw a man standing on the other side. The stranger fired his gun at them, and Swaney's friend fell immediately even as he was drawing his own pistols. As the horses panicked, Swaney spurred his own mount and sped away before he could be molested.[55]

Some of the highwaymen on the Trace posed as Methodist ministers, an easy subterfuge thanks to the distinctive black dress worn by such preachers, and thus clad they easily gained the trust of their victims. A few robbers claimed to practice sermons and hymns to perfect their impersonation, and one named James Copeland later boasted that he spent two days teaching one of his henchmen "how to pray and sing, and give that long Methodist groan, and 'Amen'."[56] Generally, even after the subduing of Mason, travelers understood that once they reached Red Bluff Stand at the Choctaw boundary, they were leaving law behind. As late as 1820 Timothy Terrell, heaving north for Nashville, stopped at Red Bluff for the night and saw a number of horses and men gathered around the inn. That night they held a mock trial of some poor lone traveler from New York whom they so frightened that he ran away leaving behind his clothing. Terrell was in his room sleeping that same night when there came a knock at the door and a whispered warning that he was in danger. He slipped outside and hid in the slave quarters, suffered several narrow misses during the night as the thugs tried to find him, and then ran away with the dawn. Innkeeper Gregg refused to offer him any aid, and later claimed that the men at his stand were only post riders, and that Terrell was insane.[57]

• • •

Insanity, real or supposed, played an undoubted role in the most famous death ever to take place along the Trace, and surely the most mysterious. Meriwether Lewis had made himself one of the most famous men in America when he and his companion William Clark completed their mission to explore the newly acquired Louisiana Territory for President Thomas Jefferson. In reward the president made Lewis governor of much of the new region, a position Lewis only finally assumed in March 1808, making his headquarters at Saint Louis. Everything went wrong for him almost at once. Administration frustrated him, and his contentious fellow appointees made governing a nightmare. On top of that he invested heavily, and unwisely, in land speculations, plunging himself into debt, and then considerably exceeded his authority by spending thousands of dollars in government funds without authorization. Learning that his activities were under a cloud, he decided to go to Washington, D.C., to present his case in person. He sold everything he had to satisfy some of his debts, and on September 4 set off south by boat, intending to sail down the Mississippi to Fort Pickering, where Memphis would later stand. From there he would ride east until he struck the Trace, then take it on to Nashville.

Along the route it became increasingly evident to those he met that Lewis's difficulties were weighing terribly on his mind, threatening to engulf him. He stopped a few days at New Madrid, apparently in ill health, but seemed recovered on September 25, when he continued his journey. When he reached Fort Pickering, however, the brave explorer appeared on the verge of insanity. Captain Gilbert Russell took Lewis into his quarters and cared for and watched over him, thinking him a danger to himself. The post doctor cared for him as he could, while Russell actively prevented Lewis from committing suicide. When Lewis seemed better after several days, Russell asked Major James Neely to accompany him on the road.

They left Fort Pickering September 29, accompanied by two servants, and rode into the Chickasaw country for two or three days. Once again Lewis showed signs of derangement, and they paused for two days while he rested. Finally they reached the Tennessee River on October 8, crossed, and proceeded on up the Trace. When two of their horses ran off, Lewis sent Neely after them while he and the servants proceeded on to Grinder's stand, arriving at sunset October 10. Robert Griner was away, but his wife and a slave girl named Malindy were there, and the sight of Lewis almost immediately frightened them. He asked her for food and whiskey but neither ate nor drank very much.

He asked her for some gunpowder and apparently got some, for Neelly seems to have kept it from him. Alarmed at Lewis's behavior, Mrs. Griner finally took Malindy and retired to the kitchen in a separate building, while the two servants went to sleep in the stable. Lewis was left entirely alone. As the dark hours passed slowly by, she heard him raising his voice and pacing as if talking to someone.

And then they all heard shots—some said two, others said three. Lewis's servant ran to the house and found him lying on the floor with two horrible wounds, one in the head, the other in his chest. "I have done the business my Good Servant," said Lewis. "Give me some water." The black gave him some, than ran away. Later Malindy heard Lewis stagger outside the house and the sound of a gourd scraping the dry water bucket as he cried for more water. Not until dawn on October 11 did the poor man finally expire.[58]

There was no question in the minds of Neelly or Mrs. Griner or any of Lewis's friends who met with him in his last days, that his death was a suicide. His two pistols lay beside him. He had repeatedly given signs of derangement. His personal and public world was collapsing around him, and at Fort Pickering he more than once actually seemed to Russell on the verge of taking his life. His closest friends, including Jefferson, never questioned that the wretched man met his end at his own hands. Yet, within a few years, as the Griners moved away and the principals disappeared or died off, rumors started that there was more to those shots than suicide. Some speculated that Robert Griner had come back and shot Lewis to rob him. Others said the servants had something to do with it. Men soon recalled knife wounds, and some even rumored that assassins had been sent by Lewis's political enemies. It was all nothing more than the natural romance and lurid imaginings that the Trace and the people of the Southwest seemed naturally to attract.[59]

No greater example of the twisting of fact into fancy when linked with the violent edge of the territory could be found than that surrounding the man once called the "Great Western Land Pirate," John Murrell. With his own hands he killed some four hundred men. More than a thousand robbers and villains followed his orders. He slit his victims' stomachs open, took out their entrails, then filled the cavity with stones to sink the bodies in swamps. He passed counterfeit scrip while dressed as a minister and commanded a widespread army of malefactors that he called the Mystic Clan of the Confederacy. Their plan was to incite a region-wide slave insurrection on Christmas Day 1835, and while the white community ran in panic or tried to deal with the revolt, Murrell and his clan would pillage town and country alike.[60]

It was all the stuff of nonsense. Murrell was born in Virginia in 1806, and by the age of sixteen was indicted for "riot" in Williamson County, Tennessee. The next year authorities charged him with horse theft. Though described as "quite a nice looking fellow," the tall, fair Murrell could not stay out of trouble, nor was he apparently smart enough to keep from getting caught. From 1823 to 1828 he was in and out of jail repeatedly, whipped once, and ordered branded another time. Locals thought of him only as a nuisance and petty thief, a braggart who rarely had two coins to rub together, and neither the brains nor the brass to organize anything more than a bungled attempt to steal a couple of slaves, which is what finally landed him in the state penitentiary in 1834. Ten years later he would be dead of tuberculosis.[61] But Virgil A. Stewart, apparently one of Murrell's few genuine friends and an accomplice on the bungled slave raid who testified against him at the trial, authored a small pamphlet in which he virtually invented an incredible life of crime and villainy. It sold widely and made Stewart something of a literary hero for a time. Indeed, the entire Murrell legend derives from nothing but Stewart, whom John F. H. Claiborne by 1860 pronounced an imposter, and his whole body of Murrell lore "one of the most extraordinary and lamentable hallucinations of our times."[62]

It was somehow fitting for the era and the place. The Natchez Trace, which brought so many of them there, and which bore so much of the responsibility for the early settlement of the Southwest, naturally attracted dark stories. Myth hung about its reaches like the moss dangling from the oaks along its path. The villains, real and imaginary, who plied its byways and spread their mayhem and their legend throughout the Old Southwest were after all just another brand of opportunists, like everyone else who came seeking fortune. Even Stewart, who more than anyone else invented the saga that would subsequently mark the Trace as one of the most evil-ridden places in America, was only doing what all the others had done: They took what they found and tried to make of it something for themselves.

❧ 14 ❧

The Road to the Indian Nations

The growing white communities and civilization at the northern and southern ends of the Trace sat like bookends on either side of the greatest part of the Old Southwest, the Indian lands. Ironically, for all the dark tales told of shadowy doings in the territory, most somehow involved those great and largely unknown lands of the Choctaw, Chickasaw, and Creek. Yet in the main these were the safest grounds for a white to tread, especially in Mississippi. The Indians made war on each other, but with the exception of the Creek they remained at peace with the whites, remarkably patient in the face of repeated provocation. Indeed, when whites committed depredations against flatboatmen or overland travelers and tried to take refuge in the Choctaw lands, the Indians helped to hunt them down and turn them over to civil authorities.[1]

Going as far back as the whites could remember, the Choctaw showed only the open hand of peace. In 1777 the explorer William Bartram left Mobile on a trip through the interior, filled with trepidation that he might encounter "cruel captivity, and perhaps being murdered by the Choctaws." But from the time his guides set up their first war whoop on approaching the outskirts of "the Nation," Bartram found the Choctaw nothing but friendly—in the Indian way. All along his trail up the Alabama he passed one Indian town after another, and while he was often fearful, he yet found that the worst his Indian hosts would do was try to steal some of his trade goods when he turned his back. "Being everywhere treated by the inhabitants with marks of friendship," he felt almost as if he were one of them. It was the same when he passed into the Creek nation, and at their great village Attassee he was even privileged to attend a council of their chiefs, including an evening of drinking and smoking and some ancient ritual that involved a strong black tea, all performed in a conical council house with even the rushes and canes on the earth laid out in a ceremonial pattern.

"The assembly being now seated in order, and the house illuminated," said Bartram, "two middle aged men, who perform the office of slaves or servants, pro tempore, come in together at the door, each having very large conch shells full of *black drink*, and advance with slow, uniform and steady steps, their eyes or countenances lifted up, singing very low but sweetly." The slaves sang their song as the king and the others present drank. Then the king offered tobacco, himself lighting the first pipe, blowing a puff of smoke heavenward, one to each of the cardinal points of the compass, then one toward his white guests. Bartram marveled at the organization of the Indians he met, their sense of nationhood and kingship, their provision for ambassadors and guests, their communications. He was not the first, nor would he be the last, to see striking parallels between their political and social organization and that of his own people.[2]

Just a few years later, in 1792, Stephen Minor left Natchez on a journey into the Choctaw country to negotiate land titles with two chiefs named Sulushmastabe and Iaghanahuma, both of whom he found to be men of sense and judgment, and both of whom treated him with unfeigned civility. They in turn led him to the great mingo, or chief, Franchimastabe, who assembled all of his chiefs and warriors, and who proved to be an intelligent and thoughtful negotiator. Most of all, Franchimastabe showed a keen sense of fairness, to white and Indian alike, and in his dealings with Minor refused to grant any concessions to the Spaniards that might endanger the welfare of other non-Spanish settlers who had married into his nation or who were operating as traders. So long as such people lived in his lands, said the mingo, they should have his protection. Minor even found portraits of George Washington, William Penn, and other prominent Americans in some of the chiefs' houses, signifying the regard they felt for their new United States neighbors.

Franchimastabe also proved to be an eloquent statesman, for when he spoke to the assembly of chiefs, he showed a considerable command of oratory. He was also no fool. When Minor made his requests, accompanied by white beads as a sign of peace and promises of friendship from his Spanish overlords, the mingo replied that "having been deceived many times by other Governors I do not know whom to believe." When Minor offered more promises, Franchimastabe responded that time, not promises, would only prove if the Spanish assurances were good. Moreover, to Minor's argument that Spain held hegemony over all these lands, including those of the Choctaw, because the British had ceded them all in the peace following the recent war, Franchimastabe reminded him that the land had never been Britain's to give. "I have always loved the Whites and wished to be in good standing with them," he said, yet when Minor pressed for the sale of certain of their lands, he declined. The Choctaw had sold land before, he said, and all the whites offered them were beads, shiny medals, and pieces of paper. He gave ground that was eternal, and they gave only useless ornaments. Minor tried hard to counter him, reminding the mingo that the Spanish traders in Natchez brought weapons, powder, shot, blankets, and more to the Choctaw. "Why then do the red men have to love a piece of land which is of no value to them?" he argued.

Franchimastabe and his chiefs prolonged the debate for hours, not out of perverseness but from the Choctaw's insistence that everyone be heard, that every opinion be aired. In the end Minor tried rather clumsily to bribe him with gifts, and the chief replied, "I always thought that in the end you would find the sure road to my heart," but he may have been speaking sarcastically, for all that he actually asked of the lieutenant was a saddle, some whiskey, and a pair of tweezers, hardly a rich haul. More likely, when Franchimastabe finally gave in and allowed the Spaniards to have the land they sought, he did so at the instance of his subchiefs and suiting his own inclination, his resistance until then largely being based on rumors of assassination by his young warriors, who resented any cession to the whites. Then Minor tried to press his advantage by asking if the new Americans to the north had been in contact with the Choctaw. Indeed they had, said the mingo, whereupon Minor warned him to beware the Yankees. They would ask only a little land, but then would want more and more, and eventually try to push the Indians entirely away from their ancestral grounds. The irony of his saying that about the Americans even while trying to do it himself seems to have eluded Minor.[3]

It was only a few years later that Francis Baily had his own encounter with the Choctaw. Like everyone else, he found them friendly toward whites. His first meeting seemed frightening enough, hearing them come whooping along the Trace, their hands displaying fresh scalps taken in battle against some Indian enemies west of the Mississippi, but then they immediately invited Baily to come into their camp and share their meal, shook his hands, and offered him their peace pipe. Indeed, at every encounter with the Choctaw, and later with the Chickasaw, Baily met nothing but courtesy and friendliness, even if occasionally he did have to watch his packs and his hat.[4]

In fact men throughout the Southwest spoke of the friendliness of the "Chatahs," the Choctaw, and it was well that they could, for the tribe occupied much of the ground between the Mississippi and Tombigbee, and as far north as the Chickasaw line. They had some fifty substantial villages and a number of smaller ones, and at their height perhaps numbered twenty-five thousand. Yet they were not warlike, at least not where the whites were concerned. Indeed, their name meant something like "charming voice," testimony to their love of singing. They could be terrible in battle against their ancestral enemies, but where their white neighbors were concerned, they mostly preferred to fight alongside rather than against them. When the war with Britain came in 1812, their great chief Pushmataha actually enlisted a regiment of his braves and led them as lieutenant colonel in Andrew Jackson's subsequent campaigns.[5]

The white settlers in the territory knew the Choctaw mostly by their chiefs, and generally knew them better than they did their more distant neighbors the Chickasaw. Pushmataha earned widespread respect from most of the newcomers, but another chief, Musculature, seems to have commanded their greatest regard. The Choctaw divided themselves into three "districts," and Musculature succeeded his father as mingo of the northeastern section in 1809. He had been a war chief in some of the raids across the river against the Osage, perhaps leading the party that Baily encountered in 1798 on the Trace returning from a raid. He made his home in what would later be called Mashulaville, in Noxubee County, on the border with Alabama, northeast of Jackson. When his father, Homastubbee, died in 1809 and Mushulatubbee succeeded him, he immediately befriended the whites, joining them in their war against the Creek in 1813–14. Even when friction with whites tried his patience, the chief continued to think the best of them. Any man was welcome at his door, and to take a spoon and eat from the cooking pot with himself and his wives and children.

One evening in 1825 three Alabamians rode into the Choctaw nation to buy some animals and called at the chief's house to ask if they could stay the night. Mushulatubbee invited them in, but only two accepted, ate a meal at his table, and slept in his beds. The other slept outdoors and the next morning the chief found him making his own corn mush. "You hog!" the mingo yelled. "You no gentleman! Saunders and Lacey, they *gentlemen!!* They eat at my table and sleep in my bed. You hog. You eat corn and sleep under tree." The man had offended him by refusing his celebrated hospitality to whites.

Mushulatubbee had another side, however, and as with so many of his fellow Indians, it involved drink. No one then understood that these aboriginal peoples lacked certain enzymes to allow their systems to handle alcohol even in moderate quantities. Rather, whites simply assumed all Indians to be drunkards, and this mingo was no exception. He was often seen in white communities, where his name and his portly frame led to his nickname "Tubbee." "He invariably got drunk when he came to town," recalled one witness. Often his friend Gideon Lincecum took him in tow and gave him one of his own concoctions of brandy and red pepper that he thought would cure the Indian of drink, but Mushulatubbee merely sat in the market house sipping the fiery "Number 6," as Lincecum called it, apparently with no effect. That done, he asked for more whiskey.[6]

He kept a portrait of Andrew Jackson on his wall and always wore his blue War of 1812 uniform when he went out, proud of his association with the Americans. By 1819, anxious to emulate his white friends, he moved from his prairie village and engaged a carpenter to build him a new four-room, two-story house. Thereafter he feuded with his friend the builder and refused to pay him, but as a mark of the amity that the old chief engendered in others, when he went to town and got drunk, the builder took him home to care for, and in the process they settled their differences.[7]

Several others among the Choctaw attracted the respect and regard of the whites. Apushimataha especially became endeared to Lincecum, who entertained him often at his home. He also made quite a hit with the ladies. At a dance at Lincecum's house, Apushimataha asked for an interpreter, and through him spoke of having heard of the Bible, and of angels that looked just like men and women. Pointing to some young women present whom he had been watching, he said, "I have been observing these six bright and most elegantly beautiful beings all night, and I have come to the conclusion that if there are any such beings as angels, a thing I never before credited, these must be some of them." He asked if he could touch them to make sure they were human, and the giggling girls agreed. "It's folks, for I can feel it very distinctly," he said afterward, a wry smile on his face.

Unfortunately, he, too, could not handle drink, but knew it. He refused ever to take a sip when business was at hand. But when time lay on his hands and whiskey was nearby, he would not leave it alone. "He was an inveterate drunkard," lamented his friend Lincecum. Moreover, Apushimataha loved to gamble, and would bet all he owned on a game of ball or a horse race. Still, to the end of his days the dissipated chief would say that "neither I nor my father nor any of my ancestors ever drew bow in anger against the people of the United States. We have been true in our friendship; we have held your hand so long that our fingers, like the claw of an eagle, will not let go."[8]

When a Choctaw did harm a white, the remorse and shame could be terrible. A drunken man named Louie handed an Indian called Atoba his pistol to examine, and when it accidentally fired, Louie fell dead. The next day Atoba asked for the pistol that he might use it to kill himself in his humiliation. Lincecum happened to be involved, and asked why Atoba would kill himself when it had clearly been an accident. "Life for life is the law," Atoba replied. When word of his intent got around, other Indians from some distance came to witness the event. Finally, to avoid its turning into a carnival, Atoba changed the place of his end, and only Lincecum was invited to watch. "I am a man and a warrior," said the poor Choctaw, but still Lincecum persuaded him to wait until he could be brought to a trial, assuming that his innocence would be established and that Atoba's own sense of guilt might be satisfied. Lincecum reckoned without the Choctaw sense of honor.

Atoba came to trial, accompanied by three hundred of his fellow braves and some chiefs. At first the sight of them panicked the people of Gainesville, but at once the Choctaw hitched their horses, leaned their rifles against trees, and walked among the gathered crowd, shaking hands and exchanging greetings in their accustomed manner. Then came the taking of testimony, and all of it clearly indicated Atoba's innocence. Unfortunately Louie had been a Kaintuck, and a number of his drunken friends were here anxious to see Atoba die. When it became evident that a verdict would probably acquit him, they began to talk loudly of mobbing the Indians assembled there. Apushimataha was present and heard this, and arose before the court to warn that someone must stop the talk or there would be bloodshed. "Their aim is to break up the peace and friendly intercourse that has always obtained between the Chahtas and the American white people," he said. "It must be prevented." When a judge warned him that his own talk might lead to bloodshed, the chief replied: "Speak not to me of blood. I was raised in blood." The jury acquitted Atoba in the end, which satisfied Lincecum and the Choctaw. But it did not satisfy Atoba or the boatmen. Within a month he was found drowned in the river, either a suicide or a homicide.[9]

It took the actions of another Choctaw to put an end to the "life for life" ethic of their people, for it claimed far too many lives in return for accidents like Atoba's or Jack Pitchlyn's. Greenwood Le Flore, son of the stand keeper Louis Le Fleur, was born in 1800, and came young to chieftainship in 1822, when his northwestern Choctaw elected him their mingo. Thomas Jefferson sent him a sword and a medal inscribed "Peace and Prosperity" by way of congratulation, and Le Flore ever after said with pride that he and his people had never raised their weapons against the Americans. Instead he fought the selling of whiskey to his people, even punishing his own brother for engaging in the traffic, strove for their education, and instituted trials to establish the difference between intent and accident in cases of personal injury. When a man on horseback found his animal suddenly turn ungovernable and it raced through a crowd, killing an Indian man, Le Flore prevented the rest from taking the hapless rider's life in return. "If you kill him, you kill me first," he shouted. That stopped them, and it stopped their age-old policy of vengeance.[10]

Relations with the Chickasaw proved more tangled for the whites, thanks to the sometime hostility between the former and the Choctaw, and the frequent warfare of all of them with the Creek to the east. The Chickasaw, too, followed a mingo and his council, though their king led not by unquestioned right but rather by his eloquence and inspiration. "The people of this nation are tall straight in their limbs, & large in size, more so than any of the southern tribes," Dr. Rush Nutt noted after a visit in 1805. "No people exercise more hospitality than the Indians, or with a better will, & live as if all things were in common." They shared the Choctaw law of reprisal, even for accidents, and had but one established crime, murder, and only one penalty. "They are a proud, haughty, jealous people," thought the doctor, "not most friendly to the whites." They were largely under the sway of the half-breed George Colbert, who seems to have manipulated their impressions of Americans largely for his own ends, especially to prevent them opening their land to more stands than his own and his family's.[11]

By contrast the Creek occupying the northeastern part of the territory, and on into southern Tennessee, took a much different attitude toward the whites—toward everyone, for that matter. Warfare was more a way of life for them. They warred with the Chickasaw and other neighboring tribes, and when the whites came, they showed a far less pacific disposition than others. As early as 1796 Indian agent Benjamin Hawkins noted of them that they "always have been funny and are in the habit of destroying hogs or cattle whenever they trespass on the fields under cultivation." When finally they allowed a trader to establish in their midst, it was only with continued grumbling, even against their mingo who made the agreement. In 1796 whites made a treaty with them that seemed to satisfy the Creek for a time, but when Hawkins asked himself "what would most likely the soonest disturb this friendly disposition of the Indians," he already knew the answer, and whites were already doing it. Being so close to the spreading Georgia and Tennessee settlements on the north and east, the Creek found a constant encroachment on their lands by squatters, and a steady stream of horse and livestock theft. Since they had the misfortune to live in closer and earlier proximity to Yankee ambitions, they naturally developed a much different attitude than the Choctaw and Chickasaw, who for so long were insulated by distance and rather benevolent British and Spanish colonial management.[12]

In fact the Creek had attacked frontier settlements in Tennessee as early as 1780, though probably in alliance with the British during the Revolution. Chickasaw arose in retaliation, and the warfare between the two tribes flared along the upper Trace for a time.[13] Yet even the Creek could be made into passive neighbors—at times—with careful diplomacy and equitable treatment. Hawkins bore more responsibility than any other for making them as friendly as they were to Americans. Starting from his first visit in 1796, he would spend the next two decades living among them and trying to turn them to white men's ways. Few of them farmed, and he brought to them knowledge of agriculture in the hope that if they became dependent on the land and crops, the men would not rove widely in hunting parties that inevitably clashed with whites. Moreover, if tied to land under cultivation, the Creek might also be more willing to cede large tracts of now unneeded hunting land to the United States. He also saw that, unlike the Choctaw and Chickasaw, the Creek had no very well developed tribal government. Their only rule derived from an annual festival during which elder men spoke of suggestions, and the rest could take or leave them as they pleased. Using his own influence as a dispenser of trade goods, Hawkins attempted to make some mingoes more powerful as a source of law, and then advised them on how to govern.

Hawkins's experiments worked to a considerable degree, with the notable exception of 1813–14, when the Creek joined with their old friends the British in making war on the United States. Despite the agent's best efforts, they had seen continual erosion of their lands by squatters, cheating by unscrupulous traders despite Hawkins's attempts to ensure that only honest men obtained trading licenses, and repeated raids on their horses and cattle. Even then, when the war came, those Creek living in most frequent contact with Hawkins did not go to war. He had shown the good sense to try to remake the tribe by using its own institutions. He did not impose a European style of government on them; he simply took the loose system they already had and maneuvered it into greater strength. When it came to farming, he recognized that it was the women who did what little was done at the outset, and so he educated them, gaining their confidence thanks to his being the only man ever to pay much attention to them. Then he left it to them to convince their husbands, as eventually they did.[14]

After Hawkins's death in 1816, the government trading house or "factory" moved to the Chattahoochee River, actually in Alabama for the first time. Once there it continued the factory policy, dating back to 1795, and the creation of the Indian trading houses to provide the Creek with goods at low prices that only covered their cost, with no profit, in order to "manifest the liberality and friendship of the U. S. and thus between ties of interest and gratitude to secure their attachment and lay the foundation of lasting peace." Factors could raise or lower some prices on certain items in order to better satisfy Indian demands, but once they set prices they pretty much stuck to them. "The Indians will then know what to depend on, and not have their jealousy excited by the apprehension of unfair dealings which a fluctuation of prices would be apt to beget." Moreover, factors were to be on their guard against unscrupulous independent traders who would charge higher prices, or extend credit to the Indians and then coerce them for repayment at exorbitant interest. "It would have been extremely desirable to carry on this trade without the use of rum," said the original instructions, "but from an apprehension that the habits of the Indians in this respect could not be controlled, that article may be provided."

The factor sold blankets, fabric, thread, handkerchiefs, scissors and knives, mirrors, locks, rifle parts, cutlery, needles, saddles, and more—some goods reflecting the actual needs of the people, and others showing the direction in which the whites hoped to turn them. As a part of their agreements in land cessions and for the establishment of such trading houses, the government also agreed to provide the Creek and other tribes with an annual gift. In the case of the Creek it was twenty-five thousand dollars outright and three thousand per year along with blacksmiths' tools, though in bad economic years the Indian payments usually fell to the bottom of the budget.[15]

Similar agencies went up among the Chickasaw and Choctaw, and for the former the agency became virtually the capital of their nation, as all gravitated to it for trade and information. The government located it almost at the very midpoint of the Trace between Natchez and Nashville, near the site of future Pontotoc, and it rapidly grew in the number of its buildings and activities. It soon became an extremely popular overnight stop on the road, so much so that Indians complained that the factor spent so much time tending to travelers that he ignored his principal charge to supply the needs of the Chickasaw. Samuel Mitchell was the first agent appointed by Washington, and he located the place and started the work of erecting its buildings, including an imposing brick main house. The government wanted to have representatives among the Indians, and the nine men who successively operated the Chickasaw Agency generally served that need well. Besides overseeing the factory, each had to make certain that treaties were obeyed by both sides, report infractions, administer some local justice, and oversee some education, especially in agriculture, spinning, and weaving. He taught them to plant and harvest cotton, work gins, operate smithies, and more, though in 1818 Congress passed the Indian Civilization Act, which transferred funds and responsibility for such endeavors to those missionaries who would soon be going into the Indian nations.[16]

The Choctaw trading house opened in 1803, after the factor Joseph Chambers arrived in Natchez with his shipment of trade goods, and then moved them down the Mississippi and over to Mobile, then upriver to Fort Saint Stephens on the Tombigbee, where he began building his store and warehouse that spring. He took over an abandoned Spanish church and a derelict blockhouse for his first store, and thus was able to get into operation with relative dispatch, installing his thirteen thousand dollars' worth of goods in May and opening his doors. Thereafter some twenty thousand dollars in merchandise a year passed through Chambers's hands. He enjoyed excellent relations with Governor Claiborne and seems to have won the amity of the Choctaw rather quickly as well. Indeed, business proceeded such that within a year he asked George Gaines to come work with him, and a few years later Gaines succeeded him as factor. He it was who for years would sell scarlet and blue cloth, cashmere, "Elastic Cloth," linsey-woolsey, calico, and London jeans, thread, buttons, Bibles, fishhooks and line, shoemaking tools, knives and saws and hammers, buckles and harness for men and beasts, carpenter's tools, guns, shoes, axes, shovels and hoes, whips, decorative plumes, beads and brooches, and more. In spite of having to pay heavy duties to the Spaniards in Mobile, through whose port the goods had to come to reach him, still the factor did a good business and kept his prices down. In fact, when he found a piece of damaged or inferior goods, he pointed out the defect to the purchaser and lowered the cost accordingly. Even Creek sometimes made the long trek to Fort Saint Stephens to trade with Gaines. As in virtually all the Old Southwest factories, Gaines did his business in barter. Four deerskins bought one and one-half pounds of gunpowder and eight musket flints; fifty-four assorted deer, coon, and fox pelts bought muslin, lead, handkerchiefs, knives, blankets, flints, and pigments. In a whole winter of hunting a Choctaw might take more than two hundred deerskins and receive just over one hundred dollars' worth of trade goods for them. In return the Choctaw never wavered in their loyalty to the United States. It was to Fort Saint Stephens and to factor Gaines that Pushmataha came to volunteer himself and his braves to fight with General Jackson.[17]

All the dealings with the Indians of the Southwest carried with them a measure of fear and suspicion. Some settlers tried to reassure their friends and family in the East. "Lately I put a line on its passage, which, I hope, relieved you from anxiety about my scalp," Moses Fisk wrote in 1812 from Tennessee. "There is no danger here, nor prospect of danger, though I have no desire to have you imagine, that I consider danger as very terrible."[18] Even some of the Choctaw and Chickasaw occasionally turned rogue, usually under the poison of whiskey or else to avenge a wrong done by a white, and the Creek could turn deadly at any time. Back in 1789 they had raided as far west as the Mississippi, burning and killing as they went.[19] The next year even some Choctaw rose up and tried to force the Coles Creek settlement to abandon its homes.[20]

With their attempts at bringing such people away from violence and down to the soil, the Anglos did not rely just on gifts and retraining. They brought to bear another weapon that some thought might be the most powerful of all—religion. During the years of British dominion in the Southwest, the Episcopal church made little or no effort to establish missions among the natives. As early as 1769 James Adair lamented this oversight and urged authorities to let him go to "our old friendly Chickosahs" as a missionary. He deplored that the only men then bringing the gospel to the heathen were amateurs, unschooled, and unofficial, for whose presence the only defense offered was that it was "better to have the ground plowed by asses, than to leave it a wa[s]te full of thistles."

Some years later in 1787 came the Society for Propagating the Gospel among the Heathen and Others in North America, and other missionary societies followed in an outburst of evangelistic fervor around the turn of the century. In 1798 the New York Missionary Society sent the Reverend John Bullen to the Chickasaw, and after his extensive tour through their country, and meeting with all of the principal headmen in the several villages and towns, he believed that there was good ground there for spreading the word and saving souls. Few could read or write, and most still looked to old witch doctors and shamans rather than more modern medicine for their cures. When he delivered his report to his sponsoring society, Bullen found them sympathetic to his desire to return and open a formal and permanent mission among the Chickasaw. He came back with a blacksmith and a mechanic, and soon started to build a school, a church, and some workshops, but then the Chickasaw fell out with one of his assistants, and Bullen dejectedly gave up. Behind him he left a barrel of Bibles and Testaments awaiting him in a Fort Pickering warehouse, uncollected. They would sit there, their shipping instructions, "to the Chickasaw Nation," clearly visible on the hogshead, for another twenty years before they were opened, to be found worm-eaten and ruined.[21]

In 1819 the Presbyterians took up the torch once more, appointing the Reverends David Humphries and T. C. Stuart, who initially went to the Creek. The Indians at first welcomed their proposal to establish schools, but then revealed a paranoia born of long association with the white man by expressing "fears that there was something behind which they did not understand," saying "it might be to get a foot-hold among them, and then make efforts to get their lands," Humphries reported. The Creek finally rejected the missionaries' offer, and so "we therefore, set our faces for the distant West." In July 1820 they reached Levi Colbert's and learned fortuitously that a few days hence there would be a great Indian ball game some miles distant, and all the major chiefs would be there. The missionaries attended, addressed the assembled mingoes, and secured their permission to establish schools. Along the way, however, Humphries had a crisis of faith and determined that he did not feel the call to minister to the Chickasaw. Stuart agreed to take the mission on his own.[22]

Stuart established his Chickasaw mission on the old Trace a few miles from the Chickasaw Agency. For two years he and his associates worked at building their church, school, and farm buildings, calling the place Monroe Station after the incumbent president, James Monroe. There in his small sixteen-by-sixteen-foot log church, Stuart preached through an interpreter to his Indian congregation. In the dim light of a single window, and through the murky atmosphere (thanks to the smoky fireplace), he tried to win souls. He opened his school for children in 1822, and the next year commenced a boarding school for youths who lived too far away to walk daily to and from home. More than fifty enrolled, many of them half-breeds, though the proportion of full-blooded Chickasaw gradually increased. Stuart ran his school like many of the "Lancastrian" academies in Natchez, the older pupils being required to help instruct their juniors.

After a time many more students sought admission than Stuart could handle, and eventually the popularity of education took hold sufficiently that the Chickasaw themselves met in 1824 to raise funds for constructing more schools within their lands. They erected one at Tockshish that same year, and soon engaged a Presbyterian preacher to come and take charge. The Indians placed another school at Pigeon Roost, and a fourth in the northwest corner of Alabama. All the schools and missions grew up along the old Trace, and while they operated there were virtually no vacancies, so great was the demand for education. The missionaries quickly learned that the boarding concept worked the best, for it kept children away from home and the sometimes unencouraging ways of parents now too old to see the benefit of learning, or to encourage it.[23]

The Chickasaw missions always suffered from inadequate funding, even when the Indians themselves voted an appropriation of twenty-five-hundred dollars a year from tribal funds. Yet they were a necessary adjunct to the business of winning souls. Moral and religious instruction went to the pupils along with practical and elementary learning, though Stuart deplored that he made very few conversions. His first was a black woman, and thereafter he used her as interpreter for his preaching. In December 1824 he baptized his first Chickasaw, and thereafter more came into the fold. Still he reported that "comparatively few" of his pupils ever took his faith, though years later many of them became Methodists. Perhaps that is what led him to complain that the Chickasaw were "with few exceptions, universally an ungrateful people." Revealing as much as anything his own entrenched prejudices as a white, he concluded that they could not be broken from the vice of drinking, and lamented that in his seventeen years among the Chickasaw, he only knew one man who would neither drink nor smoke. No wonder he confessed that he felt "ashamed and deeply humbled that so little was accomplished."[24] By 1827 he was concluding negotiations with the American Board of Commissioners for Foreign Missions to take over running the Chickasaw operation. Over an eight-year period he had baptized only 151, and inducted even fewer as members of the church.

Still, Stuart and his fellows brought some enlightenment to their flocks. In time they engaged ministers who preached in the native tongue. He formed a Bible society, and got two temperance groups in operation, but it was always an uphill struggle. Then came 1830 and political events that affected all the Indians of the Southwest dramatically. In the face of what was to happen, the Chickasaw lost almost all interest in religion or education alike. Yet in later decades they would turn overwhelmingly to Christianity and the ways that met the white man's definition of civilization, thanks in no small part to the foundation laid at the little log stations along the Trace by Stuart and his companions. The men who would lead the nation in the decades after 1830 almost all received their education from the mission, and for that, at least, Stuart could have felt some pride had he but allowed himself.[25]

The Cumberland Presbyterians, not to be outdone by those from South Carolina and Georgia who sent Stuart, also dispatched missionaries, led by the Reverend Robert Bell, who established his mission at Cotton Gin Port. By 1825 there would be more than forty mission schools in the Southwest as a whole, involving the Presbyterians, with their mission settlements; the Baptists, concentrating on higher education; and the Methodists, who limited their efforts to conversions, claiming to have baptized more than a thousand.[26]

Conversions seemed much easier to glean among the Choctaw, perhaps because of their location and more lengthy and frequent contacts with whites going back to the early French explorers. The idea of establishing a formal mission among them by Americans seems to date from 1806, when students in New England conceived the notion, but it was not until 1810 that the American Board of Commissioners for Foreign Missions took shape and began the halting process. Congress gave some aid when it appropriated money for educating the Indians, and then in 1817 the board sent examiners through the territory to sound the interest of the natives themselves. As happened with Stuart and Humphries, their agent found the Creek less than enthusiastic, "but the Chickasaws and Choctaws showed not only a readiness, but an ardent desire to have establishments," reported the Reverend Elias Cornelius. Consequently the board sent Cyrus Kingsbury the following year to open a Choctaw mission. Within two years he could look out over eight log cabins, a dining hall and kitchen, a school, a mill, a smithy and shop, barns, granaries, and more, all along the Yalobusha River at what he called the Elliott Mission. Around the station he cleared about sixty acres of land and had more than two hundred head of cattle and other livestock grazing. Of his human flock he had more than seventy Choctaw boys and girls studying in the accepted Lancastrian method. It was an excellent start. The school even had a library worth four hundred dollars.

Instruction began in April 1819, and when the students were not in the classroom, they worked out in the fields or studied blacksmithing. Mushulatubbee came to see progress in 1820 and expressed himself as delighted. "Our hearts are glad to see our children improving so fast," he said through an interpreter. Already the Choctaw showed their support with a donation of seven hundred dollars and several score cattle. Once they saw the progress of the mission, they went even farther, agreeing to take six thousand dollars of their annual funds and donate them to the support and spread of the mission schools.[27]

Buoyed by this success the board authorized another mission, and Kingsbury set out to locate it, finding the ideal spot not far from the Choctaw border with the Chickasaw, near Pigeon Roost stand on the Trace. He called it Mayhew Mission, in honor of Thomas Mayhew, a missionary of earlier days to the Indians of Massachusetts. In a short time they erected almost the mirror of the earlier mission, and soon were joined by other missionaries arrived from the East. They opened their school with twelve pupils, but the number grew steadily, and soon satellite schools opened elsewhere in the nation, including one in the home of Mushulatubbee. A church for Mayhew had to wait until 1821, when the Church of Christ opened its doors under generally Congregationalist principles, but with Presbyterian organization. The ministers, including Kingsbury, occupied themselves with nettlesome questions like the advisability of learning the native languages, or what they could do to elevate "the real Indian" as opposed to the half-breed and white inhabitants of their region.

Kingsbury opened more churches in ensuing years, as the Choctaw openly embraced the white man's religion. In 1830 alone he received 155 converts into the church. A visitor to Mayhew found the missionaries kind and humble, disinclined to complain of the discomforts they suffered in the wilderness. They kept their mission beautifully clean, inspiring the impression "of primitive Christianity" in the way they shared all things alike. Several families lived there, each in its own cabin, while a doctor, teacher, farmer, and mechanic labored in his respective vineyard. They sat in rude furniture, dined on simple pewter, and ate almost exclusively what they could raise or what the Choctaw brought them. The girl students sat learning their needlework, spinning, knitting, and cookery, while the boys practiced their carpentry, chair making, smithing, hunting, bookkeeping, elementary law, and the like. It was universally acknowledged that they need not bother with the classics, mathematics, or languages other than simple sums and English.[28] "Industry and economy are strikingly seen throughout the whole establishment and cannot fail to be incorporated with the habits of youth," said the visitor. As for the Sabbath, the children spent their day learning Scripture from memory or else in services. Unfortunately, much of the doctrine and reason for the Scripture seemed to evade them, as missionaries confused rote learning with understanding. The latter, too, would come in time.[29]

Of course it was a terribly condescending and paternalistic

approach, ably put into words by Secretary of War John C. Calhoun in 1820 when he said that the Indians "should be taken under our guardianship; and our opinion and not theirs should prevail, in measures intended for their civilization and happiness."[30] They were seeking to educate and Christianize the Indians not so much for their own intrinsic betterment, but in order to make them less troublesome for Washington to deal with, and less of a presumed burden on the state. Backed by this attitude, Kingsbury went on to establish several more missions in the 1820s. By 1830 he had thirteen of them in operation, but then, as with the Chickasaw, the events of that year suddenly brought a change in Choctaw attitudes that signaled the end of the mission system. Two years later the Choctaw mission closed and all its personnel left for other fields, with nothing to take with them but some furniture and livestock. Some sixty-six men and women labored in the several stations during the fourteen years of the mission's operation. Five were preachers, twelve teachers, eight farmers, seven mechanics, and one a doctor. They spent an average of ten thousand dollars a year on their enterprise, almost half of it supported by the Choctaw themselves, and some of the rest by congressional appropriation. They gave some education to more than fifteen hundred boarding students and another thousand who walked to school from their homes. It was a record to which the board looked with pride, and which the government took to be proof that, as Calhoun said, "they certainly demonstrate that no insuperable difficulty is in the way of a complete reformation of the principles and pursuits of the American Indian."[31]

Only by unmaking and then "reforming" Indian society and culture could the United States imagine a peaceful accommodation with the natives, it seemed. In short, whites must remold the Choctaw, Chickasaw, and Creek into their own image. The effort in the Southwest was more successful than anywhere else in the young nation, and especially among the Choctaw, but chiefly because of their long association with whites, and their essentially non-nomadic style of life. It was an easier adjustment from hunting to planting for them than for other tribes, and so with the conversion to the white God. Both transitions enjoyed considerable facilitation from the fact that so many of the mingoes were half-breeds, men with a foot in each camp already. When men like Fulsom and Colbert and Le Fleur and others adopted the white man's ways, they provided an easy example for their Indian people to follow. Moreover, all of these Indians had seen the French and the British and the Spanish come and go. They knew how rapacious these whites could be when it came to land. Yet by being accommodat-

ing and nonthreatening, they managed for several generations to fore-
stall major encroachments on their tribal territory, and perhaps hoped
thereby to continue to keep the white expansion at bay.

If so, they were tragically mistaken. Back in 1796, standing on the
verge of the territory in Tennessee and looking southwestward, Moses
Fisk said with satisfaction that *"generally,* this country answers my
expectation. . . . The Indians have always been troublesome. Many settlers were driven back, and the rest have been obliged to live very
compactly. Peace now opens the way for their spreading. From this
tract to Florida, from Miss river to the Alleg. mountains, the land
belongs to the Indians: and they are very tenacious of it, and jealous of
encroachments."[32]

While both the Spaniards and the British negotiated some
marginal land cessions from the peoples of the Trace region, it awaited
the coming of the newly independent Americans before real pressure
to yield lands appeared. Tens of thousands of poor farmers looked
yearningly southwestward in the days immediately after the end of the
Revolution. What they saw were millions of acres of excellent land,
occupied by comparatively minuscule populations of chiefly woodland
peoples who barely used the soil at all. When they felt that land could
be—should be—theirs, and at little or no cost, concern for the original
dwellers that was never high, dwindled even more. The land should be
in the hands of people who knew how to exploit it, they felt. Meanwhile, in Congress and the cabinet other considerations of an international nature arose. With the acquisition of independence, and then the
organization of the Mississippi Territory, the new United States had
foreign neighbors on its southwestern borders, neighbors who once
owned that territory themselves and would undoubtedly like to have it
back. There was nothing very secure about American independence at
that moment. Any European power, seeing the weakness of the new
nation and coveting those rich western lands, could pose a new threat,
especially with the territory so sparsely settled and, therefore, unable
to defend itself, much less act as a buffer against any invasion of the
American heartland. Secretary of War Henry Dearborn agreed in 1803
with thousands of others that opening the Indian lands was the solution. "Plant on the Mississippi a population equal to its own defense,"
he said, and the United States would find thereby a safety valve for its
westward ambitions, its land-hungry young adventurers, and a defense
of the back door to America.[33]

Settlers did not wait for the government to say they might go.
From the very first, squatters moved in on the fringes of Choctaw,

Chickasaw, and Creek lands, as well as taking root on some of the federal land already ceded by the Indians but not yet put on the block for sale. Every effort to make them adhere to laws and established boundaries met ridicule. Worse, the men in the region themselves could see—or believed—that major portions of the ground legally available in the established counties would not suit the plow, while most of the Choctaw land especially looked fertile. In Adams County in 1806 a grand jury declared that 80 percent of county ground was inferior to what could be had in the Indian nations. They called on the government to nullify native claims to those lands.[34]

Only the Creek seem to have taken the measure of the whites from the outset. Their animosity toward Europeans went back centuries to the first explorers. Though subsequently they gave land to the British in return for rifles, and then took sides with Spain in its squabble with the English on the Alabama frontier, they never either understood or fully trusted their "allies." Following independence the United States tried to make friends of them with a 1790 treaty that offered fifteen hundred dollars a year in return for two thousand square miles of their land. Unfortunately, as in so many subsequent dealings, the money or goods in lieu of cash too often went to a few chiefs and some of their white or half-breed counselors, while the Creek peoples saw little or no benefit from the trade. The factories established by Hawkins and others eased relations somewhat, especially since these men dealt honestly with the Indians. This paved the path for more treaties in 1796 and 1802 that allowed construction of forts, and ceded large tracts around each post, plus another five thousand square miles. Often now an agreement provided a special annual sum personally for the chiefs—an undisguised bribe.[35]

For the next decade the Creek resisted further treaties or cessions, however. But then their unfortunate alliance with the British in the War of 1812, and their disastrous defeat at Horseshoe Bend, Alabama, in 1814, left them virtually at the mercy of the Americans. Even before the war concluded, General Andrew Jackson dictated to them a treaty on August 9, 1814, that forced them to relinquish tens of thousands of square miles comprising the entire central third of Alabama. Only in eastern Alabama did they retain a precarious hold on a homeland, and that eroded piece by piece in subsequent treaties. In 1818 they gave up one and one-half million acres in Georgia and Alabama for less than ten cents an acre. Then in 1825, while negotiating—essentially forcing—yet another agreement, Washington announced for the first time a new policy.

By now—as periodic outbreaks erupted, frontier families met

quick and violent ends, and incursions on their remaining lands continued in spite of treaties—it had become evident to the Americans that
these Creek would always be a danger in their midst, even to the last
warrior. Washington decided that the best way to deal with the problem was to remove it, literally. "The several Indian tribes within the limits of any of the states of the Union should remove to the territory to be
designated west of the Mississippi river," they said, "as well for the better protection and security of said tribes, and their improvement in civilization." Such a policy would open all Indian land east of the river to
settlement, putting the Creek in a region where there should be no further clash with expanding whites. Seemingly, Washington did not anticipate in 1825 that white settlement might just hop the river and
continue its forced march westward. Moreover, authorities were not
disposed to take into account the emotional toll of being separated forever from ancestral homelands, or the fact that even though it would
offer the Creek new land for old acre for acre, the ground west of the
Mississippi was vastly different in look, character, and fertility. On the
other hand, such a policy did address a hard reality. Whites wanted
Indian land and were going to go after it regardless of treaties and
laws. At least a policy of Indian removal would lessen or eradicate violent clashes and leave the Indians in some peace, if only for a generation, and on an arid, treeless landscape as foreign to them as the surface of the moon.[36]

The Creek agreed at first, having little choice, but within months
they realized that they had been duped by agents having no authority
to sign for them. They murdered the chief negotiator who represented
them, and a new treaty came about. It ceded less land for the moment,
but still provided that a delegation of chiefs would be taken west of the
great river to help choose where they should move, and included
the massive bribe of one hundred thousand dollars to the associates of
the murdered agent, who still had considerable influence with the
tribe. Moreover, the Creek were to receive nearly a quarter million dollars immediately and an annuity of twenty-two thousand for their support once they were moved. Another agreement in 1827 took care of
yielding what little remained of tribal land in Georgia, and the last ones
in 1832 turned over virtually all that was left in Alabama. The government promised to pay the expenses of their removal west, give each
family a rifle and accoutrements, a blanket, and even more payments to
the tribes and their chiefs. At the same time the treaties granted each
family a half section of their lands for a five-year period, that they might
sell it and keep the proceeds before moving. Unfortunately, after the
treaties thousands of settlers simply moved onto those lands despite

continued Indian ownership, daring Creek and Washington alike to remove them. Knowing full well that the Indians would all be gone within five years, settlers had little motivation to pay for what they could squat on, and so long as angry Creek did not kill them first, they knew that eventually the land would be theirs. Many did fall to Indian bullets and arrows, but always the military intervened on the side of the settlers. Finally, by 1837, all but a few made the trip west, and the next year there were no more Creek to be seen in the Southwest.[37]

If the story differed with the Choctaw and Chickasaw, it was only in terms of degree, and thanks to their peaceful nature, events exerted less of a sense of urgency on the whites. Indeed, the Choctaw did not find themselves asked to make their first formal land cession to the Americans until 1805 and the Treaty of Mount Dexter. Before then they only had to allow construction of the Trace mail road, and grant licenses to operate stands, most of them run by Choctaw or half-breeds anyhow. The Mount Dexter agreement, however, called for more than rights of way. This time the government asked for large chunks of land bordering the established counties of Mississippi and along the river north of Natchez. Silas Dinsmoor, as Choctaw agent, spent two hundred dollars on raisins, mace, cinnamon, nutmeg, pickles, "and other things in like proportion," to prepare for entertaining the negotiators, teasing one who remembered an unsuccessful earlier dinner by adding that "we shall have it in our power to wipe out the remembrance of the anchovies by the success of this treaty."[38]

In fact the Americans got less than they wanted. The Choctaw agreed only to land along the southern border with West Florida, and President Jefferson rejected the treaty. Three years later, however, he pulled it out in answer to a threat from Spain on that border, thus using an Indian agreement as a diplomatic tool for a change, instead of merely for land acquisition.[39] That kept Washington at bay—helped by war with Great Britain—until 1816, when the sudden rush of new immigrants to the region along the Trace placed renewed pressure on the Choctaw. At the same time the Choctaw resurrected a long-standing dispute over some Alabama lands claimed by the Creek, and when the latter ceded the ground to the United States in 1814, the Choctaw protested that it had not been theirs to give. The result was another Choctaw treaty in which, for ten thousand dollars in goods and the relocation of the Choctaw trading house to a more convenient site, the tribe relinquished its claims.[40]

Just a few years later, in 1820, Andrew Jackson met with the Choctaw chiefs at Doak's stand, with Dinsmoor and Wailes present to arrange the meeting. Mississippi was a state now, and it wanted more of the Choctaw domain. The chiefs, in essence, were given no choice but to hand over more than five million acres in return for land west of the Mississippi in the Arkansas Territory, where some Choctaw already lived. They resisted until Jackson threatened that he would ignore them and deal only with their brethren on the other side of the river, taking their agreement as binding on *all* Choctaw. The only alternative, said Jackson, was that with Mississippi now a state, the Choctaw would have to cease governing themselves and instead, like all other citizens, live under the jurisdiction of the state legislature. That of course could mean disaster, land seizure without even compensation. "When we had land to spare, we gave it, with very little talk," protested the chiefs.[41] Now they had no more they did not need. No one listened. Finally Jackson simply bullied them with threats of military invasion. Faced with this coercion, the leaders at Doak's stand found no alternative but to give in.[42]

Of course it was not enough. In fact, the Treaty of Doak's Stand became virtually the prototype for Indian removal treaties, even before Washington adopted removal as a policy and first applied it to the Creek. The Choctaw, however, never losing their faith in Washington, sent Pushmataha to the capital in 1824 to ask for concessions, but he died on the day before Christmas. In the end authorities did agree to exchange the Arkansas land—already heavily infiltrated by white squatters—for equivalent territory farther west in what would one day be Oklahoma. At least no one had gotten there ahead of the Indians. Moreover, with the policy of general removal being just announced, the Choctaw delegation succeeded for a time in having its implementation postponed, but inevitably it could only be temporary.[43]

For their neighbors to the north the Chickasaw the story could not but be the same. They, too, ceded ground in an 1805 treaty. Then in 1816 they gave up all of their land north of the Tennessee River.[44] Then came 1818 and a major treaty negotiated largely by George Colbert. Acting virtually as a prime minister to the main mingo, he took repeated payments from the government as part of the cessions he helped negotiate. In 1816 he got forty-five hundred dollars to share with his brother Levi, and a tract of Indian land north of the Tennessee that would be his own to sell for his own profit. Now two years later the Americans offered the same, and more.[45] He met with Jackson and others near his old stand that September, and during the ensuing days the whites presented a request for over five million acres of tribal land in Tennessee. Again they offered money or land across the Mississippi in exchange, and finished by saying with no effort at diplomacy that if the Chickasaw did not agree, settlers would move in anyhow. To Colbert they reiterated the promise that the ground called "Colbert's Reserve" should be his to sell despite any treaties. George and Levi wanted to do so right away, and lacking federal funds for the purchase, Jackson pledged his own, to be reimbursed later. Buying Colbert effectively secured the assent of the tribal chiefs.[46]

Then came Jackson's election to the presidency in 1828. In a few months he made his policy plain, and it was the same that he had stated in the past as a negotiator: The Indians of the Southwest must remove west of the Mississippi, or else become subject to state law like any other citizen. In 1830 Congress passed a removal act in response to Jackson's request, while Indian cooperation seemed guaranteed by the continuing self-serving nature of some of their chiefs, especially Greenwood Le Flore, who now became chief of all the Choctaw and offered to accept removal in return for a guarantee that he could remain on his own land. At the same time Mississippi's legislature passed a law extending its jurisdiction over all natives within its boundaries. In effect, the cultural and territorial integrity of the Choctaw and Chickasaw ceased to be recognized.[47]

After consultation with all of his mingoes—and with his own interests—Le Flore and others agreed to meet with white negotiators at Dancing Rabbit Creek in Noxubee County, near the Alabama border. A host attended, from Gaines the factor to Le Flore and most of his chiefs and hundreds of warriors. Gaines brought provisions sufficient to feed three thousand for a week or more, and the first two days passed in friendly gatherings preparatory to the negotiations. But when talks actually commenced, it quickly became apparent that Le Flore did not speak for all his chiefs. At least two of them, followed by all their warriors, left the council in disgust. One of the white negotiators in charge suggested to Gaines that he should order further food supplies to the camp halted unless the Indians became more sympathetic.

As the days went on, a half-festive, half-ominous atmosphere pervaded the grounds. A cluster of frontier rowdies came to watch, setting up makeshift saloons and gambling games on the periphery of the Choctaw camps, missing no chance to profit by the natives. More militant Choctaw, their anger fueled by drink, talked openly of disrupting the proceedings, even of assassinating the negotiators on both sides.[48] But of course there was never a doubt that there would be a treaty. The only question was how many mingoes would sign the document. In the end the Choctaw ceded all of their remaining land east of the Mississippi and agreed to move within the next two years. Le Flore and a few other leaders got substantial bribes, and the only concession to the average Indian family was an article allowing them to remain in Mississippi if they chose, but limiting them to a grant of 640 acres per head of household, with smaller amounts for each child. But those staying behind would then be subject not to their own law but that of Mississippi.[49]

The hypocrisy of it all was staggering, even by Jacksonian standards. "It is not your lands, but your happiness that we seek," said chief negotiator John Eaton at the outset. "We seek no advantage; we will take none." But when the leaders showed reluctance, he very quickly let them know who had the power. They had no choice, he said. If they did not sell and remove, the president would order an invasion within twenty days. They could no more resist, he said, than "for a baby to expect to overcome a giant."[50]

In the end the Choctaw realized that. What they did not expect was that William Ward, appointed land agent to handle the claims of those Choctaw who elected to remain, would prove so incompetent or corrupt that most of their legal titles were botched and destined for years of litigation. He rejected some applications without cause, lost others, and simply tore up and destroyed some. While several hundred registered with him, he only ever filed the claims of a mere sixty-nine.[51]

Thus through intimidation and threat, bribe and seduction, the United States added the Choctaw domain to Mississippi and Alabama. When his people castigated Le Flore himself for his venality in the affair, he asked in return, "Which is worse, for a great government to offer a bribe or a poor Indian to take one?"[52] Given just how little choice any of them had in the matter, his fellow Choctaw did not really begrudge him his pieces of silver.

Gaines and others went west almost at once to start looking for suitable ground. The Choctaw would be the first to leave their old lands, more than twelve thousand of them crossing the river, while a scant six hundred remained to become citizens of Mississippi. A few years later the Creek followed, reluctant and militant to the end. Only force by the army finally ushered all but a few of them west. That left the Chickasaw. Jackson met with them personally at Franklin, Tennessee, in 1830, and they agreed to removal after locating agreeable grounds, but their surveyors could not find land that suited them, and the president resorted to the old threats of force. In October 1832 at Pontotoc Creek they signed their last treaty and soon thereafter started to move. They, at least, received the most generous terms from Washington, perhaps because they put up the least resistance. Yet for all of them, whether the peaceful Choctaw and Chickasaw, or the warlike Creek, the removal from their ancient homelands proved equally bitter. Indeed, for many it would be deadly, with outbreaks of disease on the journey, and hardship and privation unimagined in spite of government promises to move them in the most "humane" fashion possible. The move started in the winter of 1831–32, with the ground frozen and many of the Indians barefoot. Overwhelmingly they walked the hundreds of miles, some drowning as they waded the swamps along portions of the great river. Some of their horses froze to death, standing still erect like statues. Their teachers closed their schools and the missionaries shut their churches.[53] Even some in Jackson's military, including General Edmund Pendleton Gaines, surveyor of the old Trace so many years before, protested the removal, compromising his own standing with the president, and to no avail.[54] As the sad and embittered Indians of the Southwest trudged their way westward, they blazed a new route to be used but once, and some of it over the old path once called the "Road to the Chickasaw and Choctaw Nations." Those nations existed no more, swallowed by the irresistible hunger and opportunism of white America on the march. Their new road they called the "Trail of Tears."[55] The last of them to take it were some of the Creek. In 1837 Chief Eufaula, one of final mingoes to depart, spoke before the Alabama legislature on his way. "I go to the far West, where my people are now going," he said. "In these lands of Alabama, which have belonged to my forefathers, and where our bones lie buried, I see that the Indian fires are going out—they must soon be extinguished." He knew he could not fight it, and moreover he told them that he left without bitterness. "I came to say farewell to the wise men who make the laws, and to wish them peace and happiness in the country which my forefathers owned, and which I now leave to go to other homes in the West. I leave the graves of my fathers—but the Indian fires are going out, almost clean gone—and new fires are lighting there for us."[56]

⋙ **15** ⋘

The Road to War

It was a region always steeped in either the potential or the actuality of conflict. Indeed, only with the removal of the Indians in the 1830s, long after the breakup of the Old Southwest territory into states, and when the frontier had moved elsewhere, did the last potential for warfare in the land along the Trace disappear. The territory had been the pawn of kings, its fate and possession fought over repeatedly, though usually in other places and by other peoples. Yet the Southwest saw more than enough of hostilities within its own borders to turn its ground as dark and bloody as any on the American continent.

Before its occupation by the United States, the territory's military activity—though intense when it came—was infrequent and limited. The massacre by the Natchez in 1729 gave the French their first—and by no means last—embarrassing defeat in the New World. That humiliation spread to the Americans with the failure of Willing's expedition half a century later, and while Aaron Burr's adventuring can hardly be termed an act of warfare, yet at his approach the frontier militia girded itself as if preparing for war.

Indeed, preparation constituted the overwhelming bulk of military action prior to the second war with Great Britain. The Spaniards, French, British, and Americans all looked on the area as either a frontier bulwark or else a doorway for invasion, and shifted their meager garrisons and built their fortresses accordingly. Initially the Spanish explorers like De Soto made no efforts at defense, since they made no efforts either at settlement. They were literally passing through, and left it to the French at the end of the seventeenth century to take active steps to use arms to hold the province.

The servants of King Louis XIV wasted little time. In future Alabama they built Fort Dauphin in 1701 to protect what became the settlement at Mobile. They constructed Fort Louis the next year on the Mobile River, and there made the first capital of French Louisiana. A few years later they moved the fort to Mobile itself; the Spanish took it from them in 1780 in one of the few actions to be seen by any of these French defenses. More than three decades later it fell yet again, this time to General Wilkinson in 1813, during an undeclared conflict between the United States and Spain that led to the acquisition of Spanish West Florida. Fort Alabama went up in 1715 on the Tallapoosa and Coosa Rivers, to have its name changed later to Fort Toulouse. It never felt the sting of hostile fire, but when the French gave it up to the British in 1763 they spiked their cannon and almost destroyed the works before they left, and the English never bothered to rebuild. The last French fort was Tombecbe, erected in 1735 on the Tombigbee near the Choctaw and Chickasaw lands, and it too fell to the British in 1763, to be reoccupied and renamed Fort York. But then, in 1780, when the Spanish took much of the region, they occupied the fort and renamed it yet again, this time calling it Fort Confederation, but when the San Lorenzo Treaty forced the Spaniards out of the interior in 1795, it passed to the Americans.

Before then the Spaniards also built Fort Saint Stephens on the Tombigbee in order to guard their frontier against incursion by the spreading settlement of Americans, but in 1799 a boundary survey determined that it lay in the territory ceded to the United States, and once more the Europeans had to abandon their works. A few years later, in 1813, the Yankees built their own bastion, Fort Republic. In fact, once they took over the Alabama lands, the Americans pressed even more strenuously the work of rimming their domain with fortifications to protect against both Indian uprising and foreign incursion. They put Fort Stoddert on the Mobile River, where the later Federal Road would cross on its way to the Mississippi, and used the place as a staging point for control of the eastern part of the territory, including Wilkinson's 1813 expedition to take Mobile.[1]

Mississippi, of course, saw its own spate of fort building, starting with Fort Rosalie in 1716 and extending up the river to Fort Saint Peter at the mouth of the Yazoo. Fort Bute followed in the lower extremity of the territory, and when Britain took over, the British quickly either occupied and renamed them—as with Fort Rosalie becoming Fort Panmure—or abandoned them, as with Fort Bute. When the war came with the rebelling Atlantic seaboard colonies, the British outposts in the territory were nothing more than a jot on the story of the main war. Willing's expedition was of no military importance and excited little in the way of enlistments of the inhabitants on either side, though some eighty Natcheans joined with him for a time, more for plunder than for patriotism. The Spaniards responded as soon as their king joined the war against Britain, and easily retook the forts and the region along the great river.

Still, through it all the Southwest was barely even the stage for its fate, much less a major player. The most serious thing approaching warfare waited until 1782, as the Americans and the British were already talking peace, when James Colbert and perhaps six hundred white and Chickasaw confederates formed a small army to raid Spanish outposts and settlers, again in the name of the colonies, and in the main for their own gain. Colbert soon stopped his uprising, however, and peace settled on the Southwestern frontier for nearly two decades.[2]

The coming of peace did not avert the eyes of several nations from New Orleans, the Mississippi, and the dream of interior empire in America, of course. Given the continuing weakness of the region's defenses, the question seemed only to be who could hold onto it best. In fact, Jefferson addressed this as early as 1786, when he spoke of the desire for Spanish West Florida. "These countries cannot be in better hands" at the moment, he said. "My fear is that they are too feeble to hold them till our population can be sufficiently advanced to gain it from them piece by piece."[3]

Throughout the 1780s and 1790s both Spain and Britain had agents operating in the shadows along the Trace, from Natchez to Tennessee, seeking to influence western Americans to break loose from their new government east of the Alleghenies and help in retaking the Southwest for one foreign power or the other. Then, in 1803, France sold its Louisiana territory to the United States largely out of fear that Britain would invade and take it first. Since Spaniards still largely occupied New Orleans, President Jefferson feared that they might not willingly yield it to him, regardless of agreements with Paris. The only surety seemed to be the presence of sufficient American force to guarantee the transfer. There were a few U.S. troops at Fort Adams who could be sent downriver, but hardly enough. Authorities in Washington decided to call on the western territory for volunteers to form a hasty army if needed. Orders went to turn out the militia in the Mississippi Territory, while to West Tennessee went a request for five hundred mounted troopers. Governor John Sevier responded immediately, promising several times that number if needed. While this first five hundred would go overland by the Trace, Andrew Jackson was to oversee the transport of fifteen hundred more down the rivers.

On November 30 the Nashville *Tennessee Gazette* announced that the mounted detachment was present and ready to leave, with more companies for the boat expedition coming in weekly. Finally the horsemen set out on the Trace. For the first time the old route, even now just seeing the beginnings of its clearing, was about to host not a war party of Chickasaw or Creek, but a phalanx of whites marching to do battle if necessary with fellow whites. Even now it still looked to many, in its unfinished condition, to be "only a path that serpentined through the boundless forests." On south they rode, south to battle and glory, so they mused, riding single file the hundreds of miles to Natchez. When finally they reached Washington on December 22, they met the news that it was all for nothing. There would be no glory. Even as the Mississippi militia turned out to join with them, all received word that the Spaniards intended no impediment to the occupation of New Orleans. In fact, they had turned it over to Governor Claiborne and General Wilkinson the day before.

It was disheartening news to rumbunctious young frontiersmen, most of them too young to have fought in the Revolution and anxious now to see some adventure. The best Natchez could do was to give their officers a festive dinner, "where we drank a number of patriotic toasts and spent the day with great accord and pleasantry." Some of the men worn out or sickened by the long hard march went into the hospital at the new Fort Dearborn at Washington, while others had the pleasure of witnessing Stephen Minor turning over Concord Post, a last Spanish holdout garrison on the fringe of the territory. That done, there was nothing for the Tennesseans but to start the long march back home. In two weeks they were back in Nashville, covered with dust if not glory.[4]

It had been the first real military expedition not only for the new state of Tennessee, but also the first to pass through the Mississippi Territory or to call out the militia guarding the land along the Trace. Nearly a decade would pass before these men and their kind found themselves summoned again. Meanwhile the militia groups like the Adams Troop of Dragoons and the rest in Natchez continued to muster and parade.[5] When an isolated group of Creek made trouble, militia or Slicks went after them. But mostly people in the Southwest watched affairs abroad. "It is believed that the Tomahawk buried by our fathers with the British has lain but unquietly," George Gaines mused in March 1809, "and that altho' it has grown rusty under the earth it will have to be resumed—We are waiting with great anxiety."

Indeed they were. The peace with England had never been easy, and now renewed pressures on the western lands, in addition to violations of American rights at sea, made relations more strained. Americans wanted Canada and more of what remained of British territorial holdings. Militaristic "war hawks" in Congress pressed for an aggressive stance, while men in the Southwest wanted the British out of the Floridas, where they interfered with merchant traffic. There were also lingering—and well-founded—beliefs that the English intentionally fomented trouble with the Indians. "In case of a war with G. B. we expect to have warm work here," Gaines continued, "and should she land many Troops in the W. Floridas we shall not be disappointed, for the Creeks, a most powerful Nation of Indians, often express a partiality for the B. Government." Yet Gaines, like others in the territory, knew that their lot in any such war would be a dangerous one. "Surrounded as we will be by enemies on all sides we can only hope to save ourselves by gathering together in Forts & until we get help from Georgia Tennessee & Kentucky."[6]

Others saw unhappy portents. In Natchez that same 1809 John Adair advised Secretary of State James Madison that "the Govt of the U. S. has many Enemys; and but few warm friends here." The inhabitants of New Orleans, overwhelmingly French, felt little love for the Americans. The few British in the territory cared less for the United States and would rise against it given the opportunity. "British agents are now amongst these people," he warned, stirring them to rebel and try to unite the country to England once more.[7] In response to the increased threat, Alabamians went on building more forts, both to protect themselves from the British without, and the Creek within.[8]

Finally came the declaration of war, news not ill received in the Southwest. "None, as it seems to me, was ever juster," said Moses Fisk. "And we never make peace, till our rights at sea, as well as at land, are acknowledged."[9] Word of the state of war first reached New Orleans in July and spread upriver quickly. People held Britain and its maritime policies to blame for the recent economic slump. Others saw war as a chance to finally drive the English out of the Floridas. Yet there were also internal fears attendant. They felt little excitement over any major British army appearing on their shores. The real fighting would be in the East and at sea. But should their militia and volunteers be called together either to go to the East, or else to meet some threat—most likely at New Orleans—it would mean leaving the interior largely unguarded against Indian uprising or the threat of slave revolt.[10] Be that as it might, with word of war the men in the countinghouses and the dogtrots began to turn out, rifles in hand. "The War of 1812 was approaching," said Gideon Lincecum. Naturally he had to leave whichever of his myriad careers he then plied in order to enlist.[11]

The Southwest Territory adopted much the same sort of militia system as did the states to the east. Men aged eighteen to fifty were liable to service, an individual to be mustered in his home county under an officer generally called "colonel" despite any real rank, and elected by his own men. Law did not yet impel men to step forward, but with the common threat to all on the frontier, any man who stayed at home risked condemnation and ridicule and sometimes simply had to remove to other parts where word of his cowardice did not precede him. Those who decided to serve turned out in their hunting shirts and breeches, their muskets and long rifles on their shoulders. David Crockett answered the call, despite urgent pleas from his wife not to go to war. "It was mighty hard to go against such arguments," he confessed, "but my countrymen had been murdered, and I knew that the next thing would be, that the Indians would be scalping the women and children all about there, if we didn't put a stop to it. . . . The truth is," he went on, "my dander was up, and nothing but war could bring it right again."

Crockett went to Winchester, Tennessee, to find quite a number of men gathered to enlist and more of a crowd turned out to witness the historic occasion. Finally the volunteers paraded themselves in some rude sort of order and a local lawyer spoke to them, promised to enlist himself, and then asked rhetorically, "Who among us felt like we could fight." Crockett stepped forward among the first to sign up for ninety days. Militia units in the Trace region turned out only in response to immediate threats or emergencies, and with the hazard passed, returned to their homes. These volunteers would create no standing armies even while the nation was at war.[12]

There was to be no training and little or no drill. Once enlisted, the several county companies went to some central rendezvous, as at Huntsville, Alabama, for Crockett. In the end a regiment might grow to thirteen hundred, as did his Tennessee outfit, many of them mounted "and all determined to fight, judging from myself, for I felt wolfish all over. . . . I verily believe the whole army was of the real grit," Crockett recalled.[13] They certainly looked fierce, if motley. They carried their own guns, weapons of every kind from shotguns to horse pistols. A few with no guns simply rested cornstalks on their shoulders while waiting for a rifle to be issued, leading wags to dub some of these frontier outfits "cornstalk militia."

They tried some rudiments of drill when they were all together in the rendezvous, but it was largely a fruitless enterprise. No one knew the proper commands or even how to pronounce them. Captains summoned their men by shouting, "Oh, yes! Oh, yes!" in the manner of the "Oyez!"—Hear ye!"—of the French and British courtroom, and ordered them to take their places in line. That done, they tried to teach men the mere basics—how to turn to the right and left, how to "dress" their ranks. The instinct of the frontier to make things simple and uncomplicated turned much of the military vernacular into more recognizable words. "Halt" simply became "stop," for instance, and that suited the militia well enough and accomplished the same purpose. When they did try to march in formation, a host inevitably lost the rhythm or simply failed to see the purpose of it all, and instead idled along at their own step, though keeping up in the long, loping stride of the western man. After all, they enlisted to fight, not to become parade ground soldiers. Not a few of them came barefoot, their heads covered by every description of cap, their clothing everything from linsey-woolsey to buckskin. Men smoked in the line. Others marched with umbrellas overhead. And when they finished drill for the day, they immediately broke into groups to talk politics, swap stories, or barter with each other for everything from tobacco to farm lots. All distinctions of rank broke down immediately. Generals and privates sat together, drinking from the same jug. Vendors hastily established on the fringes of the parade ground sold little delicacies, and ersatz entertainments like cockfighting and shooting contests passed the rest of the time.[14]

A remarkable thing about the way these rude organizations worked was the unspoken organization and discipline within them, over and beyond whatever smatterings of such their officers tried to drum into them. Most volunteers came forward already loyal to or trusting in certain natural leaders from their own neighborhoods. While they might take a leisurely attitude toward the orders of some braided and plumed militia or regular general, they would follow unquestioningly the leadership of men who had helped raise their cabins, led them on a successful hunt, or bested the local bully in a fight. They worked best on a raid or expedition with a discrete goal, rather than on long periods of inactive garrison duty, when most would likely just leave and go home. Then, too, they served best when actively defending their home ground, and seemed increasingly reluctant to stay under arms the farther they marched from their own hearths. Still, Tennesseans, for instance, seemed to understand that by fighting for the Lower Mississippi they were keeping the British and Indians from appearing at their homes at the north end of the Trace.

The Old Southwest would not see a single substantial battle with the British except the fight at New Orleans in 1815, and that—though actually outside the traditional boundaries of the territory—still intimately involved the men and fate of the whole region. The first real action came in February 1813, when Washington ordered General Wilkinson to move against and take Mobile from the Spaniards. On April 10 the general and a tiny "army" of six hundred reached their goal, and five days later, without a shot being fired, the overwhelmingly outnumbered Spanish garrison surrendered. That removed a long-standing sore spot for Alabamians and at the same time drove potentially hostile Europeans, who might have taken advantage of the war with Britain, out of the Southwest for good.[15]

It was little more than a sideshow, but then Jackson raised 2,500 volunteers in Tennessee. "Every man in the western Country turns his eyes intuitively upon the mouth of the Mississippi," he told them. "To the people of the Western Country is then peculiarly committed by nature herself the defense of the lower Mississippi." The place for that defense, of course, was New Orleans. Despite a brutally harsh winter, Jackson did not waste time. He put his 670 mounted volunteers under Colonel John Coffee and ordered him to take them south on the Trace to Natchez. Jackson himself would put the remaining 1,830 on boats and go with them down the Cumberland to the Ohio, thence to the Mississippi and on down the great river.

For the men on the Trace it was a trying trip. "When duty requires, all who wish to act justly, will and must obey," Coffee told his wife. "I flatter myself I shall have a pleasant trip although the weather is as yet bad." His real concern was for Jackson. "I fear he will be froze up in the river." On January 19, 1813, Coffee finally set out, taking six days to reach the Tennessee River. He needed two days to get his men and animals across in the freezing temperatures. As soon as he encountered George Colbert and his family at the ferry, however, he found them accommodating and friendly, though Colbert would charge the government exorbitantly for ferrying and feeding the men. "We march slow," Coffee complained. "Not more than from 20 to 23 miles per day." Meanwhile he heard from northbound travelers on the Trace that the people of Mississippi welcomed their coming, though they knew of no enemy yet present for them to fight. That did not deter his volunteers. They were "perfectly careless and easy, quite chearful." By February 3, with rain and snow impeding their travel and miring the road, they reached the Chickasaw Agency. All along the way the Indians proved friendly and helpful, bringing them foodstuffs and encouragement. If anything dampened their spirits at all, it was the continuing intelligence from men met along the way that there were no British in sight below Natchez. "I know not what we are to do," Coffee mused. "Perhaps nothing."

Finally, on February 16, the mounted contingent rode into Natchez, and that very same day Jackson and his river expedition arrived under the hill.[16] For the men on the boats it had been a trying time. They left January 10 and made slow progress down stream, barely twenty miles a day. When they reached the Ohio they found great chunks of ice running with the current so quickly that they feared danger to the boats and did not move for three days. Hail and snow pelted them, while freezing winds beset them every day. Jackson's frustration showed in his dealings with Learner Blackman, who rode in his boat as chaplain to the army. "I find the Gen. cannot bare much opposition," the preacher noted after they disagreed on religious procedures. "He is a good General but a very incorrect Divine."

Along the way Jackson had to bury at least three of his men, not a bad tally considering the severity of the weather and the hazard of the long journey. They saw on either bank the evidences of the recent New Madrid earthquakes and experienced some of the heavier aftershocks. One of the boats hit a sawyer and sank without loss of life, and Blackman was kept busy with constant prayer, going from boat to boat to assure the volunteers of the Almighty's blessing on their enterprise. At last they arrived to find Coffee waiting for them, his men and mounts still panting from their journey.[17]

While Jackson put his men in camp outside Washington, he chafed at finding orders not to go farther. For the next month they waited to hear what they were to do. "We cannot here see any probable prospects of an enemy in any part of this country," Coffee wrote at the end of the month. "Seeing no prospects of any thing to do increases the anxiety to return home." He read his volunteers well. They enlisted to fight, not to sit in the snow in Mississippi. "Under a hope that we could render our country important services, we consented to the sacrifice of leaving our homes, our families and all our individual interest, but in that hope I now suppose all will be disappointed." After nearly a month of waiting, finally Jackson got word from Washington, D.C. His expedition was cancelled. He and his army were simply to retrace their steps and go home. Jackson almost exploded and would never appreciate the view of Congress that no danger now existed, and therefore no need for the volunteers. Already in neighboring Alabama the Creek were starting to escalate their depredations and attacks on outlying settlements, once more allied with their old friends the British. "Our men would have gone home better satisfied could they have had one stump of a fight," complained Coffee. "We had just begun to learn how to do duty when we shall be discharged."[18] In the end Jackson put his whole command on the Trace and headed north again on March 22, the general himself walking along with the men while the sick used his horse. He shared every hardship with them, and in return the men along the Trace gave him a nickname to last through posterity, Old Hickory.[19]

Yet he would be back, and many of these Tennesseans along with him. If the British Redcoat did not yet pose a visible threat to the Southwest, his allies did. Indeed, the people on this frontier were about to find themselves fighting their own private war, certainly connected to the international conflict, but growing out of other causes and conducted by other rules. Its roots went back to 1811, when the great Shawnee chieftain Tecumseh traveled south through the territory trying to stir resentment against the whites and to persuade Chickasaw, Choctaw, and Creek alike to join with him in a great Indian confederacy to rise and drive out the Yankee invaders. "Brush from your eyelids the sleep of slavery," he shouted, "and strike for vengeance and your country." The Americans took their land, desecrated their holy places, despoiled their women. "Let the white race perish!" he exhorted them. They must be pushed back to the ocean shores, then driven across it to the places from which they came. "Burn their dwellings—destroy their stock—slay their wives and children, that the very breed may perish. War now! War always! War on the living! War on the dead!"[20]

It was a powerful message of hate and vengeance, made the more so by its delivery from one of the most eloquent native men of his time. Tecumseh brought with him an aura of violent holiness, enhanced by the presence of his brother, called the Prophet. Yet when they spoke to the Chickasaw, their words met deaf ears. These Indians would not turn against the Americans. Nor did the Choctaw give him an overwarm welcome. But when he went to the Creek, their long-standing antagonism toward the Americans, plus the agitation of British agents, made them more than receptive. More prophets arose among the Creek themselves, and a season of growing frenzy, signaled by dancing and chanting, soon had the Alabama-Georgia frontier in a state of panic. Not all the Creek heeded Tecumseh's message, but more than enough did, and at their dances they now passed around their red sticks, ceremonial symbols of war. Finally the tribe split, the "Red Sticks" choosing war with the whites, and the others arguing its futility. At first the former waged a limited war of raid and terror on the latter, trying to coerce them into the confederacy with Tecumseh. Then, in June 1813, some of them attacked but failed to kill a post rider on the Federal Road.

If they were not ready for outright bloodshed yet, they would be soon. When a war party went to Pensacola to get weapons from the Spaniards, a hastily mustered force of militia from the territory, one hundred strong, marched to attack. At Burnt Corn Creek they struck the surprised Indians and routed them at first, but then the Creek turned and delivered a humiliating counterattack that left two militiamen dead. It was the first "battle" in the Creek conflict, a war within a war, and the source of the greatest danger to white settlers ever to arise in the Old Southwest.[21]

Soon afterward a regiment of volunteers from Baton Rouge reached the Alabama Territory to find settlers abandoning their homes and farms, and whole communities in a panic. The people of the Tensaw, Tombigbee, and Alabama Rivers left their villages and flocked to the several forts and stockades, and there they huddled for safety against the Red Stick menace. One of those stockades was a hastily erected palisade called Fort Mims, at the meeting of the Alabama and Tombigbee. A scanty 120 militia and a few hundred settler families occupied the place and seemed to entertain at first little fear of molestation even when scouting reports came in during August reporting a large number of Creek in the vicinity. Better intelligence seemed to indicate that another fort farther north was threatened. On August 30, nevertheless, its commander, Major Daniel Beasley, assured General Ferdinand Claiborne, commanding territorial volunteers, that by the morrow his position would be "in such a state of defense that we shall not be afraid of any number of Indians." He spoke a bit too soon.[22]

Even as Beasley's dispatch rode out toward Claiborne, the rider carrying it miraculously passed through perhaps seven hundred or more Creek who lay hiding in a ravine only a few hundred yards from the eastern gate to the stockade. Worse, that gate stood open now, some said because no one apprehended any trouble, and others maintaining that through neglect it was actually stuck open by drifting sand. At noon the drum beat the call to the midday meal. Some of the settlers and militia may have been drunk. Beasley himself may have been indulging. No one was vigilant. No one saw or heard the Creek swarm arise and rush toward the stockade. Only when the Red Sticks were less than one hundred feet from the gate did someone cry the warning.

Beasley himself rushed to try to close the gate, but he died in the effort as the warriors ran over and past him into the interior. A company just inside the gate fell to a man, and then the Indians rushed the guardhouses around the periphery. Within minutes all the officers fell, and the militiamen and the women and children fortified themselves inside their buildings. One by one the Creek scoured them out, some with fire, others by shooting in through the portholes. After three hours, not many whites remained, and at the point of being burned alive, they cut their way through the palisade on one side and ran for the woods. Few made it, only fifteen in all getting safely away from the carnage. Behind them the Creek engaged in an orgy of bloodletting, releasing the pent-up hostility of generations and the frenzy of their fevered months of war preparations.[23]

The disaster at Fort Mims sent an electric shock through the frontier. At least 247 died in the horrible massacre, and a score or more of women, children, and slaves were taken away as captives. It was a score too high to leave unsettled, and when the first rush of panic waned, the southwesterners arose in numbers bent on vengeance, and in the same currency that the Red Sticks gave. It was "a most bloody butchery," said Crockett, and it was what impelled him and hundreds of other Tennesseans to volunteer. "When I heard of the mischief which was done at the fort, I instantly felt like going, and I had none of the dread of dying that I expected to feel."[24] Men praised the stand of the Mims defenders far beyond what was, in all likelihood, a terrified and unorganized scramble to survive. "Their valor at least was sealed in a glorious death," the Natchez press proclaimed.[25] "Brother Tecumseh devised crimes the perpetration of which would harrow up the soul freeze the blood & cause the hair to bristle up like the back of the faithful porcupine," a Natchez man told a friend.[26] Informed of the tragedy, Jackson, back home in Tennessee, reportedly said, "Long shall the creeks remember Fort Mims in bitterness and tears."[27]

"Never did we behold Nashville in such a bustle as it has been for several days past," one editor remarked in late September. Tennesseans in hundreds poured out to volunteer, and the governor asked Jackson to command an expedition to destroy the Creek threat for good. "The volunteers to the Creek nation, are in motion in every direction, burning with anxiety, to be off against the enemy of their country."[28] Even the old stand keeper John Gordon, from the Duck River crossing of the Trace, came forward, Jackson making him captain of a company of spies. To some five thousand Tennessee militia who volunteered, Jackson's call for "retaliatory vengeance" met receptive ears.

In the territory, meanwhile, General Claiborne moved his own militia eastward toward the Tombigbee, while Governor Holmes issued the call for more. Pushmataha brought some of his Choctaw to aid in the campaign, and on December 23, at a spot called Holy Ground near Fort Saint Stephens, the Mississippians delivered to the Creek their first vengeful blow. Thereafter as more and more volunteers converged on the Creek land from north, east, and west, the prospect looked increasingly grim for the Indians. At least eight thousand angry whites were coming for them, many commanded by an unrepentant Indianophobe, Jackson.

Jackson himself set out in October 1813, and for four weeks his small army slogged south through increasingly bad weather, plagued by inadequate supplies and equally poor planning. Still, on November 2 portions of them won a lopsided victory at Tallushatchee, north of Talladega. A week later Jackson struck some one thousand Creek who were attacking Talladega, and destroyed a third of them, putting the rest to flight. A series of battles then followed, delayed by ever-worsening supply conditions and the sometimes near-mutiny of portions of the volunteers. At one point much of the command, their term of service expired, simply left and went back to Tennessee. An undaunted Jackson kept on with those remaining. He suffered two small but embarrassing near-defeats in January, when the Creek surprised his tired and hungry command. Still, he emerged with renewed prestige, and his men with increased confidence and determination to put an end to the Red Sticks for good. As his command steadily grew once more until it numbered nearly five thousand, he moved south toward the main Red Stick fastness on the Tallapoosa River, in what was known as Horseshoe Bend.

It was a brutal kind of warfare that these frontiersmen waged on the Creek, very little different from the Indian way itself. They both fought by the same ethic—risk of self as little as possible until there is a clear advantage, then push that advantage all the way without remorse. It was, after all, the same law they all used in hunting or simply in fighting the wilderness itself. At the Tallushatchee fight, with some one thousand Tennesseans facing two hundred surprised Creek, no sentiments of civilized warfare emerged. Crockett told of how he saw a woman blocking the door to a house into which some forty-six warriors had run for refuge. When she fired an arrow at the Americans, they riddled her with a volley, then went to work on the inmates. "We shot them like dogs," he said without remorse, and then they set the building afire. "I recollect seeing a boy who was shot down near the house," said Crockett. "His arm and thigh was broken, and he was so near the burning house that the grease was stewing out of him." They all watched as the twelve-year-old tried fruitlessly to pull himself away from the flames.[29]

As Jackson advanced, men in the territory, like Gaines, took heart. "We have so much confidence in you Tennesseans," he told a friend, "that now that Jackson has actually begun to drub our cruel foes we feel ourselves tolerably safe." Then came the word of the Battle of Horseshoe Bend. On March 27 Jackson struck, and though the Creek were placed in a good spot behind surprisingly strong fortifications, they never really had a chance. Against their thousand or more warriors, Jackson could concentrate nearly four times that number, plus artillery. At the end of the day more than nine hundred braves lay dead, and virtually all the rest had been captured. The defeat broke the back of the Creek uprising, and though some continued to hold out for a few months more, the war was all but over. Many surrendered to Jackson, while more just put down their arms and returned to their woodland haunts, the dreams of Tecumseh shattered in the nation's blood.

For their part, the men of the Southwest rejoiced. "Since the battle of the Horse Shoe, on Tallapoosa," said George Gaines, "we have been in high spirits."[30] Finally on August 9, 1814, the Creek made a treaty that ended their resistance, concluding the vicious little war within a war that the southwesterners fought almost by themselves.

But there was still another fight to finish. Major Thomas Hinds and a battalion of Mississippi dragoons joined Jackson, and together they moved on Mobile and then Pensacola. Jackson and his volunteers were making their own war policy now, acting in large part without orders from Washington and sometimes ignoring those he received. Then in November he learned that the British were finally marshaling forces for the long-feared and -anticipated major invasion on the Gulf Coast. Sixty ships and fourteen thousand soldiers in them were going to attack New Orleans. There the fate of an American Southwest might be settled once and for good.

Events moved with seeming lightning speed. Jackson left Mobile on November 22 and marched on the old Federal Road. Meanwhile every available militia unit from the territory sped south to the Crescent City, including the several troops from Natchez, Washington, Woodville, and more. Mississippians met with Tennesseans, Choctaw, Creoles, black companies, and even bayou pirates in the scramble to defend the city, for all understood that even if it were outside the land along the Trace, its fall would open both the river and the old road as highways of invasion for a victorious British army. This time, for a change, even the often wily Natchez planters took a stand rather than waiting to see which way the wind blew.

Jackson gave them a victory, of course. On January 8, neither knowing that the United States and Britain had concluded a peace two weeks before, the British attacked Jackson and suffered perhaps the most one-sided defeat in American history. On the side of the victors it was a win constituted of luck, favorable weather, sound leadership, and the courage of thousands of southwesterners—red, white, and black— and the accuracy of their arms. It would not be the last fight of the war, or even of the war in this region, however, for a few weeks later the British made a move against Mobile that fell just short of taking the city before word of the signing of the Treaty of Ghent arrived. But New Orleans was virtually the end of any threat to the United States, and to the Old Southwest in particular. It also virtually made Andrew Jackson, a man of the Southwest, who would one day be *the* man of the nation, bringing with him to prominence all the old ethics of ruggedness, courage, unsophistication, and opportunism that characterized these men and women at the end of the Trace. New Orleans had been their fight, and their victory was not just the winning of the battle. With it, and in Old Hickory, they won recognition on their own national stage for the first time, and began to play what would in a few years' time come to be a leading role in its affairs.

When word of New Orleans spread upriver, euphoria and relief moved with it. In Natchez the city illuminated itself in celebration, with crowds gathering to shout "Jackson!" and "Victory!"[31] A few weeks later in early March came rumors that a treaty had been signed, but confirmation waited a few more days yet.[32] Gallant heroes like the Natchez Riflemen and Hinds' company came marching home triumphantly, to enthusiastic receptions.[33] The frontier was safe. The Creek were broken. Trade could move unimpeded by the British once more, and even the Spaniards had finally been driven from West Florida. For the rest of Jackson's army, when the time came for the volunteers to go home, they set out on the Trace with buoyant step for Tennessee. In April, travelers on the old road passed brigade after brigade of them. Hundreds of the sick and weary fell out along the way, to be cared for by the stand operators and the Choctaw and Chickasaw. Indeed, never in its history had so many men been on the old path at one time.[34]

Of course, the end of the War of 1812 did not mean the end of military activity in the territory. While the Choctaw and Chickasaw never made trouble, pockets of disgruntled Creek would continue to rise from time to time to commit some isolated depredation before being hunted down by local militia or Slicks. In 1817 they killed a few settlers near the Georgia line, and a muster soon put men in the field to find and punish the offenders. Then, in 1836, they made their last stand of resistance, putting much of Alabama briefly into a fright. Militia dogged them and then tracked them to the vicinity of Hobdy's Bridge. With no more than a hundred men on each side, the "battle" was almost bloodless initially, as the attacking volunteers put the Creek to flight. But then the Indians turned to make a stand. Having no bullets, they rammed nails down their rifle barrels and fired them at the whites. The "unearthly" whining of the flying nails put a fright into the attackers at first. Southwestern whites could be just as superstitious as their native foes, but once they learned what made the noise, the militia kept on advancing. Finally the Creek withdrew entirely, beaten but not dispersed.

Instead, the few holdouts determined to make their way to their cousins the Seminole, deep in the distant Florida Everglades. In March 1837 militia caught up with them on the Pea River in southeastern Alabama. No more than 200 warriors, hungry, demoralized, and accompanied by their families, made their stand against the militia of several counties. Perhaps 250 whites commenced the attack, a part of them in fact turning in flight when an intended withdrawal became a minor rout. But then their main body advanced and swept everything before them. They took and plundered the Creek camps. "For some time after the capture of the camp an indiscriminate slaughter of women, children, old men and warriors ensued," recalled one unashamed participant, Green Beauchamp. They believed that Indian dead totaled 150 or more. Women and children who survived became slaves. Of the men, said Beauchamp, "no warriors were made prisoners."[35] The few who escaped did eventually reach the Seminole. Only the removal of the remaining Creek finally ended all such need for fifes and drums.

Warfare came rather naturally to these southwesterners, but it was—ironically—the kind practiced by their Indian foes. They left their homes for a limited time to meet a limited threat, dealt with it, removed it, and then went back to their hearths. They fought to win and to survive, not to gain plaudits for their behavior. The safest enemy was a dead one, however killed, and if in the blood lust of battle they also killed women and children, they told themselves that they were only savages anyhow, and that today's child could wield a tomahawk as a warrior tomorrow. The southwesterners never developed a true martial spirit. Only the social elite who paraded in gaudy uniforms in the cities' private militia companies ever developed any real love of regimented service, and even that was more for show than anything else. For the rest, as with many another—perhaps every—aspect of civilization in the old territory, a uniform ran counter to their main aims, which were always prosperity, opportunity, property, and independence.

Afterword

The Road West

In the seemingly brief span of two generations a civilization emerged and flourished in the Old Southwest and was ready to jump its bounds. But then, in the spread of American settlement, a generation was a long time. Indeed, for many of these hardy, rebellious, violent, and overwhelmingly opportunistic people, a generation was too long. They did not have that much time to wait. A continent was exploding around them, and if they did not grab their piece of it quickly, they feared they might lose out forever; if they did not take hold of something in one place, they had to move to another with no backward glance.

They were short-term people with long-range goals, and they revealed it in everything they did. They used the old Trace only so long as they had to, and allowed it to die without a thought when something faster and better came along. In the main, roads to them were to be used only once, and that was to get closer to the edge of the frontier, where the land was cheap or free. Steamboats and rails and the rest were new, and to these people the new was always important, whether for making their lives a little easier or their route to profit more secure. They were not city builders. Cities were too permanent, and only those who got there first had a chance of securing the most profitable footholds. In all the Southwest only Natchez became a major city by 1830, and aside from the wealthy planters who maintained town homes, a surprising number of its inhabitants were not cut from the same cloth as the frontiersmen. They came from the North or the East and came to trade, to share in the opportunity sure enough, but not to share the real culture of the men who tied themselves to the land. Even

321

the incipient industrialists showed little interest in permanence. Not a single lasting manufacturing or industrial enterprise opened its doors during the territorial or early statehood years. Industry took too long and took too many roots. A good crop only took a year, and its roots were as movable as the seeds of the cotton.

"Roots" was a word around which most of their civilization swirled. Ties and loyalties extended little beyond the family, especially for the hardscrabble settlers in their dogtrots, who learned the hard way that self-reliance was the surest reliance. Intense loyalty sprang up in those smoky cabins—tested in hunger and hardship, tempered in the face of death from Indians and the elements. No surprise, then, that for many it was difficult if not impossible to extend that loyalty on a broader scale into a genuine sense of community. In Natchez and Mobile and Jackson, where real society developed, it flourished mostly among the professional, the educated, the well-to-do, and those who came to the Southwest after the work of winning it was done. The city broadcloth and the backwoods buckskin never mixed well, each restrained by a suspicion of the other and a competition for much the same fortune. To the degree that education became prized, it was not for its own sake, but only as preparation, as another weapon in the battle for opportunity. Most of the settlers, seeing little advantage in it, gave it scant attention.

Religion offered more immediate rewards, it seemed, and the immediate was always uppermost in their minds. Certainly their gods made none of them rich. But in the simple camp-meeting kind of faith that most of them practiced, they found a tremendous emotional release from the tension and uncertainty of frontier living. Moreover, theirs were gods who rewarded the good and punished the evil—easy, uncomplicated notions that suited well the essential simplicity of wilderness life. Their religion was like their cotton in a way. Having found a crop, a road to prosperity, they felt little inclination to look for another so long as that lasted. Similarly, the words of their preachers gave them what they needed for the moment—simple codes of behavior, rigid rights and wrongs, a certain pathway to salvation. There might be others, but being shown one, they were content.

Even the violence in their blood revealed their essential nature. Immediate retaliation for wrong or injustice—whether it take the form of the urge for revenge or the needs of law and order—brought the swiftest reward. If frontier isolation from more established forms of justice encouraged the Slicks and their like, even more did such vigilantism serve their own sense of right and order. Felons could escape, either by running or by the mysteries of the legal process. Immediate retribution eclipsed such possibilities. More to the point, it took advantage of what always lay uppermost in the minds of these people—opportunity. On a personal scale, their resort to individual redress, whether by bushwhacking in the night or going "over the river" at dawn, worked toward exactly the same end. The speediest justice was the best, and in time what began as an expedient became a code of personal behavior.

Virtually their whole lives and civilization fit into the framework of simplicity, exploitation of opportunity for the fortunate, and uprooting for those not yet finding that fortune. Ironically, theirs was a culture entirely reliant on outsiders, those who brought their ideas with them and tried to make the territory bend to their mold. The one people who did not fit into the scheme, who shared neither the values nor the sense of transience, was the one that met them on their arrival. Their culture offered the newcomers nothing except their role as a threat and foe—and of course their millions of acres of land. By not fitting in and by standing in the way, the Choctaw, Chickasaw, Creek, and the rest therefore had to go. Like the poor Natchez so many decades before, in the end they all went.

These new men in the Southwest were no more or less evil or maliciously inclined than any others would have been in their place. Their prejudices were the prejudices of their time. Their excesses were those of all sparsely settled new frontiers. Their grasping and ambition were a part of their essential characters as Americans, a people born two centuries before when a nucleus of Europeans first escaped the bonds of a millennia of obstacles and began to entertain something quite new for them—a sense of hope, an expectation that life could be better for them than for their forebears. That was what initially set Americans apart from their Old World relations, and first to last it was the driving force behind the opportunism that characterized so much of their behavior in the New World. At their worst and at their best, the men who trudged along the Trace or floated down the rivers in their broadhorns were doing the same things their fathers and grandfathers had done in Virginia and New York. What made them distinctive in the Old Southwest is that they lived at a time when the westward impulse suddenly accelerated dramatically in the aftermath of American independence. It took Americans a century and a half to bridge the Appalachians. In the very next generation they pressed all the way to the Mississippi in the most dramatic exodus in history to date.

Once there they paused to catch their breath while the United States began for the first time to feel gathering strength in its adolescence. They risked and failed, profited and plundered, took what they could, endured what they must. The Old Southwest, like the stands along the Trace, served in a way as a stopover, a way station on the westward road of empire. It was as if they rested here to develop themselves, regroup their energies, test their muscles, and steel their resolve for the even greater challenge that lay literally within sight, just across the wide Mississippi. And when they were ready, when no more European threats hazarded their way, when the Indians had been subdued, when their weapons and their technology equipped them for the test, they went to the banks of the muddy stream. Once on the other side there was nothing to stop them but more Indians, more wilderness, or their own frailty, until they reached the Pacific.

By the 1830s men were already on the new roads—or more accurately, once more following faint Indian and bison tracks across a new wilderness, more prairie than woodland now, more arid, filled with fresh wonders. Even before the Indians' removal, the latest talisman of fortune on southwestern lips was the word "Texas." Land was almost free. Mexican overlords were seemingly indulgent—and in any case could probably be pushed out in time. The ground was fertile and the grasslands could sustain whole armies of livestock. It was a place for those who failed to find fortune in the Southwest to look anew, and regardless of the kind of fortune they sought.

David Crockett of Tennessee, for instance, let his wits and his charm and his smattering of frontier fame carry him into national politics, where he came up against much more sophisticated and wily fellows than he. In the end he lost a bid for reelection to Congress in 1835, and casting about for what he should do next—having tried exploring, milling, farming, soldiering, and officeholding—he reverted to what a southwesterner always knew best. "You may all go to hell," he told men who voted against him, "and I will go to Texas."[1] Already there were signs of a potential conflict between American settlers and Mexican authorities. He wanted to go not to get involved in another war but to look at the land, find a piece of it, and move his family to join him. On his way there he stopped in Arkansas, impressing some as "an eccentric Westerner and a man of great energy and daring."[2] But then, those words could have described most of them.

Samuel Clark certainly spoke of most of them when he sat on the west bank of the Mississippi in 1839 and watched the legion of settlers crossing the river and pressing west. "The roads hereabouts are crowded," he said, "with emigrants to Texas from Arkansas, Missouri, Kentucky, Alabama, Georgia & Mississippi. . . . The country is filling up fast."[3] He might even have seen Crockett in that exodus, and certainly when Crockett arrived in the new country the eccentric Tennessean saw evidence of the tide of immigration. In fact, many had come from much greater distances than he, and quite a few had crossed his path before in their mutual peregrinations through the old land of the Trace now left behind. One of them, in fact, had started in Georgia and tried South Carolina, Tennessee, and Alabama, before crossing the river. David Crockett may have thought he would be in the vanguard of the rush, but he would have been wrong: Gideon Lincecum got there ahead of him.

NOTES

Abbreviations Used in the Notes

AHQ   *Alabama Historical Quarterly*
JMH   *Journal of Mississippi History*
NTC   Natchez Trace Collection, Center for American History, Eugene C. Barker Texas History Center, University of Texas, Austin
NTPL   Natchez Trace Parkway Library, Tupelo, Mississippi
PMHS   *Publications of the Mississippi Historical Society*
TAHS   *Transactions of the Alabama Historical Society*

Chapter 1   The Road to Empire

1. Brian M. Fagan, *The Journey from Eden* (New York, 1990), pp. 204–6.
2. Ted Morgan, *Wilderness at Dawn: The Settling of the North American Continent* (New York, 1993), p. 39.
3. Marcel Giraud, *A History of French Louisiana,* vol. 1, *The Reign of Louis XIV, 1698–1715* (Baton Rouge, La., 1974), pp. 72–73.
4. R. S. Cotterill, *The Southern Indians* (Norman, Okla., 1954), pp. 6–7; D. Clayton James, *Antebellum Natchez* (Baton Rouge, La., 1968), pp. 3–4.
5. Cotterill, *Southern Indians,* pp. 14–15.
6. Morgan, *Wilderness at Dawn,* pp. 200–202.
7. Giraud, *French Louisiana,* p. 192; James, *Antebellum Natchez,* p. 4.
8. James, *Antebellum Natchez,* pp. 6–8.
9. Joseph Mathurin Pellerin to his cousin, 1719, Howard-Tilton Memorial Library, Tulane University, New Orleans.
10. Ibid., pp. 10–12.
11. Eron O. Rowland, ed., "Peter Chester, Third Governor of the Province of West Florida Under British Dominion, 1770–1781," *PMHS* (1921), p. 77.
12. Philip Pittman, *The Present State of the European Settlements on the Mississippi* (London, 1770; reprint, Memphis, 1977), pp. 37–39.
13. Rowland, "Peter Chester," p. 77.
14. Ibid., pp. 16–20.

15. Robert V. Haynes, "James Willing and the Planters of Natchez: The American Revolution Comes to the Southwest," *JMH* 37 (Feb. 1975), pp. 5–39 passim.
16. Mrs. Dunbar Rowland, "Mississippi's Colonial Population and Land Grants," *PMHS* (1916), pp. 411ff.
17. Kenneth Scott, ed., "Britain Loses Natchez, 1779: An Unpublished Letter," *JMH* 36 (Feb. 1964), pp. 45–46.
18. John F. McDermott, ed., *The Spanish in the Mississippi Valley, 1762–1804* (Urbana, Ill., 1974), pp. 11–12.
19. James, *Antebellum Natchez,* p. 26; Anna Lewis, ed., "Fort Panmure, 1779, as Related by Juan de la Villebeuvre to Bernardo de Galvez," *Mississippi Valley Historical Review* 18 (Mar. 1932), p. 547.
20. Jack D. L. Holmes, "Juan De la Villebeuvre: Spain's Commandant of Natchez During the American Revolution," *JMH* 37 (Feb. 1975), pp. 107–8.
21. Holmes, "De la Villebeuvre," pp. 109–10.
22. James, *Antebellum Natchez,* pp. 40–42.
23. Franklin L. Riley, "Spanish Policy in Mississippi After the Treaty of San Lorenzo," *PMHS* 1 (1898), pp. 55ff.
24. B. L. C. Wailes, *Report on the Agriculture and Geology of Mississippi* (Philadelphia, Pa., 1854), pp. 115–16.
25. Franklin L. Riley, "Transition from Spanish to American Rule in Mississippi," *PMHS* 3 (1900), pp. 310–11.

Chapter 2 The Road to Natchez

1. J. F. H. Claiborne, *Mississippi as a Province, Territory and State* (Jackson, Miss., 1880), p. 128n.
2. Francis Baily, *Journal of a Tour in Unsettled Parts of North America in 1796 & 1797* (London, 1856), pp. 346–49.
3. Dawson A. Phelps, "Travel on the Natchez Trace," *JMH* 15 (July 1953), p. 156.
4. Baily, *Journal,* p. 351.
5. Ibid., pp. 350–54.
6. Ibid., pp. 354–61.
7. Ruth E. Butler, Olaf Hagen, and Randle B. Truett, *The Natchez Trace: Its Location, History and Development* (NTPL, 1936), p. 175.
8. Baily, *Journal,* pp. 362–70.
9. Dawson A. Phelps, "Tockshish," *JMH* 13 (July 1951), pp. 138–42.
10. Baily, *Journal,* pp. 370–72.
11. Ibid., pp. 372–74.
12. Michael H. Bureman, *An Historical Overview of the Natchez Trace* (NTPL, 1985), p. 172.
13. Baily, *Journal,* pp. 376–79.
14. Butler, Hagen, and Truett, *Natchez Trace,* p. 180.
15. Baily, *Journal,* pp. 380–96.
16. Jill K. Garrett, *Historical Sketches of Hickman County, Tennessee* (Columbia, Tenn., 1978), p. 5.

17. William B. Turner, *History of Maury County, Tennessee* (Nashville, Tenn., 1955), pp. 40–41.
18. Baily, *Journal*, pp. 396–411.
19. Dawson Phelps, *Natchez Trace: Variant Locations,* (n.p., n.d.), p. 3; Dawson Phelps, *The Natchez Trace in Williamson and Davidson Counties, Tennessee* (NTPL, 1946), p. 2.
20. Quoted in Lena Mitchell Jamison, "The Natchez Trace: A Federal Highway of the Old Southwest," *JMH* 1 (Apr. 1939), p. 83.
21. Ibid., pp. 83–84.
22. Joseph Habersham to Abijah Hunt, Nov. 20, 1799, Letter Book I, Post Master General's Office, Record Group 28, National Archives, Washington, D.C.
23. Jamison, "A Federal Highway," pp. 84–85.
24. Habersham to Matthew Lyon, Mar. 12, 1801, Letter Book K, Record Group 28, National Archives.
25. Habersham to Henry Dearborn, Mar. 12, 1801, ibid.
26. Jamison, "A Federal Highway," pp. 90–93.
27. Ibid., pp. 94–95.
28. Ibid., pp. 96–98.
29. Phelps, *Natchez Trace: Variant Locations,* p. 13.
30. Douglas Edward Leach, "John Gordon of Gordon's Ferry," *Tennessee Historical Quarterly* 18 (Dec. 1959), pp. 323–37.
31. Dawson A. Phelps, "Stands and Travel Accommodations on the Natchez Trace," *JMH* 11 (Jan. 1949), pp. 48–51.
32. Dawson A. Phelps, "Colbert Ferry and Selected Documents," *AHQ* 25 (Fall–Winter 1963), pp. 206–13.
33. Phelps, "Stands and Accommodations," pp. 40–41.
34. Ibid., pp. 19–21.
35. Ibid., p. 15; Bureman, *Historical Overview,* p. 172.
36. Phelps, "Stands and Accommodations," pp. 15–17, 24–26; Bureman, *Historical Overview,* p. 78.
37. Phelps, "Stands and Accommodations," pp. 28, 31, 37, 42–44, 49–51; Garrett, *Historical Sketches*, p. 105; Olaf T. Hagen, *Grinder's Stand* (NTPL, 1933), pp. 5–9.
38. Dawson A. Phelps, *Gordon's Ferry* (NTPL, 1945), p. 9.
39. Phelps, "Stands and Accommodations," pp. 51–52, 52n; Bureman, *Historical Overview,* p. 173.
40. Bureman, *Historical Overview,* pp. 173–74.
41. Dawson A. Phelps, "The Natchez Trace in Tennessee," *Tennessee Historical Quarterly* 13 (Sept. 1954), pp. 199–200.
42. Dawson A. Phelps, "The Natchez Trace in Alabama," *Alabama Review* 7 (Jan. 1954), p. 25.

Chapter 3 The Road to Travel

1. Phelps, "Travel," pp. 157–58.
2. John W. Monette, "The Progress of Navigation and Commerce on the

Waters of the Mississippi River and the Great Lakes, A.D. 1700 to 1846," *PMHS* (1903), pp. 486–87.

3. Receipt of A. Thomas, Apr. 15, 1808; receipt of Evan Jones, June 2, 1806; receipt of James Kichnal, June 13, 1811, NTC.

4. John F. McDermott, ed., *Before Mark Twain: A Sampler of Old, Old Times on the Mississippi* (Carbondale, Ill., 1968), pp. 3–4.

5. Ibid., p. 5.

6. Ibid., p. 485; Phelps, "Travel," p. 161.

7. Leland D. Baldwin, *The Keelboat Age on Western Waters* (Pittsburgh, 1941), pp. 44–45.

8. Receipt, May 4, 1811, NTC.

9. Zadoc Cramer, *The Navigator* (Pittsburgh, 1814), pp. 34–38.

10. Robert J. Holden, *Travelers on the Natchez Trace: A Study of the Ohio River Valley Boatmen, Their Life and Characteristics, as Described by Contemporary Observers* (NTPL, 1977), p. 16.

11. Ibid., pp. 16–17.

12. Arthur P. Hudson, *Humor of the Old Deep South* (New York, 1936), p. 56.

13. McDermott, *Before Mark Twain*, p. 6.

14. Holden, *Travelers*, pp. 18–19.

15. "A Diary of a Journey," *Journal of the Presbyterian Historical Society* 21 (Dec. 1943), p. 174.

16. McDermott, *Before Mark Twain*, pp. 7–8.

17. John R. Bedford, ed., "A Tour in 1807 Down the Cumberland, Ohio and Mississippi Rivers from Nashville to New Orleans," *Tennessee Historical Magazine* 5 (July 1919), pp. 109–15.

18. Henry Ker, *Travels Through the Western Interior of the United States from the Year 1808 up to the Year 1816* (Elizabethtown, N.J., 1816), pp. 24–25.

19. Ibid., pp. 25–26.

20. Ibid., pp. 39–40.

21. John Bradbury, *Travels in the Interior of America* (Liverpool, England, 1817), pp. 196–97.

22. Ibid., pp. 199–206.

23. Myron L. Fuller, *The New Madrid Earthquake* (Washington, D.C., 1912), pp. 18–21.

24. Baldwin, *Keelboat Age*, p. 82.

25. Monette, "Progress," p. 489.

26. Ibid., pp. 489–90n.

27. Excerpt from Edouard de Montule, *Travels in America, 1816–1817,* in Research–Natchez Miscellaneous Correspondence, 1937–1952, NTPL.

28. Ker, *Travels*, p. 41.

29. Bedford, "A Tour in 1807," p. 116.

30. Michael F. Beard, *Prices and Credit in Territorial Natchez and its Hinterland, 1806–1818: A Report for the Natchez Trace Parkway* (NTPL, Apr. 22, 1980), p. 31.

31. Natchez, Mississippi, *Herald and Natchez City Gazette*, May 23, 1804.

32. Butler, Hagen, and Truett, *Natchez Trace,* pp. 185–86.

33. Ker, *Travels*, p. 42.

34. Natchez, Mississippi, *Herald and Natchez City Gazette*, Jan. 21, 1804; rates of ferriage across the Mississippi, June 28, 1809, NTC.

35. Phelps, "Travel," p. 160.

36. Beard, *Prices and Credit*, p. 42.

37. Phelps, "Travel," p. 160.

38. Holden, *Travelers*, p. 17.

39. Hudson, *Humor*, p. 58.

40. Baldwin, *Keelboat Age*, p. 87.

41. Ibid., pp. 110–12.

42. Ibid., pp. 113–14.

43. Franklin Riley, "Extinct Towns and Villages of Mississippi," *PMHS* 5 (1902), p. 345.

44. Butler, Hagen, and Truett, *Natchez Trace*, pp. 187–88.

45. Rush Nutt, *Portions of a Diary of a Tour Through the Western Part of the U.S.* (Entry for Aug. 1, 1805).

46. William B. Wait, ed., *Travel Diary of William Richardson from Boston to New Orleans by Land, 1815* (New York, 1938), p. 11.

47. William Willis to William Miller, Dec. 3, 1817, Barnes-Willis Family Papers, NTC.

48. Francis X. Martin to John Hamilton, Mar. 22, 1811, Howard-Tilton Library, Tulane University, New Orleans.

49. Louise G. Lynch, *Newspaper Excerpts 1822–1835, Williamson County, Tennessee* (n.p., 1985), pp. 27, 28; Thomas East, Account Book, 1839, Tennessee State Library and Archives, Nashville.

50. William Willis to———Barnes, June 16, 1817, Barnes-Willis Family Papers, NTC.

51. Willis to Barnes, June 16, 1817, ibid.; Natchez, *Mississippi Republican*, July 2, 1817.

52. Hudson, *Humor*, p. 59.

53. Wait, *Richardson*, p. 11.

54. Harriet C. Owsley, ed., "Travel Through the Indian Country in the Early 1800's: The Memoirs of Martha Philips Martin," *Tennessee Historical Quarterly* 21 (Mar. 1962), pp. 73–74.

55. Peter Joseph Hamilton, "Early Roads of Alabama," Thomas M. Owen, ed., *TAHS, 1897–1898* (Tuscaloosa, 1898), pp. 48–49.

56. Ibid., p. 50.

57. Henry DeLeon Southerland Jr., "The Federal Road, Gateway to Alabama, 1806–1836," *Alabama Review* 39 (Apr. 1986), p. 104.

58. "Lewis' Tavern at Fort Bainbridge," *AHQ* 17 (Spring–Summer 1955), p. 78.

59. "Principal Stage Stops and Taverns in What Is Now Alabama Prior to 1840," *AHQ* 17 (Spring–Summer 1955), pp. 80–86.

60. Jack D. Elliott Jr., "Leftwich's 'Cotton Gin Port and Gaines' Trace' Reconsidered," *JMH* 42 (Nov. 1980), pp. 356–58.

61. Yancey M. Quinn Jr., "Jackson's Military Road," *JMH* 41 (Nov. 1979), pp. 335–50.

62. Dawson Phelps, "The Robinson Road," *JMH* 12 (July 1950), pp. 155–61.

63. Leonard V. Huber, *Beginnings of Steamboat Mail on Lower Mississippi* (State College, Pa., 1960), p. 3.
64. James Thomas Flexner, *Steamboats Come True* (Boston, 1944), pp. 341–43.
65. Hudson, *Humor*, pp. 293–94.
66. William Kenner to Stephen Minor, Jan. 20, 1812, quoted in Huber, *Steamboat Mail*, pp. 3–7.
67. Natchez, *Mississippi Republican,* Dec. 14, 1814.
68. Ibid., Mar. 1, 1815.
69. McDermott, *Before Mark Twain*, p. 9.
70. Monette, "Progress," pp. 497–99; J. H. Scruggs Jr., comp., *Alabama Steamboats 1819–1869* (Birmingham, 1963), pp. 4ff.
71. McDermott, *Before Mark Twain*, pp. 11–12.
72. Jack N. Nelms, "Early Days with the Alabama River Steamboats," *Alabama Review* 37 (Jan. 1984), p. 16.
73. McDermott, *Before Mark Twain*, pp. 58–63.
74. Ibid., p. 43.
75. Receipt of C. B. Green, July 26, 1819; receipt of Judge Dutton, Oct. 14, 1832; receipt of John Dutton, Apr. 22, 1832; receipt of Turnbull, Oct. 9, 1830; receipt of William Davis, May 9, 1817; receipt of Hartwell and Vick, Apr. 26, 1823; receipt of Mr. Dutton, Dec. 26, 1830, Natchez Trace Steamboat Collection, NTC.
76. Receipt of Madam Girault, Mar. 21, 1822: receipt of Mr. Butler, June 12, 1826, Natchez Trace Steamboat Collection, NTC.
77. Natchez Steam Boat Company Stock Certificate Book, 1815–1820, Mississippi Department of Archives and History, Jackson.
78. Stock certificate, Nov. 10, 1818, NTC.
79. Compact, July 4, 1818, NTC.
80. Articles of Compact, n.d. (ca. 1820), NTC.
81. Wood, Pentecost & Co. Ledger, Sept. 28, Oct. 7, 10, Dec. 9, 1835, NTC.
82. Seymour Dunbar, *A History of Travel in America* (New York, 1937), vol. 3, p. 1051.
83. Eugene Alvarez, *Travel on Southern Antebellum Railroads, 1828–1860* (University, Ala., 1974), pp. 26–29.
84. Samuel Clark to John S. Russworm, Dec. 15, 1839, John S. Russworm Papers, Tennessee State Library and Archives.

Chapter 4 The Road to the Fields

1. Everett Dick, *The Dixie Frontier: A Social History* (New York, 1948), p. 61.
2. Moses Fisk to Timothy Green, Jan. 2, 1796, Moses Fisk Papers, Tennessee State Library and Archives.
3. Martin to Hamilton, Mar. 22, 1811, Tulane.
4. Dick, *Dixie Frontier*, p. 53.
5. James Hall, "A Brief History of the Mississippi Territory," *PMHS* 9 (1906), pp. 550–51.
6. Thomas D. Clark and John D. W. Guice, *Frontiers in Conflict: The Old Southwest, 1795–1830* (Albuquerque, N.Mex., 1989), p. 70.
7. Ibid., pp. 79–80.

8. Robert V. Haynes, "The Disposal of Lands in the Mississippi Territory," *JMH* 24 (Oct. 1962), pp. 226–27.

9. Haynes, "Disposal of Lands," pp. 230–33; Clark and Guice, *Frontiers in Conflict*, p. 78.

10. Edward Turner to Albert Gallatin, Sept. 2, 1803, Apr. 1, 1804, Edward Turner Letterbook 1803–1805, Rosamond E. and Emile Kuntz Collection, Tulane.

11. Gallatin to Turner, Jan. 25, 1804; Turner to Gallatin, Sept. 2, 1803, Jan. 7, 14, Apr. 6, 27, 1804, ibid.

12. Haynes, "Disposal of Lands," pp. 240–41.

13. H. S. Halbert, ed., "Diary of Richard Breckenridge, 1816," *TAHS, 1898–1899* (Tuscaloosa, 1899), p. 146.

14. Ibid., p. 151.

15. Hall, "Brief History," pp. 552–56.

16. Jack D. L. Holmes, "Livestock in Spanish Natchez," *JMH* 23 (Jan. 1961), pp. 15–17.

17. Clark and Guice, *Frontiers in Conflict*, p. 104.

18. Lynch, *Excerpts*, pp. 45ff; Clark and Guice, *Frontiers in Conflict*, pp. 107–8.

19. Richard A. Bartlett, *The New Country: A Social History of the American Frontier, 1776–1890* (New York, 1974), pp. 191–92.

20. Holmes, "Livestock," pp. 18–20.

21. Ibid., pp. 27–29.

22. Marschalk to Levin Wailes, Dec. 19, 1822, Levin Wailes Papers, NTC.

23. Claiborne, *Mississippi*, p. 140; James H. McLendon, "The Development of Mississippi Agriculture," *JMH* 13 (Apr. 1951), pp. 76–77; John H. Moore, "Mississippi's Search for a Staple Crop," *JMH* 29 (Nov. 1967), pp. 376–77.

24. McLendon, "Mississippi Agriculture," pp. 77–78; Claiborne, *Mississippi*, p. 140.

25. Willis G. Clark, *History of Education in Alabama, 1702–1889* (Washington, D.C., 1889), p. 33.

26. Moore, "Staple Crop," p. 379.

27. Claiborne, *Mississippi*, p. 143.

28. Ibid., p. 143.

29. Moore, "Staple Crop," p. 379; McLendon, "Mississippi Agriculture," pp. 78–79.

30. Stephen Bullock to William McKee, Feb. 15, 1811, Stephen Bullock Papers, NTC.

31. Claiborne, *Mississippi*, p. 143.

32. Hall, "Brief History," p. 562.

33. Receipt of B. D. Hosed, Nov. 8, 1819, Amos Alexander Papers: Ledger of Willis & Barnes, May 1828, Barnes-Willis Family Papers, NTC.

34. Claiborne, *Mississippi*, p. 144.

35. Receipt of E. Montgomery, Jan. 26, 1819, Alexander Papers; receipt of W. R. Bay, Dec. 11, 1824, Natchez Trace Steamboat Collection, NTC; ledger of Willis and Barnes, May 1828, Barnes-Willis Family Papers, NTC; John F. Morrison, *A Brief History of Early Lawrence County, Tennessee* (Lawrenceburg, Tenn., 1968), p. 8.

36. Claiborne, *Mississippi*, p. 141n.

37. McLendon, "Mississippi Agriculture," p. 80.
38. Ibid., pp. 141–42.
39. Ibid., pp. 80–81.
40. Hall, "Brief History," pp. 554–55.
41. Moore, "Staple Crop," p. 385.
42. Hall, "Brief History," p. 555.
43. C. H. Dencker to M. White, Dec. 24, 1822, Charles H. Dencker Letter Book, 1818–1825, NTC.
44. James, *Antebellum Natchez*, pp. 136–38.
45. Ibid., p. 45.
46. Claiborne, *Mississippi*, pp. 144–45.
47. James, *Antebellum Natchez*, pp. 45–46; Claiborne, *Mississippi*, p. 145n.
48. James, *Antebellum Natchez*, pp. 196–97.
49. Isabell Howell, "John Armfield, Slave-Trader," *Tennessee Historical Quarterly* 2 (Mar. 1943), pp. 10–11.
50. Samuel Coborn to A. Barnes, June 25, 1828, Barnes-Willis Family Papers, NTC.
51. *Niles' Weekly Register*, Apr. 12, 1828.
52. James, *Antebellum Natchez*, p. 197.
53. Alfred H. Stone, "The Early Slave Laws of Mississippi," *PMHS* 2 (1899), pp. 134–35.
54. Robert G. Sherer, *Subordination or Liberation? The Development and Conflicting Theories of Black Education in Nineteenth Century Alabama* (University, Ala., 1977), p. 1.
55. Stone, "Slave Laws," pp. 136–41.
56. Ibid., pp. 143–44.
57. Receipt of Robert R. Ray, Oct. 13, 1819, Alexander Papers; receipt of Samuel Chamberline, 1835, Henry Tennent Papers, NTC.
58. Note, n.d. [1817], John Buell Papers, NTC.
59. Ray Holder, ed., "On Slavery: Selected Letters of Parson Winans, 1820–1844," *JMH* 46 (Nov. 1984), pp. 324–27.
60. Terry L. Alford, "Some Manumissions Recorded in the Adams County Deed Books in Chancery Clerk's Office, Natchez, Mississippi, 1795–1835," *JMH* 33 (Feb. 1971), pp. 39ff.

Chapter 5 The Road Home

1. Clark and Guice, *Frontiers in Conflict*, pp. 172–74.
2. "Autobiography of Gideon Lincecum," *PMHS* 8 (1904), pp. 451–54.
3. Ibid., pp. 455–68 passim.
4. Ibid., pp. 469–71.
5. Dick, *Dixie Frontier*, p. 25.
6. Clark and Guice, *Frontiers in Conflict*, pp. 178–79.
7. James A. Shackford, *David Crockett, The Man and the Legend* (Chapel Hill, N.C., 1956), p. 36.
8. David Crockett Memorandum, Jan. 1, 1817, Mississippi Department of Archives and History, Jackson.

9. David Crockett, *A Narrative of the Life of David Crockett of the State of Tennessee* (reprint, Knoxville, 1973), pp. 132, 133.
10. Ibid., pp. 144–45 and n.
11. Dick, *Dixie Frontier*, pp. 27–28.
12. John Q. Anderson, "The Narrative of John Hutchins," *JMH* 20 (Jan. 1958), p. 3.
13. Dick, *Dixie Frontier*, pp. 27–28.
14. Anderson, "Narrative," p. 4.
15. Receipt of Hugh Watson, August 14, 1819, Alexander Papers, NTC.
16. McDermott, *Before Mark Twain*, pp. 100–101.
17. Mary M. McBee, comp., *The Natchez Court Records, 1767–1805: Abstracts of Early Records* (Ann Arbor, Mich., 1953), p. 4.
18. Receipt of Miller Brown, Mar. 24, 1821, Alexander Papers, NTC.
19. Beard, *Prices and Credit*, p. 12.
20. Emery Wilson Cash Book, n.d., NTC.
21. Ibid., p. 7.
22. Ibid.; Stirling and Gillaspie Blacksmith Record, 1821, NTC.
23. Fuller and Sylvester Day Book, Dec. 26, 1817, Feb. 7, 1818, Benjamin Fuller and Joseph Sylvester Papers, NTC.
24. Ibid., Mar. 31, May 26, July 10, 13, 1818; Adams County, Miss., Drug Store Ledger, pp. 107, 186, 179, NTC.
25. Fuller and Sylvester Day Book, Feb. 28, Apr. 2, 1818.
26. Wilson Cash Book, NTC.
27. Adams County Drug Store Ledger, p. 114, NTC.
28. Virginia K. Jones, ed., "The Bowie Letters, 1819 and 1821," *AHQ* 22 (Winter 1960), pp. 235–36, 237, 239.
29. Alma Carpenter, "A Note on the History of the Forest Plantation, Natchez," *JMH* 46 (May 1984), pp. 130ff.
30. Arthur H. DeRosier Jr., "Carpenter's Estimate on the Building of 'The Forest,'" *JMH* 27 (Aug. 1965), pp. 261–64; Carpenter, "A Note," pp. 135–36.
31. Carpenter, "A Note," p. 135.
32. Marius M. Carriere Jr., "Mount Locust Plantation: The Development of Southwest Mississippi during the Frontier Period, 1810–1830," *JMH* 48 (Aug. 1986), pp. 187ff; Eastern National Park & Monument Association, *Mount Locust on the Old Natchez Trace* (n.p., n.d.), pp. 1ff.
33. McBee, *Natchez Court Records*, p. 4.
34. Jones, "Bowie Letters," p. 236.
35. Stirling and Gillaspie Blacksmith Record, accounts of John Oden, William Harper, Mr. Felps, and Mince & Bennet, Cooks & Gilbert, Samuel Ferguson, John Hardin, John Davis, 1821, NTC.
36. Mack Swearingen, "Luxury at Natchez in 1801: A Ship's Manifest from the McDonough Papers," *Journal of Southern History* 3 (May 1937), pp. 188–89.
37. Joe Gray Taylor, *Eating, Drinking and Visiting in the South* (Baton Rouge, La., 1982), pp. 4–11.
38. Grady McWhiney, *Cracker Culture: Celtic Ways in the Old South* (Tuscaloosa, Ala., 1988), pp. 74–75.

39. J. F. C. Claiborne, "Trip Through the Piney Woods," *PMHS* 9 (1906), pp. 533–35.
40. Taylor, *Eating*, pp. 11–12.
41. Jones, "Bowie Letters," p. 236.
42. Receipt of A. De France, Oct. 13, 1819, Alexander Papers, NTC.
43. McWhiney, *Cracker Culture*, pp. 80–82.
44. Taylor, *Eating*, p. 12.
45. Mississippi Historical Records Survey, *Adams County (Natchez), I: Minutes of the Court of General Quarter Sessions of the Peace, 1799–1800* (Jackson, 1942), item 20; receipt of Josiah Steen, Sept. 1, 1819, Alexander Papers, NTC.
46. Receipt of J. Robtiele, June 21, 1819, Alexander Papers: James Archer to Abram Barnes, Oct. 24, 1812, Barnes-Willis Family Papers, NTC.
47. Beard, *Prices and Credit,* pp. 12, 13; receipt of James Barthe, Mar. 20, 1819, Alexander Papers, NTC.
48. Receipt of A. De France, Oct. 13, 1819; receipt of A. Hull, Feb. 5, 1820, Alexander Papers, NTC.
49. Receipt of James Shaw, Feb. 5, 1820, ibid.
50. Receipt of Israel Leonard, Oct. 9, 18———, ibid.
51. Owsley, "Martha Philips Martin," p. 77.
52. "Autobiography of Gideon Lincecum," pp. 457, 476–78.
53. Claiborne, "Trip Through the Piney Woods," p. 534.
54. Thomas Crawford to H. Tennent, Aug. 1, 1835, Henry Tennent Papers, NTC; Rhoda Coleman Ellison, ed., "A Pioneer Alabama Doctor's Ledger," *AHQ* 43 (Winter 1981), p. 316.
55. Adams County Drug Store Ledger, pp. 5, 7, 50, NTC.
56. Beard, *Prices and Credit,* p. 29; Adams County Drug Store Ledger, pp. 154, 175.
57. Ellison, "Doctor's Ledger," pp. 316–17; Ben Smith to Barnes, June 19, 1825, Barnes-Willis Family Papers, NTC.
58. Adams County Drug Store Ledger, pp. 5, 7, 50, 162, 164, 173, 175; Beard, *Prices and Credit,* p. 30.
59. Ibid., pp. 2, 37, 65, 69, 70, 89, 91, 112, 116, 119, 145, 171, 173, 175; account of Dr. Willis, 1820, NTC.
60. Adams County Drug Store Ledger, p. 153; receipt of William Dixon, 1836, Tennent Papers, NTC.
61. James Smylie to A. Barnes, June 14, 1814, Barnes-Willis Papers, NTC.

Chapter 6 The Road to Community

1. Alexis de Tocqueville, *Democracy in America* (reprint, New York, 1969), vol. 2, p. 536.
2. Charles D. Lowery, "The Great Migration to the Mississippi Territory, 1798–1819," *JMH* 30 (Aug. 1968), pp. 177–78.
3. Ibid., pp. 179–80.
4. Ibid., pp. 182–84.
5. Samuel Clark to Virginia Sawyers, Jan. 29, 1836, Russworm Papers.

6. Michael F. Beard, "Natchez Under-the-Hill: Reform and Retribution in Early Natchez," *Gulf Coast Historical Review* 4 (Fall 1988), p. 30.

7. Henry Smith, *Virgin Land* (New York, 1950), pp. 251–52.

8. Beard, "Natchez Under-the-Hill," p. 29.

9. James F. Doster, "Early Settlements on the Tombigbee and Tensaw Rivers," *Alabama Review* 12 (Apr. 1959), pp. 85–88.

10. Ibid., p. 88.

11. Stephen B. Weeks, *History of Public School Education in Alabama* (Washington, D.C., 1915), pp. 11–12.

12. Chriss H. Doss, "Early Settlement of Bearmeat Cabin Frontier," *Alabama Review* 22 (Oct. 1969), pp. 271ff.

13. Stuart Seely Sprague, "Alabama Town Production During the Era of Good Feelings," *AHQ* 36 (Spring 1974), pp. 15ff.

14. Riley, "Extinct Towns," pp. 313, 336ff.

15. Jesse M. Wilkins, "Early Times in Wayne County," *PMHS* 6 (1902), pp. 268–69.

16. Dick, *Dixie Frontier,* p. 150.

17. Owen Roberts, "Richard Thomson: Was He the First English-Speaking Settler in the Natchez District?" *JMH* 39 (Feb. 1977), pp. 64–69.

18. Jack D. L. Holmes, "Anne White Hutchins—Anthony's Better Half?" *JMH* 37 (May 1975), pp. 203–6.

19. Arthur H. DeRosier Jr., "Natchez and the Formative Years of William Dunbar," *JMH* 34 (Feb. 1972), pp. 30ff.

20. "A Genuine Account of the Present State of the River Mississippi," *PMHS* 9 (1906), p. 330.

21. Baily, *Journal,* pp. 279, 283.

22. Ibid., pp. 284–86.

23. Natchez, Mississippi, *Herald and Natchez City Gazette,* Oct. 31, 1803.

24. Turner to Albert Gallatin, Feb. 3, 1804, Turner Letter Book, Kuntz Collection.

25. Christian Schultz, *Travels on an Inland Voyage* (New York, 1810), vol. 1, pp. 142–44, 143, 146.

26. Fortescue Cuming, "Sketches of a Tour to the Western Country," in Reuben G. Thwaites, ed., *Early Western Travels* (Cleveland, Ohio, 1904), vol. 4, pp. 320ff.

27. Jedediah Morse, *The American Gazetteer* (Boston, 1810), n.p.

28. Daniel C. Vogt, "Poor Relief in Frontier Mississippi, 1798–1832," *JMH* 51 (Aug. 1989), pp. 184–88.

29. James, *Antebellum Natchez,* pp. 81–88.

30. Brown, *Western Gazetteer,* p. 231; Thomas Nuttall, "Journal of Travels into the Arkansas Territory During the Year 1819," Thwaites, *Early Western Travels* (Cleveland, Ohio, 1905), vol. 13, p. 302.

31. Natchez, *Mississippi Republican,* Mar. 5, 1818; agreement with Peter Lemons, Jan. 23, 1810, Bullock Papers, NTC.

32. Jedediah Morse, *The Traveller's Guide, or Pocket Gazetteer of the United States* (New Haven, Conn., 1820), p. 133.

33. R. W. Jones, "Some Facts Concerning the Settlement and Early History of Mississippi," *PMHS* 1 (1898), p. 86.

34. Brown, *Western Gazetteer,* pp. 233–37.
35. "Gaines' Reminiscences," *AHQ* 26 (Fall–Winter 1964), pp. 185–86.
36. Beard, *Prices and Credit,* p. 40.
37. Guy B. Braden, "A Jeffersonian Village: Washington, Mississippi," *JMH* 30 (May 1968), pp. 135ff.
38. Susanna Smith, "Washington, Mississippi: Antebellum Elysium," *JMH* 40 (May 1978), pp. 143ff.
39. Percy L. Rainwater, ed., "The Memorial of John Perkins," *Louisiana Historical Quarterly* 20 (Oct. 1937), p. 973.
40. Anderson, "Narrative," p. 5.
41. Cuming, "Tour," p. 319.
42. Beard, *Prices and Credit,* p. 34.
43. Receipt of S. Hopkins, Apr. 1812, Burnet Papers, NTC.
44. Thomas Barnes to Abram Barnes, Feb. 25, 1813, Barnes-Willis Family Papers, NTC.
45. Natchez, Mississippi, *Herald and Natchez City Gazette,* Feb. 1, 1805.
46. "Diary of a Journey," p. 178.
47. Beard, *Prices and Credit,* p. 39.
48. Account with George Selser, 1805–1806, Bullock Papers; William B. Smith Account, Dec. 21, 1810, NTC.
49. Walter B. Posey, "The Public Manners of Ante-Bellum Southerners," *JMH* 19 (Oct. 1957), pp. 219ff.
50. Rainwater, "Perkins," p. 973.
51. Hall, "Brief History," p. 558.
52. Hudson, *Humor,* pp. 468–69.
53. Bedford, "Tour," pp. 116–18.
54. Rainwater, "Perkins," p. 973.
55. Natchez, *Mississippi Republican,* Oct. 27, 1813.
56. "Diary of a Journey," pp. 179–80.
57. Natchez, *Mississippi Republican,* Dec. 15, 1813.
58. Joseph A. Jackson, *Masonry in Alabama: A Sesquicentennial History, 1821–1971* (Montgomery, 1970), pp. 12, 169–70.
59. Ibid., p. 37.
60. James, *Antebellum Natchez,* p. 256.
61. Laura D. S. Harrell, "Horse Racing in the Old Natchez District, 1783–1830," *JMH* 13 (July 1951), pp. 123–24.
62. Laura D. S. Harrell, "Jockey Clubs and Race Tracks in Antebellum Mississippi, 1795–1861," *JMH* 28 (Nov. 1966), p. 304; Natchez, *Mississippi Messenger,* Oct. 22, 1807.
63. Harrell, "Horse Racing," pp. 126, 129.
64. Harrell, "Jockey Clubs," pp. 313–15.
65. Harrell, "Horse Racing," pp. 130–31.
66. Ibid., pp. 134–37.
67. "Autobiography of Gideon Lincecum," pp. 483–85.
68. Beard, *Prices and Credit,* p. 39.
69. James, *Antebellum Natchez,* p. 258.
70. Dick, *Dixie Frontier,* p. 160.
71. Ibid., pp. 142–47.

72. Bayou Sara, La., *Record,* 1819, NTC.
73. Benjamin Smith to Abram Barnes, Oct. 5, 1816, Barnes-Willis Family Papers, NTC.
74. Greenville, Miss., Store Ledger, 1824, NTC.
75. Ibid.; Clark and Wren Mercantile Business Ledger, 1830: Natchez, Miss., Store Ledger, 1824–1825, NTC.
76. Various receipts, May 24, 1819, Aug. 14, 1819, Jan. 25, 1820, Mar. 9, 1823, Alexander Papers; receipt of E. Williams, Feb. 5, 1816, Burling Family Papers, NTC.
77. Various receipts, May 28, 1819, July 1, 1819, July 3, 1819, Sept. 28, 1819, May 12, 1820, Alexander Papers, NTC.
78. Receipt of Mr. Lee, Nov. 9, 1809, F. Allden Papers; receipt of William Shipp, Aug. 4, 1819, Alexander Papers; receipt of Francis Allden, June 2, 1811, Bullock Papers; Charles H. Dencker Letter Book, 1825; Greenville, Miss., Store Ledger, Dec. 22–24, 1825, NTC; Beard, *Prices and Credit,* p. 31.
79. Receipt of F. Borland, Feb. 2, 1827, Minor Family Papers; account with Burbridge & Smith, 1816, Bullock Papers; Clark and Wren Mercantile Business Ledger, pp. 63ff, NTC.
80. Greenville, Miss., Store Ledger, Dec. 24, 1825; receipt of Francis Allden, June 2, 1811, Bullock Papers; statement of stock on hand, Aug. 1830, Clark and Wren Mercantile Business Ledger, NTC.
81. Weeks, *Education,* p. 14.
82. Anderson, "Narrative," p. 4.
83. Charles H. Dencker to George Gunther, Jan. 20, 1820; Dencker to M. White, Sept. 4, 1824, Dencker Letter Book, NTC.
84. Shop account, 1820, Stirling and Gillaspie Papers, NTC.
85. Mary J. Welsh, "Recollections of Pioneer Life in Mississippi," *PMHS* 4 (1901), p. 349.
86. Natchez, *Mississippi Republican,* Nov. 3, 1812, July 2, 1817.
87. James F. McCaleb, "Easter on the Natchez Trace," Port Gibson, *Reveille,* Mar. 21, 1940.
88. Julian Lee Rayford, *Chasin' the Devil Round a Stump* (Mobile, Ala., 1962), pp. 21, 25, 26.
89. Ibid., pp. 33ff.
90. Lynch, *Excerpts,* pp. 22–23.
91. James, *Antebellum Natchez,* pp. 114–15.
92. "A Diary of a Journey," pp. 184, 185.

Chapter 7 The Road to God

1. McDermott, *Before Mark Twain,* p. 191.
2. Natchez, *Ariel,* May 3, 1828.
3. Hall, "Brief History," p. 557.
4. Doster, "Early Settlements," p. 85.
5. Frances A. Cabaniss and James A. Cabaniss, "Religion in Ante-Bellum Mississippi," *JMH* 6 (Oct. 1944), pp. 191–92.
6. Percy L. Rainwater, "Conquistadores, Missionaries, and Missions," *JMH* 27 (May 1965), p. 124.

7. Joseph M. Pellerin to his cousin, 1719, Tulane.
8. Marriage certificate of Henry D'Orgon and Marie Deverges, Apr. 26, 1753; baptismal certificate of Henriette Marie D'Orgon, Dec. 17, 1768, Kuntz Collection, Tulane.
9. Jack D. L. Holmes, "Irish Priests in Spanish Natchez," *JMH* 29 (Aug. 1967), pp. 169ff.
10. Ibid., p. 180.
11. Cuming, "Sketches of a Tour," p. 322; Cabaniss and Cabaniss, "Religion," p. 193.
12. Frances Preston Mills, "Amos Ogden of the Ogden's Mandamus, Late Captain of the Rangers," *JMH* 41 (May 1979), p. 183.
13. Rainwater, "Conquistadores," p. 129
14. Z. T. Leavell, "Early Beginnings of Baptists in Mississippi," *PMHS* 4 (1901), pp. 245–46.
15. Leavell, "Early Beginnings," pp. 248–50; Rainwater, "Conquistadores," p. 130.
16. Leavell, "Early Beginnings," p. 252; Cabaniss and Cabaniss, "Religion," p. 194; Rainwater, "Conquistadores," p. 131.
17. Albert James Pickett, *History of Alabama and Incidentally of Georgia and Mississippi from the Earliest Period* (N.p., 1851), p. 473.
18. Natchez, *Mississippi Republican,* Oct. 27, 1818.
19. Hugh C. Bailey, "Alabama's First Baptist Association," *Alabama Review* 14 (Jan. 1961), pp. 31ff.
20. Rainwater, "Conquistadores," pp. 131–32; Cabaniss and Cabaniss, "Religion," p. 195.
21. Rainwater, "Conquistadores," pp. 135–36.
22. Ibid., pp. 137–39.
23. *North American Review* 1 (1815), p. 68.
24. Charles B. Galloway, "Thomas Griffin—A Boanerges of the Early Southwest," *PMHS* 7 (1903), pp. 155–58.
25. T. L. Haman, "Beginnings of Presbyterianism in Mississippi," *PMHS* 10 (1909), pp. 207–11.
26. Ibid., pp. 212–14; Rainwater, "Conquistadores," pp. 141–42.
27. Rainwater, "Conquistadores," pp. 143–45.
28. Natchez, *Mississippi Republican,* May 28, 1817.
29. Rainwater, "Conquistadores," p. 146.
30. S. H. Hodge to J. W. Baldridge, Sept. 1834, Tennessee State Library and Archives.
31. James H. B. Hall, "The History of the Cumberland Presbyterian Church in Alabama Prior to 1826," *TAHS, 1899–1903* (1904), pp. 365ff.
32. Ibid., pp. 382–83.
33. Cabaniss and Cabaniss, "Religion," p. 197.
34. McWhiney, *Cracker Culture,* pp. 186–88.
35. Cabaniss and Cabaniss, "Religion," p. 197.
36. McDermott, *Before Mark Twain,* pp. 191–95.
37. Paul Cunningham to his brother, Mar. 3, 1796, Tennessee State Library and Archives.

38. *General History of the Baptist Church,* Historical Records Survey, IV-L-2, Box 1, Tennessee State Library and Archives.
39. Hall, "Cumberland Presbyterian Church," p. 387.
40. Robert M. McBride, "A Camp Meeting at Goshen Creek," *Tennessee Historical Quarterly* 22 (June 1963), pp. 137–41.
41. "Reports on Revivals and the State of Religion in Christian Countries," Society of Inquiry and Missions, Tennessee State Library and Archives.
42. Hall, "Cumberland Presbyterian Church," p. 387.
43. *General History of the Baptist Church,* pp. 27–33.
44. Lucille Griffith, "Anne Royall in Alabama," *Alabama Review* 21 (Jan. 1968), p. 63.
45. Walter B. Posey, "The Earthquake of 1811 and its Influence on Evangelistic Methods in the Churches of the Old South," *Tennessee Historical Magazine,* series 2: 1 (Jan. 1931), pp. 109–11.
46. Pickett, *Alabama,* pp. 464–65.
47. Lynch, *Excerpts,* pp. 64ff.
48. Claiborne, "Trip Through the Piney Woods," pp. 535–37.
49. Hudson, *Humor,* pp. 469–70.
50. Natchez, *Intelligencer,* Oct. 6, 1801.
51. Natchez, Mississippi, *Herald and Natchez City Gazette,* May 23, 1804.
52. John and Sarah Burns Divorce, Dec. 19, 1806, NTC.
53. Natchez, *Mississippi Republican,* Oct. 27, 1813.
54. Cabaniss and Cabaniss, "Religion," pp. 212–16.
55. Ibid., pp. 219–20.
56. Moses Fisk to John Fisk, Nov. 14, 1812, Fisk Papers.
57. Ray Holder, "Parson Winans' Pilgrimage to 'The Natchez,' Winter of 1810," *JMH* 44 (Feb. 1982), pp. 65–66 and n.
58. Griffith, "Royall," p. 62.
59. Benjamin Chase to Levin Wailes, Apr. 9, 1832, Levin Wailes Papers, NTC.
60. Holder, "Winans," pp. 47–49.
61. Ibid., pp. 58–61.
62. Ibid., pp. 63–66.
63. John R. Williams, ed., "Frontier Evangelist: The Journal of Henry Bryson," *Alabama Historical Quarterly* 412 (Spring–Summer 1980), p. 17.
64. Ibid., pp. 22ff.
65. Dawson A. Phelps, "Excerpts from the Journal of the Reverend Joseph Bullen, 1799 and 1800," *JMH* 17 (Oct. 1955), p. 258.
66. Ibid.
67. Ibid., pp. 271ff.
68. John H. Evans, "Location and Description of the Emmaus Mission," *PMHS* 6 (1902), pp. 411–13.
69. James, *Antebellum Natchez,* p. 246.
70. Charles B. Galloway, "Lorenzo Dow in Mississippi," *PMHS* 4 (1901), pp. 235–39.
71. Lorenzo Dow, *The Dealings of God, Man, and the Devil, As Exemplified in the Life, Experiences, and Travels of . . .* (Norwich, Conn., 1833), pp. 183–84.
72. Galloway, "Dow," p. 241.

73. Ibid., p. 184.
74. Holder, "Winans," p. 65n.
75. Lorenzo Dow, *Vicissitudes in the Wilderness; Exemplified in the Journal of Peggy Dow* (Norwich, Conn., 1833), pp. 43ff.
76. Holder, "Winans," p. 65.
77. Ibid., pp. 64–65 and n.

Chapter 8 The Road to Knowledge

1. Crockett, *Narrative,* p. 49.
2. Alfred B. Butts, "Public Administration in Mississippi," Dunbar Rowland, ed., *PMHS*, centenary series, 3 (1919), p. 21.
3. Hall, "Brief History," p. 557.
4. Galloway, "Griffin," p. 161.
5. James, *Antebellum Natchez,* p. 217.
6. Butts, "Administration," p. 21.
7. Doster, "Early Settlements," p. 85.
8. Dick, *Dixie Frontier,* p. 180.
9. *Washington Republican and Natchez Intelligencer,* Apr. 9, 1817.
10. "Autobiography of Gideon Lincecum," pp. 455–56.
11. Ibid., pp. 459–64.
12. "The Autobiography of James H. Maury," *JMH* 5 (Apr. 1943), p. 94.
13. Dick, *Dixie Frontier,* p. 171.
14. Ibid., p. 172.·
15. Welsh, "Recollections," pp. 352–53.
16. Dick, *Dixie Frontier,* p. 173.
17. J. Pierpont, *Introduction to the National Reader: A Selection of Easy Lessons* (Boston, 1828), pp. iii–vii.
18. For instance, Roswell C. Smith, *A Key to the "Practical and Mental Arithmetic" for the Use of Teachers* (Hartford, Conn., 1836).
19. Welsh, "Recollections," p. 353; Dick, *Dixie Frontier,* p. 175.
20. Dick, *Dixie Frontier,* pp. 176–77.
21. James, *Antebellum Natchez,* pp. 219–20.
22. Natchez, *Mississippi Republican,* Aug. 13, 20, 1817; receipt of Dr. Samuel Caswell, June 10, 1820, Alexander Papers; James Hosmer to Barnes, Oct. 1, 1818, Barnes-Willis Family Papers, NTC.
23. Natchez, *Mississippi Republican,* Sept. 24, 1817.
24. Hosmer to Barnes, Oct. 1, 1818, Barnes-Willis Family Papers, NTC.
25. Margaret Des Champs Moore, "Early Schools and Churches in Natchez," *JMH* 24 (Oct. 1962), pp. 253–55.
26. Harris G. Warren, "Vignettes of Culture in Old Claiborne," *JMH* 20 (July 1958), pp. 129–31.
27. I. M. E. Blandin, *History of Higher Education of Women in the South Prior to 1860* (New York, 1909), pp. 185, 186.
28. William B. Turner, *History of Maury County, Tennessee* (Nashville, 1955), pp. 64, 128.
29. Virginia M. Bowman, *Historic Williamson County* (Nashville, 1971), p. 3.
30. Rainwater, "Maury," pp. 94–95.

31. Lynch, *Excerpts,* p. 34.
32. Weeks, *Education,* p. 24.
33. James Smylie to Barnes, May 17, 1815, Barnes-Willis Family Papers, NTC.
34. Beard, *Prices and Credit* p. 36.
35. Receipt of J. B. Florian, Mar. 15, 1811, Minor Family Papers, NTC.
36. Lynch, *Excerpts,* p. 34.
37. Weeks, *Education,* pp. 17–19.
38. Clark and Guion, *Frontiers in Conflict,* pp. 229–30.
39. Clark, *Education,* p. 31.
40. Weeks, *Education,* p. 48.
41. Ibid.
42. Lee C. Cain, "Founding Public Schools in Alabama—A County Led the Way," *AHQ* 38 (Winter 1976), pp. 244–46; Weeks, *Education,* pp. 26–27.
43. Butts, "Public Administration," pp. 23–24.
44. Richard A. McLemore, "The Roots of Higher Education in Mississippi," *JMH* 26 (Aug. 1964), pp. 208–9.
45. J. K. Morrison, "Early History of Jefferson College," *PMHS* 2 (1899), pp. 179–82.
46. Dawn Maddox, "The Buildings and Grounds of Jefferson College in the Nineteenth Century," *JMH* 35 (Feb. 1973), p. 39.
47. Charles Norton to David Holmes, Aug. 11, 1811, Benjamin C. Wailes Papers, NTC.
48. Maddox, "Buildings," p. 40.
49. Beard, *Prices and Credit,* p. 36.
50. Natchez, *Mississippi Republican,* Apr. 28, 1813.
51. Morrison, "Jefferson College," p. 185.
52. Natchez, *Mississippi Republican,* Aug. 13, 1817.
53. Maddox, "Buildings," pp. 40–41.
54. Nuttall, "Journal," p. 302.
55. Morrison, "Jefferson College," pp. 185–87; Ray O. Hummel Jr., *Southeastern Broadsides Before 1877* (Richmond, Va., 1971), pp. 104, 105.
56. McLemore, "Roots," p. 211.
57. William Willeford, *Mississippi & Louisiana Almanac, 1827* (Natchez, 1827), p. 18 (italics in original).
58. Morrison, "Jefferson College," pp. 187–88.
59. Smith, "Washington," p. 163; Maddox, "Buildings," p. 42.
60. Stephen Duncan to Benjamin Wailes, Oct. 2, 1832; John F. H. Claiborne to Wailes, July 21, 1833, Benjamin F. Wailes Papers, NTC.
61. Percy L. Rainwater, *A Pioneer College for Girls in the Old Southwest,* Percy L. Rainwater Collection, Mississippi Department of Archives and History, Jackson.
62. Charles B. Galloway, "Elizabeth Female Academy—The Mother of Female Colleges," *PMHS* 2 (1899), pp. 170–71.
63. Rainwater, *Pioneer College.*
64. James, *Antebellum Natchez,* p. 226.
65. Galloway, "Elizabeth Female Academy," pp. 172–76.
66. Ibid., pp. 176–78; Rainwater, *Pioneer College.*
67. Blandin, *Higher Education,* pp. 63–64.

68. Weeks, *Education,* p. 19.
69. Richard W. Griffin, "Athens Academy and College: An Experiment in Women's Education in Alabama, 1822–1873," *AHQ* 20 (Spring 1958), pp. 7–9.
70. Ralph M. Lyon, "The Early Years of Livingston Female Academy," *AHQ* 37 (Fall 1975), p. 193.
71. Weeks, *Education,* p. 24.
72. Clark, *Education,* pp. 32, 36.
73. W. H. Weathersby, "A History of Mississippi College," *PMHS,* centenary series, 5 (1925), pp. 184–85; McLemore, "Higher Education," pp. 211–12.
74. Blandin, *Education,* p. 187.
75. Tommy Wayne Rogers, "Oakland College, 1830–1871," *JMH* 36 (May 1974), pp. 143–45.
76. Clark, *Education,* p. 164.
77. Butts, "Public Administration," pp. 26, 126–27.
78. Harris Gaylord Warren, "Vignettes of Culture in Old Claiborne," *JMH* 20 (July 1958), p. 134.
79. Moore, "Early Schools," p. 255.

Chapter 9 The Road to Enlightenment

1. Moses Fisk to John Fisk, Nov. 12, 1812, Fisk Papers, Tennessee State Library and Archives.
2. Butler, Hagen, and Truett, *Natchez Trace,* p. 263.
3. Habersham to John Steele, Mar. 26, 1801; Habersham to Thomas Hutchens, May 15, 1801; Habersham to William Stothart, May 27, 1801, Letterbook K, Record Group 28, National Archives.
4. Granger to W. C. C. Claiborne, Feb. 15, 1803; Granger to Postmaster at Nashville, Sept. 27, 1803; Granger to Joslin, Sept. 20, 1803, Letterbook M, Record Group 28, National Archives.
5. Granger to Postmaster at Nashville, Nov. 6, 1804; Granger to Joseph Ficklin, July 31, 1805, Letterbook N, Record Group 28, National Archives.
6. Circular, Nov. 7, 1803, Letterbook M; Granger to Samuel Winston, Jan. 31, 1809, Letterbook P, Record Group 28, National Archives; Beard, *Prices and Credit,* p. 39.
7. R. M. Meigs to Robert Curry, Apr. 21, 1815, Letterbook T; Meigs to M. Stokes, Jan. 14, 1819, Letterbook X, Record Group 28, National Archives.
8. Dencker to George Gunther, May 8, 1820, Dencker Letter Book, NTC.
9. Granger to Edward Livingston, Nov. 5, 1804, Letterbook N, Record Group 28, National Archives.
10. Madel J. Morgan, "Andrew Marschalk's Account of Mississippi's First Press," *JMH* 8 (Apr. 1946), p. 147.
11. Natchez, *Mississippi Gazette,* Sept. [Nov.] 10, Dec. 1, 1801.
12. Ibid., p. 148; Noel Polk, ed., *Natchez Before 1830* (Jackson, 1989), p. 126.
13. Natchez, *Intelligencer,* Oct. 6, 1801.
14. Morgan, "Marschalk's Account," p. 148.
15. Natchez, *Constitutional Conservator,* Apr. 16, 1803.
16. Natchez, *Mississippi Republican,* Apr. 9, Sept. 24, 1818.

17. F. Wilbur Helmbold, "Early Alabama Newspapermen, 1810–1820," *Alabama Review* 12 (Jan. 1959), pp. 53–54.
18. Benjamin B. Williams, *A Literary History of Alabama: The Nineteenth Century* (Cranbury, N.J., 1979), pp. 13–14; Daniel Savage Gray, "Frontier Journalism: Newspapers in Antebellum Alabama," *AHQ* 36 (Fall 1975), p. 183.
19. Gray, "Frontier Journalism," p. 184.
20. Ibid., pp. 185–86; Helmbold, "Alabama Newspapermen," pp. 56–57.
21. Gray, "Frontier Journalism," pp. 186–87.
22. Helmbold, "Alabama Newspapermen," pp. 67–68.
23. Gray, "Frontier Journalism," pp. 188–89.
24. James, *Antebellum Natchez,* p. 230.
25. *Historical Sketch of Maury County* (Columbia, Tenn., 1876), p. 63.
26. Edwin A. Miles, "The Mississippi Press in the Jackson Era, 1824–1841," *JMH* 19 (Jan. 1957), pp. 1–2.
27. Gray, "Frontier Journalism," p. 189.
28. Helmbold, "Alabama Newspapermen," p. 63.
29. Receipt of William Hunt, 1824, Barnes-Willis Family Papers; receipt of Thomas Ritchie, May 18, 1813, Bullock Papers, NTC.
30. Laura D. S. Harrell, "The Development of the Lyceum Movement in Mississippi Prior to 1860," *JMH* 31 (Aug. 1969), pp. 187–88.
31. Natchez, *Mississippi Republican,* May 28, 1817, Oct. 13, 1818; McBee, *Natchez Court Records,* p. 4; James, *Antebellum Natchez,* pp. 233–34; Turner to Gallatin, Mar. 1, 1804, Turner Papers, Kuntz Collection; Greenville, Miss., Store Ledger, Jan. 3, 18———, NTC.
32. Williams, *Literary History,* pp. 58, 120–21, 142, 167.
33. James, *Antebellum Natchez,* pp. 233–34.
34. Riley, "Dunbar," p. 10 and n.; Harrell, "Lyceum," p. 189; Natchez, Mississippi, *Herald and Natchez City Gazette,* Oct. 19, 1804; James, *Antebellum Natchez,* p. 232.
35. Natchez, Mississippi, *Herald and Natchez City Gazette,* Feb. 1, 1805.
36. Harrell, "Lyceum," p. 191.
37. James, *Antebellum Natchez,* p. 232.
38. Harrell, "Lyceum," p. 197.
39. James, *Antebellum Natchez,* p. 232.
40. Harrell, "Lyceum," pp. 193–95.
41. Riley, "Dunbar," pp. 94–95.
42. Ibid., pp. 98ff.
43. James, *Antebellum Natchez,* pp. 234–38.
44. Polk, *Natchez Before 1830,* pp. 116–21.
45. Dick, *Dixie Frontier,* pp. 131–32.
46. Natchez, Mississippi, *Herald and Natchez City Gazette,* Oct. 19, 1804.
47. Joseph M. Free, "The Ante-Bellum Theatre of the Old Natchez Region," *JMH* 5 (Jan. 1943), p. 14.
48. Ibid., pp. 14–15; Natchez, *Mississippi Republican,* Dec. 1, 1813; Beard, *Prices and Credits,* p. 37; James, *Antebellum Natchez,* p. 228.
49. Hudson, *Humor,* pp. 246–47.
50. Free, "Ante-Bellum Theatre," pp. 17–18.
51. Beard, *Prices and Credits,* p. 37.

52. Free, "Ante-Bellum Theatre," pp. 19–20.
53. Ibid., p. 20.
54. William Bryan Gates, "Performances of Shakespeare in Ante-Bellum Mississippi," *JMH* 5 (Jan. 1943), pp. 28ff.
55. Williams, *Literary History,* p. 138.
56. Lynch, *Excerpts,* p. 41.
57. Hudson, *Humor,* pp. 247–51.
58. Southerland, "Federal Road," pp. 106–7.
59. Dick, *Dixie Frontier,* pp. 162–63 (italics in original).
60. Free, "Ante-Bellum Theatre," pp. 20–21.
61. Ibid., pp. 21–22; Dick, *Dixie Frontier,* p. 164.

Chapter 10 The Road to Prosperity

1. Roy P. Basler, ed., *The Collected Works of Abraham Lincoln* (New Brunswick, N.J., 1953), vol. 4, pp. 62–64.
2. Moses Fisk to John Fisk, July 15, 1801, Fisk Papers.
3. Natchez, Mississippi, *Herald and Natchez City Gazette,* Feb. 1, 1805.
4. Ibid., May 30, 1804.
5. Natchez, *Mississippi Republican,* Apr. 26, 1813.
6. Julia Ideson and Sanford W. Higginbotham, eds., "A Trading Trip to Natchez and New Orleans, 1822: Diary of Thomas S. Teas," *Journal of Southern History* 7 (Aug. 1941), pp. 378ff.
7. Jack D. L. Holmes, "Cotton Gins in the Spanish Natchez District, 1795–1800," *JMH* 31 (Aug. 1969), pp. 162–63.
8. Ibid., pp. 164–65.
9. Ibid., pp. 169–71.
10. James, *Antebellum Natchez,* p. 157.
11. Ibid., p. 158.
12. W. D. Shue, "The Cotton Oil Industry," *PMHS* 8 (1904), pp. 266–67.
13. William B. Hamilton, "The Planters Society in Claiborne County," *JMH* 11 (Jan. 1949), p. 670.
14. Dick, *Dixie Frontier,* pp. 250–51.
15. Lincecum, "Autobiography," pp. 466–67.
16. Dick, *Dixie Frontier,* p. 254.
17. Dawson A. Phelps and John T. Willett, "Iron Works on the Natchez Trace," *Tennessee Historical Quarterly* 12 (Dec. 1953), pp. 309ff.
18. Dick, *Dixie Frontier,* pp. 248–49.
19. U.S. Department of State, *Compendium of the Enumeration of the Inhabitants and Statistics of the United States, as Obtained at the Department of State, from the Returns of the Sixth Census* (Washington, D.C., 1841), pp. 214ff.
20. A. M. Muckenfuss, "History of the Application of Science to Industry in Mississippi," *PMHS* 3 (1901), pp. 242–46.
21. McWhiney, *Cracker Culture,* p. 249.
22. Claiborne, *Mississippi,* p. 300.
23. William D. McCain, "The Charter of Mississippi's First Bank," *JMH* 1 (Oct. 1939), pp. 255–57.

24. Marvin Bentley, "The State Bank of Mississippi: Monopoly Bank on the Frontier (1809–1830)," *JMH* 40 (Nov. 1978), pp. 298–302.
25. Ibid., pp. 303–4.
26. Claiborne, *Mississippi,* pp. 301–302n.
27. Robert C. Weems, Jr., "Mississippi's First Banking System," *JMH* 29 (Nov. 1967), pp. 386–89.
28. McCain, "Charter," pp. 258–63.
29. James, *Antebellum Natchez,* p. 198.
30. Claiborne, *Mississippi,* p. 300.
31. Bentley, "State Bank," p. 311.
32. Charles H. Brough, "The History of Banking in Mississippi," *PMHS* 3 (1901), p. 320.
33. Marvin Bentley, "Incorporated Banks and the Economic Development of Mississippi, 1829–1837," *JMH* 35 (Nov. 1973), pp. 381ff; Brough, "History of Banking," pp. 324–26.
34. Charles H. Brough, "History of Taxation in Mississippi," *PMHS* 2 (1899), pp. 114–17.
35. James, *Antebellum Natchez,* p. 110.

Chapter 11 The Road to Rule

1. Ellicott to Dunbar, Jan. 23, 1799, Andrew Ellicott Papers, Library of Congress, Washington, D.C.
2. Mary L. Thornton, ed., "Letter From David Ker to John Steele," *JMH* 25 (Apr. 1963), p. 136.
3. Cuming, "Tour," p. 324.
4. James, *Antebellum Natchez,* p. 76.
5. Ibid., pp. 18–19.
6. William S. Coker and Jack D. L. Holmes, eds., "Daniel Clark's Letter on the Mississippi Territory," *JMH* 32 (May 1970), p. 161.
7. James, *Antebellum Natchez,* pp. 36–38.
8. Ibid., pp. 48–50.
9. Ibid., pp. 68–69.
10. Robert V. Haynes, "The Revolution of 1800 in Mississippi," *JMH* 19 (Oct. 1957), p. 239.
11. Coker and Holmes, "Daniel Clark's Letter," pp. 159–60; James, *Antebellum Natchez,* pp. 70–71.
12. Deposition of Daniel Burnet, Nov. 22, 1797; Ebenezer Dayton to Minor, Dec. 5, 1797, Minor Family Papers, NTC.
13. Petition of Silas Payne, Dec. 1, 1797, Minor Family Papers, NTC.
14. James, *Antebellum Natchez,* pp. 73–74.
15. Daniel Burnet Statement, June 22, 1800, Daniel Burnet Papers, NTC.
16. James, *Antebellum Natchez,* pp. 74–75.
17. Coker and Holmes, "Daniel Clark's Letter," pp. 165–67.
18. Haynes, "Revolution of 1800," pp. 241–42.
19. Ibid., pp. 250–51.
20. Benjamin Johnson to Isaac Briggs, Nov. 11, 1803, Turner Letterbook, Tulane.

21. D. Clayton James, "Municipal Government in Territorial Natchez," *JMH* 27 (May 1965), pp. 148ff.
22. Thornton, "Letter from David Ker," pp. 136, 137.
23. James, *Antebellum Natchez,* pp. 106–7.
24. Milton Lomask, *Aaron Burr: The Conspiracy and Years of Exile 1805–1836* (New York, 1982), pp. 4–5.
25. Jack D. L. Holmes, "Stephen Minor: Natchez Pioneer," *JMH* 42 (Feb. 1980), p. 23.
26. Ibid., pp. 74, 209–14.
27. James, *Antebellum Natchez,* p. 108; Charles B. Galloway, "Aaron Burr in Mississippi," *PMHS* 10 (1909), p. 242.
28. Daniel P. Jordan, "Partisan Politics in Territorial Mississippi: A Staunch Republican's Direct Report, December, 1807," *JMH* 41 (Aug. 1979), pp. 236–38.
29. Cuming, "Tour," p. 324.
30. D. H. Conrad, "David Holmes: First Governor of Mississippi," *PMHS,* Centenary Series, 4 (Jackson, 1921), pp. 234–35.
31. Jordan, "Partisan Politics," pp. 238–39.
32. Southerland, "The Federal Road," p. 104; James, *Antebellum Natchez,* p. 109.
33. Natchez, *Mississippi Republican,* July 26, 1815.
34. Claiborne, *Mississippi,* pp. 363, 364, 371–73, 375.
35. James, "Municipal Government," pp. 152–53; Claiborne, *Mississippi,* pp. 376–78.
36. Natchez, *Mississippi Republican,* July 26, 1815.
37. Winbourne Magruder Drake, "Mississippi's First Constitutional Convention," *JMH* 18 (Apr. 1956), pp. 79–81.
38. Ibid., pp. 93ff.
39. Ibid., pp. 103–5.
40. Ibid., p. 110.
41. Beard, *Prices and Credit,* p. 25.
42. Account with George Selser, Stephen Bullock Papers; receipt of Christopher Rankin, Aug. 17, 1819, Alexander Papers; Burton and Caymares Writ of Attachment, Aug. 6, 1818, NTC.
43. Observations on Mr. Turner's account against E. H. Bay, circa. 1820, E. H. Bay Papers, NTC.
44. Michael de L. Landon, "The Mississippi State Bar Association, 1821–1825," *JMH* 42 (Aug. 1980), pp. 223–26.
45. Beauchamp, "Early Chronicles," p. 49.
46. Rainwater, "Autobiography of James H. Maury," pp. 96, 97.
47. Doster, "Early Settlements," p. 89.
48. Darrel E. Bigham, "From the Green Mountains to the Tombigbee: Henry Hitchcock in Territorial Alabama, 1817–1819," *Alabama Review* 26 (July 1973), pp. 218–19.
49. "Autobiography of Gideon Lincecum," p. 475.
50. Bigham, "Hitchcock," p. 219.
51. "Gaines' Reminiscences," p. 180.
52. Tocqueville, *Democracy,* vol. 1, p. 243.

53. Claiborne, "Trip," p. 492.
54. Crockett, *Narrative,* pp. 142–44.
55. "Gaines' Reminiscences," p. 181.
56. James, *Antebellum Natchez,* p. 113.
57. Charles H. Brough, "Historic Clinton," *PMHS* 7 (1903), p. 288.
58. Louis U. Loveman, comp., *Presidential Vote in Alabama 1824–1980* (Gadsden, Ala., 1983), p. 53; Edwin A. Miles, "The Mississippi Press in the Jackson Era, 1824–1841," *JMH* 19 (Jan. 1957), pp. 1–2.
59. Loveman, *Vote,* p. 53; Gray, "Frontier Journalism," pp. 188–89; Miles, "Mississippi Press," pp. 2–3.

Chapter 12 The Road to Ruin

1. William Martin to Lyman Draper, May 13, 1843, Lyman Draper Papers, Tennessee State Library and Archives.
2. Ker, *Travels,* p. 41.
3. Bradbury, *Travels,* p. 208.
4. Dawson A. Phelps and Edward Hunter Ross, "Names Please—Names Along the Natchez Trace," *JMH* 14 (Oct. 1952), p. 254.
5. Beard, "Natchez Under-the-Hill," pp. 42–43.
6. Holden, *Along the Old Natchez Trace,* p. 20.
7. Hall, "Brief History," p. 556.
8. R. McAlpine to Barnes, Aug. 25, 1824, Barnes-Willis Family Papers, NTC.
9. Beard, "Natchez Under-the-Hill," pp. 35–36.
10. Beard, *Prices and Credit,* p. 31.
11. McDermott, *Before Mark Twain,* p. 8.
12. Beard, "Natchez Under-the-Hill," p. 36.
13. Phelps, "Travel," pp. 161–62.
14. Ibid., p. 162.
15. T. B. Thorpe, "Remembrances of the Mississippi," *Harper's New Monthly Magazine* 12 (Dec. 1855), p. 30.
16. Schultz, *Travels,* vol. 1, pp. 145–46.
17. Taylor, *Eating, Drinking and Visiting,* p. 13.
18. Natchez, Mississippi, *Herald and Natchez City Gazette,* May 23, 1804.
19. Excerpt from Montule, *Travels in America, 1816–1817,* NTPL.
20. John M. Alstone Account, 1811, NTC.
21. Receipt of Francis Wood, 1811, Bullock Papers, NTC.
22. Hudson, *Humor,* p. 280.
23. Posey, "Public Manners," pp. 230–32.
24. Hudson, *Humor,* pp. 60–61.
25. W. Stuart Harris, "Rowdyism, Public Drunkenness, and Bloody Encounters in Early Perry County," *Alabama Review* 33 (Jan. 1980), p. 17.
26. Beard, "Natchez Under-the-Hill," pp. 39–40.
27. Harris, "Rowdyism," pp. 18–19.
28. Nuttall, *Journal,* p. 304.
29. Schultz, *Travels,* vol. 1, pp. 140–43.
30. Bradbury, *Travels,* p. 208.
31. Beard, "Natchez Under-the-Hill," p. 36.

32. Schultz, *Travels,* vol. 1, p. 136.
33. Beard, "Natchez Under-the-Hill," p. 43.
34. McDermott, *Before Mark Twain,* pp. 196–99.
35. Schultz, *Travels,* vol. 1, pp. 136–37.
36. Beard, "Natchez Under-the-Hill," pp. 38, 39.
37. McDermott, *Before Mark Twain,* p. 44.
38. Ibid., pp. 64–68.
39. Harris, "Rowdyism," pp. 17–18.
40. James White to Ellicott, Aug. 15, 1798, Ellicott Papers.
41. Daniel Clark to Ellicott, Aug. 5, 1798, ibid.
42. Harris, "Rowdyism," p. 19.
43. Lynch, *Excerpts,* p. 103.
44. McDermott, *Before Mark Twain,* pp. 20–25.
45. Harris, "Rowdyism," pp. 20–21.
46. Galloway, "Thomas Griffin," p. 160.
47. Thorpe, "Remembrances," p. 30.
48. Beard, "Natchez Under-the-Hill," pp. 40–41, 43–44.
49. Thorpe, "Remembrances," pp. 30–31.
50. Ibid., pp. 31–32.
51. Hudson, *Humor,* p. 474.
52. Jones, "Some Facts," p. 88.
53. Martin to Draper, May 13, 1843, Draper Papers.
54. Beard, "Natchez Under-the-Hill," pp. 29–30, 44–45.
55. Ira M. Boswell, "La Cache," *PMHS* 7 (1903), pp. 319–23.
56. William A. Love, "Lowndes County, Its Antiquities and Pioneer Settlers," ibid., pp. 365–66.
57. Natchez, Mississippi, *Herald and Natchez City Gazette,* Oct. 31, 1803.
58. Edward L. Ayers, *Vengeance and Justice* (New York, 1984), pp. 13, 14.
59. Peter A. Brannan, "Duelling in Alabama," *AHQ* 17 (Fall 1955), p. 97.
60. Wilmuth S. Rutledge, "Dueling in Antebellum Mississippi," *JMH* 26 (Aug. 1964), pp. 181–90.
61. Bette B. Tilly, "The Jackson-Dinsmoor Feud: A Paradox in A Minor Key," *JMH* 34 (May 1977), pp. 117ff.
62. Brannan, "Duelling," p. 100.
63. J. Clark to Richard Dunlap, Sept. 29, 1826, F. S. Heiskell Collection, Tennessee State Library and Archives.
64. James, *Antebellum Natchez,* pp. 264–65.

Chapter 13 The Road to Law and Order

1. Michael F. Beard, *Frontier Port on the Mississippi: A History of the Legend of Natchez Under-the-Hill, 1800–1900,* master's thesis, Louisiana State University, Baton Rouge, 1981, p. 30; Thaddeus M. Harris, "The Journal of a Tour into the Territory Northwest of the Allegheny Mountains . . . ," in Reuben G. Thwaites, ed., *Early Western Travels, 1748–1846* (New York, 1966), vol. 3, p. 358.
2. Beard, *Frontier Port,* pp. 5, 13, 21.

3. Jack D. L. Holmes, "Law and Order in Spanish Natchez, 1781–1798," *JMH* 25 (July 1963), pp. 187–88.

4. Laura D. S. Sturdivant, "One Carbine and a Little Flour and Corn In a Sack: The American Pioneer," *JMH* 37 (Feb. 1975), pp. 58–60.

5. Ibid., pp. 49–50.

6. Holmes, "Law and Order," pp. 191–92.

7. Holmes, "Livestock," pp. 23, 25–37 passim.

8. Claiborne, *Mississippi,* p. 529.

9. Holmes, "Law and Order," p. 194.

10. Claiborne, *Mississippi,* p. 529.

11. Ibid.

12. Robert V. Haynes, "Law Enforcement in Frontier Mississippi," *JMH* 22 (Jan. 1960), pp. 30–31.

13. Ibid., p. 32; John Wunder, "American Law and Order Comes to Mississippi Territory: The Making of Sargent's Code, 1798–1800," *JMH* 38 (May 1976), pp. 134–35.

14. Wunder, "American Law and Order," pp. 142–43.

15. Ibid., pp. 144–54.

16. Haynes, "Law Enforcement," p. 34.

17. Doster, "Early Settlements," pp. 89–90.

18. Haynes, "Law Enforcement," pp. 37–38.

19. Beard, *Frontier Port,* p. 64.

20. *Minutes of the Court of General Quarter Sessions,* pp. 1–3.

21. Edward Turner Docket Book, Jan. 11, 1817–Feb. 24, 1819, Turner Papers.

22. Natchez, *Mississippi Republican,* Apr. 28, 1813.

23. Ayers, *Vengeance,* p. 17.

24. Haynes, "Disposal of Lands," pp. 242–43.

25. Martin to Hamilton, Mar. 22, 1811, Tulane.

26. McCaleb, "Easter," pp. 4–5.

27. William S. Coker, "Research Possibilities and Resources for a Study of Spanish Mississippi," *JMH* 34 (May 1972), pp. 122–23.

28. Harris, "Rowdyism," pp. 21–22.

29. Joseph T. Hatfield, "Governor William Charles Cole Claiborne, Indians, and Outlaws in Frontier Mississippi, 1801–1803," *JMH* 27 (Nov. 1965), pp. 344–45.

30. James W. Bragg, "Captain Slick, Arbiter of Early Alabama Morals," *Alabama Review* 11 (Apr. 1958), pp. 125–32.

31. Harris, "Rowdyism," p. 23.

32. Bragg, "Captain Slick," pp. 133–34.

33. James P. Penick Jr., *The Great Western Land Pirate: John A. Murrell in Legend and History* (Columbia, Mo., 1981), p. 57.

34. McDermott, *Before Mark Twain,* pp. 219–20.

35. Penick, *Land Pirate,* pp. 57–58.

36. McDermott, *Before Mark Twain,* p. 220.

37. Penick, *Land Pirate,* pp. 59, 64–65.

38. Ibid., p. 65.

39. Haynes, "Law Enforcement," pp. 40–41.

40. Raymond M. Bell, *Samuel Mason, 1739–1803,* (Washington, Pa., 1985), p. 3.
41. Thorpe, "Remembrances," p. 32.
42. Butler, Hagen, and Truett, *Natchez Trace,* p. 218.
43. Claiborne, *Mississippi,* pp. 225–26.
44. Hatfield, "Claiborne," pp. 346–48.
45. Bell, "Mason," p. 10.
46. Claiborne, *Mississippi,* p. 226.
47. Butler, Hagen, and Truett, *Natchez Trace,* p. 219.
48. Ibid., pp. 220–22.
49. Ibid., p. 222.
50. Natchez, Mississippi, *Herald and Natchez City Gazette,* Nov. 14, 1803.
51. Thorpe, "Remembrances," p. 32.
52. Bell, "Mason," pp. 6–7; Hatfield, "Claiborne," p. 348.
53. Hatfield, "Claiborne," pp. 349–50; Thorpe, "Remembrances," p. 32; Claiborne, *Mississippi,* pp. 226–28.
54. Phelps, "Natchez Trace in Alabama," p. 26.
55. Holden, *Travelers on the Natchez Trace,* pp. 26–27.
56. Cabaniss and Cabaniss, "Religion," pp. 200–201.
57. Guy B. Braden, *Lower Choctaw Boundary,* n.d., pp. 9–10, NTPL.
58. Dawson Phelps, "The Tragic Death of Meriwether Lewis," *William and Mary Quarterly* 13 (July 1956), pp. 310–16; Garrett, *Historical Sketches,* p. 102.
59. No more glaring example of the kind of myth and legend, accepted as fact, that connects itself to the Trace can be found than in Jonathan Daniels's *The Devil's Backbone* (New York, 1962), which is laden throughout with exaggeration and fiction posing as fact. The inventions are not Daniels's, but merely the accumulation of hysterical legend that he unquestioningly accepted even when faced with authentic contradiction. When myth clashed with fact, he preferred the former.
60. James Lal Penick Jr., "John A. Murrell: A Legend of the Old Southwest," *Tennessee Historical Quarterly* 48 (Fall 1989), pp. 174–76.
61. Penick, *Land Pirate,* pp. 9, 14–16, 18–20, 26–28.
62. Penick, "Murrell," p. 177.

Chapter 14 The Road to the Indian Nations

1. Gideon Lincecum, "Life of Apushimataha," *PMHS* 9 (1906), p. 420.
2. "Extracts from the Travels of William Bartram," *AHQ* 17 (Fall 1955), pp. 110ff.
3. Edward Hunter Ross and Dawson A. Phelps, eds., "A Journey over the Natchez Trace in 1792: A Document from the Archives of Spain," *JMH* 15 (Oct. 1953), pp. 253ff.
4. Baily, *Journal,* p. 354.
5. N. D. Deupree, "Life of Greenwood Le Flore," *PMHS* 7 (1903), p. 141.
6. William A. Love, "Mingo Mashulitubbee's Prairie Village," *PMHS* 7 (1903), pp. 375–76.
7. H. S. Halbert, "Origin of Mashulaville," *PMHS* 7 (1903), pp. 389–93.

8. Lincecum, "Apushimataha," pp. 424–25, 481–82.

9. Ibid., pp. 424–34.

10. Deupree, "Le Flore," pp. 143–44.

11. Rush Nutt, *Portions of a Diary of a Tour Through the Western Part of the U.S.*, transcript in NTPL, pp. 10–14.

12. Marion R. Hemperley, "Benjamin Hawkins' Trip Through Alabama, 1796," *AHQ* 31 (Fall–Winter 1969), pp. 210–11, 230.

13. Phelps, "Natchez Trace in Tennessee," pp. 201–2.

14. Frank L. Owsley Jr., "Benjamin Hawkins, The First Modern Indian Agent," *AHQ* 30 (Summer 1968), pp. 7–13.

15. Nella J. Chambers, "The Creek Indian Factory at Fort Mitchell," *AHQ* 21 (1959), pp. 15ff.

16. Dawson A. Phelps, "The Chickasaw Agency," *JMH* 14 (Apr. 1952), pp. 119ff.

17. Aloysius Plaisance, "The Choctaw Trading House—1803–1822," *AHQ* 16 (Fall–Winter 1954), pp. 394–416.

18. Moses Fisk to John Fisk, Nov. 14, 1812, Fisk Papers.

19. Sturdivant, "American Pioneer," p. 60.

20. Holmes, "Law and Order," p. 195.

21. Percy L. Rainwater, "Indian Missions and Missionaries," *JMH* 28 (Feb. 1966), pp. 15–26; Harry Warren, "Missions, Missionaries, Frontier Characters and Schools," *PMHS* 8 (1904), pp. 581–82.

22. Warren, "Missions," pp. 582–83.

23. Dawson Phelps, "The Chickasaw Mission," *JMH* 13 (Oct. 1951), pp. 227–31.

24. Rainwater, "Indian Missions," pp. 36–39.

25. Phelps, "Chickasaw Mission," pp. 232–35.

26. DeRosier, "Pioneers," pp. 180–81.

27. Dawson A. Phelps, "The Choctaw Mission: An Experiment in Civilization," *JMH* 14 (Jan. 1952), pp. 35–45.

28. DeRosier, "Pioneers," p. 178.

29. William A. Love, "The Mayhew Mission to the Choctaws," *PMHS* 11 (1910), pp. 373–86.

30. Rainwater, "Indian Missions," p. 31.

31. Phelps, "Choctaw Mission," pp. 54–55.

32. Fisk to Green, Mar. 12, 1796, Fisk Papers.

33. Martin Abbott, "Indian Policy and Management in the Mississippi Territory, 1798–1817," *JMH* 14 (July 1952), p. 167.

34. Ibid., p. 168.

35. C. J. Coley, "Creek Treaties, 1790–1832," *Alabama Review* 11 (July 1958), pp. 164–66.

36. Ibid., pp. 170–71.

37. Ibid., pp. 173–75.

38. Laura Bowers, *The Choctaw Agency* (NTPL, 1966), p. 8.

39. Samuel J. Wells, "International Causes of the Treaty of Mount Dexter, 1805," *JMH* 48 (Aug. 1986), pp. 180–84.

40. Abbott, "Indian Policy," p. 169; Plaisance, "Choctaw Trading House," pp. 415–16.

41. Clark and Guice, *Frontiers in Conflict,* pp. 240–41.
42. Cotterill, *Southern Indians,* pp. 208–9; Phelps, "Stands and Travel Accommodations," p. 25.
43. Clark and Guice, *Frontiers in Conflict,* pp. 243–44.
44. Park Marshall, "The True Route of the Natchez Trace—The Rectification of a Topographical Error," *Tennessee Historical Magazine* 1 (Sept. 1915), pp. 178–79; Phelps, "Chickasaw Council House," p. 171.
45. Phelps, "Colbert Ferry," pp. 207–8.
46. Charles W. Watts, "Colbert's Reserve and the Chickasaw Treaty of 1818," *Alabama Review* 12 (Oct. 1959), pp. 272–75.
47. Clark and Guice, *Frontiers in Conflict,* pp. 244–45.
48. H. S. Halbert, "Story of the Treaty of Dancing Rabbit," *PMHS* 6 (1902), pp. 374–77; Deupree, "LeFlore," p. 145.
49. Clark and Guice, *Frontiers in Conflict,* p. 247.
50. Halbert, "Dancing Rabbit," pp. 379, 389.
51. Franklin L. Riley, "Choctaw Land Claims," *PMHS* 8 (1904), pp. 346–48.
52. Deupree, "LeFlore," p. 146.
53. Love, "Mayhew Mission," pp. 391–92.
54. James W. Silver, "A Counter-Proposal to the Indian Removal Policy of Andrew Jackson," *JMH* 4 (Oct. 1942), pp. 207–12.
55. Clark and Guice, *Frontiers in Conflict,* p. 250.
56. Coley, "Creek Treaties," pp. 175–76.

Chapter 15 The Road to War

1. William H. Jenkins, "Alabama Forts, 1700–1838," *Alabama Review* 12 (July 1959), pp. 163–70.
2. James, *Antebellum Natchez,* pp. 27–28.
3. Samuel C. Williams, "Tennessee's First Military Expedition (1803)," *Tennessee Historical Magazine* 8 (Oct. 1924), p. 171.
4. Ibid., pp. 186–88.
5. Natchez, Mississippi, *Messenger,* Dec. 24, 1807.
6. "Letters from George Strother Gaines Relating to Events in South Alabama, 1805–1814," *TAHS* 3 (1899), p. 187.
7. Reuben Durrett, ed., "John Adair's Observations on Men and Affairs in the Old Southwest, 1809," *Gulf States Historical Magazine* 1 (July 1902), pp. 16–17.
8. Jenkins, "Alabama Forts," pp. 171–72.
9. Fisk to John Fisk, Nov. 14, 1812, Fisk Papers.
10. Clark and Guice, *Frontiers in Conflict,* pp. 117–18.
11. "Autobiography of Gideon Lincecum," p. 457.
12. Crockett, *Narrative,* pp. 72–73.
13. Ibid., p. 75.
14. Dick, *Dixie Frontier,* pp. 268–71.
15. Clark and Guice, *Frontiers in Conflict,* pp. 118–19.
16. John H. DeWitt, ed., "Letters of General John Coffee to His Wife, 1813–1815," *Tennessee Historical Magazine* 2 (Dec. 1916), pp. 267–70.
17. Dawson A. Phelps, ed., "The Diary of a Chaplain in Andrew Jackson's

Army: The Journal of the Reverend Mr. Learner Blackman—December 28, 1812–April 4, 1813," *Tennessee Historical Quarterly* 12 (Sept. 1953), pp. 266ff.

18. DeWitt, "Coffee," pp. 272–73.
19. Clark and Guice, *Frontiers in Conflict,* pp. 121–22.
20. Claiborne, *Mississippi,* pp. 316–17.
21. Clark and Guice, *Frontiers in Conflict,* pp. 126–27.
22. Claiborne, *Mississippi,* p. 323.
23. Pickett, *Alabama,* pp. 534–37; Claiborne, *Mississippi,* p. 324.
24. Crockett, *Narrative,* pp. 71–72.
25. Natchez, *Mississippi Republican,* Nov. 24, 1813.
26. ——— Montgomery to John Wallis, Oct. 6, 1813, Barnes-Willis Family Papers.
27. Jenkins, "Alabama Forts," p. 175.
28. Leach, "John Gordon," p. 334.
29. Crockett, *Narrative,* pp. 88–89.
30. "Letters from George Strother Gaines," p. 189.
31. Natchez, *Mississippi Republican,* Jan. 18, 1815.
32. Ibid., Mar. 1, 1815.
33. Claiborne, *Mississippi,* pp. 345–46.
34. Wait, *Richardson,* p. 15.
35. Beauchamp, "Early Chronicles," pp. 45, 50–58.

Afterword

1. Shackford, *Crockett,* p. 212.
2. John Ray article, 1888, Tulane.
3. Samuel Clark to John Russworm, Dec. 15, 1839, John Russworm Papers, Tennessee State Library and Archives.

BIBLIOGRAPHY

Manuscripts

Library of Congress, Washington, D.C.
Andrew Ellicott Papers

Mississippi Department of Archives and History, Jackson
Adams County Court of Quarter Sessions Minutes
David Crockett Memorandum
Natchez Steam Boat Company, Stock Certificate
Percy L. Rainwater Collection

National Archives, Washington, D.C.
Post Master General Letterbooks, Record Group 28

Tennessee State Library and Archives, Nashville
David Benedict, *General History of the Baptist Denomination in America and Other Parts of the World, 1785–1812*, Historical Records Survey, Tennessee (WPA)
Paul Cunningham Letter
Lyman Draper Papers
Thomas East Account Book
Moses Fisk Papers
F. S. Heiskell Collection
S. H. Hodge Letter
"Reports on Revivals and the State of Religion in Christian Countries," Society of Inquiry and Missions
John S. Russworm Papers

Center for American History, Eugene C. Barker Texas History Library, University of Texas, Austin
Natchez Trace Collection
  Adams County, Miss., Drug Store Ledger, 1818–1820
  Amos Alexander Papers

357

F. Allden Papers
John M. Alstone Account, 1811
Barnes-Willis Family Papers
William Bay Papers
Bayou Sara Record, 1819
John Buell Papers
Stephen Bullock Papers
Burling Family Papers
Daniel Burnet Papers
John and Sarah Burns Divorce, 1806
Burton and Caymares Writ of Attachment, 1818
Clarke and Wren Mercantile Business Ledger, 1828
Samuel Davis Legal Document
Charles H. Dencker Letter Book, 1818–1825
Benjamin Fuller and Joseph Sylvester Papers
Greenville, Miss., Store Ledger, 1825–1828
Minor Family Papers
Natchez, Miss., Store Ledger, 1824–1825
Natchez Trace Steamboat Collection
William B. Smith Account, 1810
Stirling and Gillaspie Blacksmith Record
Henry Tennent Papers
Benjamin L. Wailes Papers
Levin Wailes Papers
Emery Wilson Cash Book, 1835–1837

Special Collections, Howard-Tilton Memorial Library, Tulane University, New Orleans, Louisiana

Rosamonde F. and Emile Kuntz Collection
Francis X. Martin Letter
Joseph M. Pellerin Letter
John Ray Article, 1888
Edward Turner Letterbook, 1803–1805

Theses and Dissertations

Beard, Michael F. *Frontier Port on the Mississippi: A History of the Legend of Natchez Under-the-Hill, 1800–1900.* M.A. thesis, Louisiana State University, 1981.

———. *Prices and Credit in Territorial Natchez and its Hinterland, 1800–1818: A Report for the Natchez Trace Parkway.* Natchez Trace Parkway Library, Tupelo, Miss., Apr. 22, 1980.

———. *Prices in Territorial Natchez: A Partial Listing of Wholesale and Retail Costs for the Mt. Locust Program of the Natchez Trace Parkway.* Natchez Trace Parkway Library, Tupelo, Miss., May 26, 1980.

Bell, Raymond M. *Samuel Mason, 1739–1803.* Washington, Pa., Mississippi Department of Archives and History, Jackson, 1985.

Bowers, Laura. *The Choctaw Agency.* Natchez Trace Parkway Library, Tupelo, Miss., 1966.

Braden, Guy B. *Lower Choctaw Boundary.* Natchez Trace Parkway Library, Tupelo, Miss., n.d.

Bureman, Michael H. *An Historical Overview of the Natchez Trace.* Natchez Trace Parkway Library, Tupelo, Miss., Aug. 1985.

Butler, Ruth E., Hagen, Olaf T., and Randle B. Truett. *The Natchez Trace: Its Location, History and Development.* Natchez Trace Parkway Library, Tupelo, Miss., 1936.

Hagen, Olaf T. *Grinder's Stand.* Natchez Trace Parkway Library, Tupelo, Miss., 1933.

Holden, Robert J. *Travelers on the Natchez Trace: A Study of the Ohio River Valley Boatmen, Their Life and Characteristics, as Described by Contemporary Observers.* Natchez Trace Parkway Library, Tupelo, Miss., 1977.

McCaleb, James F. *Easter on the Natchez Trace.* Natchez Trace Parkway Library, Tupelo, Miss., Apr. 17, 1808.

Madden, Robert R. *The History of Grindstone Ford.* Natchez Trace Parkway Library, Tupelo, Miss., n.d.

Nutt, Rush. *Portions of a Diary of a Tour Through the Western Part of the U.S.* Natchez Trace Parkway Library, Tupelo, Miss.

Phelps, Dawson. *Gordon's Ferry.* Natchez Trace Parkway Library, Tupelo, Miss., 1945.

———. *Natchez Trace: Variant Locations.* Natchez Trace Parkway Library, Tupelo, Miss., n.d.

———. *The Natchez Trace in Williamson and Davidson Counties, Tennessee.* Natchez Trace Parkway Library, Tupelo, Miss., 1946.

Research—Natchez. Miscellaneous Correspondence. Natchez Trace Parkway Library, Tupelo, Miss.

Southerland, Henry deLeon, Jr. *Crossing the Creeks: The Old Federal Road, 1806–1836.* Master's thesis, Stanford University, 1983.

Newspapers

Natchez *Ariel*, 1828.
Natchez *Constitutional Conservator*, 1803.
Natchez *Intelligencer*, 1801.
Natchez *Mississippi Gazette*, 1801.
Natchez, *Mississippi Herald and Natchez City Gazette*, 1803–1805.
Natchez *Mississippi Messenger*, 1807.
Natchez *Mississippi Republican*, 1812–1815, 1817, 1818.
Natchez *Washington Republican and Natchez Intelligencer*, 1817.
Niles' Register, 1790–1800.

Articles

"A Diary of a Journey." *Journal of the Presbyterian Historical Society* 21 (Dec. 1943), pp. 167–85.

"A Genuine Account of the Present State of the River Mississippi. . . ." Franklin L. Riley, ed., *Publications of the Mississippi Historical Society* 9 (1906), pp. 323–30.

Abbott, Martin. "Indian Policy and Management in the Mississippi Territory, 1798–1817." *Journal of Mississippi History* 14 (July 1952), pp. 153–69.

Alford, Terry L. "Some Manumissions Recorded in the Adams County Deed Books in Chancery Clerk's Office, Natchez, Mississippi, 1795–1835." *Journal of Mississippi History* 33 (Feb. 1971), pp. 39–50.

Anderson, John Q. "The Narrative of John Hutchins." *Journal of Mississippi History* 20 (Jan. 1958), pp. 1–29.

"Autobiography of Gideon Lincecum." Franklin L. Riley, ed., *Publications of the Mississippi Historical Society* 8 (1904), pp. 443–518.

"The Autobiography of James H. Maury." *Journal of Mississippi History* 5 (Apr. 1943), pp. 88–102.

Bailey, Hugh C. "Alabama's First Baptist Association." *Alabama Review* 14 (Jan. 1961), pp. 31–40.

Beard, Michael F. "Natchez Under-the-Hill: Reform and Retribution in Early Natchez." *Gulf Coast Historical Review* 4 (Fall 1988), pp. 29–48.

Beauchamp, Green. "Early Chronicles of Barbour County." *Alabama Historical Quarterly* 33 (Spring 1971), pp. 37–74.

Bedford, John R., ed. "A Tour in 1807 Down the Cumberland, Ohio and Mississippi Rivers from Nashville to New Orleans." *Tennessee Historical Magazine* 5 (July 1919), pp. 101–28.

Bekkers, B. J. "The Catholic Church in Mississippi During Colonial Times." Franklin L. Riley, ed., *Publications of the Mississippi Historical Society* 6 (1902), pp. 351–57.

Bell, Helen D. "The History of A County." Franklin L. Riley, ed., *Publications of the Mississippi Historical Society* 4 (1901), pp. 335–42.

Bentley, Marvin. "Incorporated Banks and the Economic Development of Mississippi, 1829–1837." *Journal of Mississippi History* 35 (Nov. 1973), pp. 381–401.

———. "The State Bank of Mississippi: Monopoly Bank on the Frontier (1809–1830)." *Journal of Mississippi History* 40 (Nov. 1978), pp. 297–318.

Bigham, Darrel E. "From the Green Mountains to the Tombigbee: Henry Hitchcock in Territorial Alabama, 1817–1819." *Alabama Review* 26 (July 1973), pp. 209–28.

Boswell, Ira M. "La Cache." Franklin L. Riley, ed., *Publications of the Mississippi Historical Society* 7 (1903), pp. 313–24.

Braden, Guy B. "A Jeffersonian Village: Washington, Mississippi." *Journal of Mississippi History* 30 (May 1968), pp. 135–42.

Bragg, James W. "Captain Slick, Arbiter of Early Alabama Morals." *Alabama Review* 11 (Apr. 1958), pp. 125–34.

Brannan, Peter A. "Duelling in Alabama." *Alabama Historical Quarterly* 17 (Fall 1955), pp. 97–109.

Brough, Charles H. "Historic Clinton." Franklin L. Riley, ed., *Publications of the Mississippi Historical Society* 7 (1903), pp. 281–312.

———. "The History of Banking in Mississippi." *Journal of the Mississippi Historical Society* 3 (1901), pp. 317–40.

————. "History of Taxation in Mississippi." Franklin L. Riley, ed., *Publications of the Mississippi Historical Society* 2 (1899), pp. 113–24.

Brown, A. J. "Choctaw Mission Station in Jasper County." Franklin L. Riley, ed., *Publications of the Mississippi Historical Society* 7 (1903), pp. 349–50.

Butts, Alfred B. "Public Administration in Mississippi." Dunbar Rowland, ed., *Publications of the Mississippi Historical Society*, centenary series, 3 (1919), pp. 7–278.

Cabaniss, Frances A., and James A. Cabaniss. "Religion in Ante-Bellum Mississippi." *Journal of Mississippi History* 6 (Oct. 1944), pp. 191–224.

Cain, Cyril E. "The First Hundred Years of Post Offices on the Pascagoula River." *Journal of Mississippi History* 11 (July 1949), pp. 178–84.

Cain, Lee C. "Founding Public Schools in Alabama—A County Led the Way." *Alabama Historical Quarterly* 38 (Winter 1976), pp. 243–49.

Carpenter, Alma. "A Note on the History of the Forest Plantation, Natchez." *Journal of Mississippi History* 46 (May 1984), pp. 130–37.

Carriere, Marius M., Jr. "Mount Locust Plantation: The Development of Southwest Mississippi During the Frontier Period." *Journal of Mississippi History* 48 (Aug. 1986), pp. 187–98.

Chambers, Nella J. "The Creek Indian Factory at Fort Mitchell." *Alabama Historical Quarterly* 21 (1959), pp. 15–53.

Claiborne, J. F. C. "Trip Through the Piney Woods." *Publications of the Mississippi Historical Society* 9 (1906), pp. 487–538.

Coker, William S. "Research Possibilities and Resources for a Study of Spanish Mississippi." *Journal of Mississippi History* 34 (May 1972), pp. 117–28.

Coker, William S., and Jack D. L. Holmes, eds. "Daniel Clark's Letter on the Mississippi Territory." *Journal of Mississippi History* 32 (May 1970), pp. 153–69.

Coley, C. J. "Creek Treaties, 1790–1832." *Alabama Review* 11 (July 1958), pp. 163–76.

Conrad, D. H. "David Holmes: First Governor of Mississippi." Dunbar Rowland, ed., *Publications of the Mississippi Historical Society*, Centenary Series, 4 (1921), pp. 234–57.

Cotterill, R. S. "The Natchez Trace." *Tennessee Historical Magazine* 7 (Aug. 1921), pp. 27–35.

Cuming, Fortescue. "Sketches of a Tour to the Western Country." In Reuben G. Thwaites, ed., *Early Western Travels*, vol. 4. Cleveland, 1904.

DeRosier, Arthur H., Jr. "Carpenter's Estimate on the Building of 'The Forest'." *Journal of Mississippi History* 27 (Aug. 1965), pp. 259–64.

————. "Natchez and the Formative Years of William Dunbar." *Journal of Mississippi History* 34 (Feb. 1972), pp. 29–47.

————. "Pioneers with Conflicting Ideals: Christianity and Slavery in the Choctaw Nation." *Journal of Mississippi History* 21 (July 1959), pp. 174–89.

Deupree, N. D. "Life of Greenwood Le Flore." *Publications of the Mississippi Historical Society* 7 (1903), pp. 141–52.

DeWitt, John H., ed. "Letters of General John Coffee to His Wife, 1813–1815." *Tennessee Historical Magazine* 2 (Dec. 1916), pp. 265–94.

Doss, Chriss H. "Early Settlement of Bearmeat Cabin Frontier." *Alabama Review* 22 (Oct. 1969), pp. 270–83.

Doster, James F. "Early Settlements on the Tombigbee and Tensaw Rivers." *Alabama Review* 12 (Apr. 1959), pp. 83–94.

Drake, Winbourne M. "Mississippi's First Constitutional Convention." *Journal of Mississippi History* 18 (Apr. 1956), pp. 79–110.

Durrett, Reuben, ed. "John Adair's Observations on Men and Affairs in the Old Southwest, 1809." *Gulf States Historical Magazine* 1 (July 1902), pp. 13–18.

Elliott, J. D., Jr. "Leftwich's 'Cotton Gin Port and Gaines' Trace' Reconsidered." *Journal of Mississippi History* 42 (Nov. 1980), pp. 348–61.

Ellison, Rhoda Coleman, ed. "A Pioneer Alabama Doctor's Ledger." *Alabama Historical Quarterly* 43 (Winter 1981), pp. 315–21.

Evans, John H. "Location and Description of the Emmaus Mission." *Publications of the Mississippi Historical Society* 6 (1902), pp. 411–13.

Evans, W. A. "Gaines Trace in Monroe County, Mississippi." *Journal of Mississippi History* 1 (Apr. 1939), pp. 100–109.

"Extracts from the Travels of William Bartram." *Alabama Historical Quarterly* 17 (Fall 1955), pp. 110–24.

Free, Joseph M. "The Ante-Bellum Theatre of the Old Natchez Region." *Journal of Mississippi History* 5 (Jan. 1943), pp. 14–27.

"Gaines' Reminiscences." *Alabama Historical Quarterly* 26 (Fall–Winter 1964), pp. 133–229.

Galloway, Charles B. "Aaron Burr in Mississippi." *Journal of the Mississippi Historical Society* 10 (1909), pp. 237–45.

———. "Elizabeth Female Academy—The Mother of Female Colleges." *Publications of the Mississippi Historical Society* 2 (1899), pp. 169–78.

———. "Lorenzo Dow in Mississippi." *Publications of the Mississippi Historical Society* 4 (1901), pp. 235–45.

———. "Thomas Griffin—A Boanerges of the Early Southwest." *Publications of the Mississippi Historical Society* 7 (1903), pp. 153–70.

Gates, William B. "Performances of Shakespeare in Ante-Bellum Mississippi." *Journal of Mississippi History* 5 (Jan. 1943), pp. 28–37.

Gray, Daniel Savage. "Frontier Journalism: Newspapers in Antebellum Alabama." *Alabama Historical Quarterly* 36 (Fall 1975), pp. 183–91.

Griffin, Richard W. "Athens Academy and College: An Experiment in Women's Education in Alabama." *Alabama Historical Quarterly* 20 (Spring 1958), pp. 7–26.

Griffith, Lucille. "Anne Royall in Alabama." *Alabama Review* 21 (Jan. 1968), pp. 53–63.

Halbert, H. S., ed. "Diary of Richard Breckenridge, 1816." In Thomas M. Owen, ed., *Transactions of the Alabama Historical Society. 1898–1899* (1899), pp. 142–53.

———. "Origin of Mashulaville." *Publications of the Mississippi Historical Society* 7 (1903), pp. 389–97.

———. "Story of the Treaty of Dancing Rabbit." *Publications of the Mississippi Historical Society* 6 (1902), pp. 373–402.

Hall, James. "A Brief History of the Mississippi Territory." *Publications of the Mississippi Historical Society* 9 (1906), pp. 539–76.

Hall, James H. B. "The History of the Cumberland Presbyterian Church in Alabama Prior to 1826." In Thomas M. Owen, ed., *Transactions of the Alabama Historical Society, 1899–1903* (1904), pp. 365–94.

Haman, T. L. "Beginnings of Presbyterianism in Mississippi." *Publications of the Mississippi Historical Society* 10 (1909), pp. 203–22.

Hamilton, Peter J. "Early Roads of Alabama." In Thomas M. Owen, ed., *Transactions of the Alabama Historical Society, 1897–1898* (1898), pp. 39–56.

Hamilton, William B. "The Planters Society in Claiborne County." *Journal of Mississippi History* 11 (Jan. 1949), pp. 67–70.

Harrell, Laura D. S. "The Development of the Lyceum Movement in Mississippi Prior to 1860." *Journal of Mississippi History* 31 (Aug. 1969), pp. 187–201.

———. "Horse Racing in the Old Natchez District, 1783–1861." *Journal of Mississippi History* 13 (July 1951), pp. 123–37.

———. "Jockey Clubs and Race Tracks in Antebellum Mississippi, 1795–1861." *Journal of Mississippi History* 28 (Nov. 1966), pp. 304–18.

Harris, Thaddeus M. "The Journal of a Tour into the Territory Northwest of the Allegheny Mountains . . . ," In Reuben G. Thwaites, ed., *Early Western Travels,* (New York: 1966), vol. 3, p. 358.

Harris, W. Stuart. "Rowdyism, Public Drunkenness, and Bloody Encounters in Early Perry County." *Alabama Review* 33 (Jan. 1980), pp. 15–24.

Hatfield, Joseph T. "Governor William Charles Cole Claiborne, Indians, and Outlaws in Frontier Mississippi, 1801–1803." *Journal of Mississippi History* 27 (Nov. 1965), pp. 323–50.

Haynes, Robert V. "The Disposal of Lands in the Mississippi Territory." *Journal of Mississippi History* 24 (Oct. 1962), pp. 226–52.

———. "Historians and the Mississippi Territory." *Journal of Mississippi History* 29 (Nov. 1967), pp. 409–28.

———. "James Willing and the Planters of Natchez: The American Revolution Comes to the Southwest." *Journal of Mississippi History* 37 (Feb. 1975), pp. 1–40.

———. "Law Enforcement in Frontier Mississippi." *Journal of Mississippi History* 22 (Jan. 1960), pp. 27–42.

———. "Life on the Mississippi Frontier. Case of Matthew Phelps." *Journal of Mississippi History* 39 (Feb. 1977), pp. 1–15.

———. "The Revolution of 1800 in Mississippi." *Journal of Mississippi History* 19 (Oct. 1957), pp. 234–51.

Helmbold, F. Wilbur. "Early Alabama Newspapermen, 1810–1820." *Alabama Review* 12 (Jan. 1959), pp. 53–68.

Hemperley, Marion R. "Benjamin Hawkins' Trip Through Alabama, 1796." *Alabama Historical Quarterly* 31 (Fall–Winter 1969), pp. 207–36.

Holder, Ray. "On Slavery: Selected Letters of Parson Winans, 1820–1844." *Journal of Mississippi History* 46 (Nov. 1984), pp. 323–54.

———. "Parson Winans' Pilgrimage to 'The Natchez,' Winter of 1810." *Journal of Mississippi History* 44 (Feb. 1982), pp. 47–67.

Holmes, Jack D. L. "Anne White Hutchins—Anthony's Better Half?" *Journal of Mississippi History* 37 (May 1975), pp. 203–8.

———. "Cotton Gins in the Spanish Natchez District, 1795–1800." *Journal of Mississippi History* 31 (Aug. 1969), pp. 159–71.

———. "Irish Priests in Spanish Natchez." *Journal of Mississippi History* 29 (Aug. 1967), pp. 169–80.

———. "Juan De La Villebeuvre: Spain's Commandant of Natchez During the American Revolution." *Journal of Mississippi History* 37 (Feb. 1975), pp. 97–129.

———. "Law and Order in Spanish Natchez, 1781–1798." *Journal of Mississippi History* 25 (July 1963), pp. 186–201.

———. "Livestock in Spanish Natchez." *Journal of Mississippi History* 23 (Jan. 1961), pp. 15–37.

———. "Stephen Minor: Natchez Pioneer." *Journal of Mississippi History* 42 (Feb. 1980), pp. 17–26.

Howell, Isabell. "John Armfield, Slave-Trader." *Tennessee Historical Quarterly* 2 (Mar. 1943), pp. 3–29.

Ideson, Julia, and Sanford W. Higginbotham, eds. "A Trading Trip to Natchez and New Orleans, 1822: Diary of Thomas S. Teas." *Journal of Southern History* 7 (Aug. 1941), pp. 378–99.

James, D. Clayton. "Municipal Government in Territorial Natchez." *Journal of Mississippi History* 27 (May 1965), pp. 148–67.

Jamison, Lena M. "The Natchez Trace: A Federal Highway of the Old Southwest." *Journal of Mississippi History* 1 (Apr. 1939), pp. 82–99.

Jenkins, William H. "Alabama Forts, 1700–1838." *Alabama Review* 12 (July 1959), pp. 163–80.

Jennings, Jesse D. "Nutt's Trip to the Chickasaw Country." *Journal of Mississippi History* 9 (Jan. 1947), pp. 34–61.

Jones, R. W. "Some Facts Concerning the Settlement and the Early History of Mississippi." *Publications of the Mississippi Historical Society* 1 (1898), pp. 85–89.

Jones, Virginia K., ed. "The Bowie Letters, 1819 and 1821." *Alabama Historical Quarterly* 22 (Winter 1960), pp. 231–43.

Jordan, Daniel P. "Partisan Politics in Territorial Mississippi: A Staunch Republican's Direct Report, December 1807." *Journal of Mississippi History* 41 (Aug. 1979), pp. 231–40.

"Kentucky Ancestors in Pioneer Days. *Kentucky Ancestors* 27 (Winter 1992–93), pp. 167–69.

Landon, Michael de L. "The Mississippi State Bar Association, 1821–1825: The First in the Nation." *Journal of Mississippi History* 42 (Aug. 1980), pp. 222–42.

Leach, Douglas Edward. "John Gordon of Gordon's Ferry." *Tennessee Historical Quarterly* 18 (Dec. 1959), pp. 322–44.

Leavell, Z. T. "Early Beginnings of Baptists in Mississippi." *Publications of the Mississippi Historical Society* 4 (1901), pp. 245–54.

Leftwich, George J. "Colonel George Strother Gaines and Other Pioneers in Mississippi Territory." *Publications of the Mississippi Historical Society*, Centenary Series, 1 (1918), pp. 442–56.

———. "Some Main Traveled Roads, Including Cross Sections of Natchez Trace." *Publications of the Mississippi Historical Society,* Centenary Series, 1 (1918), pp. 463–76.

"Letters from George Strother Gaines Relating to Events in South Alabama, 1805–1814." *Transactions of the Alabama Historical Society* 3 (1899), pp. 184–91.

Lewis, Anna. "Fort Panmure, 1799, as Related by Juan de la Villebeuvre to Bernardo de Galvez." *Mississippi Valley Historical Review* 18 (Mar. 1932), pp. 541–48.

"Lewis' Tavern at Fort Bainbridge." *Alabama Historical Quarterly* 17 (Spring–Summer 1955), pp. 78–79.

Lincecum, Gideon. "Life of Apushimataha." *Publications of the Mississippi Historical Society* 9 (1906), pp. 415–86.

Love, William A. "General Jackson's Military Road." *Publications of the Mississippi Historical Society* 11 (1910), pp. 403–17.

———. "Lowndes County, Its Antiquities and Pioneer Settlers." *Publications of the Mississippi Historical Society* 7 (1903), pp. 351–72.

———. "The Mayhew Mission to the Choctaws." *Publications of the Mississippi Historical Society* 11 (1910), pp. 363–402.

———. "Mingo Mushulitubbee's Prairie Village." *Publications of the Mississippi Historical Society* 7 (1903), pp. 373–78.

Lowery, Charles D. "The Great Migration to the Mississippi Territory, 1798–1819." *Journal of Mississippi History* 30 (Aug. 1968), pp. 173–92.

Lyon, Ralph M. "The Early Years of Livingston Female Academy." *Alabama Historical Quarterly* 37 (Fall 1975), pp. 192–205.

McBride, Robert M. "A Camp Meeting at Goshen Creek." *Tennessee Historical Quarterly* 22 (June 1963), pp. 137–42.

McCain, William. "The Charter of Mississippi's First Bank." *Journal of Mississippi History* 1 (Oct. 1939), pp. 251–63.

McCaleb, James F. "Easter on the Natchez Trace." Port Gibson, *Reveille,* Mar. 21, 1940.

McLemore, Richard A. "The Roots of Higher Education in Mississippi." *Journal of Mississippi History* 26 (Aug. 1964), pp. 207–18.

McLendon, James H. "The Development of Mississippi Agriculture." *Journal of Mississippi History* 13 (Apr. 1951), pp. 75–87.

Maddox, Dawn. "The Buildings and Grounds of Jefferson College in the Nineteenth Century." *Journal of Mississippi History* 35 (Feb. 1973), pp. 37–54.

Marshall, Park. "The True Route of the Natchez Trace—The Rectification of a Topographical Error." *Tennessee Historical Magazine* 1 (Sept. 1915), pp. 173–82.

Miles, Edwin A. "The Mississippi Press in the Jackson Era, 1824–1841." *Journal of Mississippi History* 19 (Jan. 1957), pp. 1–20.

Mills, Frances Preston. "Amos Ogden of the Ogden's Mandamus, Late Captain of the Rangers." *Journal of Mississippi History* 41 (May 1979), pp. 183–98.

Monette, John W. "The Progress of Navigation and Commerce on the Waters of the Mississippi River and the Great Lakes, A.D. 1700 to 1846." *Publications of the Mississippi Historical Society* 7 (1903), pp. 479–523.

Moore, John H. "Mississippi's Search for a Staple Crop." *Journal of Mississippi History* 29 (Nov. 1967), pp. 371–85.

Moore, Margaret Des Champs. "Early Schools and Churches in Natchez." *Journal of Mississippi History* 24 (Oct. 1962), pp. 253–55.

Morgan, Madel J. "Andrew Marschalk's Account of Mississippi's First Press." *Journal of Mississippi History* 8 (Apr. 1946), pp. 146–48.

Morrison, J. K. "Early History of Jefferson College." *Publications of the Mississippi Historical Society* 2 (1899), pp. 179–88.

Muckenfuss, A. M. "History of the Application of Science to Industry in Mississippi." *Publications of the Mississippi Historical Society* 3 (1901), pp. 235–46.

Nelms, Jack N. "Early Days with the Alabama River Steamboats." *Alabama Review* 37 (Jan. 1984), pp. 13–23.

Noll, Arthur H. "Bishop Otey as Provisional Bishop of Miss." *Publications of the Mississippi Historical Society* 3 (1900), pp. 139–45.

Nuttall, Thomas. "Journal of Travels into the Arkansas Territory During the Year 1819." In Reuben Thwaites, ed., *Early Western Travels* 13 (Cleveland, 1905).

Owsley, Frank L., Jr. "Benjamin Hawkins, The First Modern Indian Agent." *Alabama Historical Quarterly* 30 (Summer 1968), pp. 7–13.

Owsley, Harriet C., ed. "Travel Through the Indian Country in the Early 1800's. The Memoirs of Martha Philips Martin." *Tennessee Historical Quarterly* 21 (Mar. 1962), pp. 66–81.

Penick, James L., Jr. "John A. Murrell: A Legend of the Old Southwest." *Tennessee Historical Quarterly* 48 (Fall 1989), pp. 174–83.

Phelps, Dawson A. "The Chickasaw Agency." *Journal of Mississippi History* 14 (Apr. 1952), pp. 119–37.

———. "The Chickasaw Council House." *Journal of Mississippi History* 14 (July 1952), pp. 170–76.

———. "The Chickasaw Mission." *Journal of Mississippi History* 13 (Oct. 1951), pp. 226–35.

———. "The Choctaw Mission: An Experiment in Civilization." *Journal of Mississippi History* 14 (Jan. 1952), pp. 35–62.

———. "Colbert Ferry." *Alabama Historical Quarterly* 25 (Fall–Winter 1963), pp. 203–26.

———. "The Natchez Trace in Alabama." *Alabama Review* 7 (Jan. 1954), pp. 22–41.

———. "The Natchez Trace in Tennessee." *Tennessee Historical Quarterly* 13 (Sept. 1954), pp. 195–203.

———. "The Robinson Road." *Journal of Mississippi History* 12 (July 1950), pp. 153–61.

———. "Stands and Travel Accommodations on the Natchez Trace." *Journal of Mississippi History* 11 (Jan. 1949), pp. 1–54.

———. "Tockshish." *Journal of Mississippi History* 13 (July 1951), pp. 138–45.

———. "The Tragic Death of Meriwether Lewis." *William and Mary Quarterly* 13 (July 1956), pp. 305–18.

———. "Travel on the Natchez Trace: A Study of its Economic Aspects." *Journal of Mississippi History* 15 (July 1953), pp. 155–64.

Phelps, Dawson A., ed. "The Diary of a Chaplain in Andrew Jackson's Army: The Journal of the Reverend Mr. Learner Blackman—December 28, 1812–April 4, 1813." *Tennessee Historical Quarterly* 12 (Sept. 1953), pp. 264–81.

———. "Excerpts from the Journal of the Reverend Joseph Bullen, 1799 and 1800." *Journal of Mississippi History* 17 (Oct. 1955), pp. 254–81.

Phelps, Dawson A., and Edward Hunter Ross. "Names Please—Names Along the Natchez Trace." *Journal of Mississippi History* 14 (Oct. 1952), pp. 217–56.

Phelps, Dawson A., and John T. Willett. "Iron Works on the Natchez Trace." *Tennessee Historical Quarterly* 12 (Dec. 1953), pp. 309–22.

Plaisance, Aloysius. "The Choctaw Trading House—1803–1822." *Alabama Historical Quarterly* 16 (Fall–Winter 1954), pp. 393–423.

Posey, Walter B. "The Earthquake of 1811 and Its Influence on Evangelistic Methods in the Churches of the Old South." *Tennessee Historical Magazine*, series 2: 1 (Jan. 1931), pp. 107–14.

———. "The Public Manners of Ante-Bellum Southerners." *Journal of Mississippi History* 19 (Oct. 1957), pp. 219–33.

"Principal Stage Stops and Taverns in What Is Now Alabama Prior to 1840." *Alabama Historical Quarterly* 17 (Spring–Summer 1955), pp. 80–87.

Quinn, Yancey M., Jr. "Jackson's Military Road." *Journal of Mississippi History* 41 (Nov. 1979), pp. 335–50.

Rainwater, Percy L. "Conquistadores, Missionaries, and Missions." *Journal of Mississippi History* 27 (May 1965), pp. 123–47.

———. "Indian Missions and Missionaries." *Journal of Mississippi History* 28 (Feb. 1966), pp. 15–39.

Rainwater, Percy L., ed. "The Memorial of John Perkins." *Louisiana Historical Quarterly* 20 (Oct. 1937), pp. 965–89.

Riley, Franklin L. "Choctaw Land Claims." *Publications of the Mississippi Historical Society* 8 (1904), pp. 345–96.

———. "Extinct Towns and Villages of Mississippi." *Publications of the Mississippi Historical Society* 5 (1902), pp. 311–83.

———. "Sir William Dunbar—The Pioneer Scientist of Mississippi." *Publications of the Mississippi Historical Society* 2 (1899), pp. 85–111.

———. "Spanish Policy in Mississippi After the Treaty of San Lorenzo." *Publications of the Mississippi Historical Society* 1 (1898), pp. 50–66.

———. "Transition from Spanish to American Rule in Mississippi." *Publications of the Mississippi Historical Society* 3 (1900), pp. 261–311.

Roberts, Owen. "Richard Thomson: Was He the First English-Speaking Settler in the Natchez District?" *Journal of Mississippi History* 39 (Feb. 1977), pp. 63–74.

Rogers, Tommy Wayne. "Oakland College, 1830–1871." *Journal of Mississippi History* 36 (May 1974), pp. 143–60.

Ross, Edward Hunter, and Dawson A. Phelps. "A Journey Over the Natchez Trace in 1792: A Document from the Archives of Spain." *Journal of Mississippi History* 15 (Oct. 1953), pp. 252–73.

Rowland, Eron O. G. "Marking the Natchez Trace." *Publications of the Mississippi Historical Society* 11 (1910), pp. 345–61.

————. "Peter Chester, Third Governor of the Province of West Florida Under British Dominion, 1770–1781." *Publications of the Mississippi Historical Society*, Centenary Series, 5 (1921), pp. 1–183.

Rowland, Mrs. Dunbar. "Mississippi Territory in the War of 1812." *Publications of the Mississippi Historical Society,* Centenary Series, 4 (1918), pp. 7–156.

————. "Mississippi's Colonial Population and Land Grants." *Publications of the Mississippi Historical Society*, Centenary Series, 1 (1916), pp. 405–28.

Rutledge, Wilmuth S. "Dueling in Antebellum Mississippi." *Journal of Mississippi History* 26 (Aug. 1964), pp. 181–91.

Scott, Kenneth. "Britain Loses Natchez, 1779: An Unpublished Letter." *Journal of Mississippi History* 26 (Feb. 1964), pp. 45–46.

Shue, W. D. "The Cotton Oil Industry." *Publications of the Mississippi Historical Society* 8 (1904), pp. 253–92.

Silver, James W. "A Counter-Proposal to the Indian Removal Policy of Andrew Jackson." *Journal of Mississippi History* 4 (Oct. 1942), pp. 207–15.

Smith, Susanna. "Washington, Mississippi: Antebellum Elysium." *Journal of Mississippi History* 40 (May 1978), pp. 143–65.

Southerland, Henry DeLeon, Jr. "The Federal Road, Gateway to Alabama, 1806–1836." *Alabama Review* 39 (Apr. 1986), pp. 96–109.

Sprague, Stuart Seely. "Alabama Town Production During the Era of Good Feelings." *Alabama Historical Quarterly* 36 (Spring 1974), pp. 15–20.

Stone, Alfred H. "The Early Slave Laws of Mississippi." *Publications of the Mississippi Historical Society* 2 (1899), pp. 133–45.

Stone, James H. "Surveying the Gaines Trace, 1807–1808." *Alabama Historical Quarterly* 33 (Summer 1971), pp. 135–52.

Sturdivant, Laura D. S. "One Carbine and A Little Flour and Corn in A Sack: The American Pioneer." *Journal of Mississippi History* 37 (Feb. 1975), pp. 43–65.

Swearingen, Mack. "Luxury at Natchez in 1801. A Ship's Manifest from the McDonough Papers." *Journal of Southern History* 3 (May 1937), pp. 188–90.

Taylor, Thomas J. "Early History of Madison County." *Alabama Historical Quarterly* 1 (Summer 1930), pp. 149–68.

Thornton, Mary L., ed. "Letter from David Ker to John Steele." *Journal of Mississippi History* 25 (Apr. 1963), pp. 135–38.

Thorpe, T. B. "Remembrances of the Mississippi." *Harper's New Monthly Magazine* 12 (Dec. 1855), pp. 25–41.

Tilly, Bette B. "The Jackson-Dinsmoor Feud: A Paradox in A Minor Key." *Journal of Mississippi History* 34 (May 1977), pp. 117–31.

Vogt, Daniel C. "Poor Relief in Frontier Mississippi, 1798–1832." *Journal of Mississippi History* 51 (Aug. 1989), pp. 181–99.

Warren, Harris Gaylord. "Vignettes of Culture in Old Claiborne." *Journal of Mississippi History* 20 (July 1958), pp. 125–45.

Warren, Harry. "Missions, Missionaries, Frontier Characters and Schools." *Publications of the Mississippi Historical Society* 8 (1904), pp. 571–98.

Watts, Charles W. "Colbert's Reserve and the Chickasaw Treaty of 1818." *Alabama Review* 12 (Oct. 1959), pp. 272–80.

Weathersby, W. H. "A History of Mississippi College." *Publications of the Mississippi Historical Society*, Centenary Series, 5 (1925), pp. 184–220.

Weems, Robert C., Jr. "Mississippi's First Banking System." *Journal of Mississippi History* 29 (Nov. 1967), pp. 386–408.

Wells, Samuel J. "International Causes of the Treaty of Mount Dexter, 1805." *Journal of Mississippi History* 48 (Aug. 1986), pp. 177–85.

Welsh, Mary J. "Recollections of Pioneer Life in Mississippi." *Publications of the Mississippi Historical Society* 4 (1901), pp. 343–56.

White, J. M. "Territorial Growth of Mississippi." *Publications of the Mississippi Historical Society* 2 (1899), pp. 125–32.

Wilkins, J. M. "Early Times in Wayne County." *Publications of the Mississippi Historical Society* 6 (1902), pp. 265–72.

Williams, John R., ed. "Frontier Evangelist: The Journal of Henry Bryson." *Alabama Historical Quarterly* 42 (Spring–Summer 1980), pp. 5–39.

Williams, Samuel C. "Tennessee's First Military Expedition (1803)." *Tennessee Historical Magazine* 8 (Oct. 1924), pp. 171–90.

Wunder, John. "American Law and Order Comes to Mississippi Territory: The Making of Sargent's Code, 1798–1800." *Journal of Mississippi History* 38 (May 1976), pp. 131–55.

Books

Alvarez, Eugene. *Travel on Southern Antebellum Railroads, 1828–1860.* University, Ala., 1974.

Ayers, Edward L. *Vengeance and Justice: Crime and Punishment in the 19th Century South.* New York, 1984.

Baily, Francis. *Journal of a Tour in Unsettled Parts of North America in 1796 & 1797.* London, England, 1856.

Baldwin, Leland D. *The Keelboat Age on Western Waters.* Pittsburgh, 1941.

Bartlett, Richard A. *The New Country: A Social History of the American Frontier, 1776–1890.* New York, 1974.

Basler, Roy P., ed. *The Collected Works of Abraham Lincoln.* 9 vols. New Brunswick, N.J., 1953.

Blair, Walter and Franklin J. Meine. *Mike Fink, King of Mississippi Keelboatmen.* New York, 1933.

Blandin, I. M. E. *History of Higher Education of Women in the South Prior to 1860.* New York, 1909.

Bowman, Virginia McDaniel. *Historic Williamson County.* Nashville, 1971.

Bradbury, John. *Travels in the Interior of America.* Liverpool, England, 1817.

Brown, Samuel P. *The Western Gazeteer; or Emigrant's Directory.* Auburn, N.Y., 1817.

Claiborne, John F. H. *Mississippi as a Province, Territory and State.* Jackson, 1880.

Clark, ———. *General Directory.* Vicksburg, Miss., n.d.

Clark, Clarence E. *Territorial Papers of the United States.* Washington, D.C., 1937.

Clark, Thomas D., and John D. W. Guice. *Frontiers in Conflict: The Old Southwest, 1795–1830.* Albuquerque, 1989.

Clark, Willis G. *History of Education in Alabama, 1702–1889.* Washington, D.C., 1889.

Cotterill, R. S. *The Southern Indians: The Story of the Civilized Tribes Before Removal.* Norman, Okla., 1954.

Cramer, Zadoc. *The Navigator.* Pittsburgh, 1814.

Crockett, David. *A Narrative of the Life of David Crockett of the State of Tennessee.* Reprint, Knoxville, 1973.

Daniels, Jonathan. *The Devil's Backbone: The Story of the Natchez Trace.* New York, 1962.

Dick, Everett. *The Dixie Frontier: A Social History.* New York, 1948.

Dow, Lorenzo. *The Dealings of God, Man, and the Devil, As Exemplified in the Life, Experiences, and Travels of* . . . Norwich, Conn., 1833.

———. *Vicissitudes in the Wilderness; Exemplified in the Journal of Peggy Dow.* Norwich, Conn., 1833.

Dunbar, Seymour. *A History of Travel in America.* New York, 1937.

Eastern National Park & Monument Association. *Mount Locust on the Old Natchez Trace.* N.p., n.d.

The Emigrant's Guide, or Pocket Geography of the Western States and Territories. Cincinnati, 1818.

Fagan, Brian. *The Journey from Eden.* New York, 1990.

Flexner, James T. *Steamboats Come True.* Boston, 1944.

Fuller, Myron L. *The New Madrid Earthquake.* Washington, D.C., 1912.

Ganier, Albert F. *Alexander Wilson's Description of the Natchez Trace.* Nashville, 1955.

Garrett, Jill K., comp. *Historical Sketches of Hickman County, Tennessee.* Columbia, Tenn., 1978.

Giraud, Marcel. *A History of French Louisiana. Volume One, The Reign of Louis XIV, 1698–1715.* Baton Rouge, La., 1974.

Historical Sketch of Maury County. Columbia, Tenn., 1876.

Holmes, Jack D. L. *Gayoso. The Life of A Spanish Governor in the Mississippi Valley, 1798–1799.* Baton Rouge, La., 1965.

Huber, Leonard V. *Beginnings of Steamboat Mail on Lower Mississippi.* State College, Pa., 1960.

Hudson, Arthur P. *Humor of the Old Deep South.* New York, 1936.

Hummel, Ray O., Jr. *Southeastern Broadsides Before 1877.* Richmond, Va., 1971.

Jackson, Joseph A. *Masonry in Alabama: A Sesquicentennial History, 1821–1971.* Montgomery, 1970.

James, D. Clayton. *Antebellum Natchez.* Baton Rouge, La., 1968.

Ker, Henry. *Travels Through the Western Interior of the United States from the Year 1808 up to the Year 1816.* Elizabethtown, N.J., 1816.

Lomask, Milton. *Aaron Burr: the Conspiracy and Years of Exile, 1805–1836.* New York, 1982.

Loveman, Louis U., comp. *The Presidential Vote in Alabama, 1824–1980.* Gadsden, Ala., 1983.

Lynch, Louise G. *Newspaper Excerpts 1822–1835, Williamson County, Tennessee.* N.p., 1985.

McBee, Mary M., comp. *The Natchez Court Records, 1767–1805: Abstracts of Early Records.* Ann Arbor, Mich., 1953.

McDermott, John F., ed. *Before Mark Twain: A Sampler of Old, Old Times on the Mississippi.* Carbondale, Ill., 1968.

———. *The Spanish in the Mississippi Valley, 1762–1804.* Urbana, Ill., 1974.

———. *Travelers on the Western Waters.* Urbana, Ill., 1970.

McWhiney, Grady C. *Cracker Culture: Celtic Ways in the Old South.* Tuscaloosa, Ala., 1988.

Mississippi Historical Records Survey. *Adams County (Natchez), I: Minutes of the Court of General Quarter Sessions of the Peace, 1799–1801.* Jackson, 1942.

Morrison, John F. *A Brief History of Early Lawrence County, Tennessee.* Lawrenceburg, 1968.

Morgan, Ted. *Wilderness at Dawn: The Settling of the North American Continent.* New York, 1993.

Morse, Jedediah. *The American Gazetteer.* Boston, 1810.

———. *The Traveller's Guide, or Pocket Gazetteer of the United States.* New Haven, Conn., 1820.

Penick, James L., Jr. *The Great Western Land Pirate: John A. Murrell in Legend and History.* Columbia, Mo., 1981.

Phillips, Ulrich B. *Life and Labor in the Old South.* Boston, 1929.

Pickett, Albert James. *History of Alabama and Incidentally of Georgia and Mississippi from the Earliest Period.* N.p., 1851.

Pierpont, J. *Introduction to the National Reader: A Selection of Easy Lessons.* Boston, 1828.

Pittman, Philip. *The Present State of the European Settlements on the Mississippi.* Facsimile edition edited by John F. McDermott. Memphis, 1977.

Polk, Noel, ed. *Natchez Before 1830.* Jackson, 1989.

Rayford, Julian Lee. *Chasin' the Devil Round a Stump.* Mobile, 1962.

Schultz, Christian. *Travels on an Inland Voyage.* 2 vols. New York, 1810.

Schwaab, Eugene L. *Travels in the Old South.* 2 vols. Lexington, Ky., 1973.

Scruggs, J. H., Jr., comp. *Alabama Steamboats 1819–1869.* Birmingham, 1963.

Shackford, James A. *David Crockett, The Man and the Legend.* Chapel Hill, N.C., 1956.

Sherer, Robert G. *Subordination or Liberation? The Development and Conflicting Theories of Black Education in Nineteenth Century Alabama.* University, Ala., 1977.

Smith, Henry. *Virgin Land.* New York, 1950.

Smith, Roswell C. *A Key to the "Practical and Mental Arithmetic" for the Use of Teachers.* Hartford, Conn., 1836.

Sydnor, Charles S. *A Gentleman of the Old Natchez Region.* Durham, N.C., 1938.

Taylor, Joe Gray. *Eating, Drinking and Visiting in the South.* Baton Rouge, La., 1982.

Tocqueville, Alexis de. *Democracy in America.* 2 vols. New York, 1969.

Turner, William B. *History of Maury County, Tennessee.* Nashville, 1955.

U.S. Department of State. *Compendium of the Enumeration of the Inhabitants and Statistics of the United States, as Obtained at the Department of State, from the Returns of the Sixth Census*. Washington, D.C., 1841.

Wailes, B. L. C. *Report on the Agriculture and Geology of Mississippi*. Philadelphia, Pa., 1854.

Wait, William B., ed. *Travel Diary of William Richardson from Boston to New Orleans by Land, 1815*. New York, 1938.

Weeks, Stephen B. *History of Public School Education in Alabama*. Washington, 1915.

Willeford, William L. *Mississippi & Louisiana Almanac, 1827*. Natchez, 1827.

Williams, Benjamin B. *A Literary History of Alabama: The Nineteenth Century*. Cranbury, N. J., 1979.

Wright, A. J. *Criminal Activity in the Deep South, 1700–1930*. New York, 1989.

INDEX

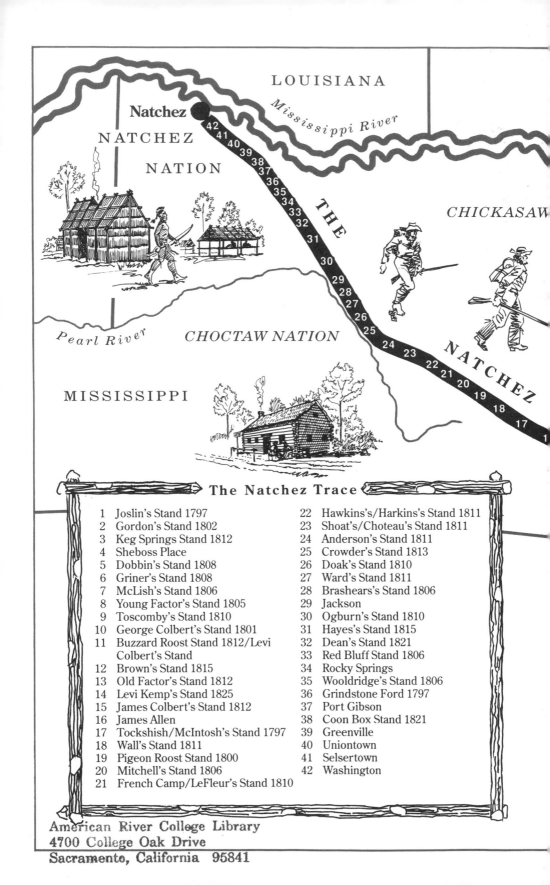

LOUISIANA

Mississippi River

Natchez

NATCHEZ

NATION

42
41
40
39
38
37
36
35
34
33
32
31

30

29
28
27

26

25

24 23
22
21
20
19
18
17

THE

CHICKASAW

NATCHEZ

Pearl River

CHOCTAW NATION

MISSISSIPPI

The Natchez Trace

1 Joslin's Stand 1797
2 Gordon's Stand 1802
3 Keg Springs Stand 1812
4 Sheboss Place
5 Dobbin's Stand 1808
6 Griner's Stand 1808
7 McLish's Stand 1806
8 Young Factor's Stand 1805
9 Toscomby's Stand 1810
10 George Colbert's Stand 1801
11 Buzzard Roost Stand 1812/Levi
   Colbert's Stand
12 Brown's Stand 1815
13 Old Factor's Stand 1812
14 Levi Kemp's Stand 1825
15 James Colbert's Stand 1812
16 James Allen
17 Tockshish/McIntosh's Stand 1797
18 Wall's Stand 1811
19 Pigeon Roost Stand 1800
20 Mitchell's Stand 1806
21 French Camp/LeFleur's Stand 1810

22 Hawkins's/Harkins's Stand 1811
23 Shoat's/Choteau's Stand 1811
24 Anderson's Stand 1811
25 Crowder's Stand 1813
26 Doak's Stand 1810
27 Ward's Stand 1811
28 Brashears's Stand 1806
29 Jackson
30 Ogburn's Stand 1810
31 Hayes's Stand 1815
32 Dean's Stand 1821
33 Red Bluff Stand 1806
34 Rocky Springs
35 Wooldridge's Stand 1806
36 Grindstone Ford 1797
37 Port Gibson
38 Coon Box Stand 1821
39 Greenville
40 Uniontown
41 Selsertown
42 Washington